CHOAN-SENG SONG is at present Associate Director of the Secretariat of the Faith and Order Commission, World Council of Churches, at Geneva. He graduated in Philosophy from National Taiwan University and received his B.D. from New College at the University of Edinburgh and his Ph.D. from Union Theological Seminary, New York. Before he joined the World Council of Churches, Dr. Song was the Principal of the Tainan Theological College, Taiwan, and also Professor of Systematic Theology. In 1976-1977 he served as Visiting Professor at Princeton Theological Seminary. His previous publications include *Prelude to a New Era* (in Chinese), *The Church—Its Task and Responsibility* (in Chinese), Asians and Blacks—*Theological Challenges, Doing Theology Today* (ed.), and *Christian Mission in Reconstruction—An Asian Analysis* (Orbis). He has also written many articles for periodicals such as *Southeast Asia Journal of Theology, Northeast Asia Journal of Theology,* and the *International Review of Mission.*

# THIRD-EYE THEOLOGY

*Theology in Formation in Asian Settings*

**Choan-Seng Song**

ORBIS  BOOKS

Maryknoll, New York 10545

Acknowledgment is gratefully extended for permission to reproduce the following:

"First Tragedy," by Trieu Vu (pp. 124–25). Copyright © 1972 by Asia Society, Inc. Reprinted from A THOUSAND YEARS OF VIETNAMESE POETRY, edited by Nguyen Ngoc Bich, translated by Nguyen Ngoc Bich, with Burton Raffel and W. S. Merwin, by permission of Alfred A. Knopf, Inc.

"A Mother's Evening Meditation," by Minh Dung (pp. 142–43). Copyright © 1974 by Asia Society, Inc. Reprinted from A THOUSAND YEARS OF VIETNAMESE POETRY, edited by Nguyen Ngoc Bich, translated by Nguyen Ngoc Bich, with Burton Raffel and W. S. Merwin, by permission of Alfred A. Knopf, Inc.

"Cry of the People," by Kim Chi Ha (pp. 185–87). From *Cry of the People*, copyright 1974 by Kim Chi Ha. Reprinted with permission of Autumn Press.

Library of Congress Cataloging in Publication Data

Song, Choan-Seng, 1929–
  Third-eye theology.

  1. Theology, Doctrinal. 2. Christianity and
other religions. 3. Asia–Religion. 4. Asia–
Civilization. I. Title.
BT78.S66    230    79-4208
ISBN 0-88344-474-7

The Catholic Foreign Mission Society of America (Maryknoll) recruits and trains people for overseas missionary service. Through Orbis Books Maryknoll aims to foster the international dialogue that is essential to mission. The books published, however, reflect the opinions of their authors and are not meant to represent the official position of the society.

To my wife, Mei-Man,
and our daughters, Ju-Ping and Ju-Ying,
who keep my theological mind from soaring
to the realm of unreality

# CONTENTS

## Part Three    The Politics of the Resurrection

# PREFACE

Mencius (ca. 371–289 B.C.), the most revered sage after Confucius in the tradition of Confucianism, once said:

Humanity is man's mind and righteousness is man's path. Pity the man who abandons the path and does not follow it, and who has lost his heart and does not know how to recover it. When people's dogs and fowls are lost, they go to look for them, and yet, when they have lost their hearts, they do not go to look for them (*The Book of Mencius*, 6A:11).

How well Mencius understood the ultimate purpose of human endeavours!

The theological treatise you are about to read is an invitation to join in the search for the lost heart. The corruption of the relations that make our life truly human, creative, and meaningful can be attributed to the loss of heart. The recovery of the heart is therefore a crucial matter for us in the twentieth century, just as it was for Mencius and his contemporaries in the fourth and the third centuries B.C. The Christian Bible, which follows God's search from the time of Adam and Eve to its culmination on the cross, gives us profound insights into God's work: the recovery of the human heart. If theology has to have a point of entry, it should be the heart. This is the basic assumption of this treatise.

Furthermore, it must be said that the recovery of the heart has been the concern of deeply religious and spiritual people everywhere. Theologians cannot begin to understand God's pain and love in their search for the lost heart until they also turn their eyes beyond their self-imposed domain of Christianity. For this reason the quest in this book is conducted with "Asian settings" in the foreground. It is in Asia, if anywhere, with its religions, cultures, and sociopolitical turmoil that God must be working without interruption to recover the lost heart. To realize and understand this, theologians need a "Third Eye," namely, a power of perception and insight that enables them to grasp the meaning under the surface of things and phenomena. On account of this, the present treatise is entitled *Third-Eye Theology: Theology in Formation in Asian Settings*.

The manuscript of this book was written while I was serving as a visiting professor of theology at the Princeton Theological Seminary during the academic year 1976–1977. I owe a heart-felt gratitude to President James McCord, who made it possible for my family and myself to spend a delightful and productive year in Princeton. Part of the manuscript was delivered as lectures at the Princeton Theological Seminary and New Brunswick Seminary. It must have been rather puzzling and perhaps shocking for my students to hear Christian theology expounded in such an unorthodox manner. But after overcoming their initial shock, they were able to join with me in the search for the lost heart with zest and zeal. I must therefore admit that I owe much to them for the stimulation and inspiration I gained from the exchange of ideas and, above all, from the fellowship in the classroom. It was for me a memorable occasion when the class at New Brunswick Seminary surprised me with a simple meal of rice they had prepared for our last session. In this way they demonstrated the sacrament of fellowship through a bowl of rice like the one I had discussed with them in the course of the seminar.

I am also much indebted to the Theological Education Fund, which enabled me to carry out this writing project through a grant. It is one of the chief aims of the Fund to encourage theological writings in the Third World. It is my hope that somehow I lived up to their expectation in this book. The Fund has now been transformed into the Theological Education Program and has a new emphasis on theological education on all six continents. But as I understand it, the Program will continue to encourage "indigenous" theological efforts. I am particularly grateful to Dr. Shoki Coe, the director of the Theological Education Fund. His all-out support of his younger colleagues in their new theological adventures will be long remembered and appreciated. He read my entire manuscript and made many comments and suggestions that showed much theological acumen.

It has been the hope of many Third World theologians that a forum might be created so that their views and ideas might come into an *Auseinandersetzung* with the theological traditions of the churches in the West. No one has offered such a forum with greater devotion that Philip Scharper, editor-in-chief of Orbis Books, Maryknoll, New York. The writing of this book owes much to his encouragement. In this connection the name of Dr. Gerald Anderson, director of the Overseas Ministries Study Center in Ventnor, New Jersey, should also be mentioned. He has been as tireless as Mr. Scharper in introducing Third World theological writings to the western world. He has been a champion of the Third World theological cause, and many of us are fortunate to have him as a friend, critic, and above all, brother in Christ. I am particularly grateful to him for reading the manuscript despite his busy schedule.

It is not possible to mention in this preface all the names of friends who have shared with me in this exciting theological pilgrimage. But on this occasion I must mention in particular Dr. Newton Thurber of the Program Agency, the United Presbyterian Church in the U.S.A. He did much to make our sojourn in Princeton possible, and for this I am grateful to him. The warmth of love he shows to people in Asia and his genuine interest in the churches and theological education of Asia have meant much to many of us over the years. He exemplifies the kind of mutuality of relationships into which people in East and West can enter because of their faith and trust in Jesus Christ.

Before concluding this preface, I must not forget to admit that the best theologians in our family are our two daughters, Ju-Ping and Ju-Ying, seven and six years old respectively at the time this book was written. They often asked questions that left my "sophisticated" theological mind at a loss. They would ask, for instance, where is God from? Is he from Asia? Perhaps he is from Taiwan (where they know we have our roots)? How does he listen to us when we pray to him? Does he have ears and eyes like ours? What does he eat—bread or rice? Or both? Vivid questions like these perplex a sophisticated mind that has lost its innocence, which is one of the basic qualities that enable us to feel touched and embraced by the love of God. Trying in vain to satisfy the "divine" curiosity of our daughters, I have to recall again and again the humbling and yet profound saying of Jesus to his disciples: "I tell you this: unless you turn round and become like children, you will never enter the kingdom of Heaven" (Matt. 18:3). What theologians need most perhaps is to regain the innocence of a child.

And my wife, Mei-Man, had as much to teach me as our daughters. Somewhere in the book I suggest that women are by instinct theological. They do not have to "learn" theology the way men do. They feel God deep inside them. They seem to be close to the source of being. If theology must somehow reflect on this source of being, a theological way must be a way of fellowship and communion, of woman and man, in suffering and joy, in despair and hope. For these reasons I dedicate this book to my wife and our daughters, hoping that what is said in it reflects something of our living together in awareness of our limitations as human beings and of our fulfillment in communion with God, the source and destination of our life.

*Geneva, Switzerland*

# INTRODUCTION

A well-known passage in the book of the prophet Joel can be cited as the point of departure for our discussion in this book. It reads:

> Thereafter the day shall come
> When I will pour out my spirit on all mankind;
> your sons and your daughters shall prophesy,
> your old men shall dream dreams
> and your young men see visions;
> I will pour out my spirit in those days
> even upon slaves and slave-girls (Joel 2:28–29).[1]

The Spirit of God and all human flesh—these are the two principal actors in this prophetic utterance. When these two actors step onto the stage before the silent but intensely expectant audience of the whole universe, the dark silence that has dominated the primordial world is broken. All human flesh becomes infused with the divine Spirit. This Spirit of God is contagious as well as creative. Men and women, regardless of age, sex, or social status, begin to dream dreams, see visions, and utter prophecy. The history of the Spirit-endowed human beings is thus begun. History as we know it is made up of the dreams, visions, and prophecies that human beings are enabled to make through the Spirit of God. History, in its most far-reaching sense, is the movement of the human spirit under the irresistible impact of the divine Spirit. It is the glorious and at the same time painful story of human spirituality caught in the bondage of the divine Spirit trying to realize its dreams, visions, and prophecies.

## The Material Forms of Human Spirituality

Human spirituality materializes itself in what human beings are able to do, build, or create. In the pyramids of ancient Egypt, the great wall of China, the Parthenon, the chief temple of Athena on the Acropolis in Athens, and in the scientific and technological achievements of the modern world, we are confronted with efforts of the human spirit to overcome the limitations of space and time. Almost all the physical and material achievements of human beings in all ages are manifestations of humanity's particular access to the source of the power of being. In

1

historical and cultural monuments we cannot but realize that in a sense human beings are immortal. They have not been able to overcome their biological conditions that impose an end to their time span. But their spirit goes on to live from one generation to another, from one achievement to another, and from the past to the future.

In religions we see the summation of this indomitable human spirit. Religion, however we define it, is a synthetic effort of the human spirit to penetrate the mystery of the world beyond this world. This is true of Hinduism, Buddhism, and Islam as well as Christianity, just to mention the so-called great world religions. A temple or a church, for example, combines in itself the spiritual aspirations of human beings with their aesthetic consciousness and architectonic ingenuity. I have already referred to the pyramids of ancient Egypt and the temple of the Parthenon in Athens, but let me now add a few more monuments. Think of the Sistine Chapel in the Vatican at Rome, adorned with a majestic interpretation of the creation by that great master Michelangelo, or consider Buddhist painting at its best in a scene of paradise from the Tun Huang grottos of the T'ang dynasty that were discovered in 1907 on the western frontier of China. Or consider one of the magnificient Shinto shrines like the Meiji Shrine in Tokyo. In religion the diverse and rich endowments of the human spirit are concentrated in one predominant theme—human beings' search for the fulfillment of their spirituality in an eternal dimension.

If referring to these religious monuments appears a little anachronistic to modern believers in secularism, then what about the liberation movements that have radically changed the understanding of men and women about themselves, their society, and the world? World War II, despite its atrocities, madness, and inhumanity, was in a true sense a birthpang that ushered in a new era of liberation for unprecedented numbers of people on Earth. China, that long-suffering nation exploited by the colonial powers, regained its autonomy. India won its independence in 1947 from British rule after two centuries of servitude. Japan was defeated but in defeat was liberated from an inordinate ambition to tyrannize other nations in Asia. Many countries in Latin America have been engaged in an up-hill struggle against the new colonialism that subjects people to political, economic, and spiritual captivity. Nor are the African nations an exception. The huge continent of Africa bristles with crises. The Africans' hard-won independence does not necessarily bring them freedom from racism, tribalism, and subtle new forms of foreign political and military influence.

I must not forget to mention the Women's Liberation Movement which, like other western commodities, is beginning to make in-roads into Asian society with its ethical and social codes that differ from those of the West, particularly those of the United States. What is most fundamental here is not just equal rights for women, equal pay and equal opportunity regardless of sex. The root problem, it seems to me, is one of spirituality. The Women's Liberation Movement is an effort on the part of women to fulfill their spirituality. As long as they have to submit to men, as long as social conventions require them to suppress their talents and longings, their spirituality is incarcerated. They are not free to develop and to create. When our creativity is restricted and suppressed, our spirituality is also endangered. That is why revolution becomes inevitable. Revolution at its best is the assertion of human spirituality against tyranny over the human spirit. The Women's Liberation Movement is a revolution seeking to transform conventional society in which women have been prevented from fulfilling their spirituality.

In this way creativity and spirituality are intimately related. One cannot do without the other. Traditional society has required certain of its members to behave spiritually without becoming at the same time creative. The Women's Liberation Movement has spectacularly proved that this is simply an impossible demand. The same is also true of the political and economic liberation of oppressed people from their oppressors. This means that liberation is a deeply spiritual matter. Basically, it is the interrelatedness between spirituality and creativity that poses a radical challenge to the institution called the church.

A church with true spirituality is a creative church. It is creative not only in matters strictly religious but must be creative also in all the areas and dimensions of human life. A truly creative spirituality is one that enables us to realize and experience the divine presence in all that we do, not only in religious worship, but also in all realms of our activities. It breaks down the barrier between the sacred and the profane, the religious and the nonreligious, the holy and the secular. To encounter other human beings in the rough and tumble of this world, to experience life in the midst of death, and to perceive meaning in the face of meaninglessness—this is spirituality.

It is this kind of spirituality that we see at work in the beginning of time. Basically, it is this same spirituality that enabled the people of Israel to view their own historical experiences in terms of the liberating power of Yahweh, their God. Furthermore, this spirituality is transformed into the power of salvation on the cross for all nations and peoples. The Christian church is to make visible and evident this spirituality of creation and redemption. Christian theology is to serve this same spirituality by making explicit the creative and redemptive meaning of *all* human historical and cultural experiences.

### Theology and the West

If this is true, the scope of Christian theology is much broader and its contents much more varied than we normally think. Christian theology, within western theological traditions, has to a large extent limited itself to the explication of the Christian faith handed down from the early church. The spirituality with which theology wrestles is the spirituality largely confined to and understood in ecclesiastical terms. The subject matter of theology, in other words, is "Christian" spirituality. It is the traditions of the church that constitute the contents of theological endeavors. And on account of the fact that Christianity has played an enormous role in western civilization, the marriage between theology and western norms of thought and life inevitably becomes the implicit assumption of doing theology in the West. It is the offspring of this marriage between theology and western civilization that have largely defined the rules of the game called Christian theology.

This has been a long marriage that was consummated in the Constantinian era. It lasted at least until the beginning of the twentieth century, although its integrity has often been threatened with disintegration. As early as the eighth century Islam made its influence felt as far west as Spain. And in the thirteenth century a Mongolian invasion was halted only at the eastern frontiers of Europe. But it was in the Enlightenment of the eighteenth century that the marriage began to show signs of fatigue and vulnerability. The spirit and mind of the Enlightenment, while still paying lip service to the decrees of the church, ventured into the unknown but exciting journey dictated by human reason. And as we all know, the force of secularization in the twentieth century has decisively shown how tenuous the marriage has been all along.

What has prevented the marriage from ending in a divorce? There is perhaps no simple answer to this question. The awareness that the church is somehow entrusted with the key to the gate of eternal life, the spirit of reform that erupts from time to time to challenge and modernize the church, great human tragedies and tribulations that drive people back to the church in search of consolation, assurance, and peace—these and many other factors have certainly contributed to the maintenance of the enfeebled marriage relationship. But there is one particular factor that can be cited as playing a significant role in prolonging the marriage between Christianity and western civilization. That factor is the western Christian mission that took the Gospel along with its western cultural accretions to Africa, Asia, and Latin America. It is in these lands and continents outside the West that the marriage was reconsecrated and strengthened. Constantinian Christianity, although beset with challenges from the secularizing West, regained its militant spirit when confronted with a spirituality entirely foreign to it. It was essentially a recapitulation of the church of the early Fathers on the continent of Europe. There was one notable exception, however. The Christianization of indigenous culture, in most cases, did not take place as it did in Europe. Confucius has never become a part of theological thinking for the Chinese church as Aristotle became dominant in the formation of Roman Catholic theology, especially that of Thomas Aquinas. A national church has not come into existence as in Sweden, England, or Germany. Still it was western missionary Christianity. This in turn means that the conduct of worship, the expression of Christian peity, and the theological reflection of the Christian faith in "missionary" lands are mostly direct extensions of their western bases.

In recent years, however, it has become increasingly obvious to many thinking people, both in the East and in the West, that the theology constructed on the marriage between Christianity and western civilization cannot serve the spirituality that grows, develops, and creates outside the framework of Constantinian Christianity. This does not deny the contributions of traditional academic theologians in the West to their churches and societies. Of course not. They have helped shape the spirituality that has blossomed into western culture. But it cannot be denied that they are limited in their ability to interpret the spirituality that lies beyond their knowledge and experience. Even a great mind such as Paul Tillich's is no exception. He appears to move in and out of theological circles, both traditional and nontraditional, with great ease. His embracing theological and philosophical mind enables him to see something ultimate in artistic and religious expressions unrelated to his own cultural and spiritual backgrounds.

This can be illustrated by a conversation Tillich had with some Buddhists in Japan. The conversation touched upon many subjects—the question of history, the concepts of the kingdom of God and Nirvana, the meaning of love and compassion, and so on. But his tendency was to relate assertions of Buddhist faith to the negative aspects of Christianity, thus pointing up positive elements in Christian faith such as the cross, *agape,* or historical identity. Toward the end of the meeting the conversation took the following turn:

The Buddhist priest asks the Christian philosopher, "Do you believe that every person has a substance of his own which gives him true individuality?" The Christian answers, "Certainly!" The Buddhist priest asks, "Do you believe that community between individuals is possible?" The Christian answers affirmatively. Then the Buddhist says, "Your two answers are incompatible; if every person has a substance, no community is possible." To which the Christian replies, "Only if each person has a substance of his own is community possible, for community presupposes separation. You, Buddhist friends, have identity, but not community."[2]

Tillich's verdict on the relationship between the identity of an individual person and community is only half true. The problem is that Tillich characteristically tried to understand Buddhism and the society shaped by Buddhist thought from his western background and experience. For him a community is based on the principle of the separation of individual identities. This is a typical western approach to community. But in Asia the reverse is the case. Community is built on the principle of unity and harmony. Community comes first, and then come the individual persons. Community gives name, that is, identity to the individual. This may not be so evident in Buddhism as a metaphysical system of thought related to life and the world, but it is clearly manifested in the ethical codes, interpersonal relations, and norms of conduct, of a society molded by Buddhist faith.

The conversation between Tillich and the Buddhist priest was conducted on a metaphysical level. Their dialogue did not lead them to the realities that constitute the substance of daily life for those under the influence of traditional Buddhist beliefs. It is thus inevitable that Tillich's observation was one-sided. Tillich and the Buddhist priest passed each other like two ships in the night. Tillich approached the subject of community from individual identity, while the assumption of the Buddhist priest was to subsume individual identity under community. They approached each other from opposite ends, and as a result, it seems that East and West did not meet.

This example shows how deeply each of us is indebted to our own culture, is shaped and conditioned by it. We are all under the power of the culture into which we are born. Our cultural heritage makes us what we are. Our views on life and the world are formed under the direct and indirect influence of our cultural traditions. True, intercultural contacts in the contemporary world have made it possible for people from diverse cultural backgrounds to appreciate and understand each other better than before. There is a conscious effort on the part of many people to overcome cultural provincialism. They expose themselves to the richness of cultural diversity and plurality. This seems to suggest that a world community of peace and understanding cannot be built on a monolithic cultural foundation but rather on cultural pluralism. The history of civilization is in one sense the history of the assimilation and rejection of foreign cultural elements. It has not evolved into a monolithic culture unifying people of different cultural backgrounds and traditions into one uniform cultural entity. Despite his great military prowess Alexander the Great failed to subsume the cultures of the Arabian desert, the Indian subcontinent, and the Nile under Greek culture. Even western culture—the heir to Greek culture—is anything but uniform and monolithic. Cultural patterns found in the Anglo-Saxon world, Germanic lands, and the Mediterranean area exhibit differences as well as similarities. Thus an observation like the following one by a Japanese writer is very much to the point:

Our sense of belonging to one world has never been keener than at present. Yet the emphasis today on this evident fact itself implies that while every individual is affected by the quickening flow of world events, he is still strongly influenced by the ways of living and thinking in his own nation and culture.[3]

The process of assimilation and rejection in the cultural evolution of a nation is in itself a fascinating subject. The point I want to stress here is that the vision of a world community must be a vision that presupposes fruitful and constructive interactions among rich and diverse cultural heritages and characteristics.

Needless to say, a religious faith that shapes and is shaped by certain cultural traditions and environments is not immune from the power of culture. In many instances a religious faith itself constitutes the power of culture. Christianity with respect to western culture, Hinduism with respect to Indian culture, Buddhism and Confucianism with respect to Chinese and Japanese culture, Islam with respect to Arabic culture are all cases in point here. That is why religious authorities and hierarchies have played important roles within social orders and political systems. The encounter of Christianity with other religions through missionary movements is therefore not simply a matter of religion in a narrow sense. The encounter cannot but be social and political as well. The Christian church, however, has been slow in realizing this. Indeed, it is the social and political awakening of the people in the Third World that has alerted the church to the sociopolitical nature of this encounter. Consequently, the churches in the Third World are forced to reappraise critically the relationship between Christian faith and the cultural forms that shape the formulation of the faith. R. H. S. Boyd summarizes this well when he says:

> The tradition which the English-speaking Churches of the West have inherited is inevitably Graeco-Roman, and more especially Latin, and it is difficult for an Anglo-Saxon or Celtic Christian to look at his faith and practice except through Latin spectacles.[4]

He calls this the Latin captivity of the church. The churches in the Third World have largely been the extension and continuation of this captive church.

### God's Silence

In this connection I wish to refer to a novel entitled *Silence (Chin moku)* by the Japanese Catholic writer Shusaku Endo. It is a historical work about the severe persecution of Catholic Christianity by the feudal government of the Tokugawas in the seventeenth century. Many Christians died as martyrs; many recanted their faith after terrible tortures and an intense spiritual struggle; and of course a great number of others quickly gave up Christianity. One of those who finally yielded to the government pressures was Father Rodrigues, a young priest from Portugal. Greatly disturbed by the rumors that his spiritual father and teacher Father Ferreira too had denied Christ, Rodrigues came to Japan with the determination to bear high the torch of the Christian faith. But in the end he too was forced to step on a *fumie*—a copper image of Christ. (Forcing suspected Christians to step on a *fumie* was a rather sinister means used by government officials to detect persons suspected of "foreign heresy.")

The novel raises many questions. Why, for instance, is God silent when his devout children cry to him from the depths of their agony and suffering? The silence of God—this is the theme of the novel. When the apostatized priest Ferreira visited Father Rodrigues in prison, he began to unburden his heart of something that must have been deep within him for many years. The old priest said:

> The reason I apostatized . . . are you ready? Listen! I was put in here and heard the voices of these people for whom God did nothing. God did not do a single thing. I prayed with all my strength; but God did nothing. . . .
> The priest shook his head wildly, putting both his fingers into his ears. But the voice of Ferreira together with the groaning of the Christians broke mercilessly in. Stop! Stop! Lord, it is now that you should break the silence. You must not remain silent. Prove that you are justice, that you are goodness, that you are love. You must say something to show the world that you are the august one. . . .
> Why is God continually silent while those groaning voices go on?[5]

God kept his silence. Christians continued to die agonizing deaths. The young priest, not being able to bear the silence of God, also apostatized. How is God to account for this silence? There is no universal answer to the universal quest into the depth of God's silence. All of us must find an answer for ourselves in our own particular context. "In 1865, when Japan was reopened, the crypto-Christians came out from their hiding, asking for the statue of Santa Maria, speaking about Christmas and Lent, recalling the celibacy of the priests."[6] Perhaps this was God's answer to the desperate question of the old priest. God was not silent after all. He continued to speak in the hearts of those crypto-Christians.

Another question that has a direct bearing upon our discussion is related to the cultural implications of Japanese spirituality for the Christian faith. This is the significance of the conversation that took place between the defeated priest and Inoue, the lord of Chikugo, who had succeeded in making the priest apostatize. For Inoue the persecution of the Christians was not just a fitful action on the part of the Japanese government. It was a cultural struggle, that is, a struggle between Japanese culture and a foreign culture represented by Catholic Christianity. By making the priest from Portugal deny the Christian faith, Inoue had won a victory over western culture. This is clear from what he said to the priest: "I've told you. This country of Japan is not suited to the preaching of Christianity. Christianity simply cannot put down roots here." Then came his verdict: "Father, you were not defeated by me. . . . You were defeated by this swamp of Japan."[7] The swamp of Japan is, of course, a metaphor for the culture of Japan.

Culture is like a living organism equipped with rejection mechanisms against the intrusion of foreign elements. The transplantation of human organs has exemplified this. Every organism needs rejection mechanisms for its own survival. The rejection of Christianity in its purely western form was a matter of survival for the culture of Japan. This is how Inoue understood it. And in a sense he was right. Christians in Japan today still constitute less that 1 percent of the whole population. The essence of Japanese spirituality is visibly and distinctly Buddhist and Confucianist. Even modern architecture reflects Japan's spiritual heritage. Its taste, contour, color, and composition of ideas can be called *sibui,* a distinctly Japanese national characteristic that has no exact equivalent in English. It can be described as a kind of quality that conveys a controlled reserve toward life and the world. It is a quality that comes from contemplating our own destiny with Stoic composure. It is exactly the opposite of being glamorous and exhibitionistic. *Sibui* is eloquent in silence, aggressive in resignation, forceful in reserve. It emanates a kind of spiritual power that enables us to cross the boundary of life and death without fear.

The formation of *sibui* spirituality comes as a result of the long years of assimilation into the fabric of Japanese society of the spirit of Chinese Confucianism and Buddhism. Perhaps it is in the practice of Zen that this *sibui* quality becomes most evident. Zen is more a way of moral and physical discipline than a system of metaphysics. It is a spirituality that permeates Japanese society and the Japanese people, not a system of philosophy monopolized by thinkers and philosophers. In Zen is summed up the spirituality known as *sibui.*

For the Chinese, the influences of Confucianism, Buddhism, and Taoism did not result in the same *sibui* quality as it did in Japan. The term *han-hsu* describes the general characteristics of those brought up in Chinese cultural traditions. *Han-hsu* is not exactly reserve, nor is it shyness. It resembles *sibui* in certain aspects, but is not so rugged as *sibui.* It is the ability to contain in ourselves our will and passion and not to give them a free reign. It is a quality of a person of wisdom and experience who knows how to stop at the right moment and at the right point. Persons with *han-hsu* do not impose themselves on others. They treat others with sincerity, and do not step over the boundaries of human decency and understanding. This *han-hsu* quality is best expressed in a saying of Confucius:

Humility is near to moral discipline (or *li*); simplicity of character is near to true manhood; and loyalty is near to sincerity of heart. If a man will carefully cultivate these things in his conduct, he may still err a little, but he won't be far from the standard of true manhood.[8]

A person of *han-hsu* is a person of *li,* namely, propriety and sincerity of heart.

Chinese spirituality is therefore *han-hsu* spirituality. It is like a tulip that has reached the stage where its beauty is not derived from unreserved openness but from restrained self-assurance. What one sees in such a tulip is not laughter but a smile, not coquettishness but gracious seduction, not open challenge but implied strength. Westerners who have not understood the *han-hsu* quality in Chinese people regard them as inscrutable. How unfortunate it is for the West to meet the East on the no man's-land of misunderstanding!

### Theology and Asian Culture

We have digressed a little. But the point I want to make is this: the Christian Gospel that seeks to lead people to the God of love manifested in Jesus Christ must find its echoes and responses from within their spirituality. By spirituality I do not mean merely something derived from a religious faith or belief. This is spirituality in a narrow sense. What I mean by spirituality is much broader, as should be already evident from our discussion so far. Spirituality is the totality of being that expresses itself in ways of life, modes of thinking, patterns of behavior and conduct, and attitudes toward the mystery that surrounds our immediate world and that beckons us on to the height beyond heights, to the depth below depths, and to the light beyond lights. Such spirituality is present both in the East and the West. And the discovery of such spirituality in the essence of Asian cultures will open the eyes of Christians to see something new in their understanding of the Gospel. It will enable them to discover fresh insights into how God is at work in nations and peoples alien to western Christian culture.

Doing theology with an Asian spirituality thus may bring about a conversion in Christians as well as in people of other faiths. This should prove to be an enrichment to the churches within the western cultural tradition. To quote R. H. S. Boyd once again:

The Indian Church has been strongly influenced by this same tradition [i.e., the Greco-Roman tradition] inherited from western missionaries, yet today it is emerging with its own distinct and fascinating cultural identity. Has this Indian Church anything to say to the West which will enable the West to rediscover its faith in a wider and richer context? Can the western Church break out of its bondage to Greek philosophy, to the Latin language, and to Roman structures?[9]

This reference to the church in India can be applied equally to other churches in the Third World. A new theological era is in the making. It makes doing theology more difficult yet more exciting, more complicated yet more enriching.

I propose to call such a theological effort "doing theology with a third eye." The term "third eye" is derived from Buddhism. According to the great Japanese Zen master Daisetz Suzuki:

Zen . . . wants us to open a "third eye," as Buddhists call it, to the hitherto unheard-of region shut away from us through our own ignorance. When the cloud of ignorance disappears, the infinity of heavens is manifested where we see for the first time into the nature of our own being.[10]

The theology with which we are familiar and in which most of us are brought up is a first- or a second-eye theology—a two-dimensional theology that is not capable of a third-dimensional insight. Because of its two dimensionality it is a flat theology. It canvasses a long stretch of terrain, which is the two thousand years of church history colored strongly by western thought forms and lifestyles.

It was Seeberg, a great German historian of the development of Christian dogmas, who observed that the Reformation represents "Christianity in the understanding of the German spirit."[11] He was right. The faith of the Reformation is the faith seen through German eyes. However definitive, influential, and far-reaching the Reformation faith may have been, there is no reason why Christians who are not heirs to the German spirit must see and interpret Christian faith through German eyes. Those who are not endowed with German eyes should not be prevented from seeing Christ differently. They must train themselves to see Christ through Chinese eyes, Japanese eyes, Asian eyes, African eyes, Latin American eyes.

This is what I mean by doing theology with a third eye. In fact, my concept is not innovative. Consider, for example, the Christian artists throughout the centuries who have tried to portray Christ. Each portrait of Christ expresses the artist's concept of Christ under the strong influence of his or her own cultural and religious background. Indeed, the effort of the religious mind to capture the face of Christ "has been influenced by the great art movements and by national and individual characteristics."[12] Accordingly, the face of Christ in art can be a typological study of the cultural, national, and ethnic influences on the different artists.[13] Compare, for example, Guido Reni's *Ecce Homo* of the decadent period of the sixteenth and the seventeenth centuries with the *Christ on the Cross* by Donatello (1386–1466), who was an artist of the early Renaissance. For Donatello and his peers of the fourteenth and the fifteenth centuries, art was to serve faith, not the other way around. In the treatment of the face of Christ, "it is not beauty they aim at but holiness."[14] The face of Donatello's Christ is:

marred by excruciating pain, but the spiritual majesty of the Sufferer remains; there is no heart-rending appeal to emotionalism, no effort to impress by exaggeration of physical suffering, and yet it is all there—the loneliness, the abandonment, the anguish, and above and within all the victory of that voluntary sacrifice which atones for the sins of the world.[15]

Guido Reni's face of Christ poses a striking contrast. It is the physical suffering that dominates Christ's facial expression. His sorrow, anguish, and pain come out so forcefully that the hope of salvation seems subsumed under them:

> This sense of anguish and suffering is expressed by Guido Reni with a power and pathos which profoundly moves the heart, but it displays an exaggeration of sentiment, which began to characterize the art of this epoch, and which was one of the evil effects of the Counter-Reformation.[16]

When we turn to Japanese artists, we seem to breathe a different atmosphere. In looking at the works of Japanese Christian artists, we should remember the *sibui* quality we discussed earlier. Let us take, for example, the *Cross of Christ* by Giichro Hayakawa.[17] On the cross Christ's outstretched arms and folded feet are nailed. But from his face we can hardly sense the kind of pain and anguish he is going through in his body and spirit. The whole picture is a paragon of tranquillity in the midst of a raging storm. The closed eyes almost shut out external intrusions into the mind of the sufferer. Christ is in deep contemplation with himself and with God. It is a profound silence that we see in Christ's face, and yet what a powerful silence! Here is Christ oblivious of his physical pain, bearing the sins of the world in his single-minded concentration on saving humankind. It is a *sibui* Christ that we encounter here, a Christ who does not show internal emotion and passion, a Christ who faces death with equanimity. Is this not a *sibui* spirituality that is seen in the Savior of the world?

Be that as it may, each portrait of Christ expresses the artist's comprehension of Christ. It portrays Christ in accord with Christ's meaning to each artist in his or her particular personal, historical, and cultural context. No artist has been able to capture the *whole* Christ, the *true* Christ, Christ as he was and is. Thus each portrait of Christ is at once a representation and a misrepresentation. This is not a surprise, for even the disciples who sat at the feet of Christ, ate with him, followed him, and lived with him formed different views of him. Some thought of him as a prophet; others regarded him as Elijah; and still others expected him to be their political liberator. No view of Christ, no picture of him, therefore, is free from falsification. Likewise, no tradition of the church is free of error, no teaching of the church by the theologians and spiritual leaders can claim to be infallible. Even the creeds of the early ecumenical councils have no absolutely binding power over members of the church in succeeding generations. In the Christian art forms we have considered here, we find one Christ in many Christs. It is the Christ of the Gospels who inspires artists of all ages to portray him, and yet no one portrait of Christ is the same as all the others. Nonetheless, the Christs in these portraits have inspired Christians of different eras to turn to the one Christ as their Savior. Thus in the history of Christian art we are impressed with the power of the incarnation residing in Christ. He was made a man of Jewish flesh but did not become captive to that flesh. He became a man of Greek flesh, of Roman flesh, of Germanic flesh, and of Anglo-Saxon flesh. This same Christ—through the works of Japanese artists, Chinese painters, or Indonesian sculptors—is beginning to assume Asian flesh as well.

Just as with art, so it is with theology. If Christian art can be thought of as a kind of visual theology, Christian theology as we normally understand it is basically a written art. If we can speak of Christian art with a third eye, we must also be able to speak of theology with a third eye. Until Christian theology has acquired this third-dimensional formulation of Christian faith, it will remain a stranger outside the western world. Black theology in the United States and Africa and liberation theology in Latin America have forcefully demonstrated this fact. Without this third dimensionality Christian theology will remain incomplete, underdeveloped, and impoverished. Fortunately although somewhat belatedly, Christian theology is now entering the era of third dimensionality. Doing theology with Asian spirituality is meant to be a contribution to the anguish and joy, to the frustration and excitement of this new theological era.

# Part One

# The Beginning of Theology

# CHAPTER 1

# THE DOUBLE DARKNESS

As long ago as the sixth century B.C., Lao-tzu, the master of aphorisms and reputed founder of Taoism in China, made the following statement:

> Impenetrable is the darkness where the heart of Being dwells,
> This Being is Truth itself and Faith itself.
> From eternity to eternity, they will never perish,
> Who saw the beginning of All?
> The beginning of All, one knows only through the perennial Spirit.[1]

The darkness surrounding the heart of Being—this has been the center of human spiritual inquiries both in the East and the West from time immemorial to the present day. Consciously or unconsciously, human beings seem to be aware of the Being from whom they derive the power and meaning of their existence. Therefore, it is only natural that they are intent on discovering who and what that Being may be. In Augustine's famous words, human souls are restless until they find rest in God. And in the process of the search for that Being, human beings become conscious of their spirituality, which relates them to that Being in a very special way. They are bound to the Being who is the source and destiny of their being. They are thus conditioned by this spirituality. They are conditioned, to use a biblical expression, by the image of God within them.

This does not mean that inquiries of the human spirit in all ages have taken the same form and expression. On the contrary! These inquiries often take vastly different forms of expression for people in different cultural situations. Why is this so? One possible answer is that the darkness surrounding the heart of Being defies a complete grasp by human beings of the mystery of that Being. In fact, religions and folklores are full of stories about those who impudently seek to penetrate the darkness of mystery to gain a glimpse of the secret of that Being. In the darkness of Being human beings are confronted with their ultimate puzzlement, anxiety, and fear. All kinds of religious images and symbols are testimonies of such an awesome encounter. Consequently, from highly developed religions like Buddhism, Hinduism, Islam, or Christianity to the primitive religions of nomads and others who live on the fringe of modern civilization, each faith has developed its own ways and systems to account for whatever insight each is enabled to gain into the mystery of Being.

Speaking of religion in Africa, Mbiti, an African religious historian, points out that within traditional life in Africa:

man lives in a religious universe. . . . Names of people have religious meanings in them; rocks and boulders are not just empty objects, but religious objects; the sound of the drum speaks a religious language; the eclipse of the sun or moon is not simply a silent phenomenon of nature, but one which speaks to the community that observes it, often warning of an impending catastrophe.[2]

It should be added that this is not a phenomenon unique to African society. A similar religious phenomenon can be observed in Asia and in other parts of the world. What we see here is a transformation of the inscrutable and mysterious Being into tangible, visible forms—a substitution that incurred the great wrath of the Old Testament prophets and of modern western missionaries.

### Mysterium Tremendum et Fascinosum

At a highly sophisticated and theological level, Rodolf Otto in his important book *The Idea of the Holy* terms this sense of reverence and awe before the objects of worship a *mysterium tremendum et fascinosum*. The *mysterium* is something before which we tremble on the one hand and experience fascination on the other. In the presence of the *mysterium* our whole being is exposed to that which defies human intellect and cognition. In Otto's own words,

the truly "mysterious" object is beyond our apprehension and comprehension, not only because our knowledge has certain irresistible limits, but because in it we come upon something inherently "Wholly Other," whose kind and character are incommensurable with our own, and before which we therefore recoil in a wonder that strikes us chill and numb.[3]

As we know, Karl Barth powerfully exploited the concept of God as the Wholly Other in the early stage of his long, distinguished theological career. With the powerful theological language at his command, Barth initiated the era of neo-orthodox theology, stressing the absolute and qualitative difference between God and human beings. In retrospect, it is only fair to say that Barth must have been impressed as much by the darkness that surrounds the heart of Being as by the finiteness and sinfulness of human beings.

In his *Epistle to the Romans,* a theological manifesto that announced his break with the nineteenth-century theology of experience, Barth emphasized the unknowability of God in language now known as dialectical. He writes:

> On the very brink of human possibility there has . . . appeared a final human capacity—the capacity of knowing God to be unknowable and wholly Other, of knowing man to be a creature contrasted with the Creator, and above all, of offering to the unknown God gestures of adoration. This possibility of religion sets every other human capacity also under the bright and fatal light of impossibility.[4]

This is a dialectical language at its best. To know God as unknowable is to confess the limitation of human cognition in matters related to God. The darkness surrounding the heart of Being proves to be impenetrable to human reason.

Not only Christian theologians have admitted the difficulty and even the impossibility of obtaining a rational knowledge of God. Lao-tzu, the ancient Chinese philosopher we have already quoted, begins his discourse on the nature of Tao thus:

> The Tao that can be told of
> Is not the Absolute Tao;
> The Names that can be given
> Are not Absolute Names.[5]

The Tao, which gives birth to all things and sustains all things, is beyond the grasp of human reason and intellect. It cannot be described in human language. Perhaps it was this recognition that turned Chinese thinkers away from metaphysical speculation on the nature of God to the appreciation of nature in Taoism, and to human relationships and conduct in Confucianism. Confucius once remarked: "Respect the heavenly and earthly spirits and keep them at a distance."[6] Is this to be taken as a piece of practical wisdom—not to offend the spirits? Perhaps it is more than that. In all probability Confucius turned away from speculations about the spirits and gods because they simply elude human rationality. Besides, there is so much with which we have to be occupied in the present world.

Confucius spent all his life trying to implement his concept of an ideal state, but his advice fell on deaf ears during the time of transition between the Ch'un Ch'iu Period (722–481 B.C.) and the Period of the Warring States (481–221 B.C.). Consequently, he turned in his later years to teaching his disciples, who at one time numbered as many as three thousand. The following conversation between the Master and one of his disciples, Tselu, is very illuminating in view of our discussion above. Once Tselu asked the Master about the worship of celestial and terrestrial spirits. In reply Confucius said: "We don't know yet how to serve men, how can we know about serving the spirits?" Tselu, however, was not totally satisfied. He went on to ask: "What about death?" And back came the Master's answer: "We don't know yet about life, how can we know about death?"[7] Was Confucius an agnostic like Bertrand Russell? Perhaps not. He believed in the existence of spirits and gods, but felt that they could not be apprehended by human reason. He taught arduously the need to show reverence toward rituals and offerings, and he himself paid his respects to the spirits and gods. It is said of him that "when he offered sacrifice to his ancestors, he felt as if his ancestors were present bodily, and when he offered sacrifice to the other gods, he felt as if the gods were present bodily."[8] The bodily presence of the spirits and gods can be experienced with our whole being but cannot be apprehended merely by our rational capacity. In this we seem to find a strange relevance in the controversy between Luther and Zwingli about the bodily presence of Christ in the Eucharist. Perhaps Confucius could have been invited to be an arbiter of this celebrated dispute in the history of the Christian church. In Confucian terms both Luther and Zwingli might have been right, for Jesus can be present both bodily and spiritually when worshipers partake of the bread and wine at the Eucharist in spirit and in truth.

What I want to point out here is that for Confucius we are not equipped with a rational tool to apprehend the spirits and gods that subsist in a mode different from ours. In this he is true to his own epistemology, for concerning human knowledge he observed: "To know what you know and what you don't know is the characteristic of one who knows."[9] For him the boundary between the knowable and the unknowable is clear and definite. A person of wisdom is one who knows where the boundary lies and does not venture to go beyond it. Within the limitation of the epistemological framework that defines and conditions our cognitive activity, we must be as humble and wise as Confucius when it comes to matters related to the Being that transcends us. All we are permitted to say within that framework is that God is. Over and above that, for example, what that Being is like, how that Being is related to us personally and to the world, are matters that require a different kind of logic or rationality. I like to call this the "logic of love." But this is to anticipate our discussion in later chapters. At present, let me simply quote Tillich, who stresses the wholly otherness of God in these words:

A phenomenological definition of the meaning of "God" in every religion, including the Christian, offers the following definition of the meaning of the term "god." Gods are beings who transcend the realm of ordinary experience in power and meaning, with whom men have relations which surpass ordinary relations in intensity and significance.[10]

The philosophical and theological language used here by Tillich is notably different from that of Lao-tzu or Confucius. But the stress on the extraordinariness of that Being who transcends human beings in power and meaning is similar. Does this not mean that the ordinary logic of reason and rationality does not stand us in good stead in our effort to apprehend and comprehend that Being? The darkness surrounding the heart of Being defies the logic of human reason.

There is a second darkness surrounding the human quest for the heart of Being. This is the darkness resulting from human *hubris* (pride) that claims to have attained the secret of God. It thus rejects other attempts at gauging the depth of the mystery surrounding the heart of Being. Consequently, the spirituality that has developed in each religion is considered to be *sui generis*. Communication between one spirituality and another becomes almost an impossible feat. One spirituality, instead of embracing another spirituality, repels it.

It has to be acknowledged that this tendency to reject another spirituality is not always found in Asia. In China Buddhism assimilated, and at the same time was assimilated into, the Chinese cultural tradition that could boast of well-developed systems of thought and belief. In Japan the same thing happened. The convergence of great spiritualities gave a new impetus to the indigenous culture and infused a new meaning of life into the people. In this way the cultural history of an Asian nation tends to evolve out of interactions among different spiritualities. Cultural traditions thus created are pluralistic and complex. By way of contrast, Christianity in Asia has to a large extent remained outside this process of assimilation. It has maintained its distinctive and monolithic character. Its impact and influence on indigenous culture have been negligible. It has not contributed in any significant degree to the shaping of the society and the politics that affect the everyday life of the people.

At long last, however, a change seems to be taking place today. As will be shown and discussed later, the Christian faith is beginning to make inroads in nations in which it constructs the basis of an entity called the Christian community. Undoubtedly this new trend has important implications. It shows that Christian spirituality and Asian indigenous spiritualities are not strange bedfellows that dream entirely different dreams. It further points to the fact that the communication between Christians and people of other faiths is not only possible but necessary. It tells us that a knowledge of what God is doing among the nations is to be gained through Christians who find themselves sharing the common visions and aspirations of life with their neighbors. This is what I call doing theology with a third eye. It is a theology open to the mysterious ways of the God who in Christ becomes human flesh in Asia. Third-eye theology is therefore an incarnational theology. Such theology allows no barriers to be set up around it to obstruct its view. With faith in the God who acts in history, it ventures into an unknown journey. Jesus Christ and God's salvation in and through him are the center of such a theology.

### The Problem of Heart-to-Heart Communication

From what has been said above, it is clear that in our theological efforts we are confronted by what I would call a "double darkness": the darkness surrounding the heart of Being and the darkness separating Christian spirituality from other Asian spiritualities. To overcome this double darkness is the task of third-eye theology, especially the darkness that makes different spiritualities unable to communicate with each other. Only when the darkness that surrounds different spiritualities is lifted can we begin to see the love and compassion of God for the world in a fuller and richer light. The following story is illustrative of what is meant here.

A Japanese Christian engaged in theological teaching in the northern part of Thailand encountered a typical example of alienation between one spirituality and another. Finding himself at the bedside of a Thai woman who was suffering from cancer, the Japanese missionary tried to talk to her about the Christian faith and Jesus Christ the Savior. A little annoyed, the woman said:

You missionaries are always trying to teach people while you really do not understand the people. The Buddhist monks are much better than you missionaries. I will call in a monk right now. I will listen to him. He will understand me. He can comfort me with his *dharma*. He can speak my own language. You are wasting your time here. Go home![11]

As the Japanese Christian missionary correctly observed, the Thai woman was not referring to a problem with the spoken language. In saying that a Buddhist monk spoke her own language, she was implying that she and the monk shared a common cultural and religious heritage, that they were on the same wavelength in spiritual matters, and that sympathy and understanding could be taken for granted within that same spiritual and cultural framework. Language is an essential vehicle for expressing and conveying the totality of what it means to be and to live and die in a certain cultural context. Language is therefore not just a matter of sound but a matter of substance, not just a problem of grammar and syntax but a problem of the mind and the spirit. Thus, when the Japanese missionary concluded self-reproachfully that the woman was objecting to his "imperialistic one-sidedness," he was missing the real issue. Maybe he was too conscious of what his western predecessors had done in the so-called mission field. Still the woman's statement posed an issue that went much deeper than that of imperialistic one-sidedness. What was at stake here, it seems to me, is this: a heart-to-heart communication did not take place between the Japanese Christian teacher and the Thai Buddhist woman. Both were anxious to penetrate the darkness of Being at a critical time in the woman's life, but the darkness between the spirituality of Theravada Buddhism and that of Christianity stood in their way. This darkness prevented them from seeing each other in the heart of Being. *Dharma* and Christ did not meet in the hearts of those two people. The woman had to call in a Buddhist monk who could speak her own language, and the Christian missionary had to go away, deeply troubled by his apparent failure to communicate to her in his own Christian language.

The central issue here is heart-to-heart communication between one spirituality and another. What is it that prevents communication from taking place freely and fruitfully among people of different religious and spiritual allegiances? The mistrust, hostility, and conflict that have developed over a long period of time—partly because of misunderstandings and distortions, and partly because of a lack of sympathy and empathy—disrupt communication. For some reason tension is particularly heightened between Christianity and other world religions. Numerous examples can be cited to illustrate this: the confrontation of Christianity with Islam in Palestine during the Crusades is a case in point. Perhaps the Crusades were conceived, motivated, and carried out by the Christian church and the kingdoms of Europe as much for political as for religious motives. It was, in any case, one of the ugliest and saddest conflicts in the history of the world. It stained the image of Christianity and strained the relationship between the two world religions.

Despite this remark, I hasten to add that I have no intention of advocating unconditional recognition and acceptance of Asian spirituality and all that it represents. Unfortunately one has to admit that the integrity of Asian spirituality is also threatened by a breakdown in heart-to-heart communication. On the whole we can say that the language of the heart has gone through a great devaluation in Asian countries. Through inner corruption on the one hand and on the other hand through the invasion of a modern technological culture based on western capitalist structures of economy and lifestyle, Asian spirituality faces the danger of disintegration. At the very least it is on the defensive. It is no longer self-evident that present-day Asia still preserves the spirituality that enables people to aspire to what is good, beautiful, and true. Disillusioned by their own affluent society, some idealistic youths may leave their western homelands in search of an oriental spirituality which, they hope, will bring peace, joy, and tranquility to their troubled bodies and souls. But as many of them soon find out, spirituality is not lying about in the streets of Calcutta, Bangkok, Peking, or Tokyo, just waiting to be picked up. There has been too much romanticism on the part of western seekers of the oriental meaning of life and also on the part of its Asian advocates. In a very strange way this becomes also evident in the West through the growth of some esoteric religious sects that claim to trace their spiritual origin to the great Asian religions.[12] As a matter of fact, the oriental religious sects that thrive on the consumerism of western society are sad caricatures of their distant spiritual ancestors.

Romanticism apart, the people in Asia are facing a crisis of spirituality that poses a baffling question concerning the meaning of human existence. The feeling is that something has departed from the spirit of Asian culture, which has somehow spent itself and is no longer capable of fulfilling its role in the increasingly demanding situation of Asia today. Asian spirituality seems to have lost its say about the complex social and political problems that confront the people in their everyday life. This is, of course, not a totally accurate assessment of what has been happening in Asia in recent decades. There is the emergence of a new vitality in Asian spirituality that seeks to help people as they wrestle with the problems of life and death and face with determination social and political changes. It must be admitted, however, that the Asian spirituality that has allowed itself to become captive to the past and lost its strength to sustain people in their daily struggle tends to be discredited by many enlightened Asians today. In this connection China can be cited as a good example.

Hu Shih, one of the most prominent champions of the Chinese Renaissance in 1919, never ceased to deplore the fatal grip of traditional Chinese spirituality on the people of China. True to a humanistic spirit based on science and democracy, he never tired of challenging the Chinese classical scholars who preached the salvation of China in terms of a revival of the traditional cultural and social values. As he poignantly pointed out:

The civilization under which people are restricted and controlled by a material environment from which they cannot escape, and under which they cannot utilize human thought and intellectual power to change environment and improve conditions, is the civilization of a lazy and non-progressive people. It is truly a materialistic civilization. Such civilization can only obstruct but cannot satisfy the spiritual demands of mankind.[13]

The turbulent history of China in the succeeding years has more than vindicated Hu Shih's indictment of the old Chinese civilization, which became uprooted from its spiritual soil in the people and as a result deteriorated.

What then about Communist China, which has carried out a radical sociopolitical transformation after long years of revolutionary struggle? What we see in China today is a single-minded pursuit of an ultimate reality defined in ideological and political terms. In his June 30, 1949, address on the occasion of the twenty-eighth anniversary of the Chinese Communist party, Mao Tse-tung stated emphatically: "We . . . declare openly that we are striving hard to create the very condition which bring about their [classes'] extinction." When this goal is finally achieved, he continued, "human society will move to a higher stage."[14] What is this higher stage? It is a classless society in which the dictatorship of the proletariat will prevail completely. Political struggle is the vehicle for the realization of this political ideology. It promises to be a long struggle, for class enemies both within China and outside are not going to surrender easily to the vision of a classless society. There is thick darkness, as it were, shrouding the Communists' sociopolitical goal—a goal that has acquired intense religious implications for the people of China. To remove the veil of darkness, Mao Tse-tung and his party advocated and engineered a continuous struggle that would involve the people of China in perpetual revolution. This is a religious crusade against the mind and the spirit of a people who have inherited the cultural and spiritual traditions of Confucianism, Buddhism, Taoism, and ancestor worship. Communism presents itself as a new spirituality promising the utopia of a classless society and fighting the traditional spirituality with formidable ideological and political weapons. The struggle has been a costly one. The spirits of Confucius and other sages are summoned up from time to time from their rest to stand trial before the court of the Communist party, which declares them to be class enemies. This is a determined attempt to wean people away from the spirituality that has played a great role in the cultural and political history of China.

Stuart Schram, a by no means unsympathetic student of Communist China, describes China under Mao Tse-tung in the following way:

Being utterly convinced that his own thought was correct, he [Mao] supposed that every one else would be better off thinking exactly as he did. In his effort to conciliate spontaneity and discipline he was therefore inclined to place the emphasis heavily on conformity.[15]

Conformity is essentially a one-way communication. The leader dictates and the masses follow. Personal relations among people also tend to become distorted on account of the need to conform to ideological and political rules. It is therefore possible to assume that in this vast school of continuous revolution that is China today, heart-to-heart communication between political leaders and the people and between individuals and their neighbors must be disrupted. Individuals must subordinate their hearts to the party's political machine and to its ideological orthodoxy. If the vision of a classless society is realized one day, the people of China as a result of their constant struggles and the rigorous need to conform would perhaps have lost their ability to talk from the heart to the heart. What kind of a utopia would this be if people have ceased to communicate in the language of the heart?

### Poverty, Injustice, and Exploitation in Asia

After this brief digression, let us now return to our evaluation of how Asian spirituality fares in the expectations of people as they constantly struggle for a more just society and a more decent life. The truth of the matter is that in Asia today a large number of people are still condemned to a life of (poverty, injustice, and exploitation) Despite gallant efforts to fight for a new lease on life, the political systems, social conventions, and cultural ethos fostered by centuries of religious spirituality do not seem to succeed in building a new basis of human existence. India, for example, is one of the countries in Asia often afflicted with famines. One can always blame an unfriendly nature and the unsatiable gods for the calamities that visit that vast land's population. But the fact is that poverty is largely the result of what human beings do. To be specific, millions of people suffer indefinitely because of rampant social and economic injustices. C. K. Kurien, an Indian economist, has analyzed the situation in the following way:

When we turn to the specifics of the Indian situation, the most striking phenomenon is the dire poverty of the many millions in our land. . . . On the basis of nutritional criteria . . . an average Indian requires goods and services worth Rs 20 a month to have a physiologically determined minimum level of living. And it was reckoned that close to 50 per cent of our population lived below even this very modest figure.[16]

The population of India is more than 600 million. This means that more than 300 million people in India have to eke out a living below the minimum level of Rs 20 a month.

Kurien's analysis points out the human factors that have contributed to this intolerable situation. He writes:

Compared to the 50 per cent of our population living below poverty line we have a small section at the top which owns and controls most of the non-labour resources in the economy and derives much of the income generated by the total economic activity in the system. Inequalities of income and wealth are common in most parts of the world, but where the vast majority of the people live in rock bottom poverty the concentration of economic resources in the hands of a few at the top gives rise to special problems. The concentration of economic resources in India is in fact glaring.[17]

Has effort toward development of the country enabled the situation to change for the better? Or is development an ideology that further strengthens the rich and powerful and impoverishes the poor and powerless? The following statement by Kurien is an answer to this.

. . . we can identify two distinct sections of population in the country. The first consists of the top 10 per cent, affluent in terms of the ownership of resources and claims on income. The second section consists of the rest, but among them the bottom 50 percent must be especially identified because of the dire poverty of their situation.

Then comes Kurien's painful conclusion: "The benefits of the growth of the past twenty years or so have gone to the top 10 per cent almost to the complete exclusion of the bottom 50 per cent."[18]

This sober study of the social and economic situation in India is a strong indictment against a society that allows the majority of its people to work and struggle for the benefit of the privileged few, a society that prides itself on its spirituality of compassion and piety as India's special contribution to the spiritual wealth of humankind. The picture presented here makes us sad and indignant at the same time. We really wonder whether the spirituality of compassion has been replaced by the spirituality of gregariousness and selfishness. What has become of the people who inherited the noble tradition of bhakti religion and the compassion of Buddha?

In 1974, when India was struck again by a widespread famine as a result of a long drought, an even grimer picture emerged. A colossal undertaking on a global level to help the starving millions with food did not seem to alleviate the threat of death. *Newsweek* magazine reported:

India has purchased 2.3 million tons of grain from the United States this year—enough to feed 11.5 million people. The imports arrive by freighter in Bombay and Calcutta—but up to 20 per cent of the incoming supply is ultimately lost to rats and rot because of India's shoddy storage facilities. Corruption seems to be low in the grain trade—partially because shipments are too bulky to be trundled away. Still, existing stocks tend to be funnelled off to the politically volatile cities where people can buy up to 4.4 pounds of grain a week in government-subsidized grain shops—in addition to what they can buy on the free market. In the countryside, particularly in famine areas like West Bengal, supplies—and subsidies—can fall to Scroogian levels. It is possible, therefore, for the . . . grain to travel 11,000 miles to India—and never fill the empty tin bowls of "a starving family."[19]

"We are in the hands of God," muttered those waiting for fate to overtake them. God, the ultimate reality, is for them not the source of life, hope, and light but a great unknown hidden behind the impenetrable veil of darkness. Their lives were reduced to agony and resignation. Darkness descended upon their emaciated bodies and empty spirits.

It is not my intention to single out India as the target of criticism. India is merely an example of what can and does happen in the rest of Asia—and in the rest of the world. There must be something wrong with a spirituality that becomes resigned and helpless in face of human calamity. Poverty, social inequality, and political injustice in many countries in Asia have cast doubt on traditional spiritual values. One of the most articulate critics of this problem is Gunnar Myrdal, a Scandinavian economist who made an intensive study of poverty in South Asia. Here is his categorical verdict:

In any case, it is completely contrary to scientific principles to follow the easy, speculative approach of explaining the peculiarities in attitudes, institutions, and modes of living and working by reference to broad concepts of Hinduism, Buddhism, or Islam, or to personality or cultural traits such as abstention, spiritualism, lack of materialism, and other allegedly "Asian values." And it is not accidental that these broad generalizations can so easily be shown to be unrealistic.[20]

This verdict of a scientifically trained western economist seems final. And in fact there is much truth in it. Asians who take refuge in their religion despite the part they themselves play—individually or collectively—in the creation of misery and suffering among members of their own society should feel indicted by such a verdict.

However true this judgment may be, it is not the whole story. The point is that the spirituality that has sustained men and women in Asia does not have to be helpless in the face of social evils and political corruption. It can sustain people in their trouble-ridden lives; it can be a force in the transformation of society; and it can inspire people to gain a vision of the future from which they may derive the meaning of existence. It is at this point that Christian spirituality and Asian spirituality can come into significant play. At various levels of life the Christian faith and other faiths can intersect to create a new dynamic for people in Asia. It is no longer simply a question of evangelizing the so-called non-Christians. Nor is it a matter of promising life in the kingdom of God to those who have accepted Christ and threatening hell to those who have refused to make a commitment to the Christian faith. It is important here for us to ask: from the Christian viewpoint, how can Christian spirituality and Asian spirituality intersect in such a way that people begin to see the historical meaning of their existence in a new light? Furthermore, how can such an intersection become a point of departure for a fresh understanding of both Christian spirituality and Asian spirituality? Out of it can a new spirituality emerge to become the foundation of a new human community?

### A Historical Intersection: Christian and Asian Spirituality

Such a historical intersection between Christianity and Asian spirituality took place in Mahatma Gandhi, the father of Indian independence. As Gandhi recollected the time when he was a young student in England, he had this to confess:

. . . the New Testament produced a different impression [in contrast to the Old Testament], especially the Sermon on the Mount which went straight to my heart. I compared it with the *Gita.* The verses, "But I say unto you, that ye resist not evil: but whosoever shall smite thee on thy right cheek turn to him the other also. And if any man take away thy coat let him have thy cloak too," delighted me beyond measure. . . . My young mind tries to unify the teaching of *Gita,* the Light of Asia and the Sermon on the Mount. That renunciation was the highest form of religion appealed to me greatly.[21]

The historical intersection of Christian spirituality and Hindu spirituality in the person of Gandhi blossomed into his principle of nonviolence. He won independence for India not by the barrel of a gun but by renouncing the use of violence. The great British Empire tumbled in India because it could not successfully resist the nonviolence of a frail and defenseless man. In Gandhi we witness a tremendous spiritual power, which manifests itself in the social and political transformation of his own nation. Thus Gunnar Myrdal's verdict on Asian spirituality cannot be accepted as final. Gandhi manifested a kind of spirituality that was deeply rooted in the soul of India and revitalized by the redemptive love of God in Jesus Christ. Although Gandhi never became a Christian in the sense of joining a Christian church, we see in him a theology of third dimensionality at work. Through what he believed and did, the darkness separating Christian spirituality and Hindu spirituality was partially overcome—only partially, because there can be no complete lifting of the veil of darkness until the last day when we shall find ourselves in the brightness of God's presence. Furthermore, by living and acting in accordance with the principle of nonviolence to the end, Gandhi was constantly reminded of Jesus who surrendered himself to the death on the cross as the supreme example of God's love. Here too the darkness surrounding the heart of God was partly lifted for him. The power of love and compassion asserts its victory in the midst of hatred and violence. "God was in Christ," says St. Paul in his second letter to the Corinthians, "reconciling the world to himself, no longer holding men's misdeeds against them, and that he has entrusted us with the message of reconciliation" (2 Cor. 5:19). This central message of the Christian faith was acted out in Gandhi's struggle for the independence of his own nation. "Rivers of blood," says Gandhi, "may have to flow before we gain our freedom, but it must be our blood."

It is therefore no accident that the towering personality and indomitable spirit of this small Indian saint made a deep impression on two prominent Christians in the West in our own day—Martin Luther King, Jr., and Dietrich Bonhoeffer. In the case of Martin Luther King, Gandhi's philosophy and practice of nonviolence in the face of social and political violence profoundly moved him. He discovered in Gandhi the tremendous impact of what Gandhi called "soul-force." Gandhi once said:

The government of the day has passed a law which is applied to me. I do not like it. If by using violence I force the government to repeal the law, I am employing what may be called body-force. I do not obey the law and accept the penalty for the breach. I use soul-force. It involves sacrifice of self. . . . [22]

The soul-force to which Gandhi refers here is the spiritual force derived from the Hindu spirituality of *ahimsa* (harmlessness, nonviolence) and the Christian spirituality of the cross. The same soul-force enabled Martin Luther King, Jr., to lead his oppressed brothers and sisters in the United States in their struggle for civil rights, in the exodus from slavery to freedom, and in the pursuit of a dream of liberation from racial prejudice and discrimination.

Martin Luther King, Jr.'s, spiritual pilgrimage thus took a curious turn. Born to a pastor's home, himself trained and educated as a pastor and theologian, he was to rediscover the great truth and power of God's love through a Hindu saint and fighter for freedom. King describes his own pilgrimage in a way that is both moving and forceful:

Then I was introduced to the life and teachings of Mahatma Gandhi. As I read his works I became deeply fascinated by his campaigns of nonviolent resistance. The whole Gandhian concept of *satyagraha* (*satya* is truth which equals love and *graha* is force; *satyagraha* thus means truth-force or love-force) was profoundly significant to me. As I delved deeper into the philosophy of Gandhi, my skepticism concerning the power of love gradually diminished, and I came to see for the first time that the Christian doctrine of love, operating through the Gandhian method of nonviolence, is one of the most potent weapons available to an oppressed people in their struggle for freedom.[23]

This is a revealing account of the transformation that took place within a dedicated Christian leader for the cause of the freedom and equality for black people in the United States. The soul-force of Gandhi was transformed into the love-force of Martin Luther King, Jr., who for the first time, to use his own words, came to see the meaning of the Christian doctrine of love. Unless he was exaggerating, and there was no reason to think that he was, this gives us a classic example of how Christian spirituality can be informed by Asian spirituality to become a life- and world-transforming power.

In a less dramatic way we also see something like this happen to a martyred theologian who after his death became known as the pioneer of a new Christianity and a new theology in the West. I am, of course, referring to Dietrich Bonhoeffer, a man destined to play a crucial role in the fate of his own nation in the 1930s and 1940s. On the one hand, there were ominous signs of the rise of demonic forces personified by Hitler and Nazi Germany. This was a frantic and diabolical effort toward the fulfillment of a messianic hope conceived totally in political terms. To his dismay and anguish Bonhoeffer witnessed the retreat of his own church from its prophetic task as a result of siding with the powers that be. In his premonition, this would plunge millions of people into unprecedented disaster. Bonhoeffer became disillusioned in the Christianity to which he owed his upbringing, education, and culture. He began to look for something outside the West that might serve as a spiritual anchor for him in the turbulent sea of German social and political upheavals. On October 17, 1933, he wrote to his brother from London where he had been barely three months as pastor of a German congregation:

... since I am becoming daily more convinced that in the West Christianity is approaching its end—at least in the present form, and its present interpretation—I should like to go to the Far East before going back to Germany.[24]

Outwardly Bonhoeffer might not be that different from western youths of today who seek to heal their disillusionment with the affluent western society by looking toward the "Far" East, but there was this profound difference—he desperately needed a spirituality that would enable him to combat the evil sociopolitical forces wrecking his country. This is how Bonhoeffer's authoritative biographer, Bethge, sees the situation:

In 1928 it was a desire for a wider experience that led to the first Indian project. In 1931 an additional factor was skepticism regarding the Western form of Christianity. And in 1934 Bonhoeffer was motivated by the desire to witness the experiment along with lines of the Sermon on the Mount as exemplified by Gandhi—namely, the purposive exercises and the Indian methods of resistance to a power that was regarded as tyrannous. . . . What he sought was a prototype for passive resistance that could induce and change without violence. What he was aiming at, therefore, was a means of combating Hitler that went beyond the aims and methods of the church struggle while remaining legitimate from a Christian stand-point.[25]

It seems strange, at first at any rate, that Bonhoeffer, who himself wrote a moving and forceful exposition on the Sermon on the Mount,[26] was looking for help from an Indian sage he never met. But he rightly realized that in Gandhi was something that crossed the rigid boundaries of alien spiritualities, something that grew out of and yet transcended a particular spirituality. From Gandhi he wanted to learn about the soul-force that might enable him to combat the body-force of Hitler. Bonhoeffer did not regard the soul-force of Gandhi as alien or contradictory to his Christian faith. On the contrary, he believed that a new spiritual force such as the one possessed by Gandhi might be able to revitalize Christianity in its western form. But his projected trip to India never materialized. His friends and colleagues counseled him against the trip. Karl Barth, in whom Bonhoeffer had been confiding as his mentor and trusted teacher, called it "the strange news" he had been hearing about Bonhoeffer for ages.[27] In a sense Bonhoeffer was ahead of his time. He was able to visualize, as no other theologian in Europe at that time did, the possibility of a new spiritual force of love emerging out of creative interactions between Christian spirituality and Hindu spirituality. If the Indian project had taken place, and if Bonhoeffer had been able to sit at the feet of Gandhi, his life course might have taken a different turn. As we know, he later took part in an assassination attempt on Hitler's life. The attempt failed; he was arrested; and after a long imprisonment he was executed shortly before the end of World War II.

Earlier I said that Christian spirituality and Hindu spirituality intersected in the person of Gandhi. They were to intersect again forcefully in Martin Luther King, Jr., and implicitly in Dietrich Bonhoeffer. At each intersection a spark of fire was kindled to illuminate the darkness surrounding God and humanity. At each intersection we are led to see the power of God's love at work in the world. And at each intersection we are met by a less cloudy vision of our ultimate human destiny in God. It is the destiny of love through pain and suffering. Mahatma Gandhi, Martin Luther King, Jr., and Dietrich Bonhoeffer all died a martyr's death. But the soul-force they shared continues to inspire and strengthen men and women in their struggle for love, freedom and justice in the world, regardless of race, culture, or religion. There is, therefore, reason to believe that this soul-force is at work in different degrees and in different ways in men and women, great and small, young and old, and Christian and non-Christian. It is the task of the theologian with a third eye to discern where such a soul-force is, to be informed by it, and to wrestle with it.

### The Trivialization of Human Issues

After this noble picture of what soul-force can accomplish in certain people, we must come back now to the brutal reality of worldliness, which can obstruct our vision of the future and blunt our sense of the divine. Let me refer to the experience of Harvey Cox, the prophet of the modern secular city. As he tells us, he was visiting a school teacher in Recife, a city in the poverty-stricken northeast of Brazil. The television set was showing an American cartoon series, *The Flintstones*. Here is Cox's immediate reaction: "The canned laughter used in the show, the banal situations, the cleverly contrived ads, the lack of contact with life, in Recife or anywhere else," made him sick. Why? Reflecting on what he saw, he came up with this answer:

Perhaps the most unsettling issue raised by *The Flintstones* in Recife is that such programs produce an inevitable trivialization of human issues. With a few exceptions, divisive issues are avoided, conflict is dissolved into personal differences, the raw edges of life disappear in a sea of gray froth. The media designed to reach the broadest possible audience thus discourages consumers from having strong feelings about anything important. It is crucial to keep the political significance of trivialization in mind, since banality seems nonpolitical. The fact is that whenever real issues can be trivialized, the status quo is strengthened.[28]

Trivialization of human issues—this is it! This is what I would call the crisis of spirituality in the present-day world. Modern technology, made readily available not only to the people in the West but also increasingly to the people of the Third World, has trivialized the human spirit. To be sure, modern scientists have made gigantic strides in their exploration of the unfathomable depths of space and of the mystery of life, but the price we must pay is the tendency to dissolve human issues into scientific and technological issues. Human quality comes to be subsumed under technological quality. The truth of the matter is that it is the human quality that made the civilizations of the past great and memorable, both in the East and in the West. In other words, civilization is made for humans, not humans for civilization. Thus when human quality is reduced in importance, as seems to be the case in modern technological culture, the human spirit is trivialized. It is such a trivialized western culture, exemplified by a cartoon series like *The Flintstones*, that is exported to the Third World. Such a culture is designed to seduce people away from the basic human and spiritual issues pertaining to the ultimate meaning of life.

We must not overlook the fact that such a trivialized western culture is not shipped out of western ports free from ideological contamination. On the contrary, it comes with an ideology focused on success in the world in terms of wealth and social status. This ideology brandishes the weapon of economic power to control the lives of individuals and of nations. Thus, in the Third World western economic power is allied with indigenous political power. This is an alliance of a trivialized western culture with a trivialized indigenous culture. In the case of the latter, human quality is lacking because the political power that has consolidated itself into a dictatorship has to eliminate all traces of human quality in order to keep people under tight control. A television cartoon series like *The Flintstones* serves as an economic and political opium that diverts people from the real issues of society, dulls their sensitivity toward injustices committed against them, and gives them a false sense of well-being. It is a religious substitute for a dream that the oppressed and the poor have no hope of turning into a reality. It is, to use a different metaphor, a kind of anesthetic that prevents them from perceiving what those in the high places are plotting against their humanity.

In this trivialized western culture, human spirituality has a formidable rival that seeks to claim the soul as well as the body of people. This is the hidden danger of the economic development that nations in the Third World are trying to achieve in competition with one another. As pointed out earlier, developmental efforts in the Third World have not benefited the poor as they should have. The reason is that such a development is often used as an instrument to bring into existence *The Flintstones* or a trivialized type of culture which keeps the poor and the oppressed contented with their fate. The urgent task facing the Third World is therefore to humanize development in such a way that economic growth is not achieved at the cost of human growth. Pope Paul VI's Encyclical *On the Development of Peoples* expressed this idea well in these words:

Development cannot be limited to mere economic growth. In order to be authentic it must be complete, integral: that is, it has to promote the good of every man and of the whole man.

And further:

We do not believe in separating the economic from the human, nor development from the civilizations in which it exists. What we hold important is man, each man and each group of men [and women], and we even include the whole of humanity.[29]

Human beings should be the goal of development. In other words, development is to serve humanity, not the other way round. From this it is clear that development cannot be limited to the so-called developing countries of the Third World. The West, which has given rise to a trivialized form of culture is as much in need of development as the Third World to which the trivialized western culture is introduced in the name of development. In such a trivialized culture both East and West are confronted with a common enemy—the dehumanization of human beings. Development in the sense of growing to full humanity must therefore be a global concern.

The trivialized culture symbolized by *The Flintstones* series is indeed symptomatic of the malaise of the world today. This culture falters on human issues and gives birth to human beings with strong economic and biological components but with insensitive, sick hearts. Sickness of heart—this is the root cause of the problems of our world at large. Christian theology must play a part in healing this sickness. But how? This is the question we shall take up in the next chapter.

# CHAPTER 2

# GOD'S HEARTACHE:
# THE BEGINNING OF THEOLOGY

## *Origin of the Creation Account*

God's heart aches. His heart aches because of an immediate danger to creation. On the one hand, there is confusion and chaos—*tohu wa-bohu* ("a darkened and devastated earth from which life and order have fled").[1] There is, on the other hand, the abyss—*tehom,* which is covered in deep darkness and defies divine intervention. Thus God has not entered the dawn of history without rivals. He is confronted by the power of evil, darkness, and death; it challenges his authority and seeks to put the world under its control. As we now know, this is the way the people of the ancient Near East—long before the appearance of the people of Israel—understood creation. It is no accident that the Priestly account of the creation in Genesis reflects deeply the ethos of the Babylonian creation myth, *Enuma elis.* In that myth Tiamat—the primordial ocean from which the Hebrew word *tehom* is derived—is a symbol of the forces of evil that are finally overcome by Marduk, the god of light. In a matchless style the majestic epic vividly describes the fierce combat between Marduk and Tiamat. On hearing Marduk's challenge and battle cry:

> In fury Tiamat cried out aloud.
> To the roots her legs shook both together.
> She recites a charm, keeps casting spells,
> While the gods of battle sharpen their weapons.
> Then joined issue Tiamat and Marduk, wisest of gods.
> They strove in single combat, locked in battle.
> The Lord spread out his net to enfold her,
> The Evil Wind, which followed behind, he let loose in her face.
> When Tiamat opened her mouth to consume him,
> He drove in the Evil Wind that she closed not her lips.
> As the fierce winds charged her belly,
> Her body was distended and her mouth was wide open.

He released the arrow, it tore her belly,
It cut through her insides, splitting the heart.
Having thus subdued her, he extinguished her life.
He cast down her carcass to stand upon it.[2]

While the cosmic battle was being fought, the gods who had chosen
Marduk to be their leader and champion looked on in terror. But when
the battle was finally won, they burst into jubilation.

Then the Lord paused to view her dead body,
That he might divide the monster and do artful works.
He split her like a shellfish into two parts:
Half of her he set up and ceiled it as sky,
Pulled down the bar and posted guards.
He bade them to allow not her waters to escape.
He crossed the heavens and surveyed the regions.[3]

The creation epic goes on to describe how Marduk marked the days,
months, and years. Thus freed from the tyranny of evil forces, the
assembly of the gods moved on to the next stage of creation.

The discovery that the creation story in the first chapter of Genesis was
not a unique revelation of the mystery of creation granted to the people of
Israel, but that it took its origin in a Mesopotamian creation myth greatly
disturbed Christians. As if to allay their disturbed minds, Old Testament
scholars were quick to show how the creation myth of a foreign origin had
been transformed to convey a meaning unique to the biblical faith. It has
been pointed out, for example, that:

while we have before us incontestable similarities in detail, the difference in
overall approach is no less prominent. The Babylonian creation story features a
succession of various rival deities. The biblical version, on the other hand, is
dominated by the monotheistic concept in the absolute sense of the term. Thus the
two are both genetically related and yet poles apart.[4]

This may be so. But there is no denying the fact that the creation story,
whether in its Babylonian form or in the Priestly version, seeks to deal with
the problems of darkness and death that confront men and women in
their daily lives. Creation is thus seen as bringing light into darkness,
turning chaos into order, and overcoming death with life. Strictly speaking therefore the creation story is concerned not so much with the origin
of the world as with the problems of life and death in human existence.

Our ancient ancestors, regardless of their culture and religion, were
very preoccupied with the question of darkness. The fear of darkness was
universally present. The inevitability of death was there.[5] To give another
example, a hymn of creation from the *Rigveda,* composed probably as far
back as 1500 or 1200 B.C. in India, was strangely similar to the book of

Genesis in its description of the primordial state of the universe:

Darkness there was: at first concealed in darkness, this All was indiscriminated chaos.
All that existed then was void and formless: by the great power of warmth was born that unit.
Thereafter rose desire in the beginning. Desire, the primal seed and germ of spirit.
Sages who searched with their heart's thought discovered the existent's kinship in the non-existent.[6]

Darkness is the evil power that separates human beings from the source of life. It is synonymous with death. Light disappears into darkness and life is swallowed up by death. In desperation we look for help from beyond ourselves. "Out of the depths I cry to thee, O Lord!" (Ps. 130:1), says the Psalmist. This is a cry for a new creation. Religious effort, including that of Christianity, begins with the need of men and women for a new day in which the power of darkness and death may be overcome.

What distinguishes faith in the Christian Bible from other faiths is therefore not the so-called *creatio ex nihilo.* Nor is it the way in which people realize that they are up against the power of evil and darkness that is dangerous to their existence. What is made very explicit in the biblical faith is the personal ways in which God responds to the fear and predicament of a human community. In other words, God's heart aches. God's heart aches because of the possible disintegration of a world still in its primitive, infant stage. God cannot contain his ache any more. He plunges right into the act of creation. He checks the power of *tehom* and lets the light shine into the darkness of the universe, thus saving creation from total destruction. A new beginning is made. And this new beginning is to sustain the world in its faltering journey toward its destination.

The Book of Psalms is full of the human cry of distress and the divine response to that cry, which is reminiscent of interactions between light and darkness, between life and death, between the power of creation and the power of chaos. Let us listen to Psalm 77:[7]

> I cried aloud to God,
> I cried to God, and he heard me.
> In the day of my distress I sought the Lord,
> and by night I lifted my outspread hands in prayer.
> I lay sweating and nothing would cool me;
> I refused all comfort (vv. 1–2).

In his great personal distress the Psalmist looks for God's intervention. He cannot bear the silence of God. He wants to hear God addressing him personally. But with no sign of God's immediate intervention, he becomes even more restless. He is now assailed by doubt:

> Has God forgotten to be gracious,
> has he in anger withheld his mercies? (v. 9)

At this point he turns to the history of his own nation in search of the assurance of God's love and salvation:

> But then, O Lord, I call to mind thy deeds;
> I recall thy wonderful acts in times gone by.
> I meditate upon thy works
> and muse on all that thou hast done (vv. 11–12).

For the people of Israel, history is never a neutral ground where no commitment is made either by God or human beings. History is not made up of objective events waiting for historians' evaluation. For individuals and for the nation, history is the product of God's saving intervention. It is where God meets people in his power and love. It is an act of faith for Israelites to turn to history when they are beset with personal difficulties and problems. To the Exodus they must turn. To the wandering in the wilderness they must return. They have to remind themselves how the river Jordan stopped its flow to let their ancestors cross from the wilderness into the land of promise. They must visualize before their mind's eye how God fought for them to secure a foothold in an alien land. In going back to history they find God's answer and hear his voice.

This is how the Psalmist of Psalm 77 transforms his personal distress into a fresh encounter with the God who works in history. His cry for help thus turns into a confession of faith in the God of history:

> Thou art the God who workest miracles;
> thou hast shown the nations thy power.
> With thy strong arm thou didst redeem thy people,
> the sons of Jacob and Joseph (vv. 14–15).

In the private chamber of agony and distress God cannot be seen or heard. The Psalmist has to open the window of his chamber to let the light of history shine into his heart and mind. There and then he sees the God of salvation; he hears the God who speaks through his mighty works in the struggles of the nations. But this is not the end of his vision. He must extend the horizon of his faith even further. That is to say, he must still go on from history to creation. Thus we hear from his mouth words that echo the account of creation in the primordial time:

> The waters saw thee, O God,
> they saw thee and writhed in anguish;
> the ocean was troubled to its depths.
> The clouds poured water, the skies thundered,
> thy arrows flashed hither and thither (vv. 16–17).

Here is the word *ocean,* or *deep,* again.[8] The power of evil and darkness is checked by God's mighty acts. Here the Psalmist makes another transition. As we have seen, he moves from his personal situation to the history of his nation. This is the first transition. Then comes the second transition. From the historical terrain he lets the imagination of his faith soar back into the beginning of time when a great cosmic battle was fought between God and the *tehom.* This is the God who won the cosmic battle that, to use the Psalmist's own words, "guided thy people like a flock of sheep, under the hand of Moses and Aaron" (v. 20).

Psalm 77 is a typical expression of faith in the Old Testament—a faith in which the individual, history, and creation are closely knitted together. What we have here is a cycle of faith, consisting of the personal, the historical, and the creational. This cycle of faith enables the biblical faith to be free from mythological preoccupation with the origin of the world. In the ancient Near East as well as in India under the influence of Hinduism, the personal and the mythological are not linked together by the historical. The marriage of the personal and the mythological results in an offspring, the mystical. India, for example, is the land of mystics. It is a land full of religious imageries and spiritual metaphors. The historical tends to be de-emphasized. The following observation is generally true as far as premodern India is concerned:

Nearly every Indian thinker seeks to live in the bosom of nature and there to have direct communion with the Absolute. He renounces the world, lives in the depths of the forest, sits under a tree or on a rock and, keeping himself aloof from all secular affairs, concentrates his thoughts on the quest for truth. There have been a few thinkers who try to seek truth while remaining in the secular world and living among people in the street. But, in India, such thinkers have been very few in number and not so influential. And the main current of the Indian civilization has been not in the cities but in the woods. It has been the civilization of the tranquil life in the forest.[9]

This is generally true, although we cannot ignore some notable exceptions such as Gandhi, who has been mentioned before. As we have seen, Gandhi tried to put his personal faith to work by involving himself in the social and political struggle of his people. In so doing, he has made his influence strongly felt not only in his own country but also abroad. At any rate, it is on the whole correct to say that a rise in historical consciousness has enabled people in Asia to grasp the meaning of religious faith as it is related to social and political changes.

### The Connection Between Creation and Redemption

In any case the story of creation is in a true sense the story of salvation loaded with cosmic and historical implications. In St. Paul's words, "The whole creation has been groaning in travail together until now" (Rom. 8:22,RSV). Creation is God's response to this cosmic groaning. And as the seer in the Book of Revelation understands it, God's work of redemption leads to the emergence of a new creation. He states: "Then I saw a new heaven and a new earth; for the first heaven and the first earth had passed away" (Rev. 21:1,RSV). He then goes on to say that God "will wipe away every tear from their eyes, and death shall be no more, neither shall there be mourning nor crying nor pain any more, for the former things have passed away" (Rev. 21:4,RSV). All this indicates that creation and redemption are in reality two sides of the same coin.[10] Where there is creation, there is redemption. Conversely, where there is redemption, there is creation. Or to put it another way, creation is God's redeeming act, while redemption is God's creating act. To separate creation from redemption is to turn creation back into a cosmogony that is a kind of primitive science trying to pry into the mystery of the origin of the universe. It must be stressed that the Bible is not primarily interested in cosmogony as such. From beginning to end its chief concern is the creating and redeeming work of God. When God acts, something new happens—a new person is born, a new community comes into being, a new heaven and a new earth, that is, a new creation, replaces the old heaven and the old earth, namely, the old creation. The whole cosmos as well as human beings in particular are sustained and renewed by this creating and redeeming God until the time of fulfillment.

Seeing creation in a close relationship with redemption, we realize that in God's creating and redeeming acts we have the very prototype of doing theology. Creation is God's redemptive response to the pain and suffering of this world. It is not so much a demonstration of God's glory as a manifestation of his love and compassion for the world. God's heart aches when the world is gripped with pain and suffering. This makes God the theologian *par excellence.* That is to say, in the heart of God we find the beginning of theology. Theology begins with God's heartache on account of the world. God does not theologize in a vacuum or in the midst of his glorious splendor and light but in confrontation with the power of *tehom,* the darkness that poses as a real threat to the birth, growth, and fruition of life. Creation redemptively carried out is God's theology in action. God the theologian is God the Creator. He is also God the Redeemer. He translates the aching of his heart into the making of life. Creation is the victory of God over *tehom.* It is the victory of heart over heartlessness, of life over death. Creation is thus the disclosure of the heart of God confronted with the powerful principle of negation. Creation, and for that matter, redemption, is the outpouring of the heart of God, the giving of God himself. It is the staking of all that God is in his involvement with the hostile elements of this world.

In this connection I must point out that God's creational and redemptive involvement with the world is not entirely foreign to Asian spirituality. It is reflected in Gautama Buddha's resolve to set out on a mission to preach the truth upon attaining his Enlightenment. This is how he reasons:

What could be a better way of living for others than to show them the path of attaining perfect bliss? What could be greater service to mankind than to rescue the struggling creatures engulfed in the mournful sea of *samsara*? . . . When the Perfect One considered how sorrow and suffering oppressed all beings, he became very compassionate, and made up his mind to preach to all mankind the eternal truths he had discovered.

> Amongst the nations I shall go
> and open the door that to the deathless leads.
> Let those that have ears to hear
> Master the noble path of salvation.[11]

In this way Buddhism became a missionary religion. The road it trod was very similar to that of Christianity. It was carried northeastward to China and Japan. To the east it entered Burma and Thailand, and to the south it found a congenial home in Ceylon. A great part of East and South Asia came under the strong influence of Buddhism. Buddhist culture imbued with Buddhist spirituality became predominant in the mind and life of hundreds of millions of people in Asia. Despite criticisms of Buddhism as a religion of negation, it is basically a religion of the heart and compassion. How then could it be totally unrelated to the love of God revealed in Jesus Christ? How could we fail to see something of God's creative-redemptive work in Buddhist spirituality?

### The Logos in Western Theology

When we come to the Prologue of John's Gospel in the New Testament, we find ourselves in a somewhat different atmosphere. There the Greek word *logos* is the linguistic vehicle for God's saving activity in the world. In the beginning was the *logos*, says John in the Prologue. This opens John's Gospel, and at the same time it also opens the door to the *logos* structure of western theology *Logos*, as C. K. Barrett points out, has a double meaning of "inward thought, and the outward expression of thought in speech."[12] That is to say, in the Greek use of the word is implied a rational structure of thought that takes an explicit form conforming to the semantic and rational structure of human communication. Here is the importance of logic, the business of which is to make sure there is correspondence between thought and speech in communication. When the word *logos* is further used in religious discourse, its basic meaning is retained. "In a theistic system," says Barrett, "it could therefore naturally be used in an account of God's self-revelation; his thought was communicated by his speech."[13] Speech thus comes to occupy a very important part in Christian theology. Especially in the Reformed tradition, speech receives primary attention.

But what is speech? First and foremost it is *human* speech. It is the words and sentences we use to communicate our thoughts and ideas. It is therefore conditioned by factors inherent in social conventions and cultural conditions. This kind of speech has to become a vehicle of divine communication. God communicates himself through human words. This is the assertion that constitutes the possibility of Christian theology. Apart from Christianity, Judaism and Islam make a similar assertion. It is no wonder because these three religions share a basic historical origin. But the problem is: How can human speech with its human conditions and limitations express the thought of God, which is not subject to these conditions and limitations? This is a basic problem which Christian theology must answer. How does theology get at this problem?

The assumption in theology is that the mind of God is reflected in the order of things, and particularly in the language human beings employ to communicate their thought. This means that human speech is considered to share the ontological nature of divine speech. Human speech is therefore not mere words. It somehow reveals the structure of God in himself. It follows that human speech employed in expressing divine truth and theological convictions comes to acquire a place of disproportionate importance in the development of Christian theological thinking. Even an iota can become a focus of vehement theological controversy. It is a well-known fact that the celebrated disputes over the two natures of Christ in the third and fourth centuries resulted in the triumph of the *homoousios* of Nicene orthodoxy over the *homoiousios* of the semi-Arian heresy. But as later became evident, the Chalcedonian formula that the Son of God is truly God and truly man and is consubstantial—*homoousios*— with the Father was not accepted without challenge. There was the so-called verbal monophysism that opposed the two natures of the Son. The crux of the matter here consisted in the fact that the verbal monophysists "took 'nature' *(phusis)* to be a synonym of 'hypostasis'. They therefore believed that there was a contradiction and an open door to Nestorianism in a formula such as that of Chalcedon which distinguishes between two natures while claiming that they subsisted in a single hypostasis."[14] Again the controversy is raised around the use of terms which have inevitable difference in connotation and usage in different cultural and semantic contexts. The following statement is therefore true:

The history of theology can be written in large part by the explanation of a series of technical terms, the understanding, misunderstanding, and final definition of which make up the development of doctrine.[15]

The power with which language binds the development of human thought to itself is impressive. Although this is not limited to Christianity alone, it is very evident in the history of Christian thought in the West. A mere iota made all the difference in the development of christological thinking in the centuries that followed.

Among contemporary theologians T. F. Torrance defends most vigorously the scientific and rational nature of theology and of the language theology employs to express theological truth. As he puts it:

Theological formulation takes place through a movement of interpretation and explanatory penetration into the inner intelligibility of the divine revelation, in which we allow our human thoughts to be moulded pliantly and obediently by the truth itself, and thus to take their basic form from the inner locution in the very being of God.[16]

There is, in other words, an inherent logicality between our theological formulation and the "inner locution" of God. What constitutes the essence of this logicality? What is the faculty in us which is most active in knowing and interpreting divine revelation? It is reason, the seat of human, and by inference, of divine rationality. "Knowledge of God," to quote Torrance again:

is essentially a *rational event*. It is not concerned at all with anything that is sub-rational or irrational. We are concerned in theology with a fully rational communication between God and man and a fully rational response between man and God. Indeed we are concerned with the very essence of rationality before which all our other experiences appear inadequately rational. . . . By rationality, we . . . mean . . . rather our ability to relate our thought and our action appropriately to objective intelligible realities. Reason is our ability to recognize and assent to what is beyond.[17]

Is this so? Granted that in theology as in science we must always be on our guard against subrational and irrational elements that obstruct and disturb our perception of objective realities. For this reason Torrance argues forcefully that what he calls scientific rationality must also be applied to theology. "Scientific rationality," according to Torrance:

is that in which we bring the inherent rationality of things to light and expression, as we let the realities we investigate disclose themselves to us under our questioning and we on our part submit our minds to their inherent connections and order.[18]

The assumption here is that essentially God is a rational Being who, like subject-matters under scientific investigation, discloses his nature to human beings. It seems that at this point a difference between scientific rationality and theological rationality must be drawn, and Torrance does draw a line between them. In theology, he tells us, "we are concerned

. . . with a *different kind of rationality* from that which we find embedded in nature."[19] How are we then to be informed by this different kind of rationality in such a way that our knowledge of God does not become just our own illusion? Torrance's answer is as follows:

If therefore we are to communicate with someone about God and to persuade him in respect of something about Him we must refer him to the divine Logos in order that he may listen to God for himself, for he cannot know God unless he lets Him bear witness to Himself and disclose Himself to him through His own Word.[20]

His conclusion:

In theological persuasion, we seek to bring others to the point where they submit their minds to the inherent rationality of the divine revelation. There they must think only as they are compelled to think by the nature of the divine realities themselves. . . .[21]

In other words, Torrance is saying that, confronted with the subject matter called God, we must realize that the analogical relation he is at pains to establish between science and theology breaks down. In the last analysis, what theology has in common with science consists in the methodological considerations which allow the subject matter to dictate the process of investigation. Here again, the analogy is a limited one. For in science the investigators both control and are controlled by the object of investigation. They are not merely passive observers or receivers of information. They operate and experiment with hypotheses and theories they have at their command. They do not approach their subject matter with their minds like a *tabula rasa*. In theology the situation is different. Torrance takes us to the presence of Reality and leaves us there, asking us to let God bear witness to us himself. But how can we be sure we are in the presence of Reality or God? What is the process of verification at this most crucial point in our knowledge of God? And furthermore, how do we know that God will address himself to us?

In the Introduction I referred to Shusaku Endo's novel *Silence*. More often than not, God is silent. God does not seem eager to speak to us when we badly need the assurance of his presence in power and love. What do we do when we do not seem to hear a word from him? My suspicion is that Torrance already knows what the inherent rationality of the Reality called God is before he takes us there. But how does he know? Did he find himself in the presence of God with a totally empty mind? Unlikely. For behind him is the tradition of the church's more than two thousand years of history. His own cultural and religious backgrounds too must have played significant roles in his knowledge of God. Thus the question is left essentially unanswered, namely, how is human rationality to be shaped by the inherent rationality of God in such a way that our thought and mind reflect the thought and mind of God? In fact, there is no easy answer to a question such as this, because the rationality of God we are discussing here has not become more accessible now than before we began our investigation. It is still a great mystery confronting us with pregnant silence.

From the discussion above it becomes clear that scientific rationality is not much of a help to us as we try to get at the mystery of the Reality that inspires our religious devotion. For what Torrance calls the "inadequately rational" makes up the content of religious experience and theological endeavor. Perhaps the term *inadequately rational* cannot accurately convey our meaning here. It is not so much what is inadequately rational as what cannot be explained in purely rational terms that engages our attention and effort. What is it then that cannot be explained in rational terms? It is the fall, it is sin, it is the cross, and it is forgiveness. The implication here is obvious: if theology is a science whose task is to explicate the rational structure of the divine-human relationships, we must qualify the word *rational* by saying that it is not scientific rationality but the rationality transformed by the saving love of God that we are talking about. But the problem is that once we start using the word in such a qualified way, we trespass on the semantic convention that makes words and concepts like *reason* or *rationality* intelligible in everyday communication. The conventions of language are bound to be impaired and the communication of meaning can easily become distorted or misunderstood. Theology has been notorious in this respect. Theologians are too often tempted to stretch the conventions of language to a breaking point on the basis that what they have to deal with cannot be expressed in ordinary terms. But the truth of the matter is that in the long tradition of *logos* theology, that is, theology dominated by reason or rationality, the structure of divine-human relationships is grasped conceptually and analytically. This results in the imposition of a severe limitation on our experience of God—the God who is not an analytical concept to begin with. In other words, scientific and philosophical frameworks that western theologians employ to get at the essence and nature of the Reality behind all realities are not conducive to penetrating the darkness surrounding the heart of Being. Rational theology, that is, theology intent on exploiting human reason to let the mystery of Being yield to human understanding, does not seem to conform to the ways in which God relates himself to the world.

### The Asian Intuitive Approach to Reality

In contrast to the conceptual and rationalistic approach to the Reality behind all realities, there is an intuitive approach that some Asians, especially the Chinese and Japanese, tend to stress in their grasp of the reality that transcends their immediate apprehension.[22] It is interesting to observe that, even in the fields of science and technology where Japan ranks high among the developed nations, the Japanese are intuitively oriented. According to Hajime Nakamura:

In the history of technology also the Japanese people have valued and still value intuitive perception *(kan)* more than scientific inferences based on postulational thinking. They were apt to rely on the dexterity of artisans rather than on exact calculation by machine.[23]

This shows that for the Japanese and Chinese, intuition rules their mind, thought, and action in an emphatic way. It is thus no wonder that religion comes to be associated more with intuition than with reason.

  . In the concept of *satori*, which is the key that unlocks the mystery of life and the world in Buddhism and particularly in Zen Buddhism, intuition is the most essential element. *Satori* is enlightenment of the mind as the mind is touched by the truth. It is an experience that leads us to the sudden realization of being in the presence of the truth we have been seeking. It can be compared to the artistic inspiration that enables an artist to grasp and apprehend what lies beneath the appearance of beauty and ugliness. In this sense theology, or more generally religion, has more in common with art than with science. Art, at its most profound expression, is religious through and through. It can become the embodiment of the sublime in the artist's mind. Theology or religion partakes of artistic profundity at its most sincere level where theology and art cross each other's path. In that intersection artistic theology is born and theological art comes into being. Both artistic theology and theological art are children of intuition. Intuition overcomes the normal framework of reason and rationality, breaks into the mystery of mysteries, and enables men and women to come to the presence of the Reality they seek.

  "*Satori*," as Daisetz Suzuki puts it:

may be defined as an intuitive looking into the nature of things in contradistinction to the analytical or logical understanding of it. Practically, it means the unfolding of a new world hitherto unperceived in the confusion of a dualistically trained mind.[24]

*Satori* opens for us a door into the dimension of things hidden from us so far. It enables us to see the reality behind and beyond phenomena and to penetrate the barriers that hinder us from seeing the true nature of things. Needless to say, this *satori* is akin to the revelation on which Christian faith depends. Revelation does not come at the end of logical reasoning. It is not bound or controlled by logic. It is not restricted by the norms within which human logic operates. It comes to you at the moment you least expect it. Think of Moses and the burning bush. To him the burning bush was a strange phenomenon at first. He had never seen anything like it. Then it turned into the disclosure of the divine commission that entrusted him with the task of leading his people out of Egypt. Or take Elijah. Utterly exhausted in his struggle with Jezebel, the ruthless and obnoxious queen, Elijah ran away and hid himself in a cave on Mount Horeb. He badly needed from Yahweh comfort and assurance which he was not going to find in an earthquake or a thunderstorm. The assurance came in a still small voice that said: "But I will leave seven thousand in Israel, all who have not bent the knee to Baal, all whose lips have not kissed him" (1 Kings: 19:18). Revelation came to St. Paul in a most unexpected way also. On his way to Damascus where he expected to arrest the followers of Jesus, he was struck by a blinding light from heaven accompanied by a voice saying to him: "I am Jesus, whom you are persecuting. But get up and go into the city, and you will be told what you have to do" (Acts 9:6). For these and many others in the history of Christianity, these are the moments of *satori* as well as revelation. Their eyes are opened through an extraordinary force which causes a deep and radical change in their whole being.

The scientific rationality that carries us up to a crucial moment when we expect to be informed by the mystery of Reality renders us helpless, as we saw earlier. But *satori* is an intuitive power that can take us across the boundary of human rationality into a world of a new vision. In Buddhism, it is true, it is stressed that we must find the Buddha-nature in ourselves; it is no use looking for it in some external principles or objects. There is thus a strongly subjective element in *satori*. But true *satori* does not shut us off completely from the external world. In Daisetz Suzuki's words:

It is one's own spiritual nature in enlightenment that responds to the external world, comes into contact with objects, raises the eyebrows, winks the eyelids, and moves the hands and legs. This Nature is the Mind, and the Mind is the Buddha, and the Buddha is the Way, and the Way is Zen.[25]

Experience of *satori* marks a new beginning in our life and in our relationship to the surrounding world. It is an experience similar to that of conversion. In Buddhism *satori* tends to be regarded purely as the work of the human spirit. But from the Christian point of view, we must say that *satori* is the work of the Holy Spirit within us. John Calvin calls it "the internal witness of the Holy Spirit."[26] Can we therefore not say that in *satori* the internal witness of the Holy Spirit is experienced as a direct and immediate movement of divine power? The Holy Spirit is thus perceived in *satori* as a power that draws us closer to the source of our being and makes us aware of the true nature of our life and the world.

What we gain in *satori* is therefore not some lofty ideas about God and about human beings. In *satori* when we are grasped by the power of the Spirit, we gain insight into the nature of realities in terms of pain and suffering. This is true of Christianity as well as Buddhism. St. Paul, for example, perceived the whole creation groaning in travail, as we previously mentioned. He goes on to say: " . . . not only the creation, but we ourselves, who have the first fruits of the Spirit, groan inwardly as we wait for adoption as sons, the redemption of our bodies" (Rom. 8:23, RSV). If this is true for those who have accepted Christ as their Lord and Savior, how much more it is also true for those who have not been initiated into the mystery of God revealed in Christ! Compare, for example, St. Paul's words with the following expression that allegedly originated with Buddha:

> How can you find delight and mirth
> Where there is burning without end?
> In deepest darkness you are wrapped,
> Why do you not seek for the light?[27]

To realize that suffering constitutes the essence of the realities of life and the world is to be initiated into the process of attaining enlightenment. In Buddhism this is summed up in the so-called Four Noble Truths. To quote again the words of Buddha, the enlightened one:

What are these Four Noble Truths? They are the Noble Truth of Suffering, the Noble Truth of the Origin of Suffering, the Noble Truth of the Extinction of Suffering, and the Noble Path that leads to the Extinction of Suffering.[28]

The search for the light can be accomplished only through the Noble Eightfold Path that leads the seeker "to peace, to discernment, to enlightenment, to Nibbana."[29]

### St. Paul's Approach to Reality

This desire to be free of the suffering of the body and to become united with the source of Being is not so strange to biblical thinking. St. Paul again, for example, is at one point much tempted by this kind of option. In his letter to the Philippians, he gives us a rare glimpse into the thoughts within the inmost recesses of his heart. "For to me life is Christ, and death gain," he reasons. Death is gain because it is the portal to the life that is Christ. Christ becomes the desire of our soul, as a hymn puts it. On him we stake everything. Death as a way to become united with him forever becomes an attractive option. Extinction of the self is a working hypothesis in our spiritual pursuit of a true life. But another thought immediately intervenes: "What if my living on in the body may serve some good purpose?" Here Paul, the herald of the good tidings, the prophet of God's saving message, is speaking. Duty calls. But he is still not clearly determined what to do. So he muses on: "Which then am I to choose? I cannot tell. I am torn two ways." For most of us steeped in the worldliness of life the choice is obvious. But Paul has reached a stage in his spiritual pilgrimage at which, if he could have his own way, he would rather choose to be with Christ than with the world. This is clear in what he goes on to say. "What I should like," he confesses, "is to depart and be with Christ; that is better by far." In the end, however, he has to drop the desire of a complete union with Christ and goes on with the task of serving his fellow human beings with the Gospel. Thus he concludes: "But for your sake there is greater need for me to stay on in the body" (Phil. 1:22-24).

I have tried to put in a sharp relief the struggle St. Paul disclosed in his letter in order to point out both the similarity and the contrast that seem to exist between Buddha and St. Paul, the two great religious leaders who have shaped the minds and hearts of millions of people all over the world in the course of centuries. For both men there is a common perception that in the present life and in the world in which we live, suffering is a brutal fact that affects us all in a fundamental way. Both see in liberation from the bondage of the body and the world the ultimate salvation. For Buddha, however, the choice is clear after his enlightenment, that is, after his attainment of insight into the nature of life and the world. He teaches and practices the ways to Nirvana with singleness of mind and heart. If he and his followers turn to the world in compassion, it is to rescue people out of their suffering and misery in order that they may also join in the blessings of Nirvana. The world is an illusion that should not retain us longer than necessary.

Essentially, this is a Bunyanesque version of Christianity. As a matter of fact, the history of the Christian church does not lack men and women who have sought the heavenly city by fleeing the earthly city. Christian, the main character in Bunyan's *Pilgrim's Progress,* tried to get away from his wife, children, friends, and neighbors in a hysterical manner. He shouted as he ran and ran as he shouted: "Life! life! eternal life!" When at last some of the neighbors caught up with him and persuaded him to return home, he replied: "I seek an inheritance incorruptible, undefiled, and that fadeth not away; and it is laid up in heaven, and safe there, to be bestowed, at the time appointed, on them that diligently seek it."[30] It does not take a profound theological mind to know that in Christian we have a faith directly opposed to that of *sola gratia,* one of the central pillars of Reformation faith. Throughout the history of the Christian church, we have to admit, salvation by works has existed side by side with salvation through faith. And an escape from the world constitutes in most cases the motivation of good works through which we hope to attain salvation. The Reformation of the sixteenth century was a revolt against salvation by works, which had reached the height of absurdity. But in varied forms it emerges again and again in the Protestant traditions of the Christian church. John Bunyan's *Pilgrim's Progress* is but a dramatic example of this. What astonishes us, however, is that Buddha and Bunyan, although centuries apart in historical origin and vastly different in cultural and religious backgrounds, had so much in common in their search for what is eternal in distinction from what is temporal.

In contrast, the world is everything but an illusion for St. Paul. The world is a naked reality that has power and authority over the life of human beings. Time and again St. Paul's path came up against the political and religious authorities of his day. He plunged right into the midst of society at the risk of his life. He rubbed shoulders with the powers that be and ended his life as a martyr. True, after Paul's conversion to Christ his spiritual orientation seemed to pull him strongly toward the other world that awaited him, the world not of the flesh but of the spirit. We saw this attitude of his a while ago. There are other passages in his letters suggesting also this strong pull away from the present to the eternal. In his exhortations to the Christians of Corinth, he made very explicit the gravitational pull toward the eternal. He said: "Meanwhile your eyes are fixed, not on the things that are seen, but on the things that are unseen: for what is seen passes away; what is unseen is eternal." To illustrate his point, he made use of the image of a building or a house. "For we know that," he wrote, "if the earthly frame that houses us today should be demolished, we possess a building which God has provided—a house not made by human hands, eternal and in heaven." Then he spoke of the conflict between life on earth and life in Christ, which is eternal. And Paul's desire to leave the world so as to be with Christ, which was expressed in his letter to the Philippians, was hinted at again, although in a quite different way. "We groan indeed," said Paul, speaking out of a strong longing normally hidden away in the depth of his heart:

we who are enclosed within this earthly frame; we are oppressed because we do not want to have the old body stripped off. Rather our desire is to have the new body put on the old body, so that our mortal part may be absorbed into life immortal (2 Cor. 5:1–4).

Here St. Paul ran dangerously close to the conclusion Buddha drew as a result of his awakening from illusion into truth. Reportedly Buddha had this to say as he reached the terrain of supreme serenity: "I am is a vain thought; I am not is a vain thought; I shall be is a vain thought; I shall not be is a vain thought."[31] The question of I, that is, the question related to the present life of which I constitute a center, loses its meaning when we are absorbed into Nirvana. Of course the consciousness of I is concrete in the sense that it depends on our tangible self, which is the body, and on its relations with other tangible selves that are also bodies. For this reason the body must be chastized and disciplined and finally become disintegrated in order that the I-consciousness may dissolve itself into the bliss of Nirvana. For centuries many oriental recluses have sought union with Nirvana in lonely deserts, on deserted mountains and forests, and by means of a strenuous discipline and self-control as they waded through the sea of bitterness in the midst of suffering humanity. Even St. Paul, who was as far from the world of Buddhist thought as a man could be, spoke of wanting to be away from the body and at home with Christ (2 Cor. 5:8). But he did not become a recluse, nor did he pursue the course of escape from the world. On the contrary, his heart constantly ached for the world. The aching of his heart took him further and deeper into suffering humanity.

What saved Paul from seeking salvation in a mysticism of the Buddhist type, or for that matter, of the Christian type, was the heritage of his Hebrew faith. The affirmation of being in his heritage of faith turned him away from the negation of being. The affirmation of being was deeply rooted in the fabric of his faith. The people of Israel grasped it as no religion of mystical orientation was able to do. To be sure, there were traces of mysticism in St. Paul, as is evident from our discussion above. This is what some call the Christ-mysticism of St. Paul.[32] But the faith he inherited from his forefathers was too much a part of his new-found faith in Christ to allow him to indulge in a mysticism for which negation of being constituted an essential component.

This faith of St. Paul's can be traced back to the beginning of Israel's formation as a distinctive national and religious unit. To the startled Moses to whom came the divine commission to lead his people out of the house of slavery in Egypt, God disclosed his name, saying, "I AM; that is who I am," or "I will be what I will be" (Exod. 3:13). The faith of the Old Testament began with the identification of the divine I. When Moses raised a question about his credentials as the leader of the liberation movement in the process of formation, he was instructed to say: "I AM has sent me to you." It is this same great I AM who was to lead the history of Israel in subsequent generations. "Thus saith the Lord,"—the declaration that always preceded utterances of the prophets—was in fact equivalent to what Moses heard in the wilderness a long time ago: "I AM has sent me to you." In the context of biblical faith, this I AM, when applied to God, should not be taken as an individualization of being. The concept of the individual as a basic unit in the conscious social structure, which developed in the West under the encouragement of Christianity and its theology, is rather foreign to the social consciousness of the Old Testament world. This I AM was the divine dynamic of solidarity with creation and humanity. This solidarity enabled the people of Israel to acquire a sense of history and to view the temporal under the perspective of the eternal. For this reason the Exodus played a crucial role throughout the history of Israel. The Exodus, as the supreme manifestation of solidarity between the divine I AM and human beings, judged, transformed, and led history. Thus the Exodus was at once historical and transhistorical. It was a superb example of how the divine and the human could intersect to create a new history, a new people, a new community, and a new vision for the future.

### The Historical and the Transhistorical in Buddhism and Christianity

For Buddhism, on the other hand, history is not conceived in terms of either being or nonbeing. I have quoted Buddha as saying: "I am is a vain thought; I am not is a vain thought." The category of being proved inadequate in Buddha's understanding of reality. When the category of being was suspended, personhood, which constitutes the center of human consciousness, was transcended. Tillich was therefore partly right when he observed that "the Ultimate in Christianity is symbolized in personal categories, the Ultimate in Buddhism is transpersonal, for example, 'absolute non-being.' "[33] It must be pointed out, however, that the transpersonal does not necessarily mean apersonal or nonpersonal. It is a merging of individual personhood with universal personhood in the bliss of Nirvana. This is best expressed in the following way: "One person is all persons; all persons are one person; one meritorious deed is all meritorious deeds; all meritorious deeds are one meritorious deed. This is called deliverance to the Pure Land by the grace of Amida."[34] It is difficult to know what this transpersonal state of being consists of. But one thing seems certain: it is a fulfillment of personhood detached from historical bondage and freed from the restrictions of the present life.

All the same, the relationship between the historical and the transhistorical determines decisively the views and attitudes of religions toward life and the world. It follows that theology, which is an active reflection on as well as a creative involvement in the meaning of faith, cannot but be strongly affected by that relationship. On the whole, it is true to say that the strength or weakness of a theology is largely determined by the nature of this relationship. Types of theology are, in fact, types of the relationship that exists between the historical and the transhistorical. We may therefore speak of a Christ-type theology and a Buddha-type theology.

As we have seen, a Buddha-type theology definitely leans towards the transhistorical because the Buddhist considers the historical to be illusory. The Buddhist, like the Christian, confronts pain and suffering as basic facts of life, as we have already discussed. What causes pain and suffering, according to Buddhist teaching, is the craving we all have for this life and world, and even for something eternal and unperishable. Hence "the Noble Truth of the Extinction of Suffering," which in part says:

For, through the total fading away and extinction of Craving (*tanha*) Clinging to Existence (*upandana*) is extinguished; through the extinction of the clinging to existence the (action-) Process of Becoming (*Bhava*) is extinguished; through the extinction of the process of becoming Rebirth (*jati*) is extinguished; and through the extinction of rebirth Decay and Death, sorrow, lamentation, suffering, grief and despair are extinguished. Thus comes about the extinction of this whole mass of suffering.[35]

In this central teaching of Buddhism, we cannot fail to see a strong pull away from the historical. The transhistorical is to be achieved through the extinction of the historical. The tension that keeps the historical and the transhistorical in conflict and pain must be broken. Once the tension is done away with, the transhistorical is cut loose from the historical. Thus, at the theoretical level at least, Buddhism is by nature world-denying or existence-denying. In the second part of this book, we shall have occasion to show how this world-denying tenet of Buddhism has to be modified under the social and political pressures of the contemporary world. At the practical level, the transhistorical cannot avoid the impact of the historical. This is one of the reasons why Buddhists in Asia increasingly find themselves involved in struggles for freedom, justice, and peace.

What concerns us here is this: when the extinction of pain and suffering is conceived and practiced in terms of a transition from the historical to the transhistorical, redemptive meaning is removed from pain and suffering. We may suffer meritoriously, but we do not suffer redemptively. That is why Buddha-type faith or theology tends to put far more stress on salvation through merit than on salvation through grace. As a matter of fact, what Gustaf Aulen calls "the Latin idea of atonement" has much in common with the Buddhist understanding of the relationship between merit and salvation. For example, Tertullian, the father of Latin theology, writes:

How absurd it is to leave the penance unperformed, and yet expect forgiveness of sins! What is it but to fail to pay the price, and nevertheless, to stretch out the hand for the benefit? The Lord has ordained that forgiveness is to be granted for this price: He wills that the remission of the penalty is to be purchased for the payment which penance makes.[36]

This is a legalistic interpretation of atonement. It is essentially an understanding of the Gospel in terms of the law. From this developed the whole medieval theology of penance. Salvation cannot be attained without penance. "Thus Penance is satisfaction, the acceptance of a temporal penalty to escape eternal loss."[37] Basically, this is a Buddhist type of theology. Even Christ was viewed in terms of the merit he was able to bestow on believers, because "by His passion and death He earns an excess of merit, and this is paid to God as satisfaction or compensation."[38] This is the way Buddhists regard the founder of their faith. It is through the merits gained by the enlightened ones plus our own merits that we are able to

escape the suffering of this world and gain entrance into Nirvana. As far
as the history of the Christian church is concerned, the Latin theory of
atonement with its emphasis on penance led to all sorts of abuses in the
conduct of the church in the Middle Ages. The most notorious of all was
the sale of indulgences to innocent believers in order to enrich the popes
and to fill the coffers of the church over which they presided. The biblical
meaning of God in Christ reconciling the world to himself was completely
lost.

The meaning of suffering as something redemptive lies in the tension
between the historical and the transhistorical. For redemption has as
much to do with the historical as with the transhistorical. Redemption is
crippled when it is severed from the historical. And suffering, considered
primarily in terms of acquiring merits, loses its redemptive meaning. It
should be stressed in contrast that suffering in the historical realm is not a
means to redemption in a transhistorical realm. This is clear, I believe, in
the suffering of Jesus Christ. In his suffering God is present to combat the
power of sin and darkness. Suffering is thus a new creation in the making.
The cross shows how a new creation must come into being through
intense pain and suffering. The whole being of God aches in Jesus Christ
on the cross. And the God who suffers is the God who redeems.

The suffering God is therefore the redeeming God. Or to put it the
other way round, the redeeming God is the suffering God. God commits
himself totally to the suffering of this world. This is fundamentally what
the incarnation is all about. As St. Paul tells us in his letter to the Philippians, Christ, the Son of God, became a human being and was obedient
unto death, even death on a cross (Phil. 2:8). The cross is God's suffering
as well as the suffering of human beings. The cross is the place where a
new creation begins in the midst of the old creation. This means that our
theology must be the theology of the cross. In the intense pain and
suffering rooted in God's strong and undefeatable love, theology ought to
find its beginning and its goal. This, in essence, is the Christ-type theology.

# CHAPTER 3

# LOVE AS THE POSSIBILITY OF THEOLOGY

Before we go any further, a clarification is in order. I have stressed the importance of the heart as contrasted with reason in doing theology. By doing theology I mean, of course, having a commitment to and an involvement in the historical expressions of Christian faith as the basis of theological reflection. That is to say, doing theology is not an act of the intellect divorced from the commitment of the heart. Lamenting the professionalization of the theological vocation to meet the demands and pressures of the academic world, Paul Minear made the following statement:

To the degree that his vocation is professionalized, the theologian tends to lose the perspective of seeing all things in the light of Christ, of viewing all nature and history afresh according to the revelation of God's wisdom and power in the death-resurrection of Jesus.[1]

Christ means the commitment and involvement of our whole being in relation to life and the world. Doing theology thus is an exercise of the whole person, not just a function of the intellect. As I said in the last chapter, theology begins and is carried out in God's aching heart in response to the aching of the human heart. Theology is born out of the birth pang of a new creation.

### The Heart in the Bible

What is the heart, according to the Christian Bible? This is no place for a detailed discussion on the biblical meaning of the heart. A few examples from the Bible will be sufficient to illustrate what the heart is in biblical faith. In Psalm 139, for instance, we find these passionate words: "Search me, O God, and know my heart! Try me and know my thoughts!"[2] To know one's heart is to know one's whole being. This is an ultimate situation which confronts us in our relationship to God. We expose ourselves entirely to God, awaiting his judgment and salvation. That is why prophets speak of the conversion of the heart as most fundamental in our life. Jeremiah declares that "all alike, the nations and Israel, are uncircumcised in heart" (Jer. 9:29). But when the day of restoration comes, Israel "shall become my people and I will become their God, for they will come back to me with all their heart" (Jer. 24:7). Ezekiel too uses a vivid language to highlight the importance of the heart in a new situation. He hears God saying to the people of Israel: "I will give you a new heart and put a new spirit within you; I will take the heart of stone from your body and give you a heart of flesh" (Ezek. 36:26). The contrast here between the heart of stone and the heart of flesh is of decisive importance. It is the contrast of a person in revolt against God and of a person in obedience to God's will. The heart of flesh is the person who has been transformed by the redeeming love of God. Thus "the heart is the seat of mental and spiritual powers and capacities." Further, "religious and moral conduct is rooted in the heart. With the heart one serves God. . . . The heart accepts the divine teachings. . . . Circumcision of heart comes with the conversion of heart."[3]

On the whole the New Testament's use of the term *heart* is in line with Old Testament usage. Besides being the locus of emotion, desire, and understanding, the heart embodies the whole person in his or her relationship to God. This is undoubtedly what Jesus means when he says: "How blest are those whose hearts are pure; they shall see God" (Matt. 5:7). The knowledge of God is closely related to the purity of heart, or the wholeness of the whole person. Paul speaks of the true circumcision as a matter of the heart, not of the flesh (Rom 2:29) just as Jeremiah did centuries before him. He can also speak of the Christians in the church at Corinth as "a letter written on our heart." They are "a letter written not with ink but with the Spirit of the living God, written not on stone tablets but on the pages of the human heart" (2 Cor. 3:2–3). The heart to which Paul refers here is, of course, not a particular part of the human body confined to a particular function. It stands for Paul as the apostle of Christ. It is his life and mission. Therefore "the heart is the centre of the inner life of man and the source or seat of all the forces and functions of soul and spirit."[4] It is "supremely the one centre in man to which God turns, in which the religious life is rooted."[5]

The emphasis laid on the heart in doing theology thus avoids emotionalism on the one hand and rationalism on the other. The heart, in the biblical sense we just investigated, accommodates within itself emotion and reason, but emotion and reason work and function in the service of the heart, which is the force of the spirit in communion with God and man. When emotion takes leave of the heart as the seat of human spirit, our theology becomes an emotional theology. We see this at cheap evangelical rallies in which the listeners' emotions are played up to a pitch where people lose control of themselves completely. On the other hand, when reason is separated from the heart, there emerges a cold theology that tries to penetrate the mystery of God with a cold logic. As Daisetz Suzuki has well said:

The human heart is not an intellectual crystal. When the intellect displays itself in its full glory, the heart still aches and struggles to get hold of something beyond. . . . The intellect is baffled. But the human heart never gets tired of its yearnings and demands a satisfaction ever more pressingly.[6]

The heart is endowed with the power to cross the boundary of reason. It perceives the transrational that eludes a rational analysis of phenomena; it experiences true life beyond a system of worldviews; and above all, it intuits the mystery of Being at the point where reason fails to grasp the latter. This means that neither emotion nor reason by itself is equipped to lead us to the presence of the heart of Being. The heart does not abrogate the function of emotion and reason in the pursuit of the truth that is God. It fulfills what they are not able to fulfill, that is, it leads the theological way to the heart of Being. In biblical faith this heart is *agape* which, according to St. Paul, is even greater than faith and hope (1 Cor. 13:13). In Asian spirituality this power of heart which is love lies hidden and remains unexplored by Christian theology. The biblical faith can set in motion this power of heart in Asian spirituality. Out of such interaction a new spirituality may emerge to take the place of the old spirituality. It is possible that out of this a new social consciousness and a new religious and moral commitment may come into being to usher in a new era for the peoples and nations in Asia.

With this clarification we must press on to explore the depth of the heart of God in which, as I said in the last chapter, theology in the true sense of the word was conceived and actualized.

Theology is not human beings speculating on the nature and essence of God. The subject of theology is God himself. He does not become the object of our theological investigation. Rather theology, when conducted by human beings, has to do with the ways of God with humanity and the world. Theology is therefore a giving account of the mystery of creation. Furthermore, it is a reflection on our experience of redemption. We simply cannot know something of God by bypassing creation and redemption. God is to be perceived and encountered at the crossroads of creation and redemption. Insofar as God in himself is concerned, we must admit that he may be a God of the philosophers and metaphysicians but not the God of believers. For this reason the birth, ministry, and cross of Jesus Christ take on tremendous significance. Jesus Christ is the crossroad of creation and redemption. In him the God who creates and the God who redeems become one. What we have in Jesus Christ is the concentration of God's creating and redeeming power. In him we are redeemed and created anew. In him an old history comes to an end and a new history begins. In the light of this supreme concentration, which is Jesus Christ, we encounter the God who created and redeemed over the long centuries before the historical event of Jesus Christ. At the same time, in the light of this concentration, we are given the assurance to meet with the God who continues to deal with the world in creation and in redemption now and in the future. Creation in redemption and redemption in creation—this is the meaning of history. And it is in history understood as the meeting place of creation and redemption that God makes himself known to us. That is why history—the history of all nations and all peoples—must be the subject matter of theology. Theology is therefore a discipline through which God enables us to encounter him as the God of creation and redemption in history. To put it differently, history as molded and charted by God's involvement should engage our theological effort.

We must now ask ourselves some questions that may carry us a little further in our discussion on the possibility of doing theology. What, for instance, is the power of the heart of God that expresses itself in creation and redemption? What is the force that transforms God's pain and suffering into acts of new creation? What prevents his pain and suffering from becoming morbid, restrictive, and destructive? And where do we look for this transforming power in our own life and in our own community or society? If theology is commitment and involvement, what makes it possible? In short, what is the power of the heart that enables us to overcome the double darkness we talked about in the previous chapter?

Let me answer these questions straightaway as follows: the power of the heart of God is *agape* or love. It is this agape-love that constitutes the power of God manifested in creation and redemption. To put it slightly differently: agape-love is everything God is and does. As the author of the first letter of John so succinctly puts it, "God is agape-love" (1 John 4:16). St. Paul dedicated a beautiful hymn to this agape-love in his first letter to the Corinthians. Perhaps this hymn of agape-love has never been surpassed in beauty, eloquence, sincerity, or profundity. "There is nothing love cannot face," says Paul, "there is no limit to its faith, its hope, and its endurance" (1 Cor. 13:7). Then comes his clarion call to put agape-love first and foremost: " . . . there are three things that last for ever: faith, hope, and love; but the greatest of them all is love" (1 Cor. 13:13). Faith without agape-love is not the faith that saves but condemns. It can be a vindictive faith, as shown in the incident of the woman caught in adultery. In the doctors of the law and the Pharisees we encounter a faith in search of its victims. Jesus would have nothing to do with it. To the frightened and mortified woman Jesus said: "Nor do I condemn you. You may go; do not sin again" (John 7:53–8:11).

Hope without love, furthermore, readily turns into an ideology that seeks to achieve its goal regardless of human cost. Hope in this way can become a ruthless power enslaving people to physical and spiritual bondage. Indeed, we must have faith and hope, but *not without love.* Agape-love redeems, heals, and creates. It is God in possession of such agape-love who "loved the world so much that he gave his only son" (John 3:16). This agape-love is not only the possibility of theology, but the alpha and omega of theology.

## Kazo Kitamori's Theology of God's Pain

At this point, I must refer to the theology of the pain of God propounded with a typically Japanese sensitivity and insight by Kazo Kitamori. His theology was as much a product of the agony and pain of his time as a result of theological reflection on the nature of Christian faith. In the 1940s Japanese culture and spirituality were undergoing unprecedented threats from the militarist government. The Japanese invasion of China had been going on for years, bringing indescribable horror and suffering to millions of Chinese. The power of darkness had completely overpowered every vestige of goodness, beauty, and truth in Japanese spirituality. The war of invasion took its toll too among the Japanese people. Reports of conquest and victory were accompanied by endless lists of Japanese troops killed on battlefields. Still the invasion continued, involving the United States and many Asian nations in the Pacific war. It was as if the gate of hell had opened and the monsters lying at the depth of the abyss of terror were suddenly released to wage vengeance on all humanity. In the Japanese invaders we saw human beings who had gone insane; we saw them turn on themselves in fierce hatred and destruction. It was the darkest hour in the history of modern Japan and Asia. And when we take into consideration what was happening simultaneously on the European front, it was the darkest hour in the history of the modern world. In such a grim world situation the theology of the pain of God was born.

As Kitamori read the Gospel in the midst of chaos and destruction, he saw the word *pain* leap out of practically every page of the Bible. God in pain—this is the God of Abraham, of Isaac, and of Jacob. This is the God of Moses and the prophets. This is the God of Christ suffering excruciating pain on the cross. "The heart of the Gospel," Kitamori confides, "was revealed to me as the 'pain of God'."[7] God is in pain because of the terrible pain the world is going through in the confusion and horror of war. Accordingly, Kitamori's theological interpretation of what God is and what he does is based on the motif of pain.

We must understand that Kitamori's emphasis on pain brings depth to our understanding of God and his relation to the world. It challenges a cheap interpretation of the Gospel as all joy, happiness, and success in the world as well as the assurance of life and glory in the world to come.

Moreover, it strikes sympathetic cords in Asian spirituality, particularly the one fostered by the Buddhist tradition. Kitamori himself writes as follows:

. . . the religious thought closest to the gospel—the pain of God which heals our wounds—is found in the Crown Prince Shotoku's *An Intepretation of Yuimakyo*, where we find religious thought which closely resembles our gospel of the pain of God who heals our pain. There we find the earth-shaking sentence: "Man's real sickness springs from foolish love; Buddha's responding sickness arises from great mercy. His suffering mercy is man's vice—man's sickness. The sickness of the great mercy saves people by absorbing their sickness. Sickness is saved by sickness."[8]

But the resemblance between the pain of God in the Christian Gospel, Kitamori goes on to declare, and the mercy of Buddha is more superficial than real. For:

it must not be overlooked that in their [i.e., Buddhists'] religious thought the echo of an alien note is heard. . . . There can be no inflexible wrath of the absolute in Buddhism, as long as it does not have the God of the first commandment. An absolute being without wrath can have no *real* pain. . . . The pain of God is his love—this love is based on the premise of his wrath, which is absolute, inflexible reality. Thus the pain of God is *real* pain, the Lord's wounds are *real* wounds. Buddhism cannot comprehend this real pain, even in the stages of thought of the Jodo and Jodo Shinshu sects about the mercy of Amida Buddha.[9]

While there is no concept of an absolute being in Buddhism, the pain and suffering that Buddha himself and Buddhist saints down the centuries have felt for humanity is nonetheless real. The problem is that Kitamori relates the absolute God to what he calls "absolute and inflexible" wrath. Even God's love, to use Kitamori's own words, "is based on the premise of his wrath." Here the God of Mount Sinai is dominant in his theological thinking. But we must ask: Is it the God of absolute and inflexible wrath that the Bible as a whole tries to convey? To be sure, the prophets of the Old Testament perceive their God Yahweh as a stern judge who judges the world on account of its wickedness and injustice. But what becomes evident and transparent in the end is the God who loves his own children despite their waywardness and sins. The prophets are never tired of calling people to return to the healing and loving embrace of God. They can do this only because for them God's wrath is neither absolute nor inflexible.

To absolutize wrath is to internalize it. This seems to be what happens in Kitamori's theology of the pain of God. In his theology there is a strong tendency to internalize God's work of salvation within God himself, seeing it as a conflict within God himself between his love and his wrath:

The pain is God in conflict within himself, God going outside of himself in Christ, God letting his son die: all of which means God conquering his wrath by his love in the interests of loving the unloveworthy.[10]

This is how Carl Michalson interprets Kitamori's theology of the pain of God. In other words, external expressions of God's salvation result from an internal conflict between love and wrath within God himself. Is it biblically and theologically commendable to internalize God's salvation in this way?

By interpreting salvation in terms of the conflict between love and wrath within God himself, Kitamori finds himself within the theological traditions of the West. Since he is himself a Lutheran, his views are particularly in the Lutheran tradition. Here his great sensitivity to Japanese spirituality seems to give way to western theological thought in which he is also versed and steeped. Just to illustrate what I mean here, I want to quote Lutheran theologian Jürgen Moltmann. In his work *The Crucified God* we find these words:

The theology of the cross must take up and think through to a conclusion this . . . dimension of the dying of Jesus in abandonment by God. If, abandoned by his God and Father, he was raised through the "glory of the Father," then eschatological faith in the cross of Jesus Christ must acknowledge the theological trial between God and God. The cross of the Son divides God from God to the utmost degree of enmity and distinction. The resurrection of the Son abandoned by God unites God with God in the most intimate fellowship.[11]

The cross, according to Moltmann, is the division of God from God to the utmost degree, while the resurrection is the union of God with God in the most intimate fellowship. But the cross and the resurrection have taken place within God, or between God and God, to use Moltmann's rather awkward expression. This is a clear example of theology constructed and developed on what I call the internalization of salvation within God himself. According to such theology, salvation takes place inside an intro-verted God. There is, in fact, too much theology here and too little salvation for poor sinners. Moltmann even speaks of the cross as "the theological trial between God and God."[12] Does this mean that the cross is a drama of God's own trial and we humans are only its spectators?

This *objective* understanding of the cross and the resurrection deprives God, it seems to me, of his intimate and personal involvement in human suffering and pain. But a more fundamental question is this: how are we to understand salvation? Are we to understand it as a dissolution of the tension between love and wrath within God himself? If the answer is yes, then what does this dissolution of the tension within God himself have to do with our own pain and our own suffering? How is it related to the forgiveness of our sins? In other words, how does this drama played within God himself become our own drama? What makes this *theological* trial become *human* salvation? If the salvation of the world consists in God's love overcoming his own wrath, do we not have to come to the absurd conclusion that the world suffers not so much from its sins as from the wrath of God? Neither Kitamori nor Moltmann, I am sure, wants to suggest this as the implication of their theology. But insofar as the wrath of God is absolutized and the cross and the resurrection are regarded as something which has taken place internally within God or between God and God, the absurdity I mentioned seems unavoidable. Thus in Kitamori and Moltmann we have a theology that goes beyond the boundary of faith to which people in the Bible bear witness.

To return to Kitamori, I want to point out further that he defines pain as "the essence of God."[13] Once wrath in God is absolutized and love is seen in conflict with wrath, pain becomes an *essential* part of God's being. Pain becomes God's essence. Thus pain acquires an ontological overtone in Kitamori's understanding of God. His God is not only the God who has pain but the God who is pain. Pain seen as an ontological element in relation to God's essence is bound to remain with God for all eternity. Pain will neither leave God nor all of creation. Pain reigns supreme! "What is the essence of the gospel?" Kitamori asks himself. His answer: "It is the cross of Christ, the pain of God, or it is God's tribulation."[14] The cross is the reality and symbol of pain. No one can question this. But there must be a difference between the cross that God in Christ is bearing for the pain and suffering of this world and the cross that embodies the conflict between God's love and his wrath, between God the Father and God the Son. The cross in the former sense is redemptive or salvific, but the cross in the latter sense is an external symbol of God's internal struggle of himself against himself. Is the cross the pain which God has inflicted upon himself in order to resolve his own internal contradiction? Is it an expression of divine masochism?

Kitamori is essentially in the tradition of western theology, which turns salvation into an intense struggle of God against God within God himself. Consequently, his theology of the pain of God, his *theologia crucis,* stops at the cross. It does not go beyond it. The cross is the final station of God's journey. Is it by accident that there is little reference to the resurrection in *The Theology of the Pain of God?* It cannot in fact accommodate resurrection; it does not have room for it. For resurrection is God's declaration of the end of pain and suffering. It is the eschatological victory over the power of pain. As the seer of the Book of Revelation puts it, God "will wipe every tear from their eyes; there shall be an end to death, and to mourning and crying and pain" (Rev. 21:4). If pain and wrath are absolute and constitute the essence of God's being, how can they be overcome? For God to have done away with pain and wrath would amount to God doing away with his own being. I am sure Kitamori has no intention whatsoever of pressing his theology of God's pain to such a logical absurdity, but how could he avoid it if he made pain and wrath into the essence of God? Moreover, I am sure Kitamori will give as much weight to the gospel of resurrection as to the theology of the pain of the cross. But if the pain and suffering of God are not seen in the perspective of resurrection, theology stops at the painful cross and the wrathful God. There will be no anticipation of a life of joy and jubilation; we are not given courage and fortitude to endure pain in joy and in hope.

It is entirely in line with his thought on the pain of God that Kitamori speaks of it as "the tragedy of God."[15] And of course the cross is the embodiment of this divine tragedy. Consequently he finds in Japanese tragedy, filled with the typical Japanese feeling of *tsurasa*—"the feeling of inevitable fate and sorrow that overhangs human life,"[16] or the feeling of an aching void that makes us helpless and weak—a comparable element that echoes the tragedy of the Gospel. Now the God of *tsurasa* is definitely much more expressive of oriental pathos than is the God of wrath. It may be, as Kitamori points out, that the element of wrath is missing in most Asian concepts of God. The desert God who pours down his wrath on the enemies of his people, the God of justice who vents his wrath on a wicked and wayward people, does not make his appearance as strongly as he does in the God of the Old Testament prophets. But there are strong indications both in the Old Testament and the New Testament that this angry God is also a God of *tsurasa*. Perhaps it is this God of *tsurasa* that eventually comes close to the heart of the biblical faith. Just a few examples will be sufficient to demonstrate the *tsurasa* nature of God in relation to his people.

### God's Search for Humanity

The account of the fall that follows closely the older version of the creation story comes up to our mind at once. Yahweh was in the garden looking for Adam and Eve who had hid themselves because of their fatal act of disobedience. "Adam, where are you?" God's voice echoed in the garden, conveying the *tsurasa* of the one who has lost the loved ones. This is God's search for humanity which He has created in his own image. The Bible taken as a whole is a witness to this search of God for humanity. This is what salvation is really about. To use a human analogy, it is like parents looking for a wayward son. In fact, this is the central theme of Jesus' parable of the father's love in Luke 15:11–32.[17] After the younger son left home and went to a far country with his inheritance, the father longed for him and waited for his return in *tsurasa*. Without that son, life became empty. The father's heart ached because of his love for the son. When he spotted his son in rags still at a distance, his heart went out to him. "He ran to meet him, flung his arms round him, and kissed him" (Luke 15:20).

God's longing for human beings is analogous to the father's *tsurasa* for his son. The *tsurasa* of God is due to his painful love for his creatures. And this *tsurasa* is the *tsurasa* of the cross where the love of God was crucified.

Salvation, as the witnesses in the Bible understand it, is God's love seeking its lost company. At the same time, it is the homecoming of human beings to the love of God. Sin makes human beings homeless and God lonely. The homeless human being and the lonely God—in these we see the powerfulness of sin. It seems to me that Shusaku Endo, the author of the novel *Silence* discussed in the Introduction, has a good insight into the lonely God who goes to seek the homeless human being. After his controversial theme of God's silence, Endo pursues the theme of God's loneliness. In a meditation beside the river Jordan he writes:

> What Jesus has to say was quite different from the teaching of the Sadducees, the Pharisees, or the prophets wearing animals' skins. The rabbis and the prophets always took human weakness to task and threatened people with God's anger and punishment. But Jesus never resorted to such measures. He said that God too was lonely, that he desired human beings just as a woman longs for a man's love. He taught that God does not hide himself in the deserted mountains and wilderness as the prophets asserted, but is present in the tears of those who suffer, in the agony of a deserted woman.[18]

Jesus' mission is the mission of a lonely God who continues his search for reunion with the homeless man until God's agape-love "fills all in all" (Eph. 1:23,RSV).

This feeling of *tsurasa* on the part of God is made no less explicit in the prophets. An oracle of the Valley of Vision in Isaiah 22 is expressive of the *tsurasa* nature of God's love and anguish for the destruction which human beings have brought down on themselves.[19] After describing the hideous battle scene in which warriors were slain and soldiers fled in panic, the oracle turns to God, who said:

> Turn your eyes away from me;
> leave me to weep in misery.
> Do not thrust consolation on me
> for the ruin of my people (Isa. 22:4).

The ethos here is unmistakable. It is a kind of excruciating feeling of void and pain at the sight of the injury and death of loved ones.

But it is especially in God's call to his people to return to him that we gain the vivid feeling of *tsurasa* that God has for them. Jeremiah, for example, is commissioned to speak to the people of Israel thus:

> Come back to me, apostate Israel,
> says the Lord,
> I will no longer frown on you.

> For my love is unfailing, says the Lord.
> I will not be angry for ever.
> Only you must acknowledge your wrongdoing,
> confess your rebellion against the Lord your God.
> Confess your promiscuous traffic with foreign gods
> under every spreading tree,
> confess that you have not obeyed me.
> This is the very word of the Lord (Jer. 3:12–13).

Love and anger, forgiveness and punishment are in intense conflict here, but it is the steadfast love of God *(hesedh)* that triumphs. Under the tremendous feeling of *tsurasa,* the *hesedh* of God seeks to win back his people. This is the Gospel of the Old Testament as well as of the New Testament.

Of all the classical prophets, however, it is Hosea who most painfully and intimately experienced God's feeling of *tsurasa* on account of his *hesedh* for his people. Israel and Judah are like the faithless woman Hosea is to marry. God, in the experience of Hosea, is almost desperate, being overcome by *tsurasa* because his people repay his love with faithlessness. God's *tsurasa* has reached its breaking point. He does not quite seem to know what to do with himself and with his people. This is all too human a way of speaking, but how else can we convey this feeling of *tsurasa* with which God is tormented? Listen to God's cry through Hosea:

> O Ephraim, how shall I deal with you?
> How shall I deal with you, Judah?
> Your loyalty to me is like the morning mist,
> like dew that vanishes early (Hos. 6:4).

Israel and Judah are punished for their sins. They will again be taken to Egypt, the house of bondage from which their forefathers had made a difficult but triumphant exodus. They will also be taken captive to Assyria, the land of foreign gods. A gruesome fate awaits their future. "For look," says Hosea:

> . . . they have fled from a scene of devastation:
> Egypt shall receive them,
> Memphis shall be their grave;
> the sands of Syrtes shall wreck them,
> weeds shall inherit their land,
> thorns shall grow in their dwelling.
> The days of punishment are come,
> the days of vengeance are come
> when Israel shall be humbled (Hos. 9:6–7).

God seems to have given up on Israel and Judah entirely. It seems that

God has determined to vent his "absolute and inflexible wrath" on his people. But in fact these words of punishment and vengeance are not so much an expression of God's wrath as of his *tsurasa,* which has turned into extreme anguish and pain. The feeling of *tsurasa* as something eroding our essence, eating up our substance, leaving us hollow and empty, becomes most explicit in what God goes on to say through Hosea, the man who yearns for the woman who has gone after other men:

> How can I give you up, Ephraim,
> How surrender you, Israel?
> How can I make you like Admah
> or treat you as Zeboyim? (Hos. 11:8)[20]

In the Japanese language there is another expression comparable to the word *tsurasa,* which in some sense reinforces it. It is the adjective *yarusenasa,* which has no obvious equivalent in English. It expresses a deep-seated longing that has no hope of immediate fulfillment. It is longing against longing, so to speak. As a result of such longing, we feel weak, not knowing what to do and where to turn. It is the love that continues to long for its partner despite all failures and disappointments. The God of *tsurasa* is also the God of *yarusenasa.* That is why he cannot give up Ephraim. Instead:

> My heart is changed within me,
> my remorse kindles already.
> I will not let loose my fury,
> I will not turn round and destroy Ephraim;
> for I am God and not a man,
> the Holy One in your midst (Hos. 11:8–9).

If this were a drama being acted on a Japanese stage before a silent audience, we could almost see how the spectators are drawn deeply and intensely into God's *tsurasa* and *yarusenasa,* and how they begin to sob and weep. They too become tormented with *tsurasa* and *yarusenasa.* This might be a drama of their own life. The *tsurasa* and *yarusenasa* of God become their own. They may even transport their own *tsurasa* and *yarusenasa* back to God. A communion between them and God in *tsurasa* and *yarusenasa* comes into being. At that moment God becomes real to them. He is in them and with them.

If this makes sense in relation to the biblical faith in the *hesedh* and *agape* of God—and I believe it does—then Jesus' cry of dereliction on the cross may be heard more as God's *tsurasa* and *yarusenasa* than as his despair. Before the final showdown between Jesus and his opponents came, we see him pour his heart out in *tsurasa* and *yarusenasa* for the city that is the symbol of God's love and presence:

O Jerusalem, Jerusalem, the city that murders the prophets and stones the messengers sent to her! How often have I longed to gather your children, as a hen gathers her brood under her wings; but you would not let me (Matt. 23:37; also Luke 13:34).

In his fierce controversy with the religious leaders of his day, Jesus had many outbursts of anger. But this was not anger pure and simple. Like Jeremiah and Hosea before him, his love for the people of his own race turned into the excruciating pain of *tsurasa* and *yarusenasa*. Thus his cry on the cross—my God, my God, why hast thou forsaken me!—is not his final call for God's wrath against his enemies, but the cry of a love that has been injured and crucified but does not give up. It is the cry of a love that forgives, redeems, and gives life.

Thus we must disagree with Kitamori when he speaks of "the love rooted in the pain of God" instead of "the pain rooted in the love of God." He actually concludes his theological discourse on the pain of God with the following meditation and prayer:

My prayer night and day is that the gospel of love rooted in the pain of God may become real to all men. All human emptiness will be filled if this gospel is known to every creature.[21]

Because of Kitamori's massive concentration on the concept and reality of pain, he has reversed the order of love and pain, making pain the root of love. This is certainly not correct from the biblical point of view, as we have tried to show above. Even in our human experience it is not quite true to regard pain as the root of love. Pain is not self-productive. By this I mean that pain is dependent on a much more essential part of human beings, which is love. You feel pain for someone because you love that person. Pain, in other words, is rooted in love.

### The Pain-Love of God

I can illustrate this by a reference to the Chinese language. In Chinese one is required to say the two words *love* and *pain* almost in the same breath. I am referring to the expression pain-love *(thun-ai)*. The force of this expression is most vividly felt when we visualize a mother holding her child in a tight embrace, plunging her lips to its cheek and almost devouring it. The mother's love for the child is so great and intense that she feels pain. Love seems to generate a kind of force very close to pain. This should not be dismissed simply as an indication of a sadistic tendency in human beings. Our experience tells us that genuine love is indeed accompanied by pain.

In different situations love transformed into pain may take on different expressions. First, love may turn into hate. The pain of love thus becomes the pain of hate. Needless to say, this is a destructive aspect of human behavior. Furthermore, a love that feels pain for its object may express itself in anger. At times anger becomes so predominant that it obliterates any love that was originally there. Anger in such a case appears to be absolute and inflexible. Even in this case, however, generically it is not anger that precedes love but love that precedes anger.

In another situation love in pain can develop into the *tsurasa* and *yarusenasa* we discussed above. Here love is in puzzlement, anguish, and conflict with itself. The heart of those filled with *tsurasa* and *yarusenasa* goes out to one who does not reciprocate their love. Their empty heart will never be filled until they win back the heart of the person they never cease to love. This kind of love will not develop into hate or anger. In this kind of love we seem to catch a glimpse of what God is like. Ultimately, the wrath of God is not seen in the Christian Bible as something inherent in God. In the last analysis the angry God is not the God of the patriarchs and the prophets, nor is he the God of the cross.

Furthermore, the love that feels pain for its object becomes a pain-love. It can be said in general that the more intense love is, the stronger the pain is; therefore the more powerful will be the pain-love. The strength of love is tested by the strength of pain-love. Pain-love is not vindictive. It does not punish for the sake of punishment. It does not turn into hate simply because of wrath, nor does it turn into wrath because of hate. It does not inflict punishment upon others as a way of appeasing its wrath. Rather it inflicts wounds on itself so that others may find wholeness and health. A mother feels pain-love for her child. Husband and wife feel pain-love for each other. Inherent in such a pain-love is self-sacrifice. Through the intensely human experience of pain-love we can surmise what God's love for the world may be like. We are thus led to say that God feels pain-love for us. This pain-love of God is what is called *hesedh* in the Old Testament and *agape* in the New Testament. John 3:16, which contains all that we need to know about the great mystery of God's saving love, can be rendered as follows: "God felt such *pain-love* for the world that he gave his only Son, that everyone who has faith in him may not die but have eternal life."[22] The cross is God's excruciating pain-love. It is rooted in the love of the God who bears pain for the world.

I believe that this kind of love constitutes the center of the Christian Gospel—Jesus Christ as the supreme expression of God's pain-love. Salvation is not to be seen as an internal struggle of God between his love and his wrath. Salvation is the external event in which God's pain-love succeeds in locating homeless people and winning them back to him. The internalization of salvation within God himself, which we saw in Kitamori's and Moltmann's theology, is not quite true to the meaning of the cross. Salvation is not God's solitary act of struggle within himself. It is the divine-human drama that actualizes itself in a new creation.

In short, Kitamori's theology of the pain of God has captured a profound element of biblical faith as well as of Asian spirituality deeply influenced by Buddhist thought. But it misses another equally profound element—the love that is constrained by pain but finally breaks it, the resurrection that turns the tragedy of life into the life of hope and celebration.

Love as understood in terms of pain-love is therefore the point of our entry into the heart of God. For God discloses himself as pain-love in human relationships, in society, and in history. Human relations are fragmentary reflections and often distortions of the pain-love of God. From the biblical viewpoint history is certainly seen as the drama of God's pain-love in action. There love is understood as the God who refuses to remain alone. Instead, he actively engages human beings in love, even though they avoid him. Thus the biblical faith has grasped the central quality of human love and views God in the light of that love. Love as we know and experience it cannot remain by itself without betraying its own nature, without ceasing to be itself. Love, if it is to remain true to itself, must seek objects to which its action can be directed. Love, in other words, fulfills itself in the object of its love. Love cannot fulfill itself until its object is fulfilled for the purpose for which it was created and instituted. The relationships created by love and with which love is surrounded are not static. There is a dynamic mutuality that enables the parties concerned to experience love as both suffering and joy, as obligation and willing sacrifice. As Daniel D. Williams puts it:

There can be no love without suffering. Suffering in the widest sense means the capacity to be acted upon, to be changed, moved, transformed, by the action of or in relation to another. The active side of love requires that we allow the field of our action and its meaning to be defined by what the other requires.[23]

I think the last sentence in this quotation is important. The meaning and action of love are to be defined by what others require. This is essentially what makes love into agape-love, that is, love for the unlovable.

This is the love that makes theology possible if we understand theology not in the sense of a rational understanding of the meaning of God but in the sense of a response in faith and hope to the manifestations of God's agape-love in the world. Its primary task is not to explore who God is in himself, but to gain a deeper insight into how God "is acted upon, changed, moved, and transformed" by human sin and the need of redemption on the part of the world. For this reason, the incarnation should constitute the center of Christian theology. The incarnation tells us how God is acted upon and moved by human beings who have become prisoners of their own sin. It also shows us how God is capable of change and transformation for the sake of human salvation. The God of pain-love is the God of change.

Even within the robust and lofty understanding of God in the Old Testament, God is often portrayed as capable of repenting of what he has done to human beings and to the world. The God of Mount Sinai, who is a God of wrath, is also the God who cannot bear the sight of human beings perishing as the result of their own sins. The God of wrath is the God of repentance. This again shows how incorrect it is to regard wrath as an absolute and inflexible part of God's nature. In this connection our attention must be drawn to the covenant God made with Noah as a covenant of repentance as much as a covenant of promise. In the aftermath of what can only be described as a holocaust caused by the cosmic flood, God's pain-love for humanity reached its most agonizing depth. "Never again," says the Lord God, "will I curse the ground because of man, however evil his inclinations may be from his youth upwards. I will never again kill every living creature, as I have done" (Gen. 8:21). The covenant which subsequently God made with Noah was his determination to keep his words. This is clear from the words which sealed the covenant at its inauguration:

I now make my covenant with you and with your descendants after you, and with every living creature that is with you, all birds and cattle, all the wild animals with you on earth, all that have come out of the ark. I will make my covenant with you: never again shall all living creatures be destroyed by the waters of the flood, never again shall there be a flood to lay waste the earth (Gen. 9:8–11).

God binds himself with a covenant as a sign of his repentance as well as his promise. The covenant is thus the reality of God's pain-love for his creation.

The binding power of the covenant is thus seen at work in God's dealing with his people. In Psalm 106, a historical lyric describing how the turbulent history of Israel alternated between the latter's obedience and God's judgment, we find the covenant playing a crucial role. The covenant does not lose its effectiveness even though the people are incorrigible and forgetful of what God has done for them. " . . . They were disobedient and rebellious still," laments the Psalmist. Then he continues:

And yet, then he [God] heard them wail and cry aloud,
he looked with pity on their distress;
he called to mind his covenant with them
and, in his boundless love, relented;
he roused compassion for them
in the hearts of all their captors (Ps. 106:45–46).

This is the way that the Old Testament faith has grasped the pain-love of God, namely, his covenant of love, his *hesedh*.

In Amos 7 we are told of dramatic encounters between Amos and God about the possible doom of Israel. Amos is shown visions of four things: locusts, fire, a plumb-line, and a basket of summer fruit. In the last two visions God's judgment on Israel seems to have reached the point of no return. But in the first two visions at least, God responds to Amos' plea with repentance. "O Lord God, what will Jacob be after this? He is so small." Amos pleads with God. "Then the Lord relented and said, 'This shall not happen.' " Even such a stern proclaimer of God's judgment as Amos has to go through in his heart a tremendous struggle caused by the tension between judgment and love. And what is more surprising, he, like the other prophets, ends up with words of promise and hope.

This pain-love that binds God to his people should not be confused with indulgence. The caution expressed in the following statement must therefore be taken into serious account:

The Old Testament thus believes that there are divine words and acts in which God's repentance is expressed. On the other hand, it is concerned that the seriousness of the message of judgment should not be weakened by this teaching. God is not a man that He should go back on his word. . . . Hence the repentance of God is not capricious. It does not overthrow the idea of judgment. It is not a false human love. On the contrary, the seriousness of the divine judgment is confirmed and established by the proclamation of divine repentance.[24]

Of course, the repentance of God is not capricious. It is entirely in conformity with his nature as pain-love. God judges because he loves. Love is the power that makes the divine judgment on sin redemptive, not destructive. Judgment will take wrathful forms, but wrath is never the basic motivation of God's judgment. The word *repentance,* when applied to God, shows how love makes God go not just halfway but all the way to meet human beings in our sins and weakness.

St. Paul seeks to express this point when he says, probably quoting a christological hymn current among the Christians of his day:

For the divine nature was his from the first; yet he did not think to snatch at equality with God, but made himself nothing, assuming the nature of a slave. Bearing the human likeness, revealed in human shape, he humbled himself, and in obedience accepted even death—death on a cross (Phil. 2:6–8).[25]

The God in Christ to whom this christological hymn bears witness is not the God of wrath, that is, not the God who becomes hardened and unchangeable on account of his wrath, but the God who changes and makes himself available to human beings because of his pain-love. All words and acts related to salvation start from this change of God in Christ into a human form. This is the heart of the Gospel—God's pain-love for his creation.

Hence, all *theo*-logical acts, that is, acts of God in the world, are acts of his pain-love. In pain-love God unites himself with human beings and in this pain-love he bears our pain and death. Our theo-*logy* is therefore derived from God's *theo*-logy. And it is this divine pain-love revealed in Jesus Christ that enables us Christians to open the door of Asian spirituality with a pronounced emphasis on love as the power that sustains human life and inspires hope for a better life in this world and in the world to come.

### Bhakti Religion and Shin Buddhism

I am referring here to the bhakti religion of India and the Shin Buddhism of Japan. Let us first take a brief look at the concept of bhakti adumbrated in the *Bhagavad-Gita,* a part of the *Mahabharata,* the sixth century B.C. epic recording the conflict between two contenders to the throne.[26] A few quotations from the *Gita* will give us an impression of how grace and devotion are emphasized as essential in our quest for salvation.

Doing continually all actions whatsoever, taking refuge in Me, he reaches by My grace the eternal, undying abode.

Surrendering in thought all actions to Me, regarding Me as the Supreme, and resorting to steadfastness in understanding, do thou fix thy thought constantly on Me.

Fixing thy thought on Me, thou shalt, by My grace, cross over all difficulties; but if from self-conceit, thou wilt not listen (to Me), thou shalt perish.

Flee unto Him for shelter with all thy being, O Bharata (Arjuna). By His grace shalt thou obtain supreme peace and eternal abode.

Abandoning all duties, come to Me alone for shelter. Be not grieved, for I shall release thee from all evils.[27]

With such words the *Gita* is concluded. For us who must execute our duty and seek fulfillment in life, there is only one source of hope and salvation, that is, bhakti "filled with love, expressing itself in reverence."[28] Commenting on the emphasis on grace and love expressed in the *Bhagavad-Gita,* Rudolf Otto says: "Here already works are not viewed as the proper way to produce redemption, but surrender of the heart to the rescuing and gracious God, and to his grace." And further: "In India as among us, faith does not appeal to one's own worthiness or service performed, but the believer appeals to the word of gracious 'promise,' which the Lord has given in the Gita."[29]

When we turn to the Shin Buddhism of Japan, we discover that the emphasis on love and compassion as the way to salvation in Nirvana is even bolder and more pronounced. It is a complete deviation from the Buddhist orthodoxy that teaches the accumulation of good works as essential to the attainment of eternal bliss. Its founder, Shinran

(1173–1263), is even reported to have said: "Even a good man will be received in the Buddha-land, how much more a bad man!"[30] Here is an unmistakable echo of the love of Christ shown particularly to sinners, prostitutes, publicans, outcasts, and the underprivileged. And of course the prodigal son in the parable of the father's love to which we referred earlier typifies the kind of people to whom God shows his love. Because of the miserable state men and women are in as a result of their sins, there is absolutely no way for them to save themselves. As a result Shinran, in a way similar to Jesus Christ, broke away from traditional Buddhism with its emphasis on asceticism and on mental and physical disciplines. In other words, he departed from a religion that had become inaccessible to the people of the street, an elite religion isolated from the realities of life. What he did was to bring salvation to the common people, that is, to the people who have to bear the burden of life and the weight of sin. To them he preached the gospel of salvation based solely on faith in the love and compassion of Amitabha Buddha. In the words of Kenneth Ch'en, Shinran taught people to place their "reliance upon absolute faith in the redeeming grace of Amitabha, to be invoked by the formula *namu Amida Butsu* (homage to the Buddha Amitabha). This faith could overcome all sin, all obstacles to salvation, because the saving power of Amitabha was unconditional."[31] This is a people's religion. It is no wonder that to this day Shin Buddhism enjoys a wide popularity in Japan.

Obviously, here is something Christians cannot lightly ignore. Francis Xavier, who started preaching Catholic Christianity in Japan in 1549, wrote home that he had met with the "Lutheran heresy" among Japanese Buddhists.[32] And it is this Shin Buddhism that makes a small crack in the gate of Karl Barth's fortified theological castle. In his treatment of religion as unbelief in *Church Dogmatics,* Barth has to admit in bewilderment:

We can regard it as wholly providential disposition that as far as I can see the most adequate and comprehensive and illuminating heathen parallel to Christianity, a religious development in the Far East, is parallel not to Roman or Greek Catholicism, but to Reformed Christianity, thus confronting Christianity with the question of its truth even as the logical religion of grace.[33]

This is a very revealing observation. Barth is puzzled and at the same time amazed to find in bhakti religion or Shin Buddhism a religion of *gratia sola,* which is the most central emphasis of the Reformed faith as contrasted to Roman Catholicism and Orthodox Christianity. This should have been here a "providential" opportunity for Barth to press his acute theological insight into the exploration of the meaning of grace and love outside the Christian context as well as within it. This should have been here a "providential" point of entry into the investigation of the nature of God's love as it manifests itself in various forms and different ways in diverse cultural settings. Unfortunately, Barth as a theologian within the

western theological traditions turns back, letting pass this golden opportunity to fathom the mystery of God's love outside the Christian tradition.
Thus he gives up grace as a criterion of a true religion.

What Barth has done is to lead us back to Jesus Christ; he hastens to
bring his christological centrism to bear on the question of a true religion.
This is what he tells us in somewhat faltering words:

> Only one thing is really decisive for the distinction of truth and error. And we call
> the existence of Yodoism a providential disposition because with what is relatively
> the greatest possible force it makes it so clear that only one thing is decisive. That
> one thing is the name of Jesus Christ. Methodologically, it is to be recommended
> that in face of Yodoism, and at bottom, of all other religions, our first task is to
> concentrate wholly upon this distinction, provisionally setting aside whatever
> other difference we think we recognize.[34]

Of course no one can question the fact that a religion of grace such as Pure
Land Buddhism has no name of Jesus Christ. But the point is that when in
Christian faith we speak of Jesus Christ, we are not invoking an abstract
name but expressing our faith in the love of God that redeems the world
through Jesus Christ. Jesus Christ is God's love incarnate, and for this
reason he is our salvation. In Jesus Christ we encounter God's love in its
most intense concentration. Our faith in him must therefore enable us to
form a positive appreciation of the quality of love and grace we find in
bhakti religion or Pure Land Buddhism, which bears some *substantial*
resemblance to the Christian experience of God's love and grace. Even
Barth as a Reformed theologian has recognized it as presenting "the most
adequate and comprehensive and illuminating" parallel to Reformed
Christianity. Why then should he turn back at this point? Why should he
find it difficult to encourage us to explore the mystery of God that must be
at work in different cultural and religious situations? Why should he feel
diffident about fathoming the mystery of God's love in the depth of
humanity since the beginning of the creation?

### Christian Theology and Asian Spirituality

The discussion above points definitely to the view that Christian theology should become engaged in the pursuit of the experience and knowledge of God with other systems of thought and faith in Asia. Needless to
say, in such an engagement Christian theology can be greatly enriched by
the world of faiths and beliefs into which it has intruded; and it can help
enrich the faiths and beliefs of Asia as well. Continuing the isolation of
Christian theology from the faiths and philosophies of Asia would not do
justice to the cultural and religious realities that in their respective ways
also reflect something of God's creation and redemption. As shown
above, some basic human experiences related to the ultimate problems of

life do transcend time and space; they overlap each other and converge on each other. As has been pointed out, an important point of convergence is to be found in love, the agape-love of God in the Bible and the pain-love of God for suffering humanity as expressed strongly in Asian spirituality. In this agape-love or pain-love is not only the beginning of theology but the very possibility of theology. In fact, this love constitutes the power of theology because it is the basic source of the dynamics with which God sets out to do the work of creation and redemption. Thus what we are engaged in here with our theological effort is not just metaphysical speculation about the nature of God. A speculative theology will not bring us any nearer to the heart of God. For theology primarily has to do with love—with the suffering and pain of love, and with the power of love that overcomes hate and despair. In this love God meets human beings, and in this divine-human encounter in love people from different cultural backgrounds and religious traditions may find the way to the heart of God and to each others' hearts.

This love enables us to enter into discourse with our contemporaries in different cultural settings as well as with personalities and events of the past. The universe of human discourse is an ever expanding universe. And its center is love and our experience of that love. Love sustains the universe of human discourse. It makes it possible for us to understand and to be understood by people outside our immediate circle. It makes our communication with God meaningful and our communication with other people human. This is the love that can even turn a heart of stone into a heart of flesh, as Jeremiah says. To be sure, love can be misunderstood, abused, and crucified. That is why Christ must suffer. For suffering is an integral part of love. But the love that suffers is a love that overcomes evil in the end. For this reason the cross proves to be a victory, not a defeat. And the love that suffers is also the love that creates a new life. Through the suffering of love an old life becomes a new life. That is why the cross is life, not death.

Furthermore, the universe of discourse with agape-love or pain-love at its center looks toward the future. The sharing of this love with people of different longings and sufferings enables us to have faith in the emergence of a world community in which people can meet one another as children of God, not as rivals in all kinds of competition such as cultural, social, political, or religious struggles. This is the vision of cosmic peace and harmony that Isaiah envisions as he says:

> Then the wolf shall live with the sheep,
> and the leopard lie down with the kid;
> the calf and the young lion shall grow up together,
> and a little child shall lead them;
> the cow and the bear shall be friends,
> and their young shall lie down together.

The lion shall eat straw like cattle;
the infant shall play over the hole of the cobra,
and the young child dance over the viper's nest.
They shall not hurt or destroy in all my holy mountain;
for as the waters fill the sea,
so shall the land be filled with the knowledge of the Lord
(Isa. 11:6–9).

Compare this with an ancient hymn to Vishnu in the *Rigveda,* an important source of Hindu thought and spirituality:

Let my inspiring hymn go forth to Vishnu. . . .
Him whose steps filled with mead, unfailing,
Revel in blissful joy; who has supported
Alone the universe in three divisions:
The earth and sky and all created beings.
I would attain to that his dear dominion
Where men devoted to the gods do revel.
In the wide-striding Vishnu's highest footstep
There is a spring of mead: such as our kinship.
We long to go to those your dwelling-places
Where are the kine with many horns, the nimble:
For thence, indeed, the highest step of Vishnu,
Wide-pacing bull, shines brightly down upon us.[35]

The natural rhythm and lyric beauty of these lines, coupled with the religious aspirations for a universal community of peace and love, make this vision of the future moving and memorable. This is another illustration of why Christian theology in Asia cannot fulfill its task until it constructs a universe of discourse with other faiths in the quest for a deeper understanding and experience of God, human beings, and the world.

Deep-rooted in human spirituality is thus the love that relates us to God and to our fellow human beings. History in a true sense is the movement of this love. In love the history of God and the history of humanity converge. History is this love in dynamic expressions. As Daniel D. Williams puts it:

We understand love when we see that it creates its own history. It changes form and brings new forms into being. This is true of the human loves and of God's love and all the loves that are interwoven in history.[36]

If history is the creation of love, we must look in history for the ways in which love does its work. In other words, history gives us clues as to how God and humanity involve each other in the work of creation and redemption. History is therefore a love story of God and humanity. The most distinguished scenario of this love story is the history of Israel. And in Jesus Christ that scenario reaches its climactic expression. But we must not stop there, for varied versions of this scenario are written throughout the history of humankind in different places and among different peoples. Until we also gain some glimpses of these other scenarios of the love story, our knowledge and experience of God's love are limited in scope and poor in content.

If history is the unfolding of the love stories between God and human beings recounted by people in different places and times, then theology has the hermeneutical task of interpreting these love stories in the light of biblical faith and bringing them into the perspective of God's love as disclosed in Jesus Christ. This will liberate Christians in Asia from the straight jacket of western theology. What the American Indian writer Vine Deloria, Jr., says about western people is equally true of Christians in the East and in the West. "A major task remains for Western man," he writes. "He must quickly come to grips with the breadth of man's experience and understand these experiences from a world viewpoint, not simply a Western one."[37] In fact, western nations have been forced more and more to learn this lesson since World War II. What we find in the arena of international politics today is no longer the western hegemony that had gone on for centuries. It is now a politics based on the balance of power that keeps the world in coexistence. The direct political and military control of the Third World by western nations came to an end with the painful exodus of the Portuguese from Angola and Mozambique in 1975. Today the last battle between white power and black power is being fought fiercely in southern Africa. It is hoped that this battle will result in the categorical end of any vestige of white domination.

In recent years the political map of the world has been radically altered, and the western nations have been forced to look at human history from a new world perspective. Similarly, our religious perception of how the God of Abraham, Isaac, Jacob, and Jesus Christ is related to human beings in history must also acquire a new world perspective. The map of human spirituality can no longer be drawn with the criteria set by Christianity in its western formulation. History is the story of God's love for *all* human beings. This means that the theological map of the Christian church must now dovetail with the religious map of a world whose contours have become more clear and distinct as a new political map of the world becomes the basis for a new management of world affairs. And the hand that guides and forms this new theological map must be a hand of love—the creating and redeeming love to which the biblical faith gives witness.

# CHAPTER 4

# THEOLOGY AS THE LOVE
# OF THE GOD-MAN IN ACTION

Love makes God divine, for God is love. It makes human beings human, for human life is sustained by love. And in Jesus Christ God as divine love and humanity as human love meet to create a new person oriented both to God and humanity. He is the love of the God-man in action. Theology, which takes its cue from Jesus Christ, must also be the love of the God-man in action. Theology does not have to do with the metaphysics of love. From beginning to end it has to do with love in action. This is the subject we want to explore in this chapter after our discussion of love as the possibility of theology in the previous chapter.

The question that comes at once to our mind is where the action of such love takes place. Action has to do with time and space. It is a happening that takes place at the crossroads of time and space. There is no action in temporal-spatial terms when it remains an idea in the mind. Action is an idea become flesh in the reality of life. The same thing is true of love as action. If love, even divine love, does not take a spatiotemporal form, it is an abstract idea that exerts no concrete influence on the life of people and the course of history. From this point of view, Jesus Christ is the massive concentration in space and time of God's love. And because of its massive concentration, the love of God in Jesus Christ has the power to accept, embrace, and transform all acts of love that have shaped human spirituality within different cultural and religious contexts.

### The Active Nature of Theology

It follows that theology as a witness to this love of the God-man in action must be also action-oriented. At this point we realize that theology is in a way analogous to scientific investigation. In general, science, although operating with a set of hypotheses deemed relevant for certain areas of research and investigation, must be conducted as much as possible in accordance with the nature and characteristics of its object. In other words, it must behave in terms of its subject matter. If scientists fail to do this, they inevitably distort the nature of their subject matter. Needless to say, the data and results they produce are unreliable. In the same way, theology, if it is to perform its function faithfully, must behave in terms of the nature of the love of the God-man in action. It must be an *active* theology based on how the love of the God-man expresses itself in the life of human beings and the world.

Despite our earlier criticism of T. F. Torrance's heavy emphasis on the place of rationality in what he calls "theological science," here I find myself in essential agreement with him when he says:

We cannot begin by forming independently a theory of how God is knowable and then seek to test it out or indeed to actualize it and fill it with material content. How God can be known must be determined from first to last by the way in which He is actually known.[1]

Christian faith begins with a basic presupposition that God is at work in history. It is on the basis of this presupposition that we approach the events of history in the hope that we may come to apprehend the inner meaning of life and history. This, I am sure, is what Torrance means when he stresses the priority of God's own self-disclosure over our knowledge of God. His further statement on this matter confirms this view:

Christian theology arises out of the actual knowledge of God given in and with concrete happening in space and time. It is knowledge of the God who actively meets us and gives Himself to be known in Jesus Christ—in Israel, in history, on earth. It is essentially positive knowledge, with articulated content, mediated in concrete experience.[2]

In theology we are involved in an experiential science, as it were. In theology we begin with where we are and what we are—that is, where God and human beings meet in space and time. We neither begin with God alone nor with humanity alone. We begin with the God-man Jesus Christ on earth. In other words, we must begin with the love of the God-man in action.

Torrance, however, seems to have overstated his case when he further tells us to refrain from questioning what we encounter in life and history. "We do not, therefore, begin with ourselves or our questions," he says:

nor indeed can we choose where to begin; we can only begin with the facts prescribed for us by the actuality of the object positively known. Anything else would be unreal and unscientific, as well as untheological.[3]

This I find difficult to agree with. If we admit, as Torrance asks us to do, that theology must begin with God's self-revelation in Jesus Christ, in

Israel, in history, and on earth, then we already know where to begin our theological investigation—we must begin with Jesus Christ. We must deal with the history of Israel, and we must grapple with everything under the sun that happens in human history and on earth. In other words, we do not wait for God to tell us where to begin. God is *already* in Jesus Christ. That is why we know how to begin with Jesus Christ. God is *already* in the history of Israel. For this reason we must study it. In the same way, God is *already* in human history and on earth. Thus the data and events we encounter there constitute the subject matter of our theological inquiry. We must put our questions—despite the fact that they are *human* questions—to what we encounter in our daily life and in human history so that the ultimate meaning of life in God may begin to take shape for us somewhat clearly. For theology to refrain from asking questions at this point is to flee back into the shelter of academic theology, which is more interested in the metaphysics of God than in the concrete acts of God in society and history. Theology in this case is truly unscientific on account of its flight from concrete facts and data to the holy of holies where the image of God is rarefied in its inaccessibility.

Where there are people, I want to assert, there theology must be. Where human suffering is, there theology must find itself. Where human joy is, there theology must be also. Theology does not take place in a vacuum. Theology is an event. It happens. What else could it be? It can be compared to the art of photography. Photographers do not create a picture out of the blue. If they are to capture the life-story of people, they must move to where the people are, that is, to where things are happening. Then with their keen sense of selectivity based on their understanding of human problems, they take the pictures that can best express the meaning of the event they are confronted with. Their photography is an interpretation of the event and the people involved in the event. Their interpretation cannot thus be created in separation from the scene where the event takes place. It must come right out of the scene itself. To the extent that their pictures grapple with the depth of the suffering and joy of an event, they communicate powerfully its message. How can theology be different from this when we are already told that God is already in Jesus Christ, in the history of Israel, in human history, and in the whole of creation?

### The Hermeneutical Circle and Active Theology

In this connection a reference to what Juan Luis Segundo, S.J., calls the "hermeneutical circle" is useful. According to him, the hermeneutical circle "is the continuing change in our interpretation of the Bible which is dictated by the continuing changes in our present-day reality, both individual and societal. . . . The circular nature of this interpretation stems from the fact that each new reality obliges us to interpret the word of God afresh, to change reality accordingly, and then to go back and reinterpret the word of God again, and so on."[4] Perhaps the word *circle* employed here is not altogether a happy one, for a circle implies a situation of enclosure and confinement. But the idea he tries to convey through "hermeneutical circle" is unmistakable. It stresses that the word of God and the reality of life interact and affect each other. The word of God in separation from reality is abstract and thus has no influence on it. At the same time, the reality of life that is not informed by the word of God is devoid of the power of transformation, which comes from the word of God. In this interaction neither the word of God nor the reality of life remains static. They change. This requires theology and sociology, for instance, to inform each other. Segundo like other Latin American theologians thus seeks to do theology in close relationship with a critical analysis of society and with a commitment to change society. It should be stressed that the hermeneutical circle as a tool of interpretation does not only bring about change in our interpretation of the word of God but also change in the way in which the word of God addresses itself to us. The impact of society causes a substantial change in our perception of the word of God with the result that the latter speaks to us in a new way. Therefore, the word of God is not a constant that does not change. This is the risk all theologians must take when they are determined to do theology in active participation with the reality of the settings in which they live.

James Cone, the most outspoken of the black theologians, has taken this risk and is ready to press the risk to its logical consequences. In his recent book *The God of the Oppressed,* he reiterates the basic rules of the game of theology according to which he wants to do his black theology. "My point," he writes, "is that one's social and historical context decides not only the questions we address to God but also the mode or form of the answers given to the questions."[5] This is in line with the argument we discussed in the previous pages. When he translates this principle of theology into the actual doing of theology as a black theologian committed to black tradition and the black community, the concept of "blackness" takes on an enormously important place. In one sense his theology is a titanic effort to exorcise the associations of the meaning of blackness and to transform it into a term with a redemptive meaning and task. For him this is not merely a linguistic exercise. It is a cultural and spiritual struggle to bring white people to their knees for the sins they as oppressors have committed against blacks. Thus in his theology *white* means literally and symbolically oppression, inhumanity, and evil, while *black* literally and symbolically stands for the oppressed, the poor, and the enslaved. In *The God of the Oppressed* Cone continues to wage war against white devils—the war he declared with the publication of his manifesto *Black Theology and Black Power* in 1969.[6]

Cone's theology is thus a passionate attempt to reconceptualize the meaning of salvation on the basis of the black experience in the United States. His message is loud and clear:

To say that Christ is black means that black people are God's people whom Christ has come to liberate. . . . To say that Christ is black means that God, in his infinite wisdom and mercy, not only takes colour seriously, he takes it upon himself and discloses his will to make us whole—new creatures born in the spirit of divine blackness and redeemed through the blood of the black Christ.[7]

Blackness is almost identified with salvation. A formidable transformation has taken place in Cone's theology—the transformation of blackness from bondage to freedom, from slavery to liberation. And the transformation is both symbolic and literal.

That is why blackness now has to define the content of Christian faith. In strong objection to other black theologians, such as Deotis Roberts, who speak of reconciliation with white people as part of the reconciliation of God in Jesus Christ, Cone contends that "only black people can define the term on which our reconciliation with white people will become real."[8] For those who believe in Jesus Christ as God's unconditional reconciliation with human beings who sin against him, this sounds like a shocking statement. One may even detect in it a spirit of vengeance. However, it is not my task here to make a theological or even a moral judgement on Cone's contention. What I want to show is that when social and historical situations are taken into serious consideration in our interpretation of the word of God, we must be prepared for a drastic change in the way the word of God speaks to us.

Active theology is thus a theology that grows out of the life of people. This was well stated by participants of the "Theology in Action" workshops held in Manila and Kuala Lumpur in 1972 and 1973 under the auspices of the Christian Conference in Asia. They in part said:

Theology is beginning to pick up theological themes in the lives of the people, to relate to social analysis and social investigation which exposes conflicts in society. Significant experiments of a new life style of Christian living can be seen. Many of us have experienced this reality in our own countries and shared these experiences at this Workshop. So we dare to hope.[9]

Theology is not to be learned but to be lived; it is not to be thought but to be experienced. And insofar as it has to do with a reflection on the nature and contents of faith, it has to grow out of the experience of faith in real-life situations. For the drama of God's pain rooted in his love does not take place in a theological debate, in a Christian conference hall, or in an evangelical rally conducted with well-trained choirs and fortified with loudspeakers. The doing of theology takes place right where a difficult decision has to be taken, be it personal or social. It is done where a value judgment has to be made, where choice between good and evil cannot be evaded. This is the strength of black theology. It is a brutal theology which, instead of avoiding head-on collisions with the brutal realities of society, faces them with passion and commitment. Theology is a relentless pursuit of what God's redemptive love means in the community of men and women whom God comes to save in Christ.

It follows that theology as the love of the God-man in action is communal in nature and expression. This is self-evident on account of the nature of love which makes theology possible and meaningful. Fundamentally, love is a communal event. That is to say, it is only within a community that the events of love can take place. This is what that rather awkward phrase *God-man* tries to convey. God's love is known primarily in the intimate communion between God and human beings. This communion is, of course, Jesus Christ. Jesus Christ is the communion of love between God and humanity. Theology is therefore not a solitary speculation on the nature of God's love. It has to do with the love of God *and* humanity. It is in this communal context that we are led to experience the redemptive nature of love as it acts in human society. This communal love is the presupposition of theology. The theology built on the foundation of this communal love is a passionate theology. It is a theology that cares and therefore makes sense. It is a theology that enables us to encounter the agony and joy of love in the midst of hatred and despair. In art and in literature this love of the God-man at work in a community is often depicted with theological profundity and sensitivity.

### Insights from the Japanese Novel Hyo-ten

*Hyo-ten (The Freezing Point),* a novel by Japanese author Ayako Miura, can be cited as an example. After it was published in 1965, it quickly became a best-seller in Japan.[10] Its author was determined to carry out a relentless conversation with the various characters she had created. The subject of the conversation was the sin that lurks in the heart of each and every one of us. She wanted to turn her characters' hearts inside out and bring out into the broad daylight the thoughts, plots, and schemes hatched in the dark corners of their souls. The novel turns out to be a tragic drama of life, showing how all of us are struggling against ourselves. There is the confrontation between the inner I and the outer I. And Miura shows that the root of this conflict and confrontation is the love in us all. In this intense struggle we see love both in its most sublime aspects and also in its ugliest aspects. This is the fearful struggle of the love of the God-man in us all.

The protagonist is a conscientious physician, Dr. Tsujiguchi, who was envied by his classmates and friends for his intellectual ability and good character. He was honest, considerate, and responsible. After graduating from medical school, he married a beautiful young woman, the daughter of his teacher, quickly established himself as the head of a large private hospital, and became the father of two children, a girl and a boy. Life seemed full of promise for the future until the day his three-year-old daughter was strangled to death by a total stranger on a river bank near their home. As the tragedy was taking place, a young eye doctor in Tsujiguchi's hospital, who had advantage of Tsujiguchi's absence, had been calling on the latter's wife, Natsu-e, to reveal to her the love he had long felt for her in secret. Natsu-e, though tempted by the other man's advances, did not fully yield to him. The tragic death of the little girl at that particular time had severe repercussions on Tsujiguchi and his wife. Natsu-e became a victim of her own sense of guilt, and Tsujiguchi was obsessed by the desire to take revenge on his wife. This obsession was intensified when he later discovered proof that Natsu-e was still not entirely indifferent to the eye doctor's persistent attentions.

Tsujiguchi soon had an opportunity to turn his obsession with revenge into action. After recovering from her initial shock, guilt, and depression, Natsu-e proposed to her husband that they should adopt a baby girl in place of the dead daughter. Now a drama of the agony and pain of love and hate began to unfold. At first Tsujiguchi was not responsive to his wife's proposal, even though Natsu-e insisted. Then by chance he heard that the infant daughter of the man who had murdered his own daughter had been put up for adoption in the hospital of his intimate friend, a gynecologist. Here was an opportunity to take revenge on his wife, Tsujiguchi thought to himself. He offered to adopt the baby girl, stating to his gynecologist friend that he wanted to put into practice the teachings of Jesus on loving one's enemy. This was a lesson he had learned in a Bible class he had attended during his college days. His friend dismissed the proposal as impracticable and tried to talk Tsujiguchi out of it. But Tsujiguchi was so determined that his friend finally agreed to the adoption on one condition: If Tsujiguchi should find the situation too difficult, the baby girl would be returned to the hospital. And of course it was agreed that the origin of the baby would be kept a complete secret from Natsu-e. In his heart, however, Tsujiguchi, reasoned:

Yes, I'll not consult Natsu-e about the adoption of this particular baby. She will love and cherish the baby without knowing her origin. The secret must be kept at all cost. What will her reaction be when one day she discovers that the baby she has brought up is the murderer's child? When she finds out that the child she has cared for for more than ten years is the murderer's daughter, she will be stricken with regret and remorse. But this is all right, isn't it? The murderer's child will grow up with love and care. At the same time, it is an attempt on my part to "love your enemy." Knowing that the girl is the murderer's child, I shall perhaps feel more pain than Natsu-e would. At any rate, I must go ahead with the plan. The day will come when Natsu-e will find out who the child is. Then she will surely rave with fury and remorse.

The drama of love is thus a drama of the conflicts and struggles in the depths of our hearts. Tsujiguchi, outwardly a well-respected doctor but inwardly a man torn with a desire for revenge on account of love, is a picture of us all.

Ironically, the redeeming factor in this drama of life is Yoko, the baby girl adopted into a home trapped by its contradictions, fears, and schemings. She grows up to be a charming, innocent, and lovable girl. Even Tsujiguchi, who at first avoided her and refused even to touch her, comes to have a warm spot for her in his heart. She is entirely incapable of thinking evil of other people. If there are angels, she is one. She does not lose her charm and lovableness even after Natsu-e begins to maltreat her when the mother learns by accident the secret of Yoko's origin. A fierce contest of will and heart breaks among the members of this peaceful family. The situation has now been reversed. Now it is Natsu-e who becomes obsessed with the desire for revenge on her husband who had allowed her to bring up the murderer's child. As to Tsujiguchi, he is now filled with regret and remorse. "Why did I let Natsu-e bring up the murderer's daughter?" he asks himself:

But at that time I just could not forgive Natsu-e. And only because I was not able to forgive her, I plunged everyone into great unhappiness. I wanted to take revenge on her, but I am the one who has become a victim of the most cruel revenge.

Even for Yoko, now nineteen, the whole thing becomes too much to bear after she comes to know the reason why Natsu-e's attitude toward her has radically changed. The burden becomes so heavy that Yoko finally loses the strength and courage to go on living. She decides to commit suicide as a way out of an impossible situation for which she is not responsible. But she does not blame anyone, not even her adopted mother. In her last will, which is in the form of a letter to her adopted parents, she writes:

All along I endured all the hardships out of the conviction that I was doing no wrong to anyone, that I was in the right and innocent. But my conviction was shattered when I learned that I am the daughter of the man who murdered your own daughter.

In reality, I did not kill anyone. I did not commit any legal offense. But the fact that my father committed a murder tells me that I too have the possibility of committing a murder. . . .

When I in this way discovered in myself the possibility of committing sin, I lost all hope in living. This Yoko [which means literally "the child of the sun"] who has tried to live happily, brightly, and openly, must have been to Mother an obnoxious person.

This is what I am thinking now. Even in the heart of Yoko, who has made every effort to live a full life, there is also a freezing point. My heart is frozen. This is my freezing point: You are the child of a condemned man. I can no longer face anyone, not even a small child. Perhaps I cannot truly live until I have learned to endure this fact. But I cannot endure it. I have lost the strength to live. I am totally frozen.

Father, Mother, please forgive my father who murdered Ruliko, your daughter.

I am struck by the word "forgive" when I say it now. Until this moment I had not thought of the need to ask others to forgive me. But I now desire forgiveness. I long to be forgiven by Father, Mother, and everyone in the world. I now crave for the authority that can pronounce forgiveness to me loudly and clearly.

Love that turns into revenge and love that seeks forgiveness when we lose our hope of living, love that confronts the freezing point at which all goodness, beauty, and truth become frozen—this is the kind of love that brings God and ourselves into a communion in which the freezing point in all of us is broken.

At the end of this tragic human drama, Tsujiguchi, Natsu-e, and their friends surround the unconscious Yoko and wait in great suffering for her to respond to the efforts to save her life. The gynecologist remorsefully confesses that Yoko in fact is not the murderer's daughter. He let Tsujiguchi adopt her in this misapprehension because he wanted to see if Tsujiguchi was capable of putting into practice Christ's injunction to love your enemy. But it is now no longer a question of deciding who is guilty of what. When Yoko responds feebly to the emergency treatment, hope begins to revive for everyone. There is now a possibility of making a new beginning. What really matters now is the love that can be a redeeming force in the life of all of us in spite of the destructive forces within us. In this powerful drama of life Miura has created an equally powerful theology of *Hyo-ten*—the freezing point that brings us face to face with God.

*Hyo-ten* is a deeply moving, thought-provoking novel that shows how the stuff of life is also the stuff of theology. We men and women are in essence theological beings. Whether we are aware of it or not, whether we care to admit it or not, we are human beings in communion with God. And the universe of relationships that surround us is an extension of our communion with God. The drama of life is therefore the drama of theology. Theologians are not just cool, objective observers of life's dramas. They, like everyone else, are part of life's dramas. Their theological reflection therefore must be a reflection of their involvement in life's dramas. Out of such reflection they may be able to point to the redemptive meaning that comes from God's own involvement in the dramas of human life. In this sense theology, whose subject matter is the love of the God-man in action, is an active and communal theology. It can be described as a *theology of relations*. Let us explore a little what we mean by the expression *theology of relations*.

## Buber and the Theology of Relations

In 1923 the brilliant Jewish philosopher and mystic Martin Buber published in Germany a profound, little book, *I and Thou,* which has had an enormous influence on theology, psychology, and education. This work contains the following bold statement: IN THE BEGINNING IS RELATION.[11] By it Buber shows deep insight into God's creation as an act of relation. The order of relations is broken down into the I-You and the I-It dimensions. The distinction between the I-You relation and the I-It relation is normative in Buber's exposition of the relations surrounding all human beings.

At first we may think that Buber has polarized the I-You relation as having to do with whatever is personal and interpersonal, while the I-It relation has to do with whatever is impersonal. In fact, polarization does exist in Buber's exposition of the structure of relations, but it is a polarization of basic human attitudes and not a polarization of categories. This means that relations are not a priori classified as either I-You or I-It. Sometimes the It-world addresses me as "You" while the You-world becomes an It to me. How does this happen? In Buber's own words:

In every sphere, through everything that becomes present to us, we gaze toward the train of the eternal You; in each we perceive a breath of it; in every You we address the eternal You, in every sphere according to its manners.[12]

Thus the I-You world and the I-It world are interchangeable.

All the same, Buber has grasped an essential aspect of human beings in their relations with others and the world around them or in their relations as communal beings. Internal and external relations determine the place of men and women in a community as well as the meaning of their existence in the world and in human history. This means that human beings who are deprived of relations fall into nonbeing. Human beings who are abstracted from their relations become disembodied beings who are detached from the universe of the triple relations among God, human beings, and nature.

We know, of course, that human beings cannot live by themselves. The *locus classicus* that stresses this basic understanding about human beings and their relations is the first chapter of Genesis, which states:

Then God said, "Let us make man in our image and likeness to rule the fish in the sea, the birds of heaven, the cattle, all wild animals on earth, and all reptiles that crawl upon the earth." So God created man in his own image; in the image of God he created him; male and female he created them (Gen. 1:26–27).

Humanity is here seen in a context of relations. To locate the place of humanity in God's creation, the threefold relations of God, humanity, and nature plays an essential role. From the beginning the Bible rules out the possibility of regarding human beings in isolation. To speak of them in separation from God is to deprive them of the basis of their life. And to consider them in abstraction from nature is to deny the affinity and fellowship they share with nature. To quote Buber again:

The basic word I-You can be spoken only with one's whole being. The concentration and fusion into a whole being can never be accomplished without me. I require a You to become I; becoming I, I say You.[13]

There is a poem by a Chinese woman probably from the Sung dynasty (960–1279 A.D.). In it she superbly expresses this I-You love. Perceiving that her husband's love for her has faded, she tries to rekindle the affection that once united her with her husband in the bond of marriage by presenting him with the following poem:

> I take a lump of clay,
> make a figurine of you
> and a figurine of me.
>
> Then I take the figurine of you
> and the figurine of me,
> crush them together,
> make them into another lump of clay.
>
> Again I make a figurine of you
> and a figurine of me,
> out of this lump of clay.
>
> There is now "You in Me"
> and "I in You."[14]

What beauty and wonder of I-You love is captured by a poetic mind! Does this not reflect something of the intensity of love that turns an I-It relation into an I-You relation? Does it also not reflect something of the love that relates the Son to the Father? According to John's Gospel Jesus prayed to the Father and said:

. . . may they all be one: as thou, Father, art in me, and I in thee, so also may they be in us, that the world may believe that thou didst send me (John 17:21).

Love has the power to shorten the time and distance that separate one person from another. In fact, love can completely overcome time and space between God and human beings. God is in Jesus Christ and Jesus Christ in God, and through Jesus Christ God is in us all.

The love that supports and sustains us all in the bond of relations is derived from the love that forms the basis of the union between God and humanity in Jesus Christ. Granted, the love we experience in our human relationships is fragmented, imperfect, and susceptible of misuse and distortion. Nevertheless, it is this love-force that seeks to overcome the time and space standing in the way of a full communion. It is this love-force that creates meaning for the life of individuals and for the history of humankind as a whole. It is no wonder that in the Bible we find again and again appeals to this love as the motivating power behind God's search for humanity.

The Song of Songs in the Old Testament should perhaps be read with this in mind.[15] What we see there is the realism of love, that is, love in its nakedness of passion and in its longing for union. It is a beautiful antiphony of love sung by the bride and bridegroom with interludes sung by their companions. At one point the bride sings:

> My beloved is mine and I am his;
> he delights in the lilies.
> While the day is cool and the shadows are dispersing,
> turn, my beloved, and show yourself
> a gazelle or a young wild goat
> on the hills where cinnamon grows (S. of S. 2:16–17).

Love creates longing for those in love. It is where the destiny of a man and a woman rests. But longing can become unbearable because we are prisoners of space and time, and space and time do interfere with the union we seek. Thus the bride continues:

> Night after night on my bed
> I have sought my true love;
> I have sought him but not found him,
> I have called him but he has not answered.
> I said, "I will rise and go the rounds of the city,
> through the streets and the squares,
> seeking my true love."
> I sought him but I did not find him,
> I called him but he did not answer (S. of S. 3:1–2).

The bride's desperation has reached a low point. She has not been able to find her true love, the love which makes her live, the love which gives meaning to her life, and the love which promises a destiny in the union with the loved one. She is now in need of any help she can find. She meets watchmen. They must surely know the whereabouts of her true love. She runs to them and asks:

The watchmen, going the rounds of the city, met me, and I asked, "Have you seen my true love?" (S. of S. 3:3)

The watchmen shake their heads. Disappointed and in despair, she falls into tears. Just as she turns away in sorrow, she catches sight of her true love. Her heart leaps with joy and she runs to him as fast as her feet can carry her. This is a moment of excitement, victory, and joy. She is in ecstasy. At last, the time and space that had cruelly separated her from her loved one are overcome. The barriers between I and You are removed. Listen now to her triumphal song:

> Scarcely had I left them [the watchmen] behind me
> when I met my true love.
> I seized him and would not let him go
> until I had brought him to my mother's house,
> to the room of her who conceived me (S. of S. 3:4).

The bridegroom responds to her in kind. From his mouth comes the most beautiful and powerful ode to the love with which God binds himself to humanity and binds one person to another. Thus he sings:

> Under the apricot-trees I roused you,
> there where your mother was in labour with you,
> there where she who bore you was in labour.
> Wear me as a seal upon your heart,
> as a seal upon your arm;
> for love is strong as death,
> passion cruel as the grave;
> it blazes up like blazing fire,
> fiercer than any flame.
> Many waters cannot quench love,
> no flood can sweep it away;
> if a man were to offer for love
> the whole wealth of his house,
> it would be utterly scorned (S. of S. 4:5–7).

The true nature of love, which is in pain and exultation, is completely exposed here. This is love in all its nakedness. Love is as strong as death and its passion as cruel as the grave. What a powerful metaphor! It makes you stagger; it makes you tremble. But at the same time it enables you to live as only human beings do: united in the communion of love with God and locked in the passion of love's agony in the community of men and women. That is why love cannot be traded with anything else, even with "the whole wealth of someone's house."

### The Particularity of Love

Both the Song of Songs and the Chinese poem referred to above are superb theology. Their subject matter is the same—love in agony and joy, love in despair and ecstasy, love in pain and exuberance! Theology should be an ode of love. It should sing the song of love. Theology without the pain and agony of love is not theology. It is a make-believe monologue directed to no one but itself. Nor is theology without joy and exultation true theology. It is an endlessly dull discourse that puts to sleep not only the audience but the speakers themselves. Such a theology has nothing to do with the God of the Christian Bible who creates the world and redeems it in passionate love. It has, of course, little in common with men and women tormented with love and destined to suffer for the sake of love. This is the meaning of theology as the love of the God-man in action. It travels between Me and You and between You and Me. It seeks You in Me and Me in You. Theology must be consummated in the marriage between Me and You. It must be the I-You love in action. Thus theology must be categorically communal. Perhaps this is the profound symbolic meaning of God as the trinitarian communion of Father, Son, and Holy Spirit. God is the communion of love. The Father and the Son in the communion of the Holy Spirit constitute the internal relationship in this communion of love. Theology is thus the language of God's love reflected in the community of men and women. To put it differently, theology is a hermeneutics of the love of the God-man active in the human community. It follows that the themes of theology must come from the human community. In Part Two we will discuss some examples that show how theology must be done within the context of a particular human community.

If love is communal in nature, it must be particular in its orientation. This means that theology, which is described as the love of the God-man in action, must be informed by historical and situational particularity. This is the next point I want to discuss.

One distinctive characteristic of love is its particular meaning and relevance. Essentially, love is not a concept but an action. It is an action verb, not a concept noun. Since action is the substance of history, love that is primarily an action must be historical. It must take historical forms. Furthermore, love as action in history should also be personal, or to use the word mentioned above, communal. The love that is historical, personal, and communal forms the basis of a human community. Herein consists the genius of the Christian understanding of the incarnation. The Word becomes flesh—this means that God's love for humanity becomes historical. It takes a personal and communal form. It becomes the basis of a new human community. In this way, the historical and personal particularity of love is crucial in the formation of a new human community as a precursor of the kingdom of God.

But the particularity emphasized here must not be taken for exclusiveness. In actual fact, this particularity is the basis of universality. I must explain what I mean. A Filipino mother, for example, loves the child she holds in her arms. Her love is directed to a particular human being—her own child. And this is the most direct way in which she can express her love. But in that particular expression of love, we also see something of the love which, say, a Polish mother, in an entirely different part of the world under a totally different historical and social setting, shows to her child. In these two particular expressions of love we realize that there is a universal quality in the love a mother shows her child. A mother does not start with the universal love of a mother for her child. Her love is a particular love directed to a particular child in a particular situation. Universality of love must therefore be based on the particularity of love. This order of love, as we may call it, cannot be reversed, at least not in our experience. Once this order is reversed, love becomes just an abstraction. We might profess to love all humanity but in practice hate our next-door neighbor.

I must stress that the particularity of love mentioned here has nothing to do with individualism. Individualism, when applied to the practice of love, leads to the exclusiveness of love. It is an egocentric love that seeks our own benefit and happiness at the expense of others. Needless to say, the particularity we are discussing here has nothing to do with such individualism. The teaching of the Chinese philosopher Mo Ti on mutual love *(chien-ai),* it seems to me, was an attempt to combat egocentric love as the basic cause of conflict and war among the rulers of his time. Born probably before Confucius died (479 B.C.) in the latter's native state, Mo Ti never became as influential as Confucius or Lao-tzu in the history of Chinese thought. Moreover, his doctrine of mutual love is often regarded as utilitarian in nature. He is often considered to be motivated more by concern for personal benefits than by moral principles such as righteousness. In other words, it pays to exercise mutual love.[16] Such a verdict may not be entirely correct. His philosophy could well have become a moral philosophy that served as the basis for a political philosophy, thus freeing China from bondage to familyism, or the family tradition. This tradition has constituted the core of China's political and social system.[17] Mo Ti, for instance, lamented the prevailing situation of confusion and conflict in his time and said:

They arise out of want of mutual love. At present feudal lords know only to love their own states and not those of others. Therefore they do not hesitate to mobilize their states to attack others. Heads of families know only to love their own families and not those of others. Therefore they do not hesitate to mobilize their families to usurp others. And individuals know only to love their own persons and not those of others. Therefore they do not hesitate to mobilize their own persons to injure others.[18]

In this vein he exposed what he considered to be the basic cause of social evil, namely, lack of love for one another. His was a lonely voice in the wilderness. But he was not deterred from pursuing his ideal of mutual love. His teaching on this subject was impressive. In answering, for example, a question about what is the way of universal (i.e., mutual) love, he replied:

It is to regard other people's countries as one's own. Regard other people's families as one's own. Regard other people's person as one's own. Consequently, when feudal lords love one another, they will not fight in the fields. When heads of families love one another, they will not usurp one another. When ruler and minister love one another, they will be kind and loyal. When father and son love each other, they will be affectionate and filial. When brothers love each other, they will be peaceful and harmonious. When all the people in the world love one another, the strong will not overcome the weak, the many will not oppress the few, the rich will not insult the poor, the honoured will not despise the humble, and the cunning will not deceive the ignorant. Because of universal love, all the calamities, usurpations, hatred, and animosity in the world may be prevented from arising. Therefore the man of humanity praises it.[19]

A naive idealism? Perhaps. But consider this teaching against the background of the ruthless struggles in the period of Warring States in ancient China, and these words sound prophetic and compassionate. Above all, Mo Ti seemed to have practiced what he preached. For even Mencius, the second-ranking sage of Confucianism and Mo Ti's opponent, had to make the following admission: "Mo Ti loved all men and would gladly wear out his whole being from head to heel for the benefit of mankind." And Chuang-tzu, the spiritual heir of Lao-tzu, is reported to have remarked: "Mo Ti was certainly a glory to the world. What he could not attain, he would never cease to seek, even though he be in privation and destitution. Ah, what a genius he was."[20] Of all the great teachers of ancient China, it is Mo Ti who came closest to teaching love as the cardinal principle that governs human beings and the world.

At any rate, it is in particular practices and applications of love that we are led to see the universal nature of love. Biblical faith puts emphasis on the universal application of love. One of the most telling examples is the story of the good Samaritan as told by Jesus in Luke 10. A lawyer had approached Jesus with a question about eternal life. He said with pride that he kept all the commandments of the law, including the article on loving God and loving one's neighbor. But as it turned out, love for the lawyer was an abstract concept. He could not see and practice it in a concrete life situation. The love he recited from the law had no particular applicability in relation to those in need. Thus his theology, if he had one, must have been a bad, abstract theology. Certainly it was not the theology of the love of the God-man in action. It was not the practice of love in response to the demands of particular situations that occupied him in his theological effort. He had a prior understanding of what love should be like from theological textbooks of the law. With that understanding he was sure that he had met all the requirements of the law concerning the practice of love. We can therefore well imagine that, when he asked Jesus who the neighbor was, he was expecting to hear Jesus confirm his own understanding of love. Seen against this background, the story of the good Samaritan becomes a very poignant story. The person who becomes your neighbor, Jesus says pointedly, has nothing to do with the description or specification of it in the book of the law. Your neighbor is the person—or the stranger if you like—whom we meet in our daily contacts. The contrasting attitudes toward the victim of a highway robbery in the story between the first two men, who belonged to the inner circle of the religious community, and the Samaritan, who was ostracized by the Jewish community, could not have been more pointed. In the final analysis what is important, Jesus seems to be saying, is neither the love written in the law nor the theology of love taught by the teachers of the law, but the love acted out in a particular situation regardless of race or creed. It is this love that brightens the world, heals wounds, and makes life worth living. The good Samaritan is the love of the God-man in action. Jesus' concluding order is unambiguous: "Go and do as he did" (Luke 10:37).

"Who is my neighbor?" This is a deeply *theo*-logical question. For we can change the question a little and ask: Who is my God? Lest there be a misunderstanding, I must stress that by turning the question about our neighbor into a question about God, I am not confusing humanity with God or God with humanity. The crucial point here is that the question of God cannot be asked in separation from the question about our neighbor. The neighbor in need is God in need. The stranger in suffering is God in suffering. Christian theology therefore is not different from metaphysics when it asks questions about God entirely outside the contexts in which questions about our neighbor occur.

The correlation between questions about God and questions about our neighbor cannot be disputed. This becomes especially self-evident when we realize that love is at the heart of this correlation. In love God relates himself to the world. Love makes God near and real to us. Love is God incarnate, and in love God interconnects with history. Love enables God to intersect with human beings on the crossroad of a particular space and time. This crossroad of love between God and human beings is the neighbor. In this sense and in this sense alone, we must speak of God in terms of humanity. Questions about God are thus questions about humanity. The questions we want to direct to God as to who he is in himself are thrown back upon us in the form of questions about our neighbor. This is precisely what Jesus did with the learned lawyer. The lawyer asked questions about eternal life. But Jesus turned his questions into a question about his neighbor. Indeed, theological inquiry begins with the question about our neighbor.

This is fundamental to the biblical knowledge of God. In his letter to the Galatians in which he defended his apostolicity with great passion, St. Paul said: " . . . but now that you have come to know God, or rather to be known by God . . . " (Gal. 4:4, RSV). Why is there this quick change from our knowledge of God to God's knowledge of us? St. Paul must have realized that it is presumptuous for us to say we know God. It is God who knows us, and our knowledge of God must begin there. Again the focus is shifted from God to human beings. If we want to know God, we must turn to humanity, that is, to our neighbor, for God loves and is close to our neighbor. *Theo*-logical questions are in reality *anthropo*-logical questions.

Therefore theology should not begin with the study of God. Rather it should start with the study of humanity, the study of people and the world, in short, the study of God's creation. Human beings with all their problems—social, political, psychological, ecological, or whatever—are subject matters of theology. The world with all its ideologies, organizations and structures, religions, arts and poetry, provides themes for a living theology. The universe with all its problems and issues calls for theological analysis and interpretation. All this points to the fact that the central concerns of theology are creation and redemption. Since this is the case, theology has no time for metaphysical questions about God. It has to direct its attention to human beings and the world. It has to discover the work of love in the human community. It has to call into question powers and ideologies that distort the communion between God and human beings and destroy the fellowship among people.

Perhaps it is the writer of the first letter of John who made this point most clear. The knowledge of God, he insisted, must begin with the practice of love among brothers and sisters. He first stressed that in love we are concerned with action and not with conceptualization. "My children," he wrote, "love must not be a matter of words or talk; it must be genuine, and show itself in action" (1 John 3:18). He then went on to affirm that God who is love discloses himself in the act of his saving mission through Jesus Christ. "For God is love," his theology of love continued, "and his love was disclosed to us in this, that he sent his only Son into the world to bring us life" ( 1 John 4:9). The incarnation was, first and foremost, the love of God in action for the world. But insofar as our knowledge and experience of God is concerned, this is still not the whole picture. What we have here is still a propositional statement which needs to be verified. How then do we go about verifying the love of God? How are followers of Christ to demonstrate that God is love? The answer John, the writer of the letter, gave is crucial to our discussion here. This is what he said:

But if a man says, "I love God," while hating his brother, he is a liar. If he does not love the brother whom he has seen, it cannot be that he loves God whom he has not seen. And indeed this command comes to us from Christ himself: that he who loves God must also love his brother (1 John 4:19–21).

Our experience and knowledge of God's love hinges on our acts of love for our brothers and sisters. To put it another way, to know God and to love him is to know and love our brothers and sisters. Love of our brother and sister is concrete and particular. This particularity of our love is a basic clue to the experience and knowledge of God. In a particular act of love God comes to humans and humans come to God. In an act of love God and humanity are interconnected. This interconnection of God and humanity takes place in all places and all times. From the Christian point of view, Jesus Christ is *the* interconnection of divine love and human love, and through him we may encounter and appreciate interconnections of love in the human community.

Since the subject of theology is this love of the God-man in action, the methods of theology must be determined by the nature and shape of this love. Fundamentally, theology does not move from the universal to the particular. It cannot approach the concrete realities of life with the general principles and articles of faith. It cannot begin with God in general and with human beings in general. In short, theology cannot treat the love of God—active in human beings, visible in human relations, and manifest in historical events—as if it could be dissected into neat components and forced into tidy formulas.

Particularity therefore plays a crucial role in doing theology. Since theology must be committed to God's acts in concrete historical situations, the life situations of men and women in particular, theologians must begin where they are. They cannot begin anywhere else. They must seek to meet Jesus Christ who is the love of the God-man in their brothers and sisters, that is, in their neighbors. Their task must be to identify redemptive meaning of events in their community. In a particular person, brother, sister, or neighbor, in their community, or in a stranger from outside their immediate community, they must try to apprehend God's agony and joy. Theology begins with humanity and ends with God. Or more correctly expressed, theology begins with a hidden God in a particular person or event, but in the process it finds itself in communion with the God in human beings and in communion with the humanity in God. And it is Jesus Christ, *the* God-man, who guides and leads theology in its witness to the saving acts of God in the living situations of men and women within a particular culture and history.

Theological particularity is the basis for doing theology with Asian spirituality, or for that matter, with any kind of spirituality. Fundamentally, in theology we are concerned with the serious business of penetrating the darkness that surrounds human spiritualities. This darkness must be illuminated by the love of God, the power that sustains all things and that makes redemptive communion with all things possible. This kind of theology gives up a false universal framework or category that has made it difficult for the Christian church to receive fresh spiritual insights from outside, and to join in the chorus sung with different styles, words, and melodies. Above all, through this kind of theological effort, theologians will be able to find themselves in a wonderful and mysterious world of human spirituality expressed in art, literature, and other cultural forms. Deeply rooted in all cultural activities is human spirituality touched by the divine spirit in search of the ultimate meaning of life. Granted that there are demonic elements in human spirituality that may be latent in cultural and religious activities. This means that theology will be also confronted by the challenge of the ultimate meaninglessness that renders life a bundle of horrible nightmares. This is particularly evident in the demonic forces released in World War II, the Korean War, and the Vietnam War. War can be said to be a synthesis of human activities, both spiritual and physical, put to the service of the demonic spirit. It is a destructively negative expression of human spirituality. Thus theology has no way of evading the issue of the ultimate meaninglessness with which demonic forces seek to replace the ultimate meaning of life. In human spirituality theology has to confront the conflict between the positive ultimate and the negative ultimate. Theology is engaged in the agony of the human spirit trying to overcome evil with the love of the God-man in action. The theology that does not reflect such an agony of the human spirit is not theology in the proper sense of the word. Theology, therefore, must first and foremost be a theology of the cross. Theology is an appointment with God at the foot of the cross.

There is a well-known prayer in the *Brihadaranyaka Upanishad:* "Lead me from the unreal to the real. From darkness lead me to light. From death lead me to immortality."[21] This must be a prayer of Christian theologians too. In confrontation with the realities of life, the task of theologians is to discern the ways which may lead them from the unreal to the real, from darkness to light, and from death to eternal life. This theological task must begin with the particular. Theologians must realize that there is no reaching the universal by by-passing the particular. In this sense, truth is particularity just as truth for Kierkegaard is subjectivity. Kierkegaard shuns objectivity not because he denies objective aspects to reality but because for him there is no possibility of attaining objectivity by by-passing subjectivity.[22] This is especially true of faith. Subjective appropriation of faith is just as important as the objective authority that faith derives from the traditions of the church or dogmas and creeds.[23]

In short, the task of theology as the love of the God-man in action is a *critical* one—critical in the generic sense of having to do with a crisis. Love after all is filled with crises. Love is a crisis that has to be faced, and love without risk is not love. Involvement in risk makes love exciting and authentic. Love is therefore a *critical* act. This is essentially what the incarnation is about. God in his love for humankind had to make a *critical* decision to become present in Jesus Christ. Ahead of Christ was the crisis of crises—the cross. The incarnation is a *critical* act taken by God in his love to meet the *critical* situation of the world. True theology therefore must be born out of a crisis. Its dynamics is the love that takes the risk of facing the critical realities of life and the world. The crisis of love calls for the doing of theology. It makes men and women theologians, for the crisis of love is the crisis of our being, the crisis of the communion that makes life possible and meaningful in relation to God and our fellow human beings. As we seek to reflect on this love and to set this love in motion, we become theologians, that is, lovers of God and humanity, and rediscover our responsibility toward God and the human community. This is the authentic doing of theology. In the following chapters we hope to show how theology can be done authentically in Asia today both among Christians and among those who remain outside the Christian church.

# Part Two

# Suffering unto Hope

# CHAPTER 5

# THE CROSS AND THE LOTUS

Suffering touches the heart of God as well as the hearts of human beings. In the suffering of humanity we see and experience the suffering of God. God and human beings are bound together in suffering. That is why we stressed in Chapter 2 that theology begins with God's heartache which is caused by human suffering and pain. In the suffering everyone of us has to go through at various stages of life, God himself suffers. Jesus Christ is the God-man in suffering. And it is this same Christ who—to use the expression of the previous chapter—is the love of the God-man in action. The cross, from the standpoint of Christian faith, is the supreme symbol of God's suffering love. It has not been surpassed even after two thousand years. In the cross we realize that suffering is not merely physical, institutional, impersonal, or secular. It is religious and human, and thus divine. Suffering is the cross God has to bear with all his creation.

Another religious symbol that over the centuries has become the focus of the religious devotion and spiritual aspirations of a vast number of people under the influence of Buddhist spirituality is the lotus.[1] The image of Buddha or Bodhisattva seated cross-legged on the lotus has been to the masses a source of comfort and peace. It stills the troubled mind and gives assurance that suffering is not the last word. It helps to maintain serenity in the midst of a turbulent life of bitterness. And it promises a life of bliss when all births cease. The lotus is to Buddhists as a religious symbol what the cross is to Christians. Radically different in every way, these two symbols point to a crucial quest of human life—deliverance.

### The Power of Symbols

Both the cross and the lotus are powerful symbols. Without the cross the faith inculcated by the humble carpenter from Nazareth would have dissipated soon after his death. By the same token, without the lotus and what it tries to communicate, the lofty teachings of Buddhism would have probably failed to captivate the devotion of the masses. As it turned out, the spirituality of the cross and the spirituality of the lotus went on to

101

conquer the realms of human life in the West and in the East respectively. In time two distinctive religions were born—the religion of the cross and the religion of the lotus. In addition, out of these two religions two distinct cultures came into being—the culture of the cross and the culture of the lotus. They took separate roads of development for centuries until the dawn of the modern era. But their paths were destined to cross. First through the missionary expansion of the western churches and then through the translation of Buddhist texts into the European languages, the two religions and cultures met on the crossroad of human history. For missionary Christianity the spirituality of the lotus was atheistic in its teaching and idolatrous in its practice—the object of divine wrath and missionary castigation. However, in Europe itself, the heartland of Christianity, Buddhism fared much better. The philosopher of pessimism, Schopenhauer, for example, found in it a striking echo of his own pessimism. He called the Hegelians who built a grandiose structure of history on ideas "simple realists, optimists, eudaemonists, shallow fellows, Philistines incarnate, bad Christians" and similar things. Then he went on to say:

the true spirit and kernel of Christianity, as of Brahmanism and Buddhism also, is the knowledge of the vanity of all earthly happiness, complete contempt for it, and the turning away to an existence of quite a different, indeed an opposite, kind. This, I say, is the spirit and purpose of Christianity. . . . Therefore, atheistic Buddhism is much more closely akin to Christianity than are optimistic Judaism and its variety, Islam.[2]

Perhaps Buddhism owes to Schopenhauer more than anybody else its reputation in the West as solely a pessimistic religion.

More recently, the encounter of these two religions and cultures took a sinister turn as they collided on the battlefields of Vietnam. The cross and the lotus quivered and groaned as the tranquility of Indochina was shattered by gunners and bombers, by demonic forces parasitic on the womb of culture. An open letter written by a group of Vietnamese to the American ambassador in 1963 affirmed that "opposition to Ngo Dinh Diem had become for many intellectuals opposition to Christianity." This expression was indicative of the religious and cultural crisis inherent in the political struggle in South Vietnam. The letter in part stated:

For us Vietnamese, to embrace Christianity means that we would be forbidden to worship our Ancestors, our deceased Parents, when this has been the most important thing in our style of life for thousands of years. . . . The Christians are hybrids, they are eccentric to Vietnamese society, they are absurd with regard to Vietnamese thought. Nor is their language even Vietnamese. . . . The young Vietnamese want to know why there are so many differences between Christianity and their culture, why this religion is so contrary to their *Volksgeist*, why so many monstrous contradictions, why so many absurd superstitions, why this severity and cruelty of the Almighty God who unceasingly curses and threatens men with such horrible words while he ought to be saving them.[3]

It is no consolation for Protestant Christians to know that these questions were directed to the Catholic church, the main body of Christianity in Vietnam that counted the ruling family of Diem among its members. What we see here is the agony of the spirituality of the lotus versus the spirituality of the cross that had been distorted in its cultural forms and misrepresented and abused by the powers that be.

At any rate, in the cross and the lotus we encounter two powerful religious symbols representing two different ways in which we grasp the world of reality behind the world of phenomena. They are the portals through which we may enter the depth of human spirituality in search of what is ultimate in life. They are pregnant with meanings that concern us in this world and in the world to come. Although life as a whole is saturated with symbols, it is in the religious realm that the symbolic character of life is intensified. For this reason religious symbols embody in themselves human spirituality in communion with the reality from which human life is derived ultimately. As Tillich well expressed the situation:

The language of faith is the language of symbols. . . . But faith, understood as the state of being ultimately concerned, has no language other than symbols. When saying this I always expect the question: Only a symbol? He who asks this question has not understood . . . the power of symbolic language. One should never say, "only a symbol," but one should say "not less than a symbol."[4]

Thus Tillich speaks of the power of symbols. In fact, life as a whole is under the spell and power of symbols. This is readily seen at a political rally in which the audience is transfixed under the spell of a powerful orator. Political demagogues in particular know almost instinctively the power of symbols and use them skillfully to sway people to their side. A leader like Hitler, for example, was able to exploit in a demonic fashion the power of symbols embodied in a political language to create a fanatical faith in despotism.

In religious symbols we have to do with the experience of revelation. What is revealed cannot be communicated or expressed literally. Literal communication cannot be applied to revelation. In fact, it drives revelation out of human experience. There is thus a basic contradiction in a literal interpretation of scriptures. Scriptures as the communication of divine revelation are highly symbolic in that they try to express what defies the normal means of human communication. Human language has to be stretched beyond its normal logic to capture something that transcends human rationality. Scriptures can thus be interpreted symbolically. This applies not only to the legends and myths of the Bible but also to its historical sections. Literal interpretations of history reveal little of the meaning which transcends history and informs the latter with revelatory significance. The Exodus in the Bible, for example, does not only refer to a historical event—the escape of a group of Hebrews from Egypt—but also to the redemption of life even for those who never participated in the historical Exodus. Therefore a literal interpretation of the Bible kills revelation. Revelation loses its meaning and power under the literalists who insist on regarding the Bible as a verbatim correspondence between what is written down and what transcends history while working within history. What Mircea Eliade, a historian of religion, has to say about symbols is very much to the point. He puts it this way:

> The symbol reveals certain aspects of reality—the deepest aspects—which defy any other means of knowledge. Images, symbols and myths are not irresponsible creations of the psyche; they respond to a need and fulfil a function, that of bringing to light the most hidden modalities of being.[5]

The deepest aspect of reality defies the conventional means of knowledge. That is why revelation must be interpreted symbolically, not literally.

It is important to bear this in mind when Christians approach other religions, including primal religions. The stereotyped judgment of other religions passed by Christians is almost invariably related to idolatry. When western missionaries went to the world beyond the West they found themselves surrounded by idols and people who worshiped them. Forgetting entirely the place images and ikons played in certain powerful traditions of Christianity, they launched crusades against the idols and their worshipers. They did not realize that idols were powerful religious symbols that stand for humanity's search for "the deepest aspect of reality." In other words, they interpreted idols literally, not symbolically. A literal interpretation of the meaning of idols resulted more often than not in a literal destruction of the idols. The burning of idols became therefore a necessary part of the conversion process. It was regarded as the manifestation of a genuine conversion from the worship of idols to the worship of the one true God. The following account is typical of the ritual of idol burning formerly carried out after the preacher or the missionary was reasonably sure that a genuine conversion had taken place. This account had as its background a small town in Korea in the early part of this century. The convert was a young Korean man, Chin Pai, for whom the time had come to demonstrate his confession of the Christian faith by burning the idols worshiped in his parents' household:

> The six Christians, including Chin Pai's mother, gathered for the burning of the idols. They piled them all up in the courtyard, first the guest-room guard spirit,

then the rags tied to the ceiling beam in the kitchen and the picture of the kitchen god, then the bunch of old straw shoes under the gate, and the rags and straw rope under the rice hulling room. . . .

From the yard they took the site god, an earthenware jar covered with a hood of thatch. They smashed the jar and burned the thatch. . . . Last of all they brought out the ancestral tablets, five of them, representing five generations. . . . Chin Pai touched a match to the pile, and as it burned, they sang one of the newly learned songs of praise.[6]

This was a bonfire celebrating a Christian victory over pagan idolatry. A clean break was made not only with the converts' religious past but also with their ancestral roots, for not even the ancestral tablets could be spared in the ritual. This was not unlike the iconoclasm that took place during the Reformation as a result of the extreme aversion Protestant Christianity felt for religious images. But if we do away with all images and symbols, then the ultimate reality they stand for is also liable to disappear from the religious consciousness of the people. This can be partly shown in the worship service of a Protestant church, especially a church that belongs to the Reformed tradition. The worship is bare and unadorned. The experience of being in the presence of a *mysterium tremendum et fascinosum* is, of course, not obtained easily.[7]

## *Jewish and Christian Reactions to the Symbols of Other Faiths*

What missionary Christianity tended to miss was the symbolic meaning of idols and images in other religions. It seldom occurred to the zealous preachers of the Gospel that the idols and images "provide 'openings' into a trans-historical world. . . . Thanks to them, the different 'histories' can intercommunicate."[8] I believe this observation by a historian of religions is relevant for Christian theology. But the fact is that the meaning and spirituality behind idols and symbols used in one religious and cultural milieu tend to elude the grasp of those brought up in another religious and cultural milieu. A statue of Buddha, in a museum in, say, London or New York, is to most western viewers no more than an object of aesthetic curiosity. For them it is not something to which they express veneration and devotion. On the other hand, a crucifix to people in a remote village in the Orient who have never come into contact with Christianity cannot appear as a symbol representing God's love in Jesus Christ for the world. It is therefore evident that idols, images, and religious symbols are incomprehensible to outsiders without interpretation. Consequently, they are bound to suffer at the hands of militant missionary religions.

It is in this connection that the treatment of idols in the Bible, especially in the Old Testament, needs to be reconsidered and reinterpreted. This is important because in most cases the Christian denunciation of idols and images takes its cue directly from the Bible. Jeremiah, for example, mocks idols in a language at once derisive and amusing:

> Do not fall into the ways of the nations,
> do not be awed by signs in the heavens;
> it is the nations who go in awe of these.
> For the carved images of the nations are a sham,
> they are nothing but timber cut from the forest,
> worked with his chisel by a craftsman;
> he adorns it with silver and gold,
> fastening them on with hammer and nails
> so that they do not fall apart.
> They can no more speak than a scarecrow in a plot of cucumbers,
> they must be carried, for they cannot walk.
> Do not be afraid of them: they can do no harm,
> and they have no power to do good (Jer. 10:1–5).

This was a prophet's version of demythologizing idols! Jeremiah exposed the false nature of idols. Idols were things fashioned by human hands. There was no life in them. They could neither move for themselves nor do harm or good. There was thus no reason to be afraid of them. If one was still in doubt as to whether idols have no power over human beings, one was shown how they were constructed out of materials imported from various countries. Thus Jeremiah went on to say:

> The beaten silver is brought from Tarshish
> and the gold from Ophir;
> all are the work of craftsmen and goldsmiths.
> They are draped in violet and purple,
> all the work of skilled men (Jer. 10:9).[9]

Idols were completely demythologized. People were exhorted to worship the one true God, the creator.

This, however, does not mean that the religious elements contained in the worship of foreign idols were entirely rejected and excluded from the religion of Israel. In fact, there are strong indications that the people of Israel adopted foreign religious feelings and beliefs into their own religion, adapting them to their needs. Thus John Gray, an Old Testament scholar, cautions us against a too-sweeping judgment on the idolatrous practices of the Canaanite religions. "In considering the condemnation of idolatry in Israel," he writes, "we must bear in mind the varying degrees in which Israel assimilated the culture of Canaan." Then he goes on to illustrate his observation by referring to the Feast of Tabernacles, which is closely related to the agricultural life of the people. He points out that the Feast of Tabernacles was associated with the New Year festival, which "was the chief seasonal festival in the peasants' year," and that "from Zech.

14:16 it is apparent that the kingship of God was a prominent theme of that festival. Psalms and passages in the prophets on this theme reveal a striking affinity in imagery and subject matter with the Ras Shamra myth of the kingship of BAAL. Here the Hebrews seized upon the Canaanite expression of faith in Providence in nature and adapted it to their own peculiar ethos as the expression of their faith in Providence in history and the moral order."[10]

It seems that such religious leaders of Israel as the prophets and priests were more astute religiously than we care to believe. On the one hand, they attacked idol worship with great vehemence. They were objects of terror (Jer. 50:38), a cause of trembling (1 Kgs. 15:13; 2 Chr. 15:16), and an abomination to the people of Israel (2 Chr. 15:8). At the same time, idols were vanity (Isa. 66:3) and a nonentity (Lev. 19:4; Pss. 96:5; 97:7; Isa. 2:8; 18:20; Hab. 2:18; Zech. 11:17).[11] But this was not the whole story. For even a very central part of the worship of BAAL related to the question of providence was incorporated into the faith of Israel in the God whose providence was at work in history and the moral order of the universe. What the prophets condemned was the "preoccupation with the material fruits of creation rather than with the nature and will of the Creator himself in idolatry in the general sense."[12] Defined in this way, idolatry, we must admit, can be said to be present in all religions implicitly or explicitly. For no religion is entirely free from the human propensity to rely on something finite as an expression of what is infinite. Being finite themselves, human beings are bound to finite objects in which the infinite is believed to be present. Thus care must be taken to distinguish between idols and images that have become the ultimate objects of worship and devotion, and idols and images through which human beings seek to grasp and express the spiritual reality on which they depend for the power and meaning of life.[13] Granted that the distinction is not always easy to make, that is still no reason for Christian believers to vent their iconoclastic zeal on the idols and images of other religions at the expense of the spiritual reality these images seek to represent. Idols and images can be, in the words of Eliade quoted earlier, "openings into a transhistorical world."

As Eliade points out, this is what happened during the Christianization of Europe. Because of its importance for our discussion here, let me quote his observation in full in the hope that it will help us grasp the theological meaning of other religions from the Christian point of view:

Much has been said about the unification of Europe by Christianity: and it is never better attested than when we see how Christianity co-ordinated the popular religious traditions. It was by means of Christian hagiography that the local cults—from Thrace to Scandinavia and from the Tagus to the Dnieper—were brought under a "common denominator." By the fact of their Christianization, the gods and the sacred places of the whole of Europe not only received common names but rediscovered, in a sense, their own archetypes and therefore their universal valencies: a fountain in Gaul, regarded as sacred ever since prehistoric times, but sanctioned by the presence of a divine or regional figure, became sacred *for Christianity as a whole* after its consecration to the Virgin Mary. All the slayers of dragons were assimilated to Saint George or to some other Christian hero; all the Gods of the storm to holy Elijah. . . . For, by Christianizing the ancient European religious heritage, it [Christianity] not only purified the latter, but took up, into the new spiritual dispensation of mankind, all that deserved to be "saved" of the old practices, beliefs and hopes of pre-Christian man. Even today, in popular Christianity, there are rites and beliefs surviving from the neo-lithic: the boiled grain in honour of the dead, for instance (the *coliva* of Eastern and Aegean Europe). The Christianization of the peasant levels of Europe was effected thanks above all to the images: everywhere they were rediscovered, and had only to be revalorized, reintegrated and given new names.[14]

Religion, like any other cultural phenomenon, is a highly complex affair. Its history is, in a sense, a history of growth through intercommunication, integration, and assimilation among diverse religious practices and beliefs. This indicates that human spirituality, despite differences in its forms and expressions, shares some basic aspirations and characteristics. Christian theology has not taken this fact seriously. Its assertion of uniqueness is often made without taking into account the very complex history of Christianity on the one hand and the contributions of other faiths and religions on the other.

Furthermore, Eliade's observation quoted above helps us to realize that human spirituality, although closely associated with a particular cultural and historical context, is capable of transcending that context. It is at once bound to it and can be freed from it. In fact, human spirituality at its deepest level transcends its own cultural and historical particularity and intercommunicates with other spiritualities. The Christianization of Europe as discussed by Eliade is a case in point. The conversion of Asia to Buddhism is another remarkable example. Joseph Kitagawa calls it the "Pan-Asianness of Buddhism." As he puts it:

Buddhism continued to grow in India's immediate neighbors and also in other areas where indigenous religions and cultures had been established. In both cases the genius of Buddhism enabled it to maintain and express its *Lebensgefühl,* which is distinct and unmistakable. Eventually, Buddhism developed into a Pan-Asian religion, closely identified with various cultures of Asia.[15]

As it made its way into other parts of Asia, Buddhism was able to transcend the "Indianness" within which it had been conceived and born. And in the course of its expansion and development throughout Asia, Buddhism has remained the religion identifiable through the symbol of the lotus just as the cross has become the symbol of the Christian faith since its inception two thousand years ago.

## Contrast Between the Cross and the Lotus

The question we must now ask is: what has the cross to do with the lotus? As early as the third century, Tertullian raised this question in relation to Jerusalem and Athens: what has Jerusalem to do with Athens? His answer was negative. Jerusalem—the city of the holy temple, the place where Jesus was crucified, the symbol of salvation revealed to the world in Christ in Tertullian's mind—had nothing to do with Athens. Athens stood for reason whereas Jerusalem was the embodiment of the sacred. Athens was a "secular" city in contrast to Jerusalem, a "holy" city. Furthermore, with its many gods and shrines Athens was a center of paganism in the ancient Mediterranean world. There St. Paul had delivered his famous sermon on the unknown God before the Court of Areopagus. "Men of Athens," he declared:

I see that in everything that concerns religion you are uncommonly scrupulous. For as I was going round looking at the objects of your worship, I noticed among other things an altar bearing the inscription "To an Unknown God." What you worship but do not know—this is what I now proclaim (Acts 17:22–23).

Thus it was Paul who in his missionary zeal sought to penetrate the depth of Greek spirituality which had blossomed into art, literature, and philosophy on the one hand and worship of every conceivable deity on the other. Paul's effort in Athens was a dramatic demonstration of the fact that Jerusalem had much to do with Athens. It can even be said to have foreshadowed the Hellenization of Christianity by leaps and bounds in the subsequent history of the development of Christian thought in the West. Tertullian's verdict was wrong. The history of Christian thought was in a true sense a history of how Greek philosophy, especially that of Plato and Aristotle, became integrated into the mainstream of Christian faith. As has been pointed out, ". . . through the whole history of Christianity in the West there runs the dynamic of the Gospel's course from the Jew to the Greek, from the Greek to the barbarian."[16]

However that may be, the cross and the lotus seem to have little in common, at first sight at any rate. The lotus springs from the surface of the water. When the wind blows and the water moves, the lotus also moves. It seems in perfect harmony with nature around it. In short, it gives the appearance of being at peace with itself.[17] In contrast, the cross strikes out powerfully, painfully, and defiantly from the earth. It penetrates space and is incongruous with nature. The lotus appeals to our aesthetic feelings, whereas the cross is revolting to the eyes of the beholder. The lotus is soft in texture and graceful in shape, while the cross is hard and harsh. The lotus moves with nature, whereas the cross stands ruggedly and tragically out of the barren earth. The lotus distinguishes itself in gentleness, while the cross is the epitome of human brutality. The lotus beckons and the cross repels. Indeed, what has the cross to do with the lotus? They represent two entirely different spiritualities which seem to be totally incompatible. They seem to have nothing in common.

But the contrast between the cross and the lotus may be deceptive. Essentially, they are two different answers to some basic questions about life and death. They seek to unravel problems and difficulties that beset us in our earthly pilgrimage. They also try to point to the fulfillment of human destiny in the eternal and blissful presence of the divine. They are not primarily concerned with a metaphysical solution to these very important problems, but with practical, day-to-day struggles in the harsh reality of society. Neither the cross nor the lotus, fundamentally speaking, is a system of thought, a set of rituals, or an institution of devotion. Originally they sprang out of the midst of the daily life of the people. They are religions of the people, but theologians—both in Christianity and Buddhism—have taken them away from the people and turned them into theological systems and religious principles bearing little relationship to the genuine fears and aspirations of the people. It is thus not surprising that the cross and the lotus do not intersect in their theological systems or ecclesiastical structures. In fact, these systems and structures only pull the two spiritualities further apart. The place for the cross and the lotus to intersect and intercommunicate is the people—the people who have to fight both spiritual and physical fears, the people who have to live and die without knowing why. Then and only then can the cross and the lotus begin to intercommunicate; they can then begin to point to the mystery that surrounds human destiny. Thus intercommunication and intercommunion of different spiritualities should begin with the people, and with the ways in which they try to cope with the problems of life and the world in sociopolitical and religious terms.

This can be illustrated, first of all, by the way Jesus and Buddha tried to communicate their message through stories and parables. Jesus gave the following reason for using parables to his disciples: "It has been granted to you to know the secrets of the kingdom of Heaven; but to those others it has not been granted" (Matt. 13:11). Then he went on to explain the meaning of the parable of the sower.[18] An abstruse mystery should not remain the monopoly of a few. Jesus mingled with the crowd and took pains to communicate the message of the Gospel to them. He definitely broke away from the religious elitism of his day and brought religion back to the people. In a sense he was the leader of a new religious movement around which the farmers and workers, the illiterate and the oppressed, could gather. He thus posed a threat to the official religion consolidated on hierarchical structures of religious orders and teachings not readily accessible or intelligible to outsiders.

In the rise of Buddhism in India we also see something of a religious reformation that returned religion from a religious elite to the people in the street. The religious and social situation of India at the time of Buddha in the sixth century B.C. was similar to that of the Jewish community in Palestine during the life of Jesus. "At the time of the Buddha," writes Kenneth Ch'en, "the dominant position in Indian society was held by the brahmans. They held the key to knowledge, and the power that went with that knowledge."[19] Brahmanism, like Judaism in Jesus' day, was the privilege of the religious leaders and the burden of the masses. As a reformer who ended up by founding a new religion, Buddha

repudiated the brahmanical claims that the *Vedas* were the sole and infallible source of religious truth. He also rejected correct performance of the rituals as means of salvation, and he disapproved of the Upanishadic emphasis on intellectual means to attain emancipation. He also protested against the iniquities of the caste system, especially the high pretensions of the brahman class, and welcomed among his followers members from not only the four castes but also from among the outcasts.[20]

Buddha was thus the first in the history of India to revolt against the caste system as the chief misfortune of Indian society.

It is therefore not surprising that Buddha tried to communicate a message of emancipation from the suffering of the world in plain language. We can hear him saying something like this:

I have taught the truth which is excellent in the beginning, excellent in the middle, and excellent in the end; it is glorious in its spirit and glorious in its letter. But simple as it is, the people cannot understand it. I must speak to them in their own language. I must adapt my thoughts to their thoughts. They are like unto children and love to hear tales. Therefore, I will tell them stories to explain the glory of the dharma. If they cannot grasp the truth in the abstract arguments by which I have reached it, they may nevertheless come to understand it, if it is illustrated in parables.[21]

It is clear from this that Buddha fully grasped the dynamics of people in religion. As Buddhism spread to China, Japan, and Southeast Asia, it became a religion of the people that created popular culture and cultivated a sense of solidarity among ordinary men and women in all walks of life. To be sure, the teachings of Buddha in their high and lofty forms never filtered down to the people unadulterated. But what is important is that Buddha brought to common men and women a sense of well-being, security, and above all a sense of destiny.

In this way a religious faith can become alive and genuine if it casts aside ecclesiastical pretensions and formidable theological systems and touches the lives and hearts of the people. As previously mentioned, both Jesus and Buddha labored to bring the light of a new faith into the lives of the people. They were close to the people, used popular language, and told stories and parables that came right out of the everyday experiences of the people. No wonder that we find in the Sutra of the Lotus Flower of the Wonderful Law the story of the lost son that bears a remarkable resemblance to the parable of the prodigal son in Luke 15:11–32.

According to the Buddhist story of the lost son, a young man left his father and went to another city where he became extremely poor. He was reduced to begging for his food. In contrast, his father grew rich and moved to a big estate where he lived in great luxury. But all the time he grieved over his lost son and said to himself:

I am old and well advanced in years, and though I have great possessions I have no son. Alas that time should do its work upon me, and that all this wealth should perish unused! . . . It would be bliss indeed if my son might enjoy all my wealth!

One day the son wandered into his father's land, and the drama of the reunion of the father and son gradually unfolded:

Then the poor man, in search of food and clothing, came to the rich man's home. And the rich man was sitting in great pomp at the gate of his house, surrounded by a large throng of attendants. . . . When he saw him the poor man was terrified . . . for he thought that he had happened on a king or on some high officer of state, and had no business there. . . . So he quickly ran away.

But the rich man . . . recognized his son as soon as he saw him and he was full of joy . . . and thought: "This is wonderful! I have found him who shall enjoy my riches. He of whom I thought of constantly has come back, now that I am old and full of years!" Then, longing for his son, he sent swift messengers, telling them to go and fetch him quickly.

The story goes on to describe how the father, who lived in a highly class-conscious society, was not able to disclose his identity to his own son and take him back into his household. The poor man had to go away without realizing that he had been in his own father's house. The father then contrived to have his son hired to work in his own household as a servant. Every day he watched with compassion as his son cleared away a refuse heap. Then one day the rich man

came down, took off his wreath and jewels and rich clothes, put on dirty garments, covered his body with dust, and, taking a basket in his hand, went up to his son. And he greeted him at a distance and said, "Take this basket and clear away the dust at once!" By this means he managed to speak to his son.

In this way, the old man made every attempt to make his son feel at home but did not reveal his own identity. In the meantime, the son proved to be a frugal, honest, and industrious man. Finally, knowing that his end was near, the old man sent for the poor man again, presented him before a gathering of his relatives, and, in the presence of the king, his officers, and the people of town and country, he said: "Listen, gentlemen! This is my son, whom I begot. . . . To him I leave all my family revenues, and my private wealth he shall have as his own."[22]

Consequently, through the father's painful and patient effort the son was reinstated in society and accepted into his father's blessing.

It goes without saying that the ethos of this Buddhist story is quite different from that of the biblical story of the prodigal son. It is Asian through and through in its emphasis on class distinctions that affect even family relations, on accumulation of wealth as a moral and social virtue, and on inheritance as a chief factor affecting the father-son relationship. These are the elements that are part and parcel of a traditional Asian society. For the people in the street such social factors provide a background against which a religious truth can be apprehended. There is in this story no reference to the son's repentance, no mention of the elder son's protest against the father's treatment of the lost son. Despite all these differences in ethos and details, the story points up the father's compassion for his son, the expression of which is very Asian in its reserve and its respect for social conventions. It stresses the acceptance of the son by the father through a ceremony in accordance with the father's social status. The resemblance of the Buddhist story of the lost Son to the biblical story of the prodigal son may be accidental. But it is evidence of the fact that deep in people's spirituality is a reflection of God's love and compassion for the world. Jesus Christ, we must admit, is not merely a reflection of God's love. He is the embodiment of that love. In any case, the father's compassion for the son in the Buddhist story may be seen as a reflection, however imperfect, of God's passionate love in the parable of the prodigal son.

### St. Paul on God's Redemptive Work in the World

This, I believe, can lead us to speak of redemptive elements in cultures and histories outside the direct influence of Christian faith. It is basic to St. Paul's perception of God's redemptive work in the world. It is clear also in his polemic against those who turn their backs on God. As Paul sees it:

For all that may be known of God by men lies plain before their eyes; indeed God himself has disclosed it to them. His invisible attributes, that is to say his everlasting power and deity, have been visible, ever since the world began, to the eye of reason, in the things he has made. There is therefore no possible defence for their conduct; knowing God, they have refused to honour him as God, or to render him thanks (Rom. 1:19–21).

This is a controversial passage, to say the least. It has been interpreted as a condemnation of everything "pagan." It is regarded as throwing a negative light on whatever is not compatible with Christian traditions and practices. Furthermore, it has been used as an argument against crediting a positive meaning to cultures and histories that have had little to do with the culture and history directly associated with Christianity.[23]

True, what St. Paul says here is an indictment of idol worshipers and those who rebel against the moral law of God. But the important thing for us to remember is that not all cultures and histories outside the sphere of Christian influence are corrupted totally with idolatry and impiety; they are not all works of a demonic power that sets itself against the God of Jesus Christ. Yes, there are demonic elements in them. But what culture and history are completely free from such elements? No religion, Christianity not excepted, is entirely free from it. Paul Tillich has put it well when he says:

Demonization of the holy occurs in all religions day by day, even in the religion which is based on the self-negation of the finite in the Cross of Christ. The quest for unambiguous life is, therefore, most radically directed against the ambiguity of the holy and the demonic in the religious realm.[24]

If we think of the corruption in the highest circles of the Christian church, of the horrible deeds of the Inquisition in the name of God, of the tragedy of the Crusades, of the disunity of the church through the centuries—if we think of all these and other evil events in the history of Christianity, we realize that Tillich is not exaggerating. Perhaps the conscience of the Christian church should have taught its members to be able to say: since even the church with its intense concentration on God's redeeming love in Jesus Christ has not been free of what Tillich calls demonization, how much more difficult has it been for other religions that have no direct knowledge of God's salvation in Jesus Christ! We therefore must admit that the Christian attitude toward other religions has in general been opposed to an open dialogue. This often results in a wholesale condemnation of other expressions of human spirituality as if they were objects of divine judgment.

Thus we should look at St. Paul's words quoted above from a different perspective. To be sure, he does not condone in the least despicable practices that debase human nature and show scorn for divine creation. That is why he condemns immorality, infidelity, and all kinds of depravity. But this does not cancel out the fact that God's love and power have been at work in the world since the beginning of creation. Human sin does not destroy God's work of creation. How could it? Otherwise sin would be stronger than the power of God. The history of the Christian church is an eloquent proof of this. The church continues to exist despite a demonizing tendency within it. The message of salvation continues to be proclaimed in spite of demonic distortions of God's love within the church.

And people continue to rally to Christ, even though the church is often divided and its pettiness as an institution is revealed. God is above all these human failures and sins. And at times he works through them. It is a source of consolation and encouragement that the truth of God has never abandoned the church in spite of the church's failure to measure up to the glory of God. If this is true with the Christian church, it must also be true with the whole of creation. The idolatry and impiety we see in cultures and histories outside Christianity really do help conceal God's truth. But there are moments and events that still disclose God's continuing presence in a society that has not been shaped by Christianity. These are what I call redemptive moments and redemptive events. While fragmentary and imperfect, they are nonetheless genuine. They reflect in some way God's redeeming love and power that have become incarnate in Jesus Christ.

To avoid any misunderstanding, let me stress that Buddha, for example, is not Jesus Christ. For that matter neither is Jesus Christ a Bodhisattva. As historical personalities Buddha and Jesus have little to do with one another. The cultural and religious contexts in which each of them carried out their missions were vastly different. But the ultimate difference from the Christian point of view comes from our faith in Jesus Christ as the direct and complete embodiment of God's saving love. The affirmation of such a faith, however, should not blind Christians to God's continuing presence and work outside Christianity. In fact, it should open our eyes to perceive a redemptive quality in moments and events in other cultures and histories that have to be considered substantively related to the work of Jesus Christ.

These redemptive moments and events, in my view, result from what St. Paul regards as God's self-disclosure in creation since the world began. Christian faith in God's redemption in and through Jesus Christ must embrace this global dimension. And the best way to appreciate the global dimension of redemptive interactions between faith in Jesus Christ and other faiths is not theoretical or doctrinal. When we realize how ordinary men and women must struggle to cope with the stresses and pressures of life and to find an ultimate meaning in our finite existence, we can begin to discern redemptive events and moments in their lives and to relate them to what God has done in Jesus Christ. Viewed in this perspective, religions and cultures outside Christianity cease to be merely objects of Christian condemnation; they begin to acquire an internal relationship with what Christians believe and do.

According to a legend, after attaining enlightenment Gautama said to a mendicant he met by chance on the road:

Having myself crossed the ocean of suffering, I must help others to cross it. Freed myself, I must set others free. This is the vow which I made in the past when I saw all that lives in distress.[25]

Compare again this vow of Buddha with Jesus' announcement at the beginning of his mission. According to Luke's Gospel, Jesus quoted the book of Isaiah and said:

> The Spirit of the Lord is upon me because he has anointed me;
> he has sent me to announce good news to the poor,
> to proclaim release for prisoners and recovery of sight for the blind;
> to let the broken victims go free,
> to proclaim the year of the Lord's favour (Lk. 4:18–19).

At first we are struck by the fundamental differences between Buddha's vow and Jesus' announcement. Buddha is a self-appointed herald of the good news he had experienced and understood after a long search that culminated in his enlightenment under the bo-tree. Jesus Christ is conscious of having been appointed and sent by God the Father. In his vow Buddha does not claim any special relationship with a deity, but for Jesus the Spirit of the Lord is present and working in him. Again the main tenet of Buddha's vow consists of emancipation from the world, which is an ocean of suffering and distress. In contrast, Jesus' announcement is filled with an active concern for the social and political conditions that victimize the innocent, the powerless, and the poor.

What we see, in other words, are two drastically different ways of understanding and appropriating the providence of God, which are not to be confused or identified. But this should not hinder us from realizing that the expression of Buddha's compassion for the masses in his vow and the way he toiled unselfishly for their emancipation from pain and suffering are not without redemptive significance. Can we not say that Buddha's way is also a part of the drama of salvation which God has acted out fully in the person and work of Jesus Christ? The histories of nations and peoples that are not under the direct impact of Christianity are not just "natural" histories running their course in complete separation from God's redemptive love and power. In this sense, there is no "natural" history. The history of a nation and the dynamics of its rise and fall cannot be explained entirely by natural forces or sociopolitical factors. There are redemptive elements in all nations that condemn human corruption and encourage what is noble and holy. Our evaluation of the history of a nation is not complete until such redemptive elements are properly recognized. From the Christian point of view, the redemptive elements in human history are witnesses to the presence in the world of the God who, in St. Paul's words "sent forth his Son, born of woman, born under the law, to redeem those who were under the law, so that they might receive adoption as sons" (Gal. 4:4, RSV). Here is a mystery the profundity of which cannot be measured or explained by the simplistic logic of a heaven and a hell brandished by zealous Christians. In my view Christian faith should at least include a readiness to acknowledge that God somehow uses the redemptive elements outside Christianity to prevent human history from going completely bankrupt, to sustain a world that often verges on destruction through such human cruelty as we witnessed in World War II in which the "Christian" West was brutally and demonically involved. Our acknowledgement of this fact should be accompanied by thankfulness to God for not leaving the world to its own destructive devices and meaningless chaos.

## The Bodhisattva and Suffering Humanity

The Buddhist concept of a Bodhisattva takes on, in this connection, an important theological meaning. A Bodhisattva occupies a place of great importance in Mahayana Buddhism as a person who follows the footsteps of Buddha in refusing to enter into Buddhahood for the sake of suffering humanity. His "prime purpose was to save mankind. He was extroverted to his fellows' needs, and his own were of no importance. He was the dedicated servant of all men, and so long as the least of them lacked enlightenment he vowed to refuse for himself that guerdon of a thousand lives."[26] The difficulty for Christians lies in the fact that a Bodhisattva is a human being. Theologically speaking, for a human being to save other human beings is a religious presumption that contradicts the basic meaning of the cross. For Christians salvation is the work of God, not of humanity. But this should not close our mind to the redemptive quality evident in a Bodhisattva, that is, the quality of putting the spiritual needs of others before our own, the readiness to enter into the suffering of our fellow human beings, and the goal toward which the human spirit should strive.

Bodhisattvas in areas under Buddhist influence perform the function of a spiritual catharsis similar to that accomplished by the prophets of ancient Israel. The crucial question is not whether Bodhisattvas are redeemers in the sense that Jesus Christ is our redeemer, for they are not. But because of them and through them people may see something of God's redemption at work in the world. Because of them and through them the world is not entirely lost. To put it positively, perhaps because of them and through them God gives hope to the world and shows his readiness to save people from destruction. The story in the Old Testament of Abraham pleading with God to save Sodom and Gomorrah can be cited as an example of my meaning. After knowing God's resolve to destroy the two wicked cities, Abraham interceded for them, asking God if he would still carry out his plan if some righteous people could be found in them. God's answer was a clear no. If there were fifty good people, thirty, even as few as ten in these cities, said God, "I will pardon the whole place for their sake" (Gen. 18:16–33). These few people constituted what I call redemptive elements for Sodom and Gomorrah. Because of them the cities would be spared and forgiven.

Let us expand this biblical story to cover historical experiences outside the biblical tradition. What redeems history—any history!—from utter nonsense and despair is the few good people we can find, even in corrupt cities like Sodom and Gomorrah, or Bodhisattvas in a society and culture like India that is outwardly and totally uninformed by a faith in Jesus Christ. The Bodhisattvas themselves are not redemptive from the viewpoint of Christian faith, but they are evidence of God's redemptive power and of humanity's hope in the future. They are witnesses to the fact that God has not forsaken the world, that the power of God's love has not been overcome by the demonic power of destruction.

At this point we recall the scene of the last judgment in Chapter 25 of Matthew's Gospel. The king on the judgment seat says to the sheep standing at his right hand:

You have my Father's blessing; come, enter and possess the kingdom that has been ready for you since the world was made. For when I was hungry, you gave me food; when thirsty, you gave me drink; when I was a stranger you took me into your home, when naked you clothed me; when I was ill you came to my help, when in prison you visited me (Matt. 25:34–36).

For the righteous these words of approval come as a complete surprise, and they do not conceal their bewilderment. They quickly reply that they have never seen the king in such misery or deprivation. They are then told that "anything you did for one of my brothers here, however humble, you did it to me" (Matt. 25:40). A conclusion we may draw is that throughout human history there are men and women who have gone about doing the king's business without being aware that they are in the king's service. Through what they are and what they do, they bring hope to those in despair, transmit light in the midst of darkness, point to life when people are threatened with death, and bring freedom to imprisoned bodies and spirits. In so doing, they knowingly or unknowingly mediate God's redemptive power to those with whom they come into contact.

It is a cause for Christians to rejoice if they are able to set aside their preconceived ideas and prejudices. They should see the mission of the church as consisting not of conquering members of other faiths but of growing with them in the knowledge and experience of God's saving work in the world. For one thing, we Christians must humbly admit that institutional Christianity alone cannot save the world. This is a historical fact as well as a theological truth that can hardly be refuted. The institutional church in Asia, with few exceptions, is a minority entity and will remain so. Its missionary work came to an end in Communist China, which has about a quarter of the world's population. Furthermore, India—the Asian nation with the second largest population in the world—is largely under the influence of Hinduism. In Indonesia the Christian church has made significant progress in terms of membership. Despite the part the church has played in building Indonesia as a nation, Islam continues to exert a dominant influence over the lives of the people.[27]

This does not mean that the churches in Asia can forego their mission and retreat into the inner sanctuaries of a Christian community sheltered from external forces at work in society and among the people. But it does mean that the mission of the Christian church in Asia can no longer be conceived of only in terms of the territorial expansion of the institutional church or a statistical increase in membership. The mission of the church is the more fundamental task of informing the Asian spirituality shaped by Asian cultures and religions with the love and compassion of God in Jesus Christ. In addition, Asian Christians together with people of other faiths and ideologies must seek to transform Asian society on the basis of freedom, justice, and equality. Sociopolitical conditions in Asia in recent decades have created a situation that not only makes such a mission of the Christian church possible but also necessary. For religions like Buddhism that are traditionally known as world-denying have been forced by external social and political events to take an active part in the life of the nations where they find themselves. This is another illustration of the way in which different cultural and religious spiritualities must seek to meet and find one another—not in the heat of theoretical and doctrinal disputes but in the very life of the nations where people live, suffer, and die.

The involvement of Vietnamese Buddhists in the tragic war that ravaged their country and ended with communist domination of the entire nation offers an illuminating example of how the "Christian" part of the world failed to work with redemptive elements in Vietnam to create a new society of freedom and hope for the people. In memory let us return to a hot summer day—the 11th of June, 1963—when a Buddhist monk, Thich Quang-Duc, burned himself to death on Phan-dingh-Phung Street in Saigon, "to call the attention of the world public to the sufferings of the Vietnamese people under Ngo-Dinh-Diem's oppressive regime."[28] In the years that followed, the self-immolation of monks continued as a protest against the cruel war and as a sacrifice for the restoration of peace. This was literally "the lotus in the sea of fire." The world was shocked by these acts of self-destruction and could not understand their meaning. The Vietnamese monk and scholar Thich Nhat Hanh recounts his conversation with an American doctor to whom he was able to explain the meaning of self-immolation by his fellow monks. "She [the American doctor] saw self-immolation as an act of savagery, violence and fanaticism, requiring a condition of mental unbalance. When I explained to her that the venerable Thich Quang-Duc was over seventy, that I had lived with him for nearly one year at Long-Vinh pagoda and found him a very kind and lucid person and that he was calm and in full possession of his mental faculties when he burned himself, she could not believe it. She could not understand because she was unable, though not unwilling, to look at the act of self-burning from any angle but her own."[29]

The inability to understand the spirit of other cultures and religions bedevils human relations, blocks intercultural communication, and creates and perpetuates the tragedy of human conflict and war. Catholicism—the dominant form of Christianity in Vietnam—was in no position to understand its Buddhist compatriots. "Certainly," writes Frances FitzGerald:

. . . the French had always shown great favoritism towards the Catholics, turning them into a self-conscious elitist minority without necessarily imparting to them a greater degree of French culture. Vietnamese Catholicism was harsh and medieval, a product of the strict patriarchate of the Vietnamese village rather than of the liberal French Church. Its churches stood like fortresses in the center of each Catholic village, manifesting the permanent defensive posture of the Catholics towards all other Vietnamese.[30]

Thus to the Christian world, both inside and outside Vietnam, the Buddhist involvement was regarded either as part of a communist conspiracy or as a way to gain self-salvation in a region of eternal bliss. The cross did not seem to meet the lotus in the sea of fire raging over Vietnam.

In his June 1965 letter to Martin Luther King, Jr., Thich Nhat Hanh further explained what it meant for a monk to immolate himself as an expression of religious faith and of social and political concern. Thich Nhat Hanh's statement has much bearing on our affirmation of the redemptive elements outside the Christian church. The letter in part reported:

What the monks said in the letters they left before burning themselves aimed only at alarming, at moving the hearts of the oppressors and at calling the attention of the world to the suffering endured then by the Vietnamese. To burn oneself by fire is to prove that what one is saying is of the utmost importance. There is nothing more painful than burning oneself. . . . During the ceremony of ordination, as practised in the Mahayana tradition, the monk candidate is required to burn one, or more, small spots on his body in taking the vow to observe the 250 rules of a bhikshu, to live the life of a monk, to attain enlightenment and to devote his life to the salvation of all beings. . . . When the words are uttered while kneeling before the community of sangha and experiencing this kind of pain, they will express all the seriousness of one's heart and mind, and carry much greater weight.[31]

The pain of suffering must accompany an act of love and compassion for others. The pain of self-immolation is a radical consequence of the symbolic pain a monk has to go through at his ordination. In this pain is included the pain of his neighbors, friends, and compatriots. And surely in this pain is reflected the pain of God who must have been present in the extreme suffering and pain of the Vietnamese people. The self-immolation of monks, if carried out in the spirit described by Thich Nhat Hanh, was a painful expression of the redemptive elements at war with destruction and inhumanity. Thich Nhat Hanh went on to say in the same letter:

In the Buddhist belief, life is not confined to a period of 60 or 80 or 100 years: life is eternal. Life is not confined to this body: life is universal. To express will by burning oneself, therefore, is not to commit an act of destruction but to perform an act of construction, i.e., to suffer and to die for the sake of one's people.[32]

Such a statement can be translated into the language of Christian eschatology. The moment of death for the monk in the act of self-immolation was an eschatological moment for him personally and for his nation. If we accept Thich Nhat Hanh's interpretation of the death of a self-immolated monk as not a destruction of life but a construction of life in the Buddhist sense, death for the monk was both the fulfillment of his religious faith in the search for eternal life and a powerful impact on the people of Vietnam to work for the transformation of society.

The eschatological moment for the monk, therefore, did not come at the end of time in an indefinite future. It came at the midstream of history. Before it were both the struggle for freedom and peace for a country devastated by war and life in the presence of the eternal God. This is not to extol death as a means to salvation or social transformation. Death as a part of the Buddhist teaching regarding the extinction of self as a way to Nirvana does not seem to play an essential role in these particular instances of self-immolation in the busy streets of Saigon in the midst of a national crisis. If Thich Nhat Hanh's interpretation is right, I am inclined to believe that the death of these monks may have had a redemptive significance. Again I must stress that the death of a self-immolated monk is not to be identified with the death of Christ on the cross. The redemptive nature of Christ's death cannot be reproduced by the death of another person. As St. Paul says, " . . . in dying as Christ did, he died to sin, once for all" (Rom. 6:10). Christ's death is for all time and cannot be repeated. It was a historical event that took place under Pontius Pilate, but its redemptive power transcended its historical framework and became effective and operative throughout history. Furthermore, Christ's death was for all of humanity. As Matthew's Gospel states: the Son of Man came "to give up his life as a ransom for many" (Matt. 20:28).

The death of a Vietnamese monk did not have such a transcendent power. It was a sacrifice offered in a hope that the agony and suffering of the people of Vietnam might come to an end. But insofar as it was a sacrifice, it partook of the redeeming power of God in Vietnam. At least, it was a part of that love of which the author of John's Gospel spoke when he wrote: "There is no greater love than this, that a man should lay down his life for his friends" (John 15:13). This great love can only come from God and is made possible through God. The monk who practiced this kind of love must have been close to the heart of God. This is the kind of love that heals wounds in old relationships and creates a possibility for new relationships. Without this kind of sacrificial love, the human community is doomed to fail and die. But the power of such a love brings hope to a community that otherwise is subject to exploitation and inhumanity. This love is therefore redemptive in nature, although it is not redemption itself as was the love of Christ on the cross. Perhaps we can say that all genuine love that contributes to the healing of human relations, transformation of society on the basis of justice and freedom, and the consolidation of whatever makes men and women truly human, is redemptive in nature. I believe this is not an oversimplification. As long as this kind of love remains at work in human society, it is possible for us to see, feel, and experience God's love not in abstract theory but in the actual lives of people. In this sense, the love and compassion of the Vietnamese monks who set themselves on fire give us a glimpse into the depths of God's agony in the face of human tragedy as well as into the power of God's redeeming love in a seemingly senseless and demonic situation.

This example from Vietnam demonstrates that Buddhism in Asia has come a long way in its sense of responsibility toward the world. The lotus still looks as peaceful as ever. But it symbolizes peace in the midst of unrest and fear. It still appears as tranquil as ever, but its tranquility is surrounded by the fire of destruction. It still looks toward Nirvana as the destination of human striving, but its Nirvana is forced to take history seriously. Here the cross can and must meet the lotus. What the cross encounters here is the lotus in the sea of fire of a political and military struggle that has destroyed Vietnam. If the cross cannot meet the lotus's thrust into a sea of suffering, how can we say the cross is God's redemption for people in all places and at all times? An observer stated:

The monks who were daring to defy both General Hguyen Cao Ky and his United States protectors were neither dupes of the Communists nor ambitious would-be office holders themselves. . . . Rather . . . they had been driven to take the stand they had by their profound compassion for their suffering people, and by the fact that there literally was no one else who could speak for the war-weary people and their longing for peace. Far from being a departure from their religious faith, their actions were impelled by it.[33]

The truth of the matter is that the Buddhist involvement in the struggle for peace in Vietnam was basically not different from the Christian concern for social justice, freedom, and peace that has come to be considered increasingly as an integral part of faith. In this common cause—whether at a local level or on a global stage—the cross and the lotus should be comrades in arms. Asian Buddhists enter human suffering through the lotus, and Christians through the cross. Whether they will meet before the throne of God's salvation and glory is not for mortals to judge. But at least they have a common entry into the ultimate question of life, which is suffering, and they share a common duty to go together through suffering with faith and hope in the salvation of all humanity.

# CHAPTER 6

# THE SEED OF HOPE IN THE WOMB

The hope of salvation—conceived in terms of both this world and the world to come—is the chief concern of humanity's religious quest. As I have shown in the previous chapter, this quest more and more takes the form of involvement in the struggle for peace and freedom in present-day Asia. Salvation no longer means simply the abandonment of this world in favor of the world to come, the giving up of the temporal in order to gain the eternal. The present ceases to be considered as a mere temporary station in the passage from the past to the future. It is informed by the past and impregnated with the future. The present therefore has to be seen under the perspective of eternity. This gives a new sense of urgency to the present. What we do here and now is of utmost importance. What we are and what we do constitute a link—and a very important link—in the course of human history. We are not accidental products of history. On the contrary, we are a part of the power that gives birth to history. Our role in history is not passive. We have a responsibility to fulfill in the passage of time. Our duty is to ensure the continuation of life without which history is meaningless. The great emphasis the people of Asia place on the continuity of family life must be seen in this perspective. Here we find an Asian outlook on salvation closely related to the experience of life in the mother's womb.

### The Young Widow of Vietnam

As a point of departure for our discussion of salvation in terms of the continuation of life, let me quote a poem by a South Vietnamese poet describing the grief and hope of a young wife who has just received the sad news of the death of her husband on the battlefield. It is called "First Tragedy."

> The yellow telegram
> with its stark typewritten letters
> announces a death

124

She knew it would be his death
still she mumbles the words
telling herself telling
herself don't
                cry
for this is common
in war who is ever free of tragedy

Just lie still lie still
you are free now my darling

Constantly thinking of the future
with a withering faith

she has painted her own portrait
the high collar the still-life round eyes
the bombs the grenades
everything is black
because nothing is left
who has not suffered in a war

In confusion she looks down
at the seed coming to life in her
coming to the misery of life
try to grow up like your father my darling.[1]

What a cruel tragedy this poem paints for all humanity! Its realism only heightens the tragic note. The poem is simplicity itself. There is no rhetoric to enhance the cruel sense of war, but how eloquent the poem is in its accusation against the futility of war! There is no appeal to sympathy for the young wife, and yet we cannot fail to see her face distorted with painful tears. There is no angry outburst against those who must be held responsible for her husband's death. Nonetheless how forceful the poem is in its indictment against them!

The telegram that carries the fatal news is yellow. What color other than yellow could be fitting for an occasion like this? The telegram must be *yellow*, because yellow in China and Japan stands for an obscene distortion of the sacred union between man and woman. It is a color that symbolizes the act of shamelessly exposing the secret parts of human consciousness in public. It is a color that can be turned into an expression of indecency. Thus the telegram that comes to the young wife is yellow, because its message has to do with the indecency of a meaningless death in a cruel war. The yellow telegram is an epitome of the dehumanization of all that is noble in humanity. It tells the whole world what damage human ruthlessness can do to a human being created in the image of God. Here is the theological meaning of war. War is the releasing of the demonic in human beings against the creation of God. It dehumanizes men and women, reducing them to statistics of deaths and injuries. It disfigures and destroys the image of God in humanity. War therefore is like an act of rape committed against God's creation. It is an act of sheer irrationality. As Frances FitzGerald puts it in her perceptive study of the people of Vietnam and the Vietnam War:

The physical suffering of South Vietnam is difficult to comprehend, even in statistics. The official numbers—859,641 "enemy," over 165,268 ARVN soldiers and about 380,000 civilians killed—only begin to tell the toll of death this war has taken. Proportionately, it is as though twenty million Americans died in the war instead of the forty-five thousand to date. But there are more to come. In the refugee camps and isolated villages people die of malnutrition and the children are deformed. In the cities, where there is no sanitation and rarely any running water, the adults die of cholera, typhoid, smallpox, leprosy, bubonic plague, and their children die of the common diseases of dirt, such as scabies and sores.

But this is not all the Vietnam War did to the people of that agricultural nation. For FitzGerald goes on to tell us:

The physical destruction is not, perhaps, the worst of it. The destruction of an entire society—"That is, above all, what the Vietnamese blame the Americans for," said one Vietnamese scholar. "Wilfully or not, they have tended to destroy what is most precious to us: family, friendship, our manner of expressing ourselves." . . . Physical death is everywhere, but it is the social death caused by destruction of the family that is of overriding importance.[2]

In all fairness we must admit that the Vietnamese themselves, especially the various political factions that lusted after power and wealth at the expense of the people, were as much to blame as the Americans for the destruction and tragedy of the Vietnam War. But the question of responsibility becomes a really heart-rending question when the death of a human community occurs. When a human community dies, people lose their sense of relatedness and belonging. They lose their essential being. They become nobodies. Traditionally, this is what it means in Asia when you lose your family connections, when you are not able to fulfill your responsibilities toward your family. With the destruction of your family, a vital part of you is also destroyed.

Against a background like this we can begin to understand the desperation of the young woman in the poem as she faces her bleak future. "Constantly thinking of the future with a withering faith," the poem says. For Asians faith is essentially a social event—the experiences of a community and of family devotion. This kind of faith finds corporate and communal expressions, for example, in festivals, spontaneous gatherings in the courtyard of a community temple, worship at the family altar, and so forth. Faith is therefore not a rational understanding of what you believe. Nor is it an expression of your will and determination to believe as an individual in isolation from the community. At least, this is the faith of the common people. When the missionaries brought Christianity to Asia, they were slow to realize and appreciate the communal character of Asian faith. "In Japan," says Masatoshi Doi, for instance, "to become a Christian means to be uprooted from the local community to which one belongs; and this very often can have disintegrating effects upon one's personality."[3] This is not only true in Japan but also in other countries of Asia. The voluntary withdrawal of Christians from their community has created a cultural gap that makes it difficult for Christians to feel, think, and behave as members of their usual community.

At any rate, with the untimely death of her husband the young wife of the poem senses that her immediate community, which is her family, has disintegrated. This must be a greater blow than she can cope with. As a result of the disintegration of her family, her faith is also about to fall apart. She now faces a lonely and uncertain future. The power that once sustained her, the power she found in her family and community, is gone. A national crisis has now become her personal crisis. A national tragedy has been turned into her personal tragedy. The disintegration of her nation becomes the disintegration of her own self, and she has no future. Her life becomes an empty present that is cut off from the past and barred from the future. She becomes a nonperson, taking refuge in a withered faith. She has reached the nadir of her existence.

Then the poem continues. "In confusion," it says, "she looks down at the seed coming to life in her." This is the genius of this poem. This is the heart of its message. In desperate confusion and grief beyond words, the bereaved wife looks down and feels the seed of a new life moving in her womb. Looking down is an unpretentious, natural act—something she does by instinct. Countless women in a similar situation have done the same thing. Hundreds and thousands of bereaved young wives in Vietnam must have done the same thing too. The seed moving within the womb, this is what Asian women instinctively turn to when faced with a crisis of family disintegration or social destruction. The vivid pulse of life from the seed in the womb is not something out of nowhere. It takes its origin in the past and it presses onward to the future. It is the seed of life from which hundreds of thousands of lives have emerged in the past. Furthermore, it is the seed of life out of which thousands and hundreds of thousands of lives will flow into the future. This seed of life, despite the death of its immediate giver, is a seed of hope for the newly bereaved wife, her family, and her society. This instinctive feeling for the seed in the womb has given Asian women the courage to live, the will to survive, and hope for the future.

Throughout long centuries of suffering, Asians have learned to stake their hopes and their future in the seed hidden within the mysterious womb of humanity. A new life is in the making to succeed the life that has just passed out of the community of the living. The seed of life in the womb is therefore the seed of hope for Asians. Their past, their present, and their future converge in the seed of hope carried in the mother's womb. The seed of life in the bereaved wife's womb is the power of hope that unites all the members of the family, including the deceased husband, in a communion of life and hope. That is why the young woman murmurs to the seed of life in her womb: "coming to the misery of life, try to grow up like your father, my darling."

For Asians, the concentration of human hope is in the womb. Through it humanity comes into touch with the mystery of life. It is there that life is created, grows, and takes form. It can almost be regarded as a happening analogous to creation. Into the darkness of the human womb the seed of life comes into being. What we see there is the life force connecting the past with the future. A new life in formation in the mother's womb is not the negation of the old life but its fulfillment. At the same time it is endowed, from its conception, with the ability to grow into the future. That life force is the dynamics of the history of a person, a family, a nation, and even of the human race. In this sense the human womb is the bearer of history. The hope that is based on the seed of life in the womb is thus rooted in the past, lives in the present, and extends into the future. Such a hope is historical, existential, and eschatological. The Asians have intuitively apprehended this close relation between human hope and the seed of life in the womb.

### Sarah, the Wife of Abraham

What the Asians have perceived anthropologically is theologically perceived by people in the Christian Bible. Take, for example, the case of Sarah. She and Abraham had not been blessed with children and both were old. Sarah had definitely passed the age of childbearing. To her the messengers of God announced the incredible news that she would give birth to a child. In this entire episode Gerhard von Rad draws our attention to the messengers' response to Sarah's skepticism: "Is anything impossible for the Lord?" (Gen. 18:14). According to von Rad, this reply "reposes in the story like a precious stone in a priceless setting, and its significance surpasses the cozy patriarchal milieu of the narrative; it is a heuristic witness to God's omnipotent saving will."[4] Of course, there are countless ways in which God can demonstrate his saving will and power. In the historical and religious consciousness of the people of Israel Yahweh their God led them out of the land of Egypt. He fought on their side against their enemies. He finally gave them the land of promise. God's salvation was a historically verifiable fact interpreted through their faith. But the saving will of God manifested through Sarah's conception and childbearing possesses a saving meaning of an ultimate kind. By virtue of the fact that Sarah and Abraham were without a child and that Sarah had already passed the stage of childbearing, there was a serious threat to the continuity of the patriarchal history through which God planned to show his saving love for the nations. In actual fact, that history had barely begun. It was therefore a crisis not only for patriarchal history but also for the way God had chosen to manifest his saving will for creation. On account of this, Sarah's womb took on great significance. The seed of life that was to be conceived and to grow there through divine intervention was to bear the meaning of salvation. Sarah's womb became an important point at which God's salvation took on a historical manifestation.

### Isaiah's Prophesy to King Ahaz

Another dramatic demonstration of God's wish to save his people by means of the seed of life in a human womb is found in the account of a confrontation between the prophet Isaiah and Ahaz, king of Judah, during the national crisis of the so called Syro-Ephraimitic war in 733 B.C. Rezin, of Damascus, and Pekah, king of Israel, were marching against Jerusalem in order to force Judah into a coalition of Palestinian states against Tiglath-pileser III, king of Assyria.

The gravity of the situation is vividly protrayed in Isaiah 7. We are told that the "king and people were shaken like forest trees in the wind" (Isa. 7:2). Confronted with a crisis of such magnitude, Ahaz on the one hand appealed for help from the Assyrian king, and on the other took steps to strengthen the city's defense. He was not about to stake the fate of the nation on the prophet's assurance of divine protection. He was therefore unmoved when Isaiah challenged him in these words: "Ask the Lord your God for a sign, from lowest Sheol or from highest heaven" (Isa. 7:10). This challenge was meant to rekindle in Ahaz his faith in the God of creation. If God is with us, Isaiah was saying, who can be against us, not to say Rezin and Pekah, who are like two smouldering stumps of firewood (Isa. 7:4)? Ahaz was adamant. "No," he replied perhaps uneasily, "I will not put the Lord to the test by asking for a sign" (Isa. 7:12). Under the heavy pressure of the developing crisis Ahaz failed to fulfill the role of spiritual leadership on which his nation had been founded and on which its greatness depended.

The response of Isaiah was immediate, sharp, and uncompromising. He declared:

Therefore the Lord himself shall give you a sign: A young woman is with child, and she will bear a son, and will call him Immanuel (Isa. 7:14).

We do not need to discuss here the different interpretations of this verse of the Old Testament.[5] Perhaps the question as to who the young woman and her child might be can never be answered. But for our purpose here, this is of no consequence. What is important for us is the fact that at the height of a national crisis the seed of life in a woman's womb was proclaimed by the prophet as being of saving significance. That seed of life was to be the hope of Judah, and Ahaz was challenged to stake the fate of his nation on it. The name of the child to be born was symbolic. He was to be called Immanuel ("God with us"). In Immanuel the hope of Judah would lie.

The hope that comes from God is therefore closely related to the process of life in which we are all involved. On account of this, there is reason to believe that the young woman of Isaiah's prophecy may be a collective term for all the women in Judah who at that time were pregnant and carrying the seed of life in their wombs. These future mothers would be witnesses to God's support for Judah at a time of crisis. In spite of the imminent danger to Jerusalem, people should not be afraid, for the coalition between Rezin and Pekah would fail. Perhaps there was a much deeper meaning here than temporary relief from an enemy's attack. As we learn from later developments in the political history of Israel and Judah, the Assyrians and Babylonians did not leave Palestine in peace. The people of Israel and Judah were taken captive to Assyria in 721 B.C., and to Babylonia in 587 B.C. Psalm 137 gives us a vivid picture of how the people of Judah went through spiritual agony in captivity:

> By the rivers of Babylon we sat down and wept
> when we remembered Zion.
> There on the willow-trees
> we hung up our harps,
> for there those who carried us off
> demanded music and singing,
> and our captors called on us to be merry:
> "Sing us one of the songs of Zion."
> How could we sing the Lord's song
> in a foreign land?
>
> If I forget you, O Jerusalem,
> let my right hand wither away;
> let my tongue cling to the roof of my mouth
> if I do not remember you,
> if I do not set Jerusalem
> above my highest joy.

This is an expression of nationalism at its best. It is religious as well as political in feeling. For many Jewish captives their faith became—perhaps for the first time—an existential experience. This political turmoil was the immediate cause of a revival of faith in Yahweh their God. The essence of this revival of faith consisted in the awareness that the Jews must look for their future in God. Never again should they trust in themselves for security, as Ahaz had mistakenly done.

But what is the visible link between a present crisis and a future promise? What is the anchor in history that can enable us to turn despair into hope? This anchor is the new life pulsating in a mother's womb, which is a sign of God's presence. It is a witness to God's acts in history and both the promise and reality of God's hope. That future life is God's hope incarnate in a human womb. Insofar as it is God's hope become flesh, it is also humanity's hope. Thus in the Old Testament as in Asian culture, hope is inseparably bound up with life. Hope cannot be detached from the continuation of life from one generation to another. My life is both temporal and eternal. It is temporal because it is set in a framework of a definite span of time—the time covering the passage of an individual from the cradle to the grave. But my life is at the same time eternal, because it is an integral, essential part of a life that stretches from eternity to eternity. Hope that is closely related to life is therefore both temporal and eternal. That is why the young Vietnamese woman in the poem can experience the life of her deceased husband in the seed of life growing in her womb. That is why Isaiah can point to the women with child in Judah's critical hour and thus proclaim a message of hope. Although Judah will not escape a national calamity in the days to come, life still exists to carry the life of the nation forward. The seed of life in the mother's womb is thus a sign given by God in history. The seed of life in the womb is the fruition of the interaction between God's hope and humanity's hope. It is Immanuel—God with us, and we with God.

### The Birth of Jesus Christ

At any rate, Isaiah's strong affirmation of hope through the birth of Immanuel is a direct adumbration of the birth of Jesus Christ some seven centuries later. Needless to say, this interpretation of Isaiah's prophecy requires a historical retrospect. This, of course, is not to say that the child mentioned in Isaiah's prophesy can be identified with Christ. Such an identification violates the integrity of the biblical texts as well as the historical settings of the two events. But Immanuel in Isaiah's affirmation can be said to be messianic in nature in the sense that Immanuel ensures the reality of God's presence and salvation. In other words, Immanuel shares the messianic mission of bringing God's salvation close to people. Immanuel is not the Messiah, not the one anointed and commissioned by God to be the Savior. He is not the son of God who has become the son of man in the sense Jesus Christ is. But because he is a sign and symbol of God's salvation, he participates in what is symbolized, namely, the fulfillment of God's salvation in and through the Messiah. This participation makes him take on a messianic quality in what he is and does. In a much less visible way, the seed of life to which the Asians look for assurance of hope and meaning also pertains to the messianic mission of hope and salvation. It is therefore incumbent on us to study in some detail the accounts dealing with the birth of Jesus.

The events surrounding the birth of Jesus Christ are remarkably similar to the cases discussed above. Our attention is drawn not to the birth itself but to the events that preceded it. In the first place, Luke's Gospel mentions that Zechariah and his wife, Elizabeth, though well advanced in years, had no children. The barrenness of Elizabeth is reminiscent of Sarah's. Yet to the barren Elizabeth, John, the precursor of Jesus, was born. The Old Testament theme of a seed of life in the mother's womb as the embodiment of hope and salvation is repeated. This is evident when an angel of the Lord announces to Zechariah news of an incredible nature. "From his very birth," says the angel:.

he [John] will be filled with the Holy Spirit; and he will bring back many Israelites to the Lord their God. He will go before him as forerunner, possessed by the spirit and power of Elijah, to reconcile father and child, to convert the rebellious to the ways of the righteous, to prepare a people that shall be fit for the Lord (Luke 1:16–17).[6]

The messianic motif adumbrated in other cases of conception, especially that of Isaiah 7, becomes unquestionably clear. Themes like reconciliation, repentance, and conversion to God are emphasized. This reinforces the fact that in the Bible the conception of life in the human womb is not considered merely as a biological process. It must be seen in relation to what God intends for humanity and the world. In this way the human womb has come to be closely associated with manifestations of God's messianic acts in history.

The most remarkable event of all, of course, is the conception of Mary through the Holy Spirit. According to Luke's Gospel, the annunciation begins with the angel's greeting: "The Lord is with you."[7] This is the theme of Immanuel which we saw in Isaiah 7. It is followed by the announcement of the conception of Immanuel to a perplexed and frightened Mary. The angel's response to Mary's questioning is significant:

The Holy Spirit will come upon you, and the power of the Most High will overshadow you; and for that reason the holy child to be born will be called "Son of God" (Luke 1:34).

With this announcement we have the translation of the Johannine theological formula of "Word become flesh" into the most profound human experience between a man and a woman. God has chosen to intervene in history through the human womb, in that depth of humanity where life is conceived and born. Because God has chosen the human womb to manifest his presence in the world and his salvation for humankind, this is his affirmation of the seed of life as the seed of hope. God has now created *the* seed of life in Mary's womb as the embodiment of the hope of God's salvation. It is a profound religious insight on the part of Luke to give his account of the birth of the Savior in this way. The human womb thus becomes the embodiment of human hope. It is where God comes to meet us, to become united with us, to be one with us. In Mary's womb the God-man is conceived and born. Mary's womb becomes a new universe, a new creation. God has entered the human womb for the creation of a new life that is both God and man, a life that will be responsible to both God and humanity, a life that binds God and humanity in a new covenant of love and redemption.

Not in vain does the young Vietnamese woman in the poem consider the seed of life stirring within her. Her immediate assurance lies in the living experience of her dead husband. But in that experience she reaches out to something beyond her husband, that is, to a life which in the Christian faith can only be given by God himself. This new life is not the negation of the life she bears from the past and will pass on to the future. It is the fulfillment of that life. Of course, she is not aware of the fulfillment of life that took place two thousand years ago in Nazareth when the angel Gabriel appeared to Mary. Nor is she aware of the link that mysteriously connects the life within her to the life in Mary's womb. But for that matter, neither Sarah nor the women with child in Judah in the time of Isaiah were conscious of the same relationship. Millions and millions of mothers who, in the most hopeless hour of their lives, have felt the movement of life within them perhaps knew little of the redemptive quality of the seeds of life in their wombs—the redemptive quality that comes from the seed of life in Mary's womb. What we have in Mary is a historical particularity endowed with universal significance because of the divine intervention and presence.

Furthermore, in the conception of Jesus through the Holy Spirit we seem to grasp the meaning of God's action in history as something concrete, experiential, and close to the reality of life. Since God chose the most intensely intimate relation between a man and a woman to realize his purpose of salvation, he has indicated how profoundly he is concerned about the salvation of the world. From the human point of view, our spiritual history is the outcome of passion. It is the expression of a passionate human involvement and of God's direct intervention in history through Mary's womb. History is the concrete manifestation of the intense confrontation and interaction between divine passion and human passion. In Mary's womb divine passion and human passion create a new life that sheds light on and redeems all histories. Thus the seed of life in

Mary's womb is the consummation of the old creation and the beginning of a new creation. Jesus Christ is the new creation, the new history, and the new human being.

Luke has a marvelous way of communicating the mystery of a new life which begins in God's passionate engagement with the world and brings about humanity's passionate response. I am referring to Mary's meeting with Elizabeth at the latter's house. This is a lyrical drama in two parts. The main actors in the first part are the babies in their mothers' wombs; the second part is the responses of the mothers to the extraordinary event taking place within them. And this two-act drama concludes with the Magnificat, which beautifully and forcefully proclaims the messianic mission of Immanuel to the world.

According to Luke's account, "when Elizabeth heard Mary's greeting, the baby stirred in her womb" (Luke 1:40). There seemed to be some invisible connection between the baby in Mary's womb and the one in Elizabeth's womb. From the start, the two babies were surrounded by a mysterious power over which their mothers had no control. They were destined to become involved in God's mission of salvation, one as the forerunner of the other. And both were to suffer martyrdom for the sake of that mission. From beginning to end they were to serve the purpose of God in the world. Guided and nurtured by the Holy Spirit, they were thus able to respond to each other while still in their mothers' wombs.

The movement of the seed of life in her womb quickly prompted Elizabeth to express herself in words of joy and hope. "God's blessing is on you above all women, and his blessing on the fruit of your womb. . . . I tell you, when your greeting sounded in my ears, the baby in my womb leapt for joy. How happy is she who has had faith that the Lord's promise would be fulfilled!" (Luke 1:42–45). God's promise takes the form of the seed of life in the human womb. This point, which has been central to our discussion in this chapter, is here confirmed again. The joy and hope embodied in the mother's womb are the joy and hope of our life and of the world. This becomes even more explicit and concrete in Mary's response to Elizabeth.

Before addressing ourselves to Mary's "Magnificat," however, I want to make a few remarks concerning the place of woman in human perception and the experience of God's redemptive love. As may already be clear to the readers of the foregoing discussion, woman has a particular role to play in God's mission of salvation. This unique role comes from her ability to keep the seed of life within her, nourish it, let it grow, and give birth to it. The throbbing of a new life within her is the throbbing of a new creation. Within her a miraculous event of creation takes place. She is made by God in such a way that she is permitted to participate directly in God's creation. She is a co-creator with God in the true sense of the word.

## The Birth of Cain

In this connection our attention is drawn to the account of the birth of Cain, the first son of Adam and Eve, after the fall. When Cain was born, Eve said: "With the help of the Lord I have brought a man into being" (Gen. 4:1). This utterance of joy is meant to explain the meaning of the name "Cain" *(Quayin)*, which is derived from the verb *qanah*—"to get"—or etymologically "to fashion," "shape," or "form." Thus Cassuto, for example, translates the verse as follows: "I have created a man equally with the Lord."[8] Consequently he ingeniously observes:

> The first woman, in her joy at giving birth to her first son, boasts of her generative power, which approximates in her estimation to the divine creative power. The Lord formed the first *man* (2:7), and I have formed the second *man*.[9]

The generative power woman possesses comes, of course, from God. It is part of God's creation of woman. Eve's joy and pride are therefore not to be interpreted as another indication of humanity's desire to be like God, which, in the thought of the Old Testament writers, constituted the cause of the fall. Rather it should be seen as genuine joy and pride on the part of Eve, and, I am sure, of Adam also, who came thus to know that even after the fall human beings are still permitted to share the creative and generative power of God. There must be an element of astonishment in it as well, in view of the traumatic experience of the fall. The fact that God is still gracious to them, that they are not totally barred from the mystery of God's creation, and that they are able to form and give birth to a child— all this is truly astonishing. And Eve must have felt this more personally and strongly than Adam because the second man had been conceived and formed in her own womb.

Of course creation is not a painless process, as we have stated in the previous chapters. This means that Eve's exclamation of joy is an exclamation of one who has just come through the creative process with great pain. Giving birth to a new life is an exciting, demanding, and excruciatingly painful part of creation. What we see in childbearing is pain rooted in the love that unites a man and a woman and makes them into one flesh. The joy of the mother and father at the birth of their child is the joy that grows out of their pain-love for each other. In the process of childbearing, the woman—not the man—goes through this pain-love of the creative act with her whole being, just as God commits his whole being to creation and redemption. Creation is an act of total commitment. In almost the same way, childbearing is also an act of total commitment with its pain, risk, struggle, and finally joy. Thus we cannot but conclude that woman is able to know and experience God as creator and redeemer in a most profound way. She seems to have a direct access to the heart of God. She does not have to speculate on the nature of God, for she experiences God with her whole being. She does not have to resort to cosmogony to explain God's creation, for within her own womb the mysterious power of generation and creation is working to give birth to a new life. She even does not have to philosophize or theologize about the nature of pain rooted in the love of God, for in childbearing she experiences physically and spiritually the pain-love of the creating and redeeming God.[10] What takes place in the human womb is the concretization of God's creative and redemptive love for the world. And the life conceived and formed there is a sign of the hope that will be greeted with joy on its arrival. Hence woman should be a fervent believer, a natural theologian, and an unsurpassed interpreter of the pain-love of God as the hope of the world. Perhaps we can call this "the theology of the womb." An exciting theological horizon may develop to witness and interpret the "Word become flesh" from the theology of the womb. This will be a powerful theology leading us to God's creative pain-love of redemption, which becomes the seed of life and takes the form of a human being in Mary's womb.[11]

After these observations we now return to Mary, who responded to Elizabeth's greeting with the words of the Magnificat—a prayer unsurpassed in its beauty, unparalleled in its vision of hope, and unmistakable in its commitment to the mission to those in pain and suffering:

> Tell out, my soul, the greatness of the Lord,
> rejoice, rejoice, my spirit, in God my savior;
> so tenderly has he looked upon his servant,
> humble as she is.
> For, from this day forth,
> all generations will count me blessed,
> so wonderfully has he dealt with me,
> the Lord, the Mighty One.
>
> His name is Holy;
> his mercy sure from generation to generation
> toward those who fear him;
> the deeds his own right arm has done
> disclose his might:
> the arrogant of heart and mind he has put to rout,
> he has brought down monarchs from their thrones,
> but the humble have been lifted high.
> The hungry he has satisfied with good things,
> the rich sent empty away.
>
> He has ranged himself at the side of Israel his servant;
> firm in his promise to our forefathers,
> he has not forgotten to show mercy to Abraham
> and his children's children, for ever (Lk. 1:46–55).[12]

This is a hymn of praise and thankfulness to God's blessing and mercy, expressing Mary's complete acceptance of the role she is to play in the work of God's salvation. It is also a hymn describing the nature of God's mission in the world through the child to be born. And finally it is also a hymn that emphasizes the seed of life in Mary's womb as the seed of hope in God's promise from Abraham to the posterity of the future.

### The Theology of the Womb

Here, it seems to me, is a theology of the womb in a compact form. First of all, it is a theology of obedience in response to God's confiding to Mary the mystery of his salvation through the seed of life in her womb. Obedience in this context is not to be understood as the subservient attitude of an inferior before the superior, a slave before the master, or a subject before the ruler. The image of God as a great monarch with full power and authority over his subjects has been predominant in traditional Christian theology. Obedience to such a God is in fact a submission in humiliation. In such a traditional image of God, the experience of God as the oppressor and of humanity as the oppressed is latent in Christian worship, discipline, and personal devotion. On the whole, it is true to say that Christian theology has been a patriarchal theology.[13] There is thus a strong tendency to emphasize wrath as an inalienable part of God's being.[14] In the first part of Mary's doxology, we are given an entirely different image of God. God is still mighty, but he is mighty in his tenderness, great in the wonderful way he deals with us. Obedience to this God is an expression of joy and praise. That is why Mary bursts out in praise that is also a doxology of obedience: "Rejoice, rejoice, my spirit, in God my savior!"

Second, the theology that grows out of experiencing God's salvation in the human womb is a theology of commitment. The whole cosmos is like a womb where a new life struggles to come into being. Filled with injustice, oppression, and hatred, the world is where God's mission of salvation strives to bring about a new life to fill it with justice, freedom, and love. As a mother commits herself totally to bringing into fruition the seed of life within her, so Christians must be committed to the emergence of a new world in which light prevails over darkness, love overcomes hate, and freedom vanquishes oppression. That is why in the second part of the Magnificat we have an expression of commitment to the messianic ministry of liberation, which is a part and parcel of the Magnificat. How else could it be? The theology of the womb is therefore the theology of liberation in the sense of bringing into being a new life and a new order.

And third, the theology of the womb is a theology of hope for both temporal and eternal life—the life of which each of us is an organic and historical part. The Magnificat expresses this concept in terms of the history of the people within which the Savior is to be born. This is a fulfillment of life that has gone before as well as an anticipation of the life to come. The theology of the womb thus relates the past and the future to the present of the life in formation in the womb. For this kind of theology no life is wasted. The life that takes its form in a particular mother is a part of universal life seeking its ultimate fulfillment in the life of God. In the seed of life conceived in Mary's womb we see the shape and form of this universal life particularized to link up with the life of the family, the nation, and the world. The ultimate meaning of life is hope. But hope that has not become a part of pulsating life is an abstract, unreal, and illusionary hope. It is life that gives to hope meaning and content. In the mother's womb hope and life become truly one. They become one flesh carrying history from one generation to another and toward eternal life in God. This must surely be the meaning of the last two lines of the Magnificat: he [God] has not forgotten to show mercy to Abraham, and his children's children, forever.

What we have here is the biblical and theological basis of the human community where the divine drama of salvation is unfolded. Frequent references to genealogy in the Old Testament are but an illustration of how salvation is apprehended in terms of communal relationships. And as a matter of fact, the Priestly account of the creation in Genesis 1:1–2:4a can be considered the genealogy of the great and comprehensive community called creation. The conclusion of the account makes this clear: "These are the generations [*toledoth*] of the heavens and the earth when they were created."[15] As Eichrodt points out:

The genealogical conception remains fundamental for the understanding of history, and is able to exert a decisive influence by making clear that the power of community to determine destiny is an essential factor in the historical drama.[16]

In other words, we have in the Old Testament a basic approach to apprehending and appropriating God's salvation in terms of community. We must view community as a historical entity like the family or nation, and also as a cosmic reality expressed in creation. And in the very center of community is the power of creation and generation of the human womb.

The genealogies in Matthew's Gospel and in Luke's Gospel substantiate the argument above. Matthew, who was conditioned by his Jewish background, locates Jesus Christ in the historical community of his people (Matt. 1:1–17). Though limited in scope, Matthew's genealogy succeeds in pointing up the communal nature of salvation centered on the person of Jesus Christ. Probably because of Luke's much wider contact with the gentile world and the influence of St. Paul's theology of mission, Luke was able to expand the genealogy of Christ back to Adam, who stands for all humanity. The implication is unmistakable: God's salvation in Jesus

Christ takes place within the community that comprises all humanity. To put it differently, because of the seed of life in Mary's womb, all people are communally and thus redemptively related. In Luke's genealogy the redemptive meaning of the Priestly version of the creation story becomes evident. By virtue of our genealogical relationship with Jesus Christ, all humanity finds itself under the power of God's saving love.

This is an effort to understand and experience God's salvation in terms of kinship. Seen in relation to Matthew's genealogy and especially to Luke's genealogy with its emphasis on Jesus Christ as its main focus, the human community is not merely a sociological phenomenon. It is not just a congregation of people gathered together on the basis of a common interest. Nor is it a formation due to some historical accident. In and through the seed of life conceived in Mary's womb all men and women are basically blood brothers and sisters. The concept of kinship is therefore fundamental to the biblical understanding of salvation. And the theology of the womb can once again make explicit God's salvation within the context of a community understood in terms of kinship and blood relationship.

The kinship that binds men and women has been broken, however. This is one of the painful prices human beings had to pay for sin. The broken kinship makes it possible for acts of enmity and savagery to take place among human beings. The classical example is Cain's murder of Abel, his brother. When questioned by God, Cain was able to ask God: "Am I my brother's keeper?" (Gen. 4:9). In reply God painfully reminded Cain that Abel's blood was crying out to him from the ground. The blood relationship was brutally injured and even destroyed. Salvation has lost its kinship meaning. This is the tragedy which human beings have brought upon themselves through sin. In the course of human history, this has never been so clear as it is in today's world where our technological and industrial development has forced us to sacrifice community and kinship in pursuit of physical and material progress. As stressed here, salvation is essentially an event associated with community and kinship. Thus when we lose community and kinship, we lose salvation too. This is the hard lesson we have learned in a world where various forces are at work to fragment the human community and destroy the community spirit built on loyalty and faithfulness to God's covenant.

Salvation therefore consists in restoring health and wholeness to the human community. This community is built on the consciousness that in God—and from the Christian point of view, in the God who came to humanity in Jesus Christ—all men and women are bound together in kinship and blood relationship. The restoration of the human community means the restoration of the kinship and blood relationship ordained by God in creation and actualized in Jesus Christ. In 1975, Section III of the Fifth General Assembly of the World Council of Churches held at

Nairobi, Kenya, was assigned the task of discussing the theme "Seekin Community." Section III's report stated in part:

We all agree that we have one solid basis, one holy reason of seeking communit with others: as fellow-creatures of God we are linked to each other, although in fallen creation sin and unbelief divide. Many of us believe and some witness to th actual experience of a common ground far beyond that of our common humanit They have found that Christ sets them free to explore a community under Go with men and women of other faiths.[17]

The perception that in creation we have a solid basis of human commu nity is an important insight. In fact, it is one of the main theses of this boo that creation should be taken into more serious consideration in ou understanding of redemption. Therefore to the insight of the report jus quoted, I must add that creation apprehended in the perspective o redemption is the true foundation of human community. Or to put another way, it is redemption divorced from creation that tends to set up barrier between the Christian community and other communities. Unt the Christian church can view the community in the light of creatio integrally related to redemption, the division between the Christia community and the rest of the human community will continue.

By tracing the birth of Jesus Christ back to Adam, Luke crossed th barrier separating the Christian community from the human communit as a whole. A solid basis for the human community could be found in creation informed with the meaning of redemption. This creation redemption complex should enable Christians to appreciate the culture and histories outside the Christian church in a more positive way Through an effort like this one, Christians will be able to contribute to th emergence of a human community in which people of diverse cultura religious, and historical backgrounds can rediscover their common kin ship and blood relationship.

In short, the theology of the womb enables us to appreciate bloo relationship and kinship as pivots of the inner structure of the huma community. The womb is the infrastructure of the community create and redeemed by God. God enters human history through the huma womb and creates a new life, laying the foundation of a new huma community built on love, justice, and peace. In it begins the kingdom o God that links all humanity in a common kinship and blood relationship

# CHAPTER 7

# THE RICE OF HOPE

For ordinary men and women hope is not a concept; it consists of tangible and concrete things. At least hope must be related to the symbols which have a direct connection with their daily lives. In Chapter 5 we discussed the importance of symbols for our religious faith. In most cases religious symbols are derived from concrete things in the lives of the people. Practically any object or thing is potentially of symbolic value. In fact, the more common an object is, the more impact the symbol derived from it may exert on people. Here is one criterion that distinguishes a popular religion from an elitist religion—or to be more accurate, a popular aspect from an elitist aspect of the same religion. In its popular expression, a religious faith assumes a less rigid form, especially with regard to the formulation of its teachings. Needless to say, this popular manifestation of a religious faith has a far greater appeal to the great majority of members of the religious community. For most believers the chief manifestations of their faith take place in rituals, festivals, and other communal acts of worship which are closely related to everyday life. On the other hand, the same religious faith may become doctrinally so sophisticated and ritually so elaborated that it loses touch with the realities that confront most people every day. A religious faith thus may become the monopoly of an elitist minority in the community. Christian theology in the traditional sense tends to become an instrument of an elitist group that shows disdain for popular expressions of faith and keeps away from them. Third World theologians have taken important steps to reverse this theological trend. They put emphasis on the living context of the people as the context of their theological effort. They believe that theology must echo the pulsations of life coming from the teeming humanity of the marketplaces, streets, theaters, restaurants, dockyards, farms, and similar areas. The pulse of life in these popular places is also the pulse of God, beating in suffering and joy, in sorrow and laughter, in despair and hope. This means that no *theo*-logy can be done unless we listen with empathy to popular artists and novelists, to merchants and peddlers. In them we can hear the authentic, spontaneous pulse of the people. It is the task of the

141

theologian to give to it a shape and to communicate with it across the boundaries of cultural and historical experiences. One of the theologian's tasks is thus to build a bridge of understanding and appreciation between life and faith.

Since hope is concrete and tangible, it must be historical. In other words, hope has to do with what has taken place in time and space. We must therefore stress the fact that hope is both the present and the future. Hope enables the present to expand into the future. In hope the present is linked to the future. We have already seen the significance of this aspect of hope in Chapter 6 when we discussed the theology of the womb. The seed of life in the mother's womb is an embodiment of human hope. What can be more historical than the coming into being of a new life? Hope is thus a historical experience. It has to do with the practical as well as the spiritual aspect of life. Hope detached from daily life is no longer hope but an illusion. And yet it is hope bound to the practical life that leads us to the transhistorical dimension of life.

### The Meditation of a Vietnamese Mother

Another Vietnamese poem, "A Mother's Evening Meditation," shows how simple Asians gain an assurance of hope in a world filled with uncertainty and death. It is the meditation of a mother who has lost her son in the war:

> I fill a bowl with new rice
> place ebony chopsticks at the side
> chase the flies way
> and often I see your face as it looked
> the last time you came home.
>
> Today the fields looked ripe,
> the empty train came back
> spouting black smoke above worn grass.
>
> I filled this bowl to the edge, placed ebony
> chopsticks at the side and chased
> the flies away. Today is the end
> of the month, you would be getting paid today
> if you were alive.
> You would be going downtown, smoking,
> sending postcards home.
>
> I fill the bowl with new rice
> look at the pair of chopsticks and your son,
> just fallen asleep.
> A wonderful child, peaceful as a pebble,
> he is half a year old now but still has no name.

This is your anniversary.
Suddenly your wife holds her head and cries—
"He died in his spring!"

I fill a bowl with new rice
and sit, noticing the signs of autumn, the fallen leaves. . . .
The child in the cradle smiles at me
I place the ebony chopsticks
chase the flies away
and wipe the streaming tears.[1]

In the unassuming language of the poet we hear the affirmation of hope in the midst of despair and the overcoming of sorrow through the vivid memory of a dead son. The whole poem is filled from beginning to end with a genuine Asian pathos. This is the language of faith and hope of an unsophisticated people. It is an unadorned expression of how the ordinary Asian copes with the cruelty of fate. What we see here is not resignation but hope, however vague that hope may be. And the presence of a half-a-year-old child in the poem serves to illuminate the vagueness of hope just as it did in the poem we discussed in Chapter 6.

But here I want to draw attention to the ritual of rice the mother performs in memory of her deceased son. In this ritual is another expression of the way Asians regard hope as something unashamedly mundane and concrete. But precisely because of this fact, hope becomes a reality that transcends even this mundane world. Hope in this case is not something to be conceptualized, idealized, or philosophized. In actual fact, it is a part of life that is embedded in what we see, touch, feel, and eat. Hope is therefore a natural part of what it means to live and die. This essentially is the meaning of the ritual of rice offered daily by countless Asians at the family altar.

For the mother in the poem the bowl of rice she prepares for her deceased son becomes a link between now and the hereafter, between the present and the future, between life and death. The bowl of rice she fills each day is the symbol and the reality of her faith and hope in eternal life. As long as she lives, she will fill her son's bowl with fresh rice every day. Her son is dead, and she is under no illusion to deny this cruel fact. But in the act of filling the bowl with rice, her son is alive. In the rice that fills the bowl is the mystery of a life that overcomes death. Through that bowl of rice her son is as real to her now as he was in the past. For her that bowl of rice speaks more eloquently than a long difficult discourse on hope. It is the concentration of what it means to live beyond death.

Not by accident rice becomes a powerful symbol of life and hope. Rice is the staple food for most Asians. It nourishes life and is its source. A bowl of rice carries Asians from one day to another day, from one year to another year, from one generation to another generation. In short, it maintains life from eternity to eternity. It is more than just a bowl of rice. The rice in the bowl, when used in a family ritual like the one performed by the mother of the poem, ceases to be a mere object of gastronomic consumption. It is life; it is hope; and it is spirit.

For this reason the bowl of rice the mother prepares for her deceased son helps her remember her son. She remembers the day her son is paid, what he does on payday, and she sees him alive and full of vigor in his small child. When her daughter-in-law, overcome with grief, sobs out the words, "He died in his spring," the mother's response is to fill the bowl with new rice and place her son's chopsticks beside the bowl. She "chases the flies away and wipes the streaming tears." Here is a simple Asian mother's answer to the tyranny of death. This is her response to a life overcome by the grief of death. The bowl of rice sustains our physical life, but it also makes it possible for us to stake our hope on a life untouched by grief and death. The bowl of rice unites the living and the dead. It is where the communion of all the members of the family—the living and the dead—takes place. Because it is the rice of union and communion, it is the rice of hope.

A bowl of sacramental rice—that is what it is. Rice is transformed into the power of memory, and the power of memory is the power of life. Memory is not only a sign of life but life itself. It is the condition of life. Without memory there is no hope for the continuation of life after our physical death. When memory ceases, absolute death occurs. For this reason there is no memory in the realm of the dead. This is an insight Bildad the Shunite tries to share with Job, who is afflicted with disease and tormented with death. When death strikes someone, says Bildad:

> His memory vanishes from the face of the earth
> and he leaves no name in the world.
> He is driven from light into darkness
> and banished from the land of the living.
> He leaves no issue or offspring among his people,
> no survivor in his earthly home . . . (Job 18:17–19).

Notice here the reference to offspring. Our offspring ensure the continuation of our life. We are thus remembered and continue to live even after our death.

Our knowledge of God too depends on memory. The dreadful thing about death is that it is capable of blotting out memory, even the memory of God. In Psalm 6 this is explicitly stated:

> For in death there is no remembrance of thee;
> in Sheol who can give thee praise?[2]

The role memory plays in life as a whole cannot thus be underestimated.

We can even go so far as to say that the perpetuation of memory is the perpetuation of life. At least, this must be what is behind the raising of monuments, the preservation of things left behind by the deceased, and the writing of autobiographies and biographies. Our physical life is short but our memory is eternal. Even our relationship with God is conditioned by memory.

## Augustine on the Theological Meaning of Memory

In his *Confessions* Augustine discusses memory with penetrating insight. Life is saturated with all kinds of memory. The fact that humanity has the capacity of memory is a constant source of amazement. The human mind is a great storehouse in which what we can see, touch, smell, experience, and reflect is gathered up and remembered. In the great storehouse of our memory we find ourselves and the world in which we live. Augustine therefore exclaims in wonder:

Great is the power of memory. It is a true marvel, O my God, a profound and infinite multiplicity! And this is the mind, and this I myself am. What, then, am I, O my God? Of what nature am I? A life various, and manifold, and exceedingly vast.[3]

For Augustine this marvelous power of memory is the power of life. It determines and shapes life. It is there that we are confronted by the mystery of life. At the same time it is there that we encounter God. Augustine is afraid at first that this discovery of the power of memory may make God superfluous. So powerful is memory that it can almost be self-perpetuating in the life to which it gives form. But he has to acknowledge that there is no knowledge of God without memory. This is how he reasons:

Thus I will pass beyond memory; but where shall I find thee, who art the true God and the steadfast Sweetness? But where shall I find thee? If I find thee without memory, then, I shall have no memory of thee; and how could I find thee at all, if I do not remember thee?[4]

Memory cannot take the place of God, and yet without memory we cannot know God. This is the dilemma to which Augustine tries to address himself. How does he get around it? Here is his answer:

And thus since the time I learned of thee, thou hast dwelt in my memory, and it is there that I find thee whenever I call thee to remembrance, and delight in thee.[5]

In other words, memory does not create God, for memory, however powerful, is not above God. It is given to us by God. It is God who places himself in our memory so that we can remember and glorify him.

Augustine was the first theologian in the history of Christian thought to explore in great depth the theological meaning of memory. At least, he showed that memory deserves as much theological attention as other Christian concepts. After all, history consists of memories and the interpretations of memories. In memory, events and experiences are registered, waiting to be put into an order that makes history intelligible. But memory does not only have to do with what has taken place. It enables us to anticipate the future and visualize what is still to come. In a sense therefore we can also say that memory is the power of the future. Memory makes it possible for us to transcend the framework of time and space by which our life is conditioned. In theological language then memory is the receptacle of divine revelation, which enables us to speak of the sacramental meaning of memory.

### The Last Supper: The Sacramental Meaning of Memory

To explain what I mean by the sacramental meaning of memory, I must now turn to the Last Supper Jesus had with his disciples on the eve of his suffering on the cross. Literally it was the *last* supper, a farewell meal. The three years of life together were now drawing to an end. Despite what Jesus had been to the disciples and had done for the people around him, despite the vision of the kingdom of God Jesus had tried to inculcate in them, they were still not able to make up their minds as to who Jesus was. They just could not accept the idea of a suffering Messiah.[6] As we shall discuss in Chapter 11, this was perhaps one of the reasons why even Peter tried to dissociate himself from Jesus after the latter's arrest. Peter, who had always been ahead of the others in demonstrating his loyalty and courage, must have found it difficult to reconcile the cross with the messiah he and his compatriots had been waiting for with great expectation. To him and also to others, Jesus' surrender must have been a great disillusionment. Their expectation was gone and their dream had vanished. Divine intervention in history to vindicate their nationalistic cause and to help restore Jewish national independence was again deferred. They had left everything to follow Jesus, and as a result of the cross had lost everything. Peter was perhaps disgusted with himself. How else can we explain the strong words Mark used to describe Peter's third denial? When the bystanders identified him as a Galilean, "he broke out into curses, and with an oath he said, 'I do not know this man you speak of.' Then the cock crew a second time" (Mark 14:70–71).[7] Jesus' defeat was Peter's personal tragedy. We must assume that he was too preoccupied with his own personal defeat to be able to grasp the redemptive meaning of suffering in the new image of the Messiah Jesus had projected.

The Last Supper was Jesus' final act to authenticate his messianic ministry and to institute a memory by which he would be recognized as the true Messiah. By taking bread and wine and giving them to his disciples with the words, "This is my body," and "This is my blood," Jesus was imparting a sacramental power that would enable his followers to grasp the full significance of his ministry. The memory with which they are to remember Jesus whenever they share bread and wine together will be a sacramental memory relating them to him in a special way. Through that sacramental memory Jesus is not only remembered but is alive. Therefore bread and wine used for such a special occasion are no longer mere bread and wine. They become bread and wine in the possession of a sacramental quality just as the rice the Vietnamese mother places in front of her deceased son takes on more than ordinary significance. The food we eat can be sacramentally transformed into the symbol and assurance of eternal life. This is evident from Jesus' discourse on the bread of heaven in John's Gospel. Jesus corrected his audience who said that in ancient days Moses gave their ancestors manna to eat in the desert. He asserted: "I tell you this: the truth is not that Moses gave you the bread from heaven, but that my Father gives you the real bread from heaven. The bread that God gives comes down from heaven and brings life to the world." Sacramental transformation has taken place in the understanding of bread. Bread is life. It partakes of the power of life that comes from God. Thus, when asked to give them this kind of life-giving bread, Jesus replied: "I am the bread of life. Whoever comes to me shall never be hungry, and whoever believes in me shall never be thirsty" (John 6:30–40). The identification of bread with life in Jesus is direct. Here a complete sacramental transformation has taken place in our understanding of bread as the source of true life in God. Jesus Christ is the life-bestowing bread. To partake of this kind of bread is to partake of the life given in him. That is why Jesus, at the Last Supper with his disciples, broke bread and gave it to them. And after Jesus is gone, the sacramental bread creates a sacramental memory through which believers find themselves in the presence of the living Christ. Bread, memory, and life in Christ, these are bound in a sacramental relationship that gives hope, faith, and love. To be caught up in this relationship is to be part of the history filled with redemptive significance.

What has been said above can be further illustrated by incidents that took place soon after the crucifixion and resurrection. The first of these incidents took place for two unidentified followers of Jesus on their way to Emmaus from Jerusalem. The subject of their conversation was the crucifixion of Jesus, which they had just witnessed. Their hearts were heavy with sorrow and pain. Even after a stranger joined them and enlightened them on the meaning of the suffering Messiah, they were still not able to comprehend it fully. It was not until they sat at table and shared the bread the stranger had broken that "their eyes were opened, and they recognized him" (Luke 24:13–32). This is a perfect example of how the participation in the breaking of bread enables us to encounter the living Christ in our memory. This is what I mean by the sacramental meaning of memory. Memory in this case is the link between the crucified Jesus and the resurrected Christ. Memory is thus a passage from death to life, from despair to hope. The memory of the Vietnamese mother in which her son is alive, and for that matter, the memory of most of us for our loved ones who have passed beyond this world, may be a reflection of this sacramental memory that takes place between Jesus and his followers, however imperfect, fragmentary, and even distorted that reflection may be. Memory makes the world become real. In memory we encounter and experience eternal life. Memory enables us to have a foretaste of life in God.

Another example is the moving story told by John in his Gospel about the renewed commission to Peter to be the shepherd of Jesus' sheep. The renewal of the commission took place after Jesus had broken bread and given it to Peter and his companions just as he had done at the Last Supper. Without question this was the re-enactment of the last meal through which Jesus instituted memory into an instrument of hope. At that breakfast by the Sea of Tiberias where Peter and other disciples had gone back to their old trade, Jesus was alive and real to them. It must have been an awesome experience, for they did not dare to speak their mind. Their silence made the presence of the living Christ even more evident. And when Peter accepted the commission to take care of Jesus' sheep, he and his fellow disciples stepped into a new history that would be informed and molded by the salvation of God in Jesus Christ.

It is therefore with good reason that St. Paul stresses the element of memory in his understanding of the Lord's Supper. After reprimanding severely the corrupt practices that accompanied the common meal of the church in Corinth, St. Paul went on to lay down what he considered to be the proper understanding and practice of the Lord's Supper:

For the tradition which I handed on to you came to me from the Lord himself: that the Lord Jesus, on the night of his arrest, took bread and, after giving thanks to God, broke it and said: "This is my body, which is for you; do this as a memorial of me." In the same way, he took the cup after supper and said: "This cup is the new covenant sealed by my blood. Whenever you drink it, do this as a memorial of me." For every time you eat this bread and drink the cup, you proclaim the death of the Lord, until he comes (1 Cor. 11:23–26).

Needless to say, this is the formula used in the celebration of the Lord's Supper in most Christian churches of the past and of the present day.

By adding the phrase "as a memorial of me," St. Paul captures a crucial element in the institution of the Lord's Supper. There are two foci to this memorial—the past and the future.[8] The past is the crucifixion of Jesus

Christ. That historical event had made the Last Supper different from all other meals. Everything at the Last Supper was transformed sacramentally. Through that meal and its memory, the crucifixion was to be understood redemptively. Just as the crucifixion made that meal different from all other meals, so did the Last Supper make the crucifixion different from all other crucifixions. Just as the Last Supper was a messianic supper, so to speak, so was the crucifixion a messianic sacrifice. And each and every time the Lord's Supper is observed, the memory of Jesus Christ enables believers to grasp the redemptive meaning of the crucifixion and experience the presence of the resurrected Christ.

But this is not all the Lord's Supper means to us. It also means the future; it points to the time to come. The memory of the resurrected Christ is the memory of one who will return in glory. That is why St. Paul wants the celebration of the Lord's Supper to be the proclamation of Christ's death *until he comes.* Here St. Paul interprets correctly the words of Jesus recorded by Mark and Matthew. Jesus said on that last occasion to his disciples: "Never again shall I drink from the fruit of the vine until that day when I drink it new in the kingdom of God" (Mark 14:25; cf. Matt. 26:29). The reference to the future is clear. The disciples are to remember Christ not only in terms of the past but also for the sake of the future. For this reason the Lord's Supper as a memorial of Jesus Christ is also future-oriented. It is our memory in anxious waiting for the revelation of the full meaning of life in God.

Thus the memory with which we are to remember Christ in the Lord's Supper is both historical and eschatological. We must stress that the historical and the eschatological in relation to the Supper are unlike the two ends of a pole which will never meet. They in fact converge in the present when the bread is broken and the wine is poured. In that sacramental moment the historical becomes eschatological and the eschatological becomes historical. Surely this must be the meaning of the real presence of Jesus Christ at the Lord's Supper. In the Lord's Supper Christ is present both historically and eschatologically. It is the remembrance of the past that ushers the future into the present. It is also the remembrance that anticipates the future, which in turn redeems the past in the present. This is the mystery surrounding the Lord's Supper. And it is the power of memory that brings this mystery home to believers.

This theological interpretation of the meaning of the Lord's Supper with its emphasis on memory is supported by New Testament scholarship. C. H. Dodd, a well-known British New Testament scholar, for example, has observed:

At each Eucharist we are *there*—we are in the night in which He was betrayed, at Golgotha, before the empty tomb on Easter Day, and in the upper room where He appeared; *and* we are at the moment of His coming, with angels and archangels and all the company of heaven, in the twinkling of an eye at the last trumpet. Sacramental communion is not a purely mystical experience, to which history, as embodied in the form and matter of the sacrament, would be in the last resort irrelevant; it is bound up with a corporate memory of real events.[9]

Commenting on such a statement, Donald Baillie says: "Such passages show magnificently how at this sacrament we have the presence, the memory and the hope all in one."[10] Here is the sacramental meaning of memory in the Lord's Supper: the crucifixion of Jesus as redemption for the world and the ultimate fulfillment of that redemption become a reality in the believer's memory of Jesus Christ. The Lord's Supper thus relates the believer to the life of Christ in a very real way. It is no ordinary memorial supper. It is the Supper through which the risen Christ becomes present in the life of the believer.

### The Missionary View of Ancestor Worship

What has the Vietnamese mother's experience of her deceased son's presence through the ritual of the bowl of rice to do with the Christians' experience of Christ's presence through the Lord's Supper? On the surface the two events have nothing in common. The ritual of the bowl of rice related to the deceased members of the family is, in fact, a widespread religious practice in Asian countries under the influence of Chinese culture. It is part of what is known as ancestor worship, which has been branded as idolatry by the Christian churches in Asia. This negative attitude on the part of both the Catholic and the Protestant churches toward ancestor worship—a deep-rooted, age-old expression of religious devotion constituting the core of the family system—has done much to alienate Christianity from indigenous culture. Speaking of the papal decree of 1704 that forbade the practice of ancestor worship for Catholic Christians, Kenneth Scott Latourette, the well-known historian, writes:

The most serious indictment which can be brought against the papal decision is that it established a tradition for making the Church unadaptable to Chinese conditions and beliefs. It tended and still tends to keep the Roman Catholic Church a foreign institution, one to which China must conform but which refuses to conform to China. . . .[11]

The turn the controversy over ancestor worship took within the Christian churches of China was an unfortunate one. On the one hand, it not only showed a failure on the part of the missionaries to understand the deeply human spiritual longings behind ancestor worship for the assurance of eternal life but it also exposed their human weaknesses. "The story of the controversy," observes Latourette, "is not a pleasant one. The jealousies; the mutual denunciations and recriminations; the evasions; all were contrary to that spirit which Christian missionaries supposedly came to China to exemplify."[12] This is perhaps just another example in the history of Christianity of how a controversy over doctrinal purity brings out the worst in defenders of the faith. Every time we come across a case such as this (and we find many such cases in the lands missionaries sought to convert to Christ), we are reminded of what Jesus said about those who considered doctrinal purity and a correct observance of the law essential to salvation: "The Sabbath was made for the sake of man and not man for the Sabbath: therefore the Son of Man is sovereign even over the Sabbath" (Mark 2:27).

On the other hand, Latourette points out one factor that had apparently not been grasped by the missionaries in China. "It is significant," he says:

that in the only countries where Christianity has triumphed over a high civilization, as in the older Mediterranean world and the Nearer East, it has done so by conforming in part to older culture. Whether it can win to its fold a highly cultured people like the Chinese without again making a similar adaptation remains an unanswered question.[13]

Latourette wrote this in 1929. Two decades later Christianity in its institutional form was eradicated from Communist China. Time was thus too short for the historical lesson mentioned by Latourette regarding the expansion of Christianity in Europe to be tested out in China. But it is probably correct to conjecture that the foundation laid by the western missionaries would have made it exceedingly difficult, if not impossible, for the churches established in China to become less alienated from Chinese culture, even if the political climate under the Nationalist government continued to remain favorable to the propagation of the Gospel. A similar comment can be made of most countries in Asia. The autonomy of an Asian church from the control of the churches in the West unfortunately does not mean automatically an emergence of new formulations of the Christian faith that take seriously the meaning of indigenous spiritual expressions. To state the situation more accurately, many persons in positions of theological and ecclesiastical leadership are still not able to see the significance of other spiritualities for Christianity in this day and age when the basic premises of the church as understood in western terms are being increasingly questioned and challenged.

This can be seen in the debate over the draft report produced by Section III at the Fifth General Assembly of the World Council of Churches in 1975. We have already referred to it earlier. The full title of this report is as follows: Seeking Community: the Common Search of People of Various Faiths, Cultures, and Ideologies. " . . . the majority of speakers were not happy with it [the draft report]," it was recorded. They believed that it would be understood as spiritual compromise (Dr. per Lønning, Church of Norway) or opposition to the mission of the Church (Bishop Michael, Russian Orthodox). There were a number of detailed criticisms, in particular to paragraphs 4 and 5, which stated that Christians should not allow their faith to add to the divisions of humanity because, as fellow-creatures of God, we are linked together.[14]

As a matter of fact, the message of redemptive love of God in Christ is compromised when a statement calling for seeking community with people of other faiths is challenged and criticized. Here again a cold-blooded logic of faith tends to blind some Christians, and as a result their loyalty to the traditional formulations of faith makes them unable to see the love of God active in human situations outside the immediate realm of the Christian church.

To return to the question posed by Latourette, I want to say that what is important is not conformity in part to Chinese culture, or for that matter, to any culture with which Christianity has come into contact. A superficial conformity tends to create a hybrid that serves neither Christianity nor the other religions. In fact it can be counterproductive, for it often leads to sidestepping the fundamental issues in favor of an outward imitation of one another. It may also prevent people of different religious convictions and persuasions from meeting each other at the deepest level of humanity where people find themselves wrestling with their basic human and spiritual needs. This is the level at which God in Christ will find us. It is there that he seeks to impart to us his message of love and hope. Evangelism—in its deepest sense of God coming all the way to meet us human beings in order to reunite us with him and with one another—takes place at this level. Evangelism in this sense goes beyond conversion to one particular form of religion. What occurs is the conversion to God who is present in the whole of his creation through his Word, Jesus Christ. In the words of John's Gospel:

the Word was with God at the beginning, and through him all things came to be; no single thing was created without him. All that came to be was alive with his life, and that life was the light of men (John 1:2-4).

### Ancestor Worship as the Commemoration of the Dead

In the light of this discussion, how are we to see the meaning of the ritual of the bowl of rice from the standpoint of the Lord's Supper? Does the Christian experience of the Lord's Supper throw some light on the daily ritual performed by that Asian mother in memory of her son? I think the answer is yes. What we are primarily concerned about at the Lord's Supper is life, not death. Although we have to remember Christ's death until he comes, it is a death that has been conquered by life. It is not the sting of death we remember when we take part in the body and blood of Christ symbolized by the bread and wine. The sting of death St. Paul speaks of in 1 Corinthians is a destructive death. It is the death that consigns living beings to oblivion, to annihilation, to nonentity. This bitter death has been overcome by Christ's death. So what we celebrate at the Lord's Table is life, not death. It is a proclamation of victory over death. St. Paul made that proclamation a jubilant one in these words: "Death is swallowed up; victory is won! O Death, where is your victory? O Death, where is your sting?" (1 Cor. 15:55). St. Paul identified death as the last enemy conquered by Christ. Thus when we look to the future beyond the Lord's Table, it is the coming of the living Christ that we await in faith and hope.

Similarly, the chief concern of the Asian mother who prepares a daily bowl of rice for her deceased son is life, not death. The tragedy of death is very much with her. She cannot hold back her tears of sorrow. Yet she tries to overcome her sense of bereavement by turning to the bowl of rice, which for her symbolizes life. That is why she visualizes her son in his full vigor and life. Her son is real and alive to her. The presence of her son, she feels, is a bodily as well as a spiritual presence. The importance of a bodily union with God, which Donald Baillie stresses alongside the spiritual union, can be applied here also. Baillie explains this by referring to interpersonal relationships. In his words:

we love the bodies of our friends as well as their souls, and when we are separated from them we long to hear the sound of their voices, to see their faces and familiar gestures, and to feel the touch of their hands.[15]

When the Asian mother fills the bowl of rice and places a pair of chopsticks beside it, she must be feeling as if she hears the sound of her son's voice, sees his face and familiar gestures, and feels the touch of his hand. The ritual of the bowl of rice is thus not a ritual of death but a ritual of life. It is not a communion with the dead but a communion with the living.[16] There is an insurmountable gulf separating the living and the dead. But in the communion through the bowl of rice, the barrier between death and life is overcome. It is the living mother and the living son that become united in bodily and spiritual communion.

At this point we must distinguish between ancestor worship as the cult of the dead and ancestor worship as the consciousness of the living presence of the dead in our lives through some ritual. Most Christians and theologians often fail to make such distinctions. Eichrodt, for example, states emphatically that ancestor worship, especially the form it takes in the cult of the dead, is definitely rejected by the mainstream of Old Testament faith. According to him:

in Israel . . . it was the shattering experience of God's will to rule which shut the gates of the kingdom of the dead, and proscribed any dealings with the departed.

Yahweh's claim to exclusive lordship covered not only alien gods but also those subterranean powers which might offer their help to men. In this way his sovereignty was deliberately concentrated on this world; it was on this earth that God's kingdom was to be set up. The direction of all his forces to this end gave a man's life its whole content and value. Hence Yahweh claimed the living for himself, and united them to his people; the dead had no further relationship with him.[17]

This means that ancestor worship, or the cult of the dead, is entirely incompatible with and even contradictory to, the worship of Yahweh as the sole Lord.

There are, however, at least two points on which we want to take issue with Eichrodt. First of all, his observation assumes that ancestor worship has largely to do with worshiping the dead as powers that are opposed to God. As a matter of fact, in most cases the spirits of the dead are not worshiped as transcendental powers. They are objects to be feared and placated. A theological judgment of ancestor worship should therefore not ignore this distinction between the worship of the dead and the placation of the dead, for "there are cases in which the dead are worshiped; but those of placation and ministration to the needs of the departed in the other world are much more numerous."[18] That is to say, ancestor worship in its popular practice indicates an underdeveloped stage of human consciousness, which sees the realm of the dead in a sense as a continuation of the realm of the living. Thus relations between the living and the dead are a form of continuing the relations among the living. That is why the dead are believed to have physical needs that must be met, and why their advice is often sought and their favor requested. This is clear from a report made on the basis of a field study of the cult of the dead in a Taiwanese village. "In studing the reciprocity that is at the heart of ancestor worship," says the report:

we shall find that the living are expected to care for the dead in payment of the debts they owe them. Beyond this, in the act of meeting this obligation, the living hope to inspire a further reciprocal response from the ancestors, to obtain through them the good life as they perceive it: wealth, rich harvests, and offspring who will ensure undying memory and sustenance in the afterlife.[19]

This does seem to show that what is involved in ancestor worship or the cult of the dead, at least in its popular form, is not so much an elevation of dead ancestors to the position of a supreme deity as a practical demand to fulfill the social and family responsibilities extended to the deceased person.[20]

It follows that ancestor worship can be viewed as an extension of familial or tribal relationships. In Israel a strong sense of familial and tribal solidarity also existed. Evidence of this is its history centered around the patriarchal structures of society. Even Eichrodt has to concede that the high regard with which ancestral graves were held in ancient Israel is a proof of the existence of ancestor worship.[21] At any rate, what took place in Israel seems to have been the transformation of ancestor worship into the worship of Yahweh, the one true God of Israel. Yahweh is the God of the patriarchs. At the inception of Moses' mission of the Exodus he was instructed to identify God to his compatriots in Egypt as "JEHOVAH the God of their forefathers, the God of Abraham, the God of Isaac, the God of Jacob" (Exodus 3:15). This God of their forefathers was to be confessed by succeeding generations. "The Lord your God," says an ancient creed in Deuteronomy, "will bring you into the land which he swore to your forefathers Abraham, Isaac and Jacob . . . " (Deut. 6:10).

→ Secondly, Eichrodt stresses that "the dead had no further relationship with God." This is a statement that is not self-explanatory, and unfortunately Eichrodt does not help us in the context of this statement to understand what he means by *the dead*. Of course, God has no dealing with the dead, if death is taken in an absolute sense of the complete cessation of life, which virtually means a complete separation from God. In fact, the fear of death in the Old Testament is caused by the thought of drifting into a nebulous realm outside the jurisdiction of God. Such a fear is genuine. We have already seen how it is expressed in the Old Testament, especially in the Psalms. But the point is that, if we consider the sovereignty of God as extending over the whole of creation, there can be no realm outside his care and control. Consequently, there should be no room for "absolute" death in a faith that confesses God as its creator and redeemer. In biblical faith, therefore, God has no further dealing with the dead, for God is the God of the living, not of the dead. Here the biological meaning of the word *dead* should yield to the theological meaning of that word. Theologically speaking, we must affirm that in dead persons God deals not with the dead but with the living. The theological meaning of death is therefore different from its physical meaning. Death occurs physically, but it does not occur *theo*-logically. This is the ultimate meaning of life after death. In God there is no death, for in death we have life. Life is the eschatological meaning of death. The author of the Book of Revelation thus tells us that when a new heaven and a new earth appear, "there shall be an end to death" (Rev. 21:4).

This digression about ancestor worship brings out an important point that has been totally neglected by Christians in their aversion to it as a cult of the dead unacceptable within the Christian church. This point has to do with the continuing presence of the deceased as essential to preserving family ties as well as basic to the belief in life after death. There are positive factors in ancestor worship that can be shared by Christians as they sit at the Lord's Table in remembrance of Christ until he comes. In the experience of the living presence of Christ as we partake of his body through the bread and wine, we ought to be concerned not merely with our own personal relation with him and our own life in him. We experience the living Christ as center of the family to which we belong, a family consisting also of those who have passed beyond this life into another life and of those who are to follow us in the future. With Jesus Christ at the center of this sacramental experience of life, we constitute together with all the members of our family a communion established on the foundation of the cross and the resurrection. The Lord's Supper must therefore be a family supper in a true and comprehensive sense. It must be a *communion* in the true sense of the word, a communion that solidifies the ties binding us all in the love of God. At the Lord's Table we rejoice in our own salvation as we partake of the bread and wine as the symbols and assurance of God's saving love made effective in us through Jesus Christ. But the Lord's Supper does not stop there. It further gives us the assurance that the loved ones who have gone before us are also present with us through Jesus Christ. The Lord's Table is therefore surrounded by both the visible and invisible members of the great family of God with Jesus Christ at the head of the Table. This is his Table, and this is his Supper. And because this is his, no one is excluded from it, not even those who have passed through death into life.

There is thus a great need to restore this familial and communal nature to the celebration of the Lord's Supper, especially in the churches of Asia where various religious beliefs and practices reflect strongly the importance of family ties as the basic social construct. Regrettably, the radical social changes brought about by industrialization and modernization have contributed much to the disintegration of the family. Christianity, because of its negative attitude toward ancestor worship, has also been regarded as a threat to the coherence of the family, especially in relation to its deceased members. However, if we consider the repeated references to forefathers in the religion of Israel and the worship of Yahweh, and if we consider particularly the emphasis on life in the resurrected Christ as an essential part of our Christian faith, the place of the deceased as integral members of a new family life in Christ does not need to be de-emphasized. Christians should not fear to say that in the sacramental experience of the presence of the living Christ in the Lord's Supper, we also experience vividly the presence of those who have already departed as being in the loving and saving care of God. The Lord's Supper is the family celebration of life in God. There is therefore no reason for the living to be anxious about the fate of the deceased or to feel the need to provide for their needs. There is, furthermore, not the slightest reason to be afraid of them, to placate them, or to seek their favor. The life in God made real to us through the Lord's Supper binds all of us, both the living and the dead, to rejoice together in our enjoyment of God.

To put it another way, the Lord's Supper through the presence of the living Christ sacramentalizes the familial and communal ties within which we find the meaning of life. God is the basis of these ties. In him our isolation, to quote Donald Baillie again,

has been overcome in Christ, and in Him we are all one with God and one with each other; and yet our unity will never be complete until we see God face to face. And thus we stand between looking back and looking forward.[22]

The Lord's Supper links our looking back to our looking ahead. It is oriented both to the past and to the future. It points to the time when we shall no longer need to be united with God and each other through partaking of the bread and wine. At that time the Lord's Supper will be discontinued, for we shall be directly in the presence of God. We shall no longer celebrate the Lord's Supper on that day of fulfillment. It is, despite its utmost importance in the life here and now, a temporary provision. It exists between the cross and the return of Christ in person. The Lord's Supper is an eschatological undertaking. It leads to the day when we shall see the spiritual body of Christ and be in the immediate company of all the members of the family of God. Thus the Lord's Supper is a promise to be fulfilled, a hope to be realized, and a vision to be actualized.

This is the message of the Lord's Supper for countless Asians who prepare the daily bowl of rice for deceased members of the family. In the Lord's Supper they will find the promise and reality of the life they are seeking through the bowl of rice. In Jesus Christ the rice they offer will be sacramentalized. He affirms their family ties. He grants them union with their loved ones. He is the assurance of the life they seek for themselves and their loved ones. Christ is the Lord of the bowl of rice. In this sense, they have no more need to seek the presence of their deceased ones in the bowl of rice. It is in Jesus Christ that the tears they shed will be wiped away and communion with their loved ones will be realized. In sharing the bowl of rice together in the presence of the living Christ, they can look forward to the day when they will find themselves in the company of all those who are bound together with their family ties and the ties of the great family of God. In this transformation of the bowl of rice into the Lord's Supper, God in Christ is acknowledged and confessed as the Lord of creation. To participate in this transformation is to participate in the mission of God. This is an evangelism that addresses itself to the needs and longings of the human spirit at its deepest level.

# CHAPTER 8

# SUFFERING UNTO HOPE

Hope is the meaning of suffering. This must be the faith that is either implicitly or explicitly present in all our spiritual and sociopolitical struggles. Hope is a spiritual force which can transform the negativity of suffering into an affirmation of life. We must therefore speak of the power of hope. This power is no less needed today than in the days of our forefathers. For an advance in scientific knowledge and the development of industrial technology have brought new pressures on human life. In addition, our knowledge of the new dimensions of human suffering raises the question as to whether human beings will one day be freed of the shackles of suffering. To find the meaning of suffering in the power of hope is, therefore, an urgent task of the churches today.

Increasingly the specialists of scientific and technological development have had to admit that human suffering has not been overcome as a result of progress in science and technology. The following observation is just one example of the increasing frustration we observe as a result of the human suffering which people, especially people in the Third World, have to face today:

Despite such fresh understandings of the nature of development, the plight of the poor remains hardly better, perhaps worse, than six years ago. The Green Revolution, while a boon, has not offset the disastrous effects of drought, floods, reduced fertilizers and the exodus from the countryside. Today more people are malnourished and starving than six years ago. The battle for improved health is plagued by shortages of health services, especially in rural areas. Forty percent of the world's people still have no access to health services.[1]

These words were written as recently as 1975. When we consider such a situation in conjunction with the United Nations prediction that by 1985 the poorer nations will have a shortfall in cereal production of 75 million tons, human suffering, particularly in Third World countries, seems to be approaching apocalyptic proportions. In addition, corruption, injustice, and inequality in these countries aggravate an already serious state of affairs.

For example, in Brazil 6% of the population controls 94% of the land; in Venezuela less than 1% of the people control 75% of the land, despite the fact that the masses live in the farms. Studies in India, Mexico and Brazil show that the poorest sections of the population have a decreasing standard of living, while the upper social echelons are increasing their material well-being. Colonialist pressures act *within* a country similar to the fashion in which they acted between the richer country and the colony previously, draining the wealth of the country into the hands of the rich, often from rural to metropolitan areas. When aid programmes are obliged to work through existing social and political groups, they tend to accentuate this process.[2]

The joy of liberation from the old colonial powers seems short-lived. People in the Third World, especially the poor and powerless masses, have found themselves again in the bondage of poverty and oppression. Small wonder that some Latin American theologians have begun talking about a theology of captivity instead of a theology of liberation![3]

### *"God of Asia"*

It seems that humanity has become the victim of its own love of progress and success. Its vision of the future is dimmed, its hope for a better life is clouded by many questions and frustrations, and its faith in God has been subdued. The following poem on the "God of Asia" is indicative of such a gloomy mood:

> You offer no joy, God of Asia
> No hope
> You are not with us
> Nor do you go ahead
> You will not comfort
> Will not welcome
> Your gentle people.
>
> You will not defend us
> from unending war
> Floods, the world's greed
> And maddened sun
> And from the strange children
> We see everywhere—
> The grey ugly children
> Swollen bellies puzzled eyes.
> Where do they come from?
>
> You part the sea, the people perish
> Strike the rock, it gushes mystery
> Forty years have become four thousand
> In this desert.

Other Gods promise more
And many leave you.
Often we would follow happy
To clothe ourselves through
Rite and discipline in hope.

Your holy men seeking you
Stared at the sun till the fires
Seared their eyes and the light
brought them lasting darkness
Content in their mummy rags.

We are not so steadfast.
Yet we will stay, God of Asia.
In pain and mystery,
Finding you as you choose.
For isn't it best to know now
There is no more.[4]

The God in this poem is distant. He is the God of illusion, not of the present reality. He is the God of despair, not of hope.

In contrast to this view of God, I would like to assert that the God of Asia is the God of hope, and as the God of hope, he is powerful. In recent years many thoughtful Christians have spoken of powerlessness as a prerequisite for the renewal of the church for its mission in the world. This has been a correct emphasis. The obsession with power that at one time dominated the rank and file of the church was a gross misrepresentation of Jesus Christ who refused earthly power and glory in fulfillment of his redemptive ministry. Ever since Christianity was sanctioned as a legitimate religion of the Roman Empire by Constantine in A.D. 313 the church has come to view itself as possessing both spiritual and secular power. Despite setbacks and persecutions, the Christian church has been a power in the history of western civilization. The Middle Ages, in particular, can be regarded as the period of the great struggle between the power of the church represented by the papacy and the power of the world represented by the Holy Roman Empire. For the church of the papacy there were times of humiliation and times of glory. On occasion the papacy was able to use the powerful weapon of excommunication to bring a ruler to his knees, as happened during the fierce rivalry between Emperor Henry IV of Germany and Pope Hildebrand. In order to obtain absolution from excommunication, Henry IV went to the castle where Pope Hildebrand was staying, "and there presented himself before the castle gate on three successive days, barefoot as a penitent."[5] The image of the church as the humble servant and follower of the crucified Christ dedicated to the mission of reconciliation and salvation was completely lost in this struggle for power between the papacy and the empire. The drama thus played to its bitterest end in the Middle Ages was a drama of a fateful union between the church and the state.

## Missionary Militancy

In a strange way, the struggle for power between the church and the state in the West was carried to foreign lands like China. It became increasingly clear that the western Christian missions, despite their zeal for the propagation of the Gospel in foreign lands, were prepared to rely on the so-called gunboat diplomacy of the western nations. For this reason missionary militancy came to be regarded by anti-Christian nationals as part and parcel of the foreign military invasion. In their eagerness to evangelize a pagan nation like China, which was considered to be the key to the conversion of other pagan lands, the early missionaries regarded the western military invasion of China as God's intervention. The missionary theology of the nineteenth century subsumed the power of the Gospel under the power of the state. The following observation amply illustrates the missionary theology of the secular powers. In an article entitled "Ends and Means: Missionary Justification of Force in Nineteenth Century China," Stuart Miller writes:

Most American missionaries made clear that they preferred to rely on the English, rather than the Japanese or Germans, to protect them and to pave the way for the evangelization of China. "Great Britain is especially the friend of the missionary as her power is felt by our celestial brethren . . . for these people tolerate Christianity only because it is backed by standing armies and battleships. So far as we can see this is God's plan for us at present," wrote H. K. Shumaker.[6]

Missionary theology such as this was of course not able to live up to the message of the crucifixion and the resurrection, which is a totally different kind of power from that displayed by armies and battleships.

Viewed from this angle of power, the modern missionary movements of the churches in the West resembled more the tribal wars waged between Israel and other nations than the mission of the cross carried out by Jesus. From a secular viewpoint the efforts of Israel to gain a foothold and establish itself in the promised land was a bloody history. The invading groups of people from the desert depended as much, if not more, on their own power and ability to fight their enemies as on the power of their faith in Yahweh their God. Yahweh was in fact worshiped as a tribal wargod. Yahweh, who was believed to reside in the ark, went out to war with the Israelite forces. Wars were waged in the name of Yahweh. "These wars," according to von Rad, "were then holy wars, in which Yahweh himself fought in defense of his own people; they were sacred operations, before which the men sanctified themselves . . . and whose termination was the ban, the assignment of the spoil to Yahweh."[7] This tradition of the holy war continued in the history of the Christian church, notably in the Crusades of the Middle Ages, and in the missionary expansion of the church in the modern era.

In a sense the history of Israel recorded in the Old Testament can be regarded as the "justification of force for tribal survival and national consolidation," to borrow Stuart Miller's words. The use of military power in the conquest of the promised land was seen in close relation to divine intervention in the life of the people of Israel. But at the same time there is in the Old Testament a quite different understanding of the history of Israel in relation to other nations and peoples. In essence, stress was placed on the fact that the blessings of the people of Israel were closely related to those of other nations. This is certainly true in the case of Abraham to whom, on leaving his own native land, God says: "I will make you into a great nation, I will bless you and make your name so great that it shall be used in blessings" for other nations (Gen. 12:2). And in the Suffering Servant of the Second Isaiah we have one who "bore the sin of many and interceded for their transgressions" (Isa. 53:12).[8]

The renunciation of force, furthermore, is shown beyond doubt in this song dedicated to the Suffering Servant:

> He was afflicted, he submitted to be struck down
> and did not open his mouth;
> he was led like a sheep to the slaughter
> like a ewe that is dumb before the shearers (Isa. 53:7).

The God of revenge who played a dominant role in the history of Israel before the Exile disappeared completely. What we have here is a different kind of God seen through the eyes of the Suffering Servant, namely, a suffering God. The God of suffering has replaced the God of revenge. And it is this suffering God, not the revengeful God, who is the God of hope.

The justification of the use of force by, for example, the early missionaries to China has been decisively repudiated by Jesus Christ himself. The temptation to use the power of this world to achieve a messianic kingdom was great. But to that temptation Jesus finally said no.[9] In Chapter 11 we shall discuss in detail Jesus' attitude toward power and authority. It is enough to state here that Jesus saw an extreme danger in any alliance with the powers of this world to achieve his messianic mission.

In contrast to Jesus' attitude towards the powers of this world, "few nineteenth century American missionaries found it strange that Christ's glad tidings should be introduced to China by the skirl of pipes, the staccato message of Gatling guns, and the roar of Hotchkiss cannon."[10] Here was the fundamental weakness of the missionaries' theology, which was not able to distinguish between the brutal power of the western states and the redeeming power of Jesus Christ. The result is that the western missionaries came to be closely associated with the political and military powers that rudely forced China to open its door to the West. In order to proclaim the power of salvation, most missionaries placed themselves under the protection and privilege of the aggressive power of the western nations. In the course of time, the missionary activities of the western churches instituted themselves into structures of power reflecting the power politics exercised by the western nations toward the Third World nations. In all fairness it must be said that if the situation had been reversed and the Gospel had been brought to the West from the East, in all probability a similar situation might have occurred. That is to say, if the nations in the East had been in a position to dominate the West, the Gospel might have been proclaimed in the West from a position of military and political strength. However, such a conjecture cannot absolve the churches of the West for their reliance on gunboat diplomacy to gain entry into the heart of the pagan East.

### The Theology of the Crucified God

How different is this God of the pompous church and the militant missions from the God of the cross! The God we encounter in Jesus on the cross is powerless and helpless. In this vast and rich universe of his, he has nothing to support him but the two cruel wooden beams representing pain, shame, and suffering. But this is precisely the God who has the power to save the world. This is the God experienced by the German theologian Dietrich Bonhoeffer in prison. Shortly before his execution he wrote:

God lets himself be pushed out of the world on to the cross. He is weak and powerless in the world, and that is precisely the way, the only way, in which he is with us and helps us. Matt. 8:17 makes it quite clear that Christ helps us, not by virtue of his omnipotence, but by virtue of his weakness and suffering. . . . Only the suffering God can help.[11]

Since Bonhoeffer's death, the powerlessness of God has become a dominant theme for some important western theologians. On the one hand, the secularized western society has successfully weakened the power and influence of the church. There are, on the other hand, some theologians who have accepted this as a challenge to embark on fresh efforts to restore the cross and all that it stands for as the very center of the church and theology. One of the most eloquent representatives of this new theology of the cross is Jürgen Moltmann. His book *The Crucified God,* to which we referred earlier, is a powerful *apologia* of the cross. The cross shows us a suffering God. Instead of the death of God, he speaks of the "death in God."[12] God does not just suffer the tyranny of death as something inflicted on him from outside. He carries the sting of death, as it were, within himself. Death is not introduced into God. Death is there right in the heart of God. The identification of God with us human beings in our suffering and death cannot be more complete than this. To be sure, God is not destroyed by death. On the contrary, God kills death. This, of course, is the message of Easter morning. But what suffering and what torment God—the God who had to carry death within himself on account of the world—had to go through! Here is how Moltmann depicts God on the cross:

He [God] became the kind of man we do not want to be: an outcast, accused, crucified. *Ecce homo!* Behold the man! . . . is a confession of faith which recognizes God's humanity in the dehumanized Christ on the cross. At the same time the confession says *Ecce deus!* Behold God on the cross! Thus God's incarnation "even unto the death on the cross" is not in the last resort a matter of concealment; this is his utter humiliation, in which he is completely with himself and completely with the other, the man who is dehumanized. Humiliation to the point of death on the cross corresponds to God's nature in the contradiction of abandonment. When the crucified Jesus is called the "image of the invisible God," the meaning is that *this* is God, and God is like *this*. God is not greater than he is in this humiliation. God is not more glorious than he is in this helplessness. God is not more divine than he is in this humanity.[13]

In this way, the identification of God with us human beings becomes complete. Weakness, helplessness, and even death, invaded God. This God bears little semblance to the God of the Old Testament who put the enemies of Israel to rout and mercilessly slaughtered them. Nor is he the God decked with the glory of earthly power. Definitely, he is not the God who needs the protection of military forces for his work in a pagan land. He is a totally different God—the powerless God crucified on the cross.

This is a dangerous theology. It is dangerous to the church, which is burdened with the glory and privilege of the past and feels constrained to retain its power and influence that have eroded in recent years. As a matter of fact, the church and its mission are under the judgment of this crucified God. To be a church of this crucified God is to be a crucified church. It is a suffering church that can give witness to the crucified God. The church that lives in affluence, the church that is contented with its wealth and resources will find it difficult to be a crucified church of the crucified God. Do we then not have to say that the church that profits from a rich and affluent society, if measured by the sufferings of the crucified God, is a long way from a suffering church, a church of the crucified God? Yes, the Confessing church that struggled against the demonic power of the Nazi regime was a suffering church, a church of the crucified God. But the Evangelical church in Germany today, which is dependent heavily on the state tax as the main source of its revenue, still needs to learn how to become a suffering church. We must therefore ask: What does it mean for a church in an affluent nation such as West Germany, Switzerland, or the United States, to follow the crucified God? How can such a church become a suffering church of the crucified God? Molmann's theology of the crucified God has no direct answers for questions like these. Can we therefore not say that Moltmann's theology of the crucified God, despite its insights and challenges, is somewhat out of his own context, namely, the context of the industrially developed and economically prosperous West Germany of today? His theology could well have been the theology of the Confessing church of Germany in the 1930s. It could have been a theology for the Barmen Declaration of 1934. But it certainly does not have its context in the rich church of a rich nation. We still need to hear from Moltmann what it means for his church in Germany to become the church of the crucified God.

The theology of the crucified God is, furthermore, dangerous to the traditional theology of the church in the West. Let us take, for instance, the concept of the vicarious suffering of Jesus Christ. It has been correct, biblically and theologically, to speak of Jesus as suffering, dying, and rising *for* the sins of the world. "First and foremost," writes St. Paul, "I handed on to you the facts which have been imparted to me: that Christ died for our sins . . ." (1 Cor. 15:3). It has been a central affirmation of the Christian faith that Christ who is sinless takes upon himself sin on our behalf. The One who shared the rich glory of God, is made humble and poor for our sake; the One who has no reason to suffer, bears suffering on account of the world; the One who dies our death, does so to give us life, and so on. Thus vicariousness has become essential in the Christian understanding and experience of God's salvation. But the fact is that we continue to sin and are victims of a sinful world. We still live in the world in which there seems to be no end to suffering and death. The vicarious sufferings and death of Jesus Christ has not done away with our sufferings and death. The doctrine of Christ's vicarious suffering leaves therefore a great gap between life as it is at present with its hopes frustrated, its dreams shattered, and the fulfillment of these hopes and dreams in the future. From the standpoint of Christian faith, how are we to account for the endless suffering in the world and the inevitable death that puts an end to our earthly existence?

It is at this point, we must admit, that the theology of the crucified God has an important insight to offer. The God who is crucified on the cross is not so much the God who vicariously suffers and dies *for* the world as the God who suffers and dies *with* the world. Here vicariousness is replaced by identification. The crucified God is the God who identifies all the way with us in our suffering and death. He suffers with us and dies with us. The tragic story of death quoted by Moltmann is a vivid illustration of what is said here. In the story a survivor of Auschwitz tells of a profound personal experience in the following scene:

The SS hanged two Jewish men and a youth in front of the whole camp. The men died quickly, but the death of the youth lasted for half an hour. "Where is God? Where is he?" someone asked behind me. As the youth still hung in torment in the noose after a long time, I heard the man call again, "Where is God now?" And I heard a voice in myself answer: "Where is he? He is here. He is hanging there on the gallows."[14]

Perhaps there is no other answer to the absurdity and inhumanity of a death like this one. And how filled this story is with such absurdities and inhumanities! Faith alone can give an answer in such a situation: God is hanging there on the gallows! This is the meaning of the cross. The cross is not to explain why we have to suffer. It tells us where God is suffering with us. The cross is our suffering become God's suffering and our pain become his pain, our despair become his despair, and our death become his death.

God is not the explanation of human suffering. He *is* human suffering. He does not suffer for us; he suffers *with* us. He does not die for us; he dies *with* us. Thus in suffering or in death, namely, in the situation of utter despair and emptiness, we are not alone. We do not suffer alone and die alone. This must be the faith that enables us to face the ultimate situations of life with equanimity. The God of our faith is the God who suffers our suffering and the God who dies our death. If this God is on our side, who can be against us? (Rom. 8:31), asks St. Paul. He then goes on to make a great confession of faith:

For I am convinced that there is nothing in death or life, in the realm of spirits or superhuman powers, in the world as it is or the world as it shall be, in the forces of the universe, in heights or depth—nothing in all creation that can separate us from the love of God in Christ Jesus our Lord (Rom. 8:38–39).

It would be hard to find a more beautiful confession of faith than this. God is the ultimate meaning of suffering, death, and life. No suffering is unimportant to God, for it is his suffering. No death is inconsequential to him, because it is his death. And no life is not dear to him because it is his life. If this God is on our side, who can be against us?

### The Suffering Love of God

This is the God who makes our suffering a suffering to the point of hope. In this God suffering and hope are linked and form a close ally. God is the power which transforms suffering into hope. It is in suffering that

God as the power of hope becomes most manifest. In suffering we are grasped by the power of hope, a power that is greater than any power of this world. The power that turns suffering into hope is a redeeming power because it is rooted in love. Where there is this power of love, there is the manifestation of God's redemption. That is why we can always afford to hope. Insofar as there is no end to this power of love, which is God himself suffering with the world in Jesus Christ, there is no end to hope. This still does not explain why there is suffering in the world. God as the power of love and hope cannot be invoked to justify the continuing presence of suffering in our lives. But he does tell us that he is determined to redeem us from hopeless suffering by suffering with us in Jesus Christ. He gives us hope by entering into our suffering. Jesus Christ is this hope incarnate—God's assurance that our suffering has its destination in God.

There is no power in the world greater than the power of hope rooted in the suffering love of God. This power of hope was tried and tested on the cross. The cross was designed to crush the power of hope and to demonstrate its powerlessness in front of the powers of this world. But God transformed the cross into a testimony of hope rooted in his redeeming love. In the words of St. Paul, "to us who are on the way to salvation it is the power of God" (1 Cor. 1:18). Indeed, the cross has continued to give witness to the power of hope through the ages. The cross is a symbol reminding the world that God is at his strongest when he seems to be at his weakest, that God is at the height of his power when he reaches the depth of helplessness.

We in fact have to agree that, before it became the cross of God, the cross was the nadir of human powerlessness and hopelessness. It was an irreversible end to everything standing for hope and the future. The cross stood for inhumanity, brutality, hell, and death. It was the last defiance of satanic power against humanity. The cross was antihuman, anti-Christ, and anti-God. In the cross was concentrated the cosmic power of negation. But by rendering God powerless, the cross itself became transformed. For on the cross what was exposed was not the powerlessness of God but the powerlessness of the power of negation. What was revealed was the power of the powerlessness of God. The demonic power of negation proved on the cross to be essentially powerless. The power of hate was consumed in its own hate and the power of death was dissolved in its own death. Thus the demonic power of negation was a self-destructive power. That is why it was powerless. In contrast, the powerlessness of God came from his inability to hate, to destroy, and to kill. That is why he was the most powerful God. He was the God who loves, who lets live, and who gives hope. The cross was therefore the victory of the powerlessness of God over the power of hate, destruction, and death. It was the triumph of love over hate, heaven over hell, and life over death. The world was saved by this powerlessness of God.

All this surely means that we cannot talk about the power of God by omitting his powerlessness, that we cannot experience the strength of God by turning away from his weakness and that we cannot embrace life by fleeing death. Here is precisely the paradox of Christian faith: when we embrace the powerlessness, weakness, and death of God hanging on the cross in Jesus Christ, we come to embrace his power, strength, and life. The mystery of the incarnation is the mystery of this paradox. What makes the church an instrument of God's salvation in the world is not its institutional strength or doctrinal orthodoxy. It is the mystery of this paradox which becomes manifest when the church of God is threatened with its own power and the power of this world. At every age the church has to learn over and over again to turn away from its own strength to the weakness of God. Conversion to the weakness of God is the *sine qua non* for the church to manifest God's strength. What is most needed in the churches of the West and in the churches of the Third World established on the western pattern is this conversion. When such a conversion takes place—it is happening in some churches in Asia today, as will be discussed in Part Three—we shall see in them the powerful church of a powerful God. Likewise, when such a conversion takes place in Christians, they too will become the powerful people of a powerful God. The history of Christianity must in reality be the history of such a powerful church with its powerful people serving a powerful God. Here is the true meaning of the power derived from the powerlessness of the cross; it is the power to become one with those who suffer. Thus it is a redemptive power.

The faith that God with his redemptive power is actively and personally involved in human suffering gives us the courage to suffer to the point of hope. In this connection we should remember the impassioned "I have a dream" speech of Martin Luther King, Jr., on August 28, 1963, at the Lincoln Memorial in Washington, D.C., before 230,000 people. This speech marked the climax of the famous March on Washington, which left an indelible mark on the struggle of black people in the United States for civil rights. Dr. King proclaimed:

I have a dream that one day on the red hills of Georgia the sons of former slaves and the sons of former slave owners will be able to sit down together at the table of brotherhood. I have a dream that one day even the state of Mississippi, a state sweltering with the heat of oppression, will be transformed into an oasis of freedom and justice.

I have a dream that my four little children one day will live in a nation where they will not be judged by the color of their skin, but by the content of their character.

I have a dream that one day every valley shall be exalted, every hill and mountain shall be made low. The rough places will be made plain and the crooked places will be made straight. . . . With this faith we will be able to hew out of the mountains of despair the stone of hope. With this faith we will be able to work together, to pray together, to struggle together, to go in jail together, to stand up for freedom together, knowing we will be free one day.[15]

This was, of course, the dream of that ancient prophet of Israel, the so-called Second Isaiah, translated into the dream of a black leader dedicated to the suffering of his own people. That ancient prophet died, but his dream lived on.

In Jesus Christ that dream became a reality. He turned the suffering of the people into hope. The Sermon on the Mount is the messianic dream turned into reality. He came to give consolation to the sorrowful, to see right prevail for those who are hungry and thirsty, and to proclaim the kingdom of God to those who suffer persecution for the cause of right (cf. Matt. 5:1–10). In this way he gives us the courage to hope. The cross is the affirmation of this courage. That is why the cross must lead to the resurrection. Life and not death is the final word of God. The cross is therefore a powerful message of God, which does not disappear into the emptiness of space. It echoes and fills the universe with its powerful chorus of Easter hymns.

The courage to hope, which is given to us through Jesus Christ, is the dynamics that enables us to create our future out of our present sufferings. The future does not come to us, but we must go to the future. This is the chief difference between human beings and other animals. For other animals the future comes to them. They are passive in relation to time, and wait passively for the future to come and swallow them up in a vast abyss of nonentity. This simply means that they have no future. The future is meaningless to them. But for human beings the future can be created. We hope, anticipate, plan, and expect. All these are the verbs primarily related to the future. They mean that we are capable of *becoming* the future. We are not under the tyranny of time. We are born into the future, we live in anticipation of it, and we die into it. We do not disappear into timelessness as our physical life comes to an end. With death we are reborn into a future that becomes God's eternity. The courage to hope enables us to live the future in the present. It enables us to bear our present sufferings in anticipation of future glory. It empowers us to see the shape of the kingdom of God in the transformation of society which many people struggle to bring about. The courage to hope brings us to the presence of God, who is our future and eternity.

Without this courage to hope there is no courage to be. This must be what Paul Tillich means when he says:

There are no valid arguments for the "existence" of God, but there are acts of courage in which we affirm the power of being, whether we know it or not. If we know it, we accept acceptance consciously. If we do not know it, we nevertheless accept it and participate in it. And in our acceptance of that which we do not know the power of being is manifest in us. Courage has revealing power, the courage to be is the key to being itself.[16]

For those who live in suffering, the courage to be must come from the courage to hope. To be in the present despite all sufferings and hardships, we must draw strength from a hope that gives a vision of the future. To live in the midst of destructive powers, we must depend on the power of hope that brings the future into the present. This power of hope is the power that makes room for the future in the present. God is this power of hope.

In order to translate what has been said above into the language of everyday life, we must turn to situations in which suffering is not a concept but a bread-and-butter issue of the people. The following story gives a setting for our further discussion.

In place X, there were people living, farming, fishing on land their forefathers had occupied for generations. They were told the government wanted the land to grow sugar for export: that they, the people, had no right to the land. They would work on the sugar fields and would be paid. So the government sold the land to the landowners and a few skirmishes later, the people yielded and complied. It didn't work out. They had enjoyed subsistence . . . [but now they were forced to live] below subsistence. Children had no educational opportunity because they had to earn wages too. The people who were profiting were the government and the sugar-owners. What had happened was that the traditional land users had been caught up in the system whereby their "third world" country was a resource supplier and a national market for the "first" world. Examples of this, of course, are legion. One thing unites them—systematic hunger, caused by exploitative power.[17]

Increasingly, it is in this kind of situation that Christians in Asia must speak of hope. How is the message of hope to be communicated in such a situation? How can God be demonstrated as the power of hope? Very often the power of the church as a well-institutionalized body becomes powerless. Its language of hope becomes faulty and empty. The God of such a church is helpless. Such a church is at a loss as to what to do for the people who are suffering. It leaves them to cope with their suffering. But the church that has left the people has also left God.

This is not the end of the story, however, for God begins where we human beings fail. The document from which the above story is quoted goes on to identify where and how God may show his power of hope:

We have to begin with people. People must know what makes them hungry, what crushes them and holds them down. If they have rights, they must know how to use them and defend them. If they have none, they must claim some.[18]

People—this is where God seeks to exercise his power of hope. In people such as those described in the story above, we are most likely to encounter

Immanuel, God with us. Where else can we find him? God takes up the cause of the suffering people as his own cause. This is the faith that is basic to the social and political involvement of Christians. In history we have to deal with oppressors and the oppressed, kings and paupers, the rich and the poor. In dealing with them, we deal with God. We argue with him, plead with him, bargain with him, and above all, live with him, suffer with him, and hope with him.

## The Power of Hope in God

The power of hope, however, does not consist merely of making people aware of their situation and their rights. It should go on to equip them for an actual change of their lot in life. Therefore

people need to be able to organize themselves. They need to have their own organization, not simply belong without much meaning to organizations of people who have land and have jobs, and who run them. Organizations are needed because nobody can combat, plunder and withstand repression alone. Organizations take many forms—labour unions in job situations, tenants' organizations, and various collective forms of production, marketing, credit and even ownership. Organizations bring solidarity, discipleship, defined strategies and purposes, bargaining power, and a capacity to develop action which deals with all aspects of a problem.[19]

This is the power of hope in action. Power is not a static concept but dynamic action. The power of hope is no exception. Hope is grasped and experienced as power when it enables people to organize themselves into a power to be reckoned with, when it changes their fatalistic suffering into suffering unto hope. In this way, the power of hope gives to the poor, the oppressed, and the exploited the courage to hope and consequently the courage to be.

The social and political implications of the gospel of hope are thus evident. The hope which has to do with the transformation of human conditions affects the lives of individuals and the community as a whole. The assertion that God is with the poor, the oppressed, and the outcasts, in short, with those who suffer under inhuman conditions, is a political as well as a spiritual assertion. The Gospel that addresses itself to moral and spiritual sins cannot but address itself at the same time to social and political sins. In the last analysis, suffering is social and political in nature as well as spiritual in content. Thus in dealing with suffering, we must see to it that hope becomes organized. And when people are organized under the power of hope, even though the realization of their hope is far off, we find that hope itself has already become a reality for them.

It hardly needs to be stressed that this gospel of hope should become the center of the ministry of the church in Asia today. To evangelize, that is, to proclaim the good news, is to enable those in suffering to have the courage to hope, and thus to gain the courage to be. To put it differently, to confess the faith is to confess God as the power of hope and the power to be, no matter how formidable and how devastating suffering may be. All this must be what is commonly known as evangelization. Evangelization is an act of empowering people with the power to suffer unto hope. It is an act which makes people aware that God does not condone social and political evil, that God does not accept suffering as the inevitable result of fate. This understanding of the task of the church is very important in Asia where people are taught by centuries of tradition and culture to believe that it is their fate to suffer. This is suffering unto despair. A new life therefore cannot begin until suffering unto despair is transformed into suffering unto hope. The task of the church is to play an active role in this transformation. This is liberation from the tyranny of fate into the freedom of the God of hope. Who can then say this is a mere social and political concern that has little to do with the church? Even for the church, as a matter of fact, there is no such a thing as a "mere" social or political concern, for liberation from the fate imposed by social and political powers is at the same time the liberation of the spirit. We have learned in Asia that there is no shortcut to the liberation of the spirit by submitting to social and political bondage. We will take up this point again in Part Three: "The Politics of the Resurrection."

There is nothing novel or strange about this understanding of the task of the Christian community. In actual fact, it is central to the biblical understanding of the historical nature of God's mission for his people in the world. The history of Israel began with the liberation of its people from the land of bondage. The Exodus became the basis of the covenant God made with the people of Israel. The covenant was the sign and reality of God's intervention in history. It broke the fate that has bound men and women to a life of enslavement. It gave a purpose to lives that otherwise had disintegrated into purposelessness. It also gave a future to people who had become prisoners of the past and slaves to the present. That is why the covenant in the Bible is very closely related to the promise—the promise of land to the patriarchs of the Old Testament, and the promise of a new life in Christ in the New Testament.[20] The mission of the church must therefore be a mission of promise and a mission of hope.

In many ways the churches in Asia have begun to grasp this message of the covenant and promise in the Bible. As an illustration we can cite another statement from Asia that deals precisely with what concerns us here. It is a 1973 statement of the Federation of the Asian Roman Catholic Bishops' Conference. Among other things it says:

A local church in dialogue with its people, in so many countries in Asia, means dialogue with the poor. For most of Asia is made up of multitudes of the poor—poor, not so much in human values and qualities, and in human potential, but poor, in that they are deprived of access to material goods and resources which they need to create a truly human life for themselves, deprived, because they live under oppression, that is, under social, economic, and political structures which have injustice built into them.[21]

Such a dialogue has indeed begun. And the center of this dialogue is the covenant and promise understood primarily in the Bible. The poor and the outcasts are essential parts of this covenant and promise. In fact the rich and the powerful are constantly warned that they may forfeit God's covenant and promise if they deal unjustly with the poor. Of course, such a dialogue is a threat to those who hold power. That is why a dialogue of this kind, although it begins with no attempt to instigate a revolt on the part of concerned Christians and citizens, often quickly results in its suppression by the government, police intimidation, and political arrests. But the fact is that the beginning of such dialogue in many parts of Asia has given Christians an enormous sense of liberation and brings about in them the experience of freedom in Jesus Christ. They testify to the fact that, in the poor and the oppressed, the rulers and oppressors are no longer dealing with powerless people but with a powerful God. They bear witness to the fact that, in the suffering of the people, those who hold power are confronted with the suffering of God; in the cry of the people, they hear the cry of God; in the death of the people, they face the death of God. Thus dialogues on social and political issues are fundamentally *theo-*logical issues. In such dialogues the rulers and the ruled, the oppressors and the oppressed, all find themselves in the presence of God, their Judge and Redeemer.

### The Riddle of Human Suffering

The foregoing discussion brings us to the point where we must stress again that suffering unto hope is not an answer to the question of why people suffer. Suffering unto hope is a testimony to God's presence in human suffering. Ultimately, why we must suffer is a question that has no answer. "Why" is, in fact, a scientific question, not a theological question. "Why" demands an explanation or explication, but not faith. It seeks to take us out of suffering instead of enabling us to meet God in our suffering. It is perfectly natural and legitimate for scientists to raise questions about the objects they are studying. The more relentless and ruthless the questioning is, the more possible it will be for the scientists to get at the nature of the objects of their research. On the basis of their questions and answers, they are able to construct hypotheses and theories to explain the structure of the universe and the complex working of atoms and protoplasm. But for the suffering that touches the depths of the human spirit, there can be no answer to the question why. Job in the Old Testament asked again and again why he, of all people, had to suffer. To his three friends who were completely overwhelmed by the pitiful state to which he had been reduced and who remained speechless for seven days and seven nights, Job asked why he had been born to suffer:

> Why should the sufferer be born to see the light?
> Why is life given to men who find it so bitter? (Job 3:2)

The moral reasoning and exhortation of his friends only succeeded in inciting Job's anger and in strengthening his determination to fight God to the bitter end. In great torment of body and spirit, he decided not to yield to the great injustice inflicted on him:

> I swear by God, who has denied me justice,
> and by the Almighty, who has filled me with bitterness:
> as long as there is any life left in me
> and God's breath is in my nostrils,
> no untrue word shall pass my lips
> and my tongue shall utter no falsehood.
> God forbid that I should allow you to be right;
> till death I will not abandon my claim to innocence.
> I will maintain the rightness of my cause, I will never give up;
> as long as I live, I will not change (Job 27:1–6).

Asking why he had to suffer and listening to the reasons given to him by his friends, he was made into a defiant man who felt trapped in the depth of his agony. In the end Job had to stop asking why. And the moment he did, he found himself embraced in the loving bosom of God.

God seems to be allergic to scientific questions. But he is infinitely patient with sinners, both those who are repentant and those who are unrepentant. As Luther puts it, God "loves what is sinful, bad, foolish, weak and hateful, in order to make it beautiful and good and wise and righteous. For sinners are beautiful because they are loved; they are not loved because they are beautiful."[22] But God seems exceedingly impatient with theologians who give him no rest with their "scientific" inquiries about his nature and his ways in the world. God cannot be the object of scientific investigation, nor can he be subjected to minute theological scrutiny. Perhaps the death-of-God theology, which was a fashion at one time, was a logical outcome of speculative theology asking scientific questions of God. God has succeeded in eluding the pursuit of death-of-God theologians. He sets himself free from the doctrinal framework that has fashioned him according to the taste and temper of theological trends and ecclesiastical traditions. He now seems to be letting us know that he is to be encountered in the places where people suffer and hope. As Bonhoeffer has put it so pointedly:

This is what I mean by worldliness—taking life in one's stride, with all its duties and problems, its successes and failures, its experiences and helplessness. It is in such a life that we throw ourselves utterly into the arms of God and participate in his suffering in the world and watch with Christ in Gethsemane.[23]

Suffering in the world is thus a part of our growth into the knowledge and experience of God who is Immanuel, God with us.

The freedom of God is the freedom to be with those who suffer in hope and unto hope. The woman who looks down and feels the seed coming into life in her womb, the mother who fills the bowl with new rice for her son each day, each of them encounters God in her suffering. The seed that stirs in the woman's womb and the rice with which the mother fills the bowl speak volumes about the hope of humanity in a world of misery and suffering. I am sure God wants us Christians to share in that seed of hope stirring in the womb of humanity. And perhaps he is calling us to be a bowl of the rice of hope and life to those struggling to be free from fear and despair. Surely this must be the meaning of the cross, which is God suffering with us human beings unto the hope of a new life in him.

# Part Three

# The Politics of the Resurrection

# CHAPTER 9

# THE CROSS
# IN THE RESURRECTION

## Easter Sunday in Seoul

On April 22, 1973, an Easter service was celebrated early in the morning in an open-air theater on top of Namsan mountain near the center of Seoul, Korea. Christ is risen! This is, and always will be, the message of Easter. The power of hell has not overcome heaven. Death has not nullified life, despair has not conquered hope, and hate has not destroyed love. As St. Paul declared:

If Christ was not raised, your faith has nothing in it and you are still in your old state of sin. It follows also that those who have died within Christ's fellowship are utterly lost. If it is for this life only that Christ has given us hope, we are of all men most to be pitied (1 Cor. 15:17–19).

Easter service since the church of the apostles has been the proclamation that Christ is indeed risen from the dead, that those who believe in him are not lost, that they are not most to be pitied of all men and women. Easter morning service is therefore the celebration of God's affirmation of life, of his creation, and of his people. It is God's yes against Satan's no, to use Karl Barth's language.[1] At the same time it is man's Amen to God's yes. Easter Day is truly the Lord's Day, the day of Christ's rebirth from the womb of death. Surrounded by complete darkness in the womb of death, God died in Christ. God in Christ died our death and we died with him. The power of darkness swallowed up the power of light. The world was without God for three days and three nights. The world without God is a hopeless world in which chaos rules and Satan takes charge. In this kind of world we would hear again and again the despairing cry of Average Woman in a play by Guenter Rutenborn, *The Sign of Jonah:*

God is guilty! That is true! True! True! I speak for all the mothers of the twentieth century! I speak in the name of all innocent children who died in the last two wars. I speak in the name of those who froze to death while fleeing for their lives. . . .[2]

The God who succumbs to the tyranny of death and has no power of resurrection must be a profound disappointment to the world in which innocent lives are constantly sacrificed on the altar of demonic power. In this kind of world we are all condemned to become victims of human insanity.

This has led Nicholas Berdayev to say:

We are entering an inhuman world, a world of inhumanness, inhuman not merely in fact, but in principle as well. Inhumanity has begun to be presented as something noble, surrounded with an aureole of heroism. No longer is every man held to be a man, a value, the image and likeness of God.[3]

How true this statement would be if the God of Jesus Christ were merely the God of Good Friday and not the God of Easter Sunday as well! Inhumanity would have replaced humanity; the image of the devil would have taken the place of the image of God in humanity; and eternal death would have destroyed eternal life. The threat of death to the God of creation is therefore a real threat. The battle in the womb of the darkness of death fought between the power of life and the power of death, between the power of destruction and the power of creation, that is, between God and Satan, must have been a fierce battle. These were horrible hours in which history came to a complete stop, for the world without God has no history. Fundamentally, death has no history. Death is the end of all things and the dissolution of history. Good Friday posed a real threat to God.

The whole universe must have watched the battle between Good Friday and Easter Sunday in horror and silence. Not until Easter Sunday dawns is that silence broken. The whole of creation bursts into a chorus of praise and jubilation: Hallelujah, the Lord is risen! He is risen indeed! The God of the cross is vindicated by the God of resurrection. A new creation begins with the resurrection. It is a creation that both promises and fulfills eternal life. In anticipation of such a life the writer of the Book of Revelation heard a voice proclaiming from the heavenly throne: "God will wipe every tear from their eyes; there shall be an end to death, and to mourning and crying and pain; for the old order has passed away" (Rev. 21:4). The power of resurrection is the power of faith, hope, and life.

But the truth of the matter is that the Christian community throughout the centuries has had to celebrate Easter under the shadow of Good Friday. The history of the church tells us that we must identify the God of the resurrection with the God of the cross. To put it differently, the resurrection must be experienced in and through the cross just as the cross must be seen in the light of the resurrection. The fact is that the resurrection has not made the cross superfluous. This is a historical reality the church has to accept. The church, together with the world as a whole, continues to bear the pain and agony of the cross in the midst of the resurrection. The cross is the meaning of the resurrection. This is God's politics of resurrection.

This must have been the experience of the men and women who assembled for that Easter morning service in Seoul in 1973. Some months earlier, in October 1972, President Park had declared martial law, suspended the constitution, dissolved the National Assembly, and proclaimed himself "president for life." The people of Korea—a people who had fought and shed blood for freedom and democracy against Japanese colonialism and the communist dictatorship of North Korea—were once again confronted with authoritarian rule in President Park's government. His political leadership was built on the absolutization of power, which is known in Korea as the "institutionalization of authority." In the words of the "Theological Declaration of Korean Christians, 1973":

The present dictatorship in Korea is destroying rule by law and persuasion; it now rules by force and threat alone. Community is being turned into jungle. . . .

The regime in Korea is destroying freedom of conscience and freedom of religious belief. There is freedom neither of expression nor of silence. There is interference by the regime in Christian churches' worship, prayer, gatherings, content of sermons, and teaching of the Bible. . . .

The dictatorship in Korea is using systematic deception, manipulation, and indoctrination to control the people. The mass media has been turned into the regime's propaganda machine to tell the people half-truths and outright lies, and to control and manipulate information to deceive people. . . .

The dictatorship in Korea uses sinister and inhuman and at the same time ruthlessly efficient means to destroy political opponents, intellectual critics, and innocent people. The use of the Korean Central Intelligence Agency (KCIA) for this purpose is somewhat similar to the evil ways of the Nazi Gestapo or the KGB of the Stalin era. People are physically and mentally tortured, intimidated and threatened, and sometimes even disappear completely. Such treatments are indeed diabolical acts against humanity.[4]

This indictment against the Park regime expresses the determination of Korean Christians to stand on the side of freedom and democracy against dictatorship. Precisely because of it, the message of the resurrection for these Christians was at the same time the message of the cross. On December 22, 1972, Eun Myung-ki, pastor of the Namun Presbyterian Church at Chunju City in North Cholla province, had been arrested in his pulpit while praying with the members of his congregation.[5] The resurrection faith of the church in South Korea found itself suddenly under the grip of the powerlessness and power of the cross.

It is thus a church of the cross that was celebrating the victory of the resurrection that Easter morning in 1973. As the service was in progress, the Rev. Park Hyung-kyu, pastor of Seoul's First Presbyterian Church, and his colleagues distributed leaflets, "calling for statesmen to repent and prayerfully entreated, 'O God, have mercy on foolish rulers!' "[6] This was their message: "Resurrection of democracy is the liberation of the people."[7] For this Resurrection Day message, Pastor Park was arrested and charged with "preparing an insurrection."[8]

In the eyes of the rulers of this world the resurrection faith with the cross at its center can be a faith of insurrection. So be it! If this be an insurrection, it is one in the hearts and minds of Christians, staged not to take over political power and form a political party, but to urge and challenge those in power to humanize and democratize their political machinery and make it capable of serving the needs of the people. Thus an insurrection shaped by the faith of the resurrection differs from an insurrection that arises out of a struggle for political power and domination. It is an act of faith that endeavors to signal hope to a people who have become victims of a ruthless dictatorial power. The struggle of Korean Christians for freedom and democracy under Park's institutionalization of power and authority is a forceful expression of the resurrection faith. It kindles the fire of hope in the midst of a suffering nation and people.

Indeed, the faith that advocates the democratization of political power in South Korea today has become a threat to the absolutization of authority carried out on the basis of an anti-Communist ideology. It is a sad fact that the political power that is waging a crusade against the communist dictatorship in North Korea has itself become dictatorial both in form and in content. It takes on a demonic character that deprives people of their freedom and integrity. It treats people as ideological tools in order to achieve its ambition for absolute power. It turns them into cogs in a political machine that depersonalizes them. Within such a political system of physical and spiritual regimentation, a mere plea for the democratization of power is regarded as insurrectionary. It becomes treason to call for the liberation of the people from the oppressive power of a repressive government. But the resurrection faith that emerges from the suffering of the cross means precisely not only liberation from physical death but also liberation from the power that dehumanizes the human spirit and treats human beings as means to achieve its political ambition.

At this point we must ask: what is the criterion that distinguishes good politics from bad politics? What constitutes the moral basis of power in political activities? Ultimately, what is politics for? The answer must be the well-being of the people. Politics is the art of ordering society in such a way that the well-being of the people is protected, respected, and enhanced. That is why rulers must rule by the consent of the people. And their consent should be expressed in a constitution formulated by a duly elected body that establishes political processes through which the people can participate in political decisions without coercion and inhibition. This is what democracy is about in essence. Democracy, which means "gov-

ernment by the people" in Greek, is one of those noble concepts that can
be corrupted by misuse. When a nation under dictatorial rule still calls
itself democratic, we no longer know what democracy really means. In
any case, the following requirements are fundamental to a democratic
polity and any government that professes to practice democracy must
take them seriously. "As a minimum, democracy is a system of government," writes Dorothy Pickles, "a set of institutions that fulfills at least two
essential requirements:

It must, first, be able to elicit as accurately as possible the opinion of as many
people as possible on who shall be their representatives and on how the country
ought to be governed. This means as a minimum, universal suffrage, political
parties, and the organization of free voting in uncorrupt elections at relatively
frequent intervals. Second, it must provide ways of ensuring that those chosen by
the public do in fact do what the electorate wants them to do or that they can be
replaced if they do not, even between elections. The fulfillment of this require-
ment entails methods of supervising the work of governments, of keeping them in
constant contact with public opinion. In other words, the process of government
in a democracy is essentially a dialogue between rulers and ruled. Dictators can
achieve power by the use of regular electoral machinery, as Hitler did, but they
then maintain themselves in power either by manipulating public opinion in their
favour or by ignoring or repressing its free expression.[9]

Judged by these requirements, many nations in the world today, especially those in Asia like South Korea, fall far short of true democracy. To
apply the word *democracy* to such nations is a monstrous abuse of language
employed by rulers to justify the concentration of power in their person at
the expense of the people.

What is of special importance in the above quotation is the following
sentence: ". . . the process of government in a democracy is essentially a
dialogue between rulers and ruled." Such a dialogue has been effectively
terminated in a dictatorial country. Dictatorship is basically a monolithic
structure of government in which the ruled can only play a passive role, a
role that consists solely in consenting to the orders of rulers. The well-
being of the people becomes subordinated to power politics in high
places. In such a situation the people are cast in different roles in accordance with the whims and needs of their rulers. At one time they
may become the objects of the rulers' sudden benignity, and at other
times the targets of their wrath. No matter what role they are forced to
play, they are victims deprived of human dignity and offered up on
the altar of authoritarian rule. We may conclude therefore that where
there is no free dialogue between rulers and ruled on methods, direc-
tions, and goals of government, democracy is dead. And when democracy
is dead—democracy understood in the sense of an uninhibited, uncor-
rupted communication between rulers and ruled—something vital to the

human spirit is also dead—dignity, honesty, love, and freedom. People then live by the dictate of the ruler, not by the voice of conscience. Dictatorship is therefore an assault on the image of God in human beings.

A voice raised on behalf of the well-being of the people under a political system that embodies the absolutization of power is thus branded as an insurrection. That voice must be suppressed and liquidated. In a sense human history is a history of the struggles between rulers and ruled, a history of conflicts between the well-being of the people and institutions of political power based on dictatorial rule. In the Old Testament we encounter the history of intensive struggles and conflicts between the Jewish prophets and the kings. The prophets of the Old Testament are frequently spokesmen for a powerless people. They are constrained to speak out against those in power on behalf of the poor and the oppressed. They often find themselves having to proclaim bad news to the rulers and pronounce God's judgment on them. For this they are treated as rebels and insurrectionists. Jeremiah is a case in point. When Jerusalem was beseiged by the Babylonians, Jeremiah counseled the nation to surrender. "Whoever remains in this city," Jeremiah said to the nation of Judah:

shall die by sword, by famine, or by pestilence, but whoever goes out to surrender to the Chaldeans shall survive; he shall survive, he shall take home his life and nothing more. These are the words of the Lord: This city will fall into the hands of the king of Babylon's army, and they will capture it (Jer. 38:2).

For the king and his courtiers who were trying desperately to ward off the Babylonian attack, this amounted to treason punishable by death. "The man must be put to death," the king's officers indignantly declared. "By talking in this way he is discouraging the soldiers and the rest of the people left in the city. He is pursuing not the people's welfare but their ruin" (Jer. 38:4).

### The Yusin Constitution

Those who hold power also speak of people's welfare, of course. But this is a pretension that has no basis in the life of the people. Dictators always know infinitely better than the people themselves what the latter need and aspire to. Of course they do, because it is they who dictate what the people should need and define what they should expect. Dictatorship is a political factory in which people's needs and desires are manufactured. The holders of absolute political power are self-appointed defenders of a welfare not desired by the people. Even the Park regime speaks of the welfare of the people. It does this after the dissolution of the National Assembly and the declaration of martial law, that is, after the dialogue between the government and the people has been effectively terminated. A critical reading of the Yusin Constitution, which was promulgated on October 18, 1972, tells us what has happened. The new Constitution says in part: the new "democratic" Republic is determined:

To promote the welfare of the people domestically, and to strive to maintain permanent world peace internationally, and thereby to ensure the security, liberty and happiness of ourselves and our posterity.[10]

Does this not remind us at once again of the words Jeremiah said in great distress? "They dress my people's wound, but skin-deep only, with their saying, 'All is well.' All well? Nothing is well!" (Jer. 6:14) How could a government really know what the welfare of the people is when people are chained to an authoritarian rule consolidated under one person? How could there be peace both domestically and internationally when those in power practice the politics of fear and intimidation?

Article 1 of the Yusin Constitution further states:

The sovereignty of the Republic of Korea shall reside in the people, and the people shall exercise sovereignty whether through their representatives or by means of national referendum.[11]

But when political dissenters are arrested, tortured, and sentenced to long prison terms or death, how can we believe that the sovereignty of the Republic resides in the people? When the life of the people is under the constant surveillance and harrassment of the Korean Central Intelligence Agency, how can we expect them to exercise their sovereignty through an election or a referendum? When the pulpit in a church is invaded by the police, prayer meetings are broken up, and Christians taken before military courts for voicing their conscience, how is it possible not to regard the new Constitution as a crude fabrication of the government to lull and deceive the minds of the people?

What the Yusin Constitution has done under martial law is to stifle the people's outcry on the one hand and on the other to turn into political martyrs those who dare to call attention to the people's outcry. A notable example is Kim Chi Ha, perhaps the most outspoken poet in Korea today, who has become a victim of Park-style democracy. His long poem, "Cry of the People," is a cry of the suppressed majority—a vivid expression of their spiritual and physical torment under the Park regime. The poem begins with a wrenching appeal:

> Hear our cry! Hear our cry!
> Crying out of aching hunger.
>
> Patience quickly running out!
> Can we long believe this ruler?

The poet then attacks the Yusin Constitution, which in his opinion is nothing more than a cruel deception to seduce the people into passive obedience:

> The Yusin signboard advertisement
> Is merely to deceive people;
>
> On democratic constitution's tomb
> Dictatorship has been established;
>
> Human rights went up in smoke;
> Now sheer survival is at stake.
>
> The people's leaders thrown into prison
> For espousing democratic rights.
>
> For their deep belief in freedom
> Students and Christians are labelled "traitors";
>
> Rule by fear and violence
> Shows total desperation.

The poem goes on to uncover the corruption in the government and vocalize the pain and agony of a people victimized by the economic situation. It speaks of the atmosphere of fear and deception that has enveloped the nation like a thick cloud. At this point the poem turns into a call to:

> Christians, independence fighters,
> Betray not now the people.
>
> In the spirit of all martyrs,
> Come forth to root out evil!
>
> You who are overloyal,
> Take courage, change your hearts!
>
> Ex-prisoners, bearing tyranny's scars,
> Rise up to greet the day!
>
> Jobless and beggars,
> Struggle for survival!
>
> Gang leaders, shoeshine boys,
> Come and join the fight!
>
> Bus drivers, train conductors,
> Claim your human rights!
>
> Opportunists, hypocrites,
> You too take a stand!
>
> Politicians, officials,
> Know the people's will!

This is a cry to mobilize the people of Korea for freedom and democracy. It is the cry of the cross. Politics under a dictatorship is a cross to be borne by the people. It is a cross on which what is best and noble in humanity is crucified. An authoritarian political power is a cross on which the rights of the ruled are suspended and destroyed by the wrongs of rulers. But Kim Chi Ha refuses to bear this cross in despair and resignation. He carries it in hope, in the spirit of the resurrection. That is why he is able to conclude his poem with an expression of courage and expectation.

> Let nothing keep you from your freedom!
> Let tyranny no longer reign!
>
> Arise, spirit of self-determination!
> Guide our destiny!
>
> And we will sing the song of peace,
> In freedom, justice, and love.[12]

This is a poem written in sweat and blood. It is the sweat and blood of a people crying out for vindication. It is an eloquent and powerful communication of the people's will to their ruler. It seeks to break the barrier of the false dialogue set up by the ruler. This is the politics of the cross carried out in the hope of resurrection.

### The Resurrection and the Transfiguration

The preceding discussion enables us to come to the following conclusion: hope in the resurrection is a historical hope. In other words, the cross closely links this hope to the movement of history. Resurrection is the link between death and life in a physical and a spiritual sense. And it is the cross which constitutes the essence of this link in history. Therefore the cross is the historical meaning of the resurrection, just as the resurrection is the eschatological meaning of the cross. The eschatological must converge with the historical in the rough and tumble of this world. This means that the resurrection should not be separated from the cross. Once it becomes separated from the cross, the resurrection divorces itself from history. When this happens, we can no longer speak of the resurrection as the fulfillment of history. The resurrection ceases in that event to be a historical hope. It loses at once its impact on the historical processes of individuals and of nations. As Moltmann puts it, "The theology of Easter hope must be changed into the theology of the cross, if it is to set our feet on the ground of the reality of the death of Christ and our own death."[13] What is involved here, however, is not only the reality of death, but the reality of the whole of history. The resurrection is the fulfillment of history; it is the partial exposure of the meaning of history filled with suffering, pain, and despair as well as a full disclosure of the mystery of history at the end of time. With the resurrection of Christ from the dead, a new history of God's dealings with the world has begun in the midst of a history that is still under the power of destruction. Under the impact of the resurrection, the cross can now be borne in hope, for a new life has already begun.

In this connection our thoughts go back to the disciples who were instructed by the risen Christ to return to Galilee where Jesus had begun his ministry. According to Matthew's account, the risen Christ told the women at the tomb early on Sunday morning: "Do not be afraid. Go and take word to my brothers that they are to leave for Galilee. They will see me there" (Matt. 28:10). This instruction seems to imply that the disciples are to start their ministry all over again from the very place where Jesus began with them three years earlier. The ministry that carried Jesus from Galilee to Jerusalem was in a true sense Jesus' own ministry. The disciples did not understand the meaning and purpose of his ministry. They had followed him for three years with hopes and expectations quite different from those of Jesus. They dreamed wild dreams that often missed completely the mark Jesus was aiming at. For them Jesus was essentially a Jewish messiah on whom they were prepared to stake their national political hope. They harbored a faith in him as the hope of their race. They labored with him because he seemed the only leader on the horizon who could realize their political dream. The cross, however, shattered their hope and expectation. Everything had to begin all over again. And the risen Christ chose to meet them at the place where he had recruited them three years before.

This meeting of the risen Christ with his disciples in Galilee is of fundamental historical significance. It drives home to the disciples that he is and will be as fully involved in history as he was before. Galilee, the site of Jesus' ministry, serves as the link between the risen Christ and the historical Jesus. The Jesus of history and the Christ of faith are essentially one. There is no Christ of faith without the Jesus of history, and the Jesus of history cannot be correctly understood and experienced apart from the risen Christ. What is to confront the disciples in Galilee is the Jesus of history now appearing as the Christ of faith. They are to meet the crucified Jesus in the risen Christ. In other words, faith in Jesus Christ is a historical faith. It is a faith which not only touches heaven but also moves the earth. Since the resurrection has not made Jesus less historical and accessible, our faith in him calls us back to our duties on the plane of history. In this way the Jesus of the cross and the Christ of the resurrection are to become united in the one person of Jesus Christ in the consciousness of the disciples in Galilee where Jesus began his mission.

Thus it is not the empty tomb but Galilee that makes the resurrection of Jesus Christ a historical event.[14] In actual fact, the empty tomb plays no significant role in the whole event of the resurrection.[15] It is neither a proof nor a disproof of the mystery related to the resurrection of Jesus Christ. It has no historical significance as far as our faith in the risen Christ is concerned.[16] We can thus only speak of a symbolic meaning of the empty tomb. The empty tomb is symbolic of the faith that a tomb is not the final destiny of human beings. It is not the last answer to the problem of life. After the resurrection of Jesus Christ, not only the tomb that had contained him must remain empty but all the other tombs must also become empty. To use the words of the author of the Book of Revelation, the empty tomb is "an end to death" (Rev. 21:4). Can we not say that the empty tomb is the death of death? Strictly speaking, therefore, we cannot speak of the resurrection life as "life after death." Rather it must be "life after life."[17] This is what the resurrection must be when we take its historical character seriously. For death is the termination of history. It closes the door to the future and bars the gate to life. The resurrection, however, has removed this deadly obstacle to life. The sting of death, as St. Paul puts it, is taken away. The resurrection is therefore life after life.

In Galilee the disciples are enabled to realize the historical connection between the Jesus they have known for three years and the Christ who now comes to them as the risen Lord. A great transformation has thus taken place in their understanding of the messianic mission of Jesus Christ. Galilee—this historic spot—provides a context for the momentous, hermeneutical transformation. Jesus Christ is no longer their prospective national hero. He is God's Son, who humbled himself to stand on the side of the poor, the outcasts, and the oppressed. The cross after all has not ended in failure and defeat. It is a divine mission that strikes at the very root of all human problems. It is God's redemptive act, which recreates our humanity out of the chaos and ruin of inhumanity. The ministry of the disciples after the resurrection of Jesus should be a ministry in service of this redemptive act of God on the cross. The cross sustained and strengthened by the power of the resurrection thus becomes the center of their apostolic ministry.

The familiar story of the transfiguration must be cited here because it seems to provide us with a paradigm illuminating the historical impact of the resurrection. The story is told in all the Synoptic Gospels (Matt. 17:1-8; Mark 9:2-8; Luke 9:28-36). Pointing out a close parallel between Mark's story of the transfiguration and his account of the resurrection, Paul Lehmann has observed:

Indeed, Mark seems deliberately to associate the transfigured and the risen Christ. The glory with which the Transfiguration exalts Jesus is the form he was believed to possess from the moment of the Resurrection, and in which he was thought to have revealed himself to his disciples. Thus, for Mark, the Transfiguration is the prefiguration of the Resurrection.[18]

If we consider the fact that the resurrection is a radical transfiguration of life, the parallelism between the story of the transfiguration and the story of the resurrection in the Synoptic Gospels, and especially in Mark's Gospel, becomes understandable. It is possible that the authors of the Synoptic Gospels read the meaning of the resurrection into the transfiguration. In the light of their extraordinary experience with the risen Christ, the disciples must have begun to realize that the resurrection was the culmination of the process of the transfiguration Jesus had gone through in the course of his earthly ministry. The life of Jesus from the beginning to the end is now perceived as the life of transfiguration. What they began to see in their postresurrection encounter in Galilee must have been the Jesus who had been transfigured from a lowly carpenter into the herald of the good news of God's salvation, from an ordinary human being into the way, the truth, and the life, from a lonely religious teacher into a bold opponent of the powerful religious hierarchy of his day, and from an insignificant man of an oppressed race into a towering figure standing without fear before the oppressor's tribunal. The story of the transfiguration must have been meant as a summation of the process of dramatic change seen in retrospect from the vantage point of the resurrection of Jesus. If this is true, the parallelism between the story of the transfiguration and the account of the resurrection serves to establish once and for all the place of the crucified and risen Christ in the consciousness of the disciples. This does not mean that the story of the transfiguration was fabricated by the authors of the Synoptic Gospels. It is a paradigm of history grounded in their deep reflection on the meaning of the risen Christ.

Our attention is further drawn to the sequence of the story of the transfiguration. Confronted with the transfigured Jesus, Peter exclaimed in terror and ecstasy: "Rabbi, how good it is that we are here! Shall we make three shelters, one for you, one for Moses, and one for Elijah?" (Mark 9:5). The voice that was heard from the cloud surrounding them totally ignored Peter's confused statement. It said: "This is my Son, my Beloved; listen to him" (Mark 9:7). This was a confirmation of Jesus' messianic mission. The transfigured Jesus is the Messiah, the God-anointed. He is not merely a messenger of salvation. He *is* salvation. But Peter did not quite understand the meaning of the messianic ministry of salvation to be carried out by the transfigured Jesus. If his suggestion had been accepted, the transfigured Jesus would have remained only a mystical experience of the three disciples. The transfiguration then would have lost its historical and political significance. Salvation would have become detached from human experiences in daily life. This means, of course, that the transfiguration would have forfeited its redemptive meaning within the historical domain. God's salvation would have been removed from humanity's historical experience.

Therefore we can almost perceive a conscious effort on the part of the

Synoptic writers to move as quickly as possible away from the isolated mountain of the transfiguration back to the crowded village where people are beset with the problems of earthly life. As it turns out, the disciples who had been left behind were unable to cope with an epileptic boy seized with convulsions from time to time. The sight of Jesus must have been a relief to them and especially to the boy's father. At the request of the father and his expression of faith, Jesus healed the boy. This is the power of the transfiguration at work. In this healing episode the historical link has been established between the mountain of the transfiguration and the world of suffering, between the transfigured Jesus and the historical Jesus, between the Son of God and the Son of Man. In this act of healing we see how the transfiguration of Jesus is translated into a redemptive event that took place in the life of the people.

As the accounts of the post-transfiguration events show, the healing of the epileptic boy was just a beginning of a whole series of incidents that led Jesus ever closer to Jerusalem. His conflict with the religious leaders intensified and the plots to arrest and put him to death thickened. The transfigured Jesus now had to face the concentrated challenge of this world. The power of the transfiguration was put to the test by the religious and political powers of the day. And as the events unfolded, the transfigured Jesus became the crucified Jesus. The transfiguration developed into the crucifixion. The true meaning of the transfiguration was painfully and sharply disclosed in the crucifixion. The crucifixion testified to and certifies the redemptive meaning of the transfiguration. The crucifixion was thus a painful but magnificent transfiguration of all the agony and suffering that threaten the disintegration of human life and the life of all creation. On the cross the transfigured Jesus transfigured sin into grace, judgment into forgiveness, and death into life. And wonder of wonders, on the cross the transfiguration and the resurrection become linked in the historical drama of God's salvation. The cross enables us to accept the transfiguration and the resurrection as a single historical experience that affects our life not only as individuals but as a part of creation.

Here we must turn to John's Gospel, which concluded the narrative of the life and ministry of Jesus with a moving account of the breakfast scene by the Sea of Tiberias (John 21:1–22). In this account, John, the author of the Fourth Gospel, seems more concerned than the Synoptic writers to demonstrate how the mission of Jesus after his resurrection was to be continued. For him the meaning of the resurrection cannot be found in a flight from historical responsibility. The resurrection of Jesus authenticated the mission of the cross as the manifestation of God's saving power. The resurrection as the historical experience of salvation must therefore be verified in history. This seems to be the chief emphasis of the conversation between the risen Christ and Peter after they had breakfasted in a deeply disquieting silence. Jesus asked Peter the same question three times: Do you love me? This "me" is the risen Christ. It is then the risen Christ whom Peter was asked to love. Peter confessed each time that he loved the risen Christ.[19] Then the great missionary command came to him in a clear and unmistakable voice: Feed my lambs and tend my sheep! The love for the risen Christ must become the feeding and tending of the people for whom Jesus had suffered and died. The encounter with the risen Christ by the Sea of Tiberias must have reminded Peter of the transfigured Christ on the mount of the transfiguration and of the crucified Jesus on the mount called Golgotha. Just as Peter had to come down from the mountain with the transfigured Christ, so he was now to carry the redemptive presence of the crucified and risen Christ into the lives of the people. Through Peter and his companions the resurrection must become a power to transform humanity and the world.

Furthermore, for the author of the Fourth Gospel the breakfast with the risen Christ must have been a re-enactment of the Last Supper. With the cross immediately before him, Jesus had sat at the supper table with his disciples trying to bring home to them the redemptive meaning of his impending death. But the disciples had failed to comprehend what Jesus said and did during the supper. When he was arrested, they fled and Peter, in accordance with Jesus' prediction, denied him three times. They thus rejected the mission of the cross. It must have been with all this in mind that John made the risen Christ say to Peter at the conclusion of breakfast:

I tell you this in very truth: when you were young you fastened your belt about you and walked where you chose; but when you are old you will stretch out your arms, and a stranger will bind you fast, and carry you where you have no wish to go (John 21:18).

This is a clear allusion to the fact that the postresurrection ministry of Peter was to end on the cross. The cross was again very much a part of the resurrection. And now with the power of resurrection felt and encountered by Peter in the presence of the risen Christ, Peter cannot run away from the cross the second time. He might have been able to deny the crucified Jesus, but he cannot deny the risen Christ. Once he has accepted the risen Christ, he has no alternative but to accept the crucified Jesus as well.

### Historical Faith and the Third World Churches

The resurrection is therefore both a celebration and a challenge. It has to be a celebration because life, not death, is affirmed as the final reality. But it must at the same time be a commitment because it commits us to the cross. This commitment to the cross is a key to understanding and appropriating the power of the resurrection. Without such a commitment the resurrection remains a mystical experience out of joint with the historical reality that defines and conditions our existence. Indeed, it is the cross that brings the resurrection into our lives. It is on the cross that we are to encounter the risen Christ suffering as the crucified Jesus. It is through the cross that we are to be embraced by the power of the new life imparted by the risen Christ. And it is in the cross that we are to be led into the mystery of the transfiguration, which will enable us to pitch our tent not on an isolated and deserted mountain but in the midst of human struggles. That is why the risen Christ issued again a command to Peter—the command that was given three years earlier when Peter was a fisherman: "Follow me!" (John 21:19). Peter and the church after him were commanded to follow the risen Christ to the cross. If we want to encounter the risen Christ, we must come to the cross. This is what the command of the risen Christ to follow him means. But the cross has been transfigured in the meantime. It is no longer the preresurrection cross but the cross of the risen Christ. It is a cross that leads not to death but to life, and that brings hope instead of despair.

The resurrection faith of a Christian community becomes a historical faith when the cross of the risen Christ becomes its central concern. Apart from this cross, there is no other way for the church or Christian community to become an effective force in the world. The church guided by the cross of the risen Christ is a historical church. An uninterrupted succession to the authority of Peter and the apostles is not what makes the church historical. A Christian community that serves primarily the cross of the risen Christ is an authentic community. It is not an inerrant interpretation of Scripture that makes it authentic. The cross of the risen Christ alone is that which makes a church and a Christian community historical and authentic.

Seen from this perspective, many churches in the Third World have become truly historical. As the cross of the risen Christ creates historical consciousness in the practice of their faith, they begin to find themselves a responsible part of the sociohistorical settings that differ radically from the settings of the lands from which their faith came. What their "mother" churches in the West say and theologize is no longer normative for them. The sociopolitical, religious, and cultural demands—in a word the historical demands—of the society to which they belong now dictate their reflections on, and practice of, the Christian faith. Until recently church history in the true sense of the word did not exist for many churches in the Third World. They formed merely a part of the history of the churches in the West. The church history class in seminaries always began, and in many instances still begins, with the Greco-Roman churches, it then turned to the Reformation in Europe, and concluded with the missionary expansion of the western churches to the Third World.[20] Christians in the Third World were taught to recognize their origins in the West but were not encouraged to wrestle with their own historical roots and destiny. But faith, detached from the history of believers, became a faith of the empty tomb, not of the risen Christ. It was a faith that sought its fulfillment after history passed into oblivion. The church with such a faith celebrated Easter Sunday as if the weekdays did not exist in God's creation. The Hallelujahs of the Easter Sunday service failed to echo Jesus' cry of dereliction on the cross and became hollow and empty. As Emerito Nacpil observed about the theological situation of the churches in the Philippines:

Jesus Christ as *Lord*—lord of salvation; lord of creation, not only of spiritual things but also of nature and of human and world history; lord of the eschaton, not only of personal destiny but also of the fulfillment and unification of all things in him—these christological theses, as well as other equally important theological themes, remain on the fringes of active faith and are underdeveloped in their theological and ethical significance.[21]

But how can a church without an intense historical consciousness tackle these essential questions of faith? How can a Christian community which has not come of age historically be able to view its task in the perspective of world history?

This trend, however, has decisively changed, thanks to the sociopolitical pressures that have brought the cross of the risen Christ right into the churches of the Third World. To give an example, in February 1976 the General Committee of the All Africa Conference of Churches, representing 114 member churches in 33 African countries, issued the "Confession of Alexandria." It in part declared:

Through the continuing work of Christ, God is charting His Highway of Freedom (Isaiah 40:3–5) from Alexandria to the Cape of Good Hope. By witnessing to the victorious power of the cross (Romans 8) we Christians in Africa are encouraged to be co-workers with all those who are called by God to participate in His work.[22]

The phrase "from Alexandria to the Cape of Good Hope" graphically sets the whole continent of Africa as the *locus* of African Christians' confession. In the early centuries of Christianity northern Africa with the cosmopolitan city of Alexandria as its center was one of the cradles of Christianity. In Alexandria the Old Testament was translated into Greek, Philo labored to interpret Judaism in the language of Hellenistic philosophy, and great Fathers of the early church such as Clement of Alexandria and Origen tirelessly expounded the Christian faith. It was also in northern Africa that the theological giants of Latin Christianity— Tertullian, Cyprian, and Augustine—laid a foundation for the theology and order of the Latin Church.[23] All this, as it turned out, was to be a preparation for the spread of the Christian faith northward across the Mediterranean Sea to Europe. Southward the great natural barrier of the Sahara Desert refused to yield to the penetration of Christianity until the dawn of the modern era. When the Christian faith made its appearance at long last south of the Sahara, it was clothed in an alien garb designed not for jungle dwellers and tribal communities but for the so-called civilized peoples of the world.

With this historical background in mind, we cannot fail to realize the significance of the fact that the African Confession was issued in Alexandria, an ancient city that was once a thriving center of Christianity. It was even more significant that the drafters of the Confession did not direct their gaze northward toward the Mediterranean Sea and beyond it to Europe. Instead, they made a complete turnabout and looked toward the southernmost tip of their vast continent, defying the Sahara Desert and embracing tens of thousands of square miles of territory to reach the Cape of Good Hope. For African Christians Africa has become their continent, its history their history, its suffering their suffering, and its joy their joy. The beating of drums is no longer considered an abominable superstition used merely to conjure up evil spirits and placate them, and hence something to be banned from the churches. It is the heartbeat of the African spirit shared by Christians in search of their destiny in God. Nor can dancing in ecstasy be regarded simply as an act of frenzy of the mind and the body. It is the human spirit in agony and joy seeking communion with a power beyond human control. It is the spirit of humanity seeking union with the Spirit of God. African Christians must be partners in this search. Thus the theology of African Christians must be a theology of Alexandria and the Cape of Good Hope; their church must be one that stretches from Alexandria to the Cape of Good Hope; and their destiny must be a destiny closely bound to their African brothers and sisters who are going through the painful process of liberation in all parts of Africa between Alexandria and the Cape of Good Hope. In short, they now hear the call "to respond to Christ on terms that are authentic, faithful and relevant to the men and women in Africa today."[24] African Christians have at last claimed Africa as their own home, accepted its heritage as theirs, and plunged into the struggle for liberation as their own struggle. In all this we see a genuine witness to the cross of the risen Christ in Africa.

### The God of History

In this chapter we began our discussion with the struggle of Korean Christians for freedom and human rights under a repressive government. We then proceeded to discuss how the cross, the resurrection, and the transfiguration must be interpreted together for the Christian faith to exercise its historical mission in the world. And as a further example the Confession of Alexandria was cited to demonstrate how African Christians are assuming their historical responsibilities in Africa today. The incarnation of the Christian faith in Third World countries has taken place. This is perhaps the most remarkable fact to be recorded and remembered in the history of Christianity during the latter part of the twentieth century. For in this period Christians outside the western world began to become "authentic, faithful, and relevant," to use the words of the Confession of Alexandria. And to become authentic, faithful, and relevant is to become historical. This is what the incarnation essentially means.

In the last analysis Jesus Christ is God's historical incarnation. Jesus Christ is everything God is in a historical setting. On account of this, he is authentic, faithful, and relevant. To put it differently, in him God becomes authentic, faithful, and relevant in relation to the world. Thus if we want to experience the authentic God, we must experience the authentic Jesus. If we seek to encounter the faithful God, we must encounter the faithful Jesus. And if we endeavor to perceive the relevant God, we must find him in the relevant Jesus. That is why Jesus said to Philip who asked him to show the Father to him: "Have I been all this time with you, Philip, and you still do not know me? Anyone who has seen me has seen the Father" (John 14:9).

In Jesus Christ God has become historical, and therefore he is the authentic, faithful , and relevant God. This is the most central message of the Bible. It is the axis around which stories and events related to the whole cosmos, and especially to the whole of humanity, revolve now and until the end of time. Because of this God, the storytellers of ancient Israel could advise us that God had heard the cry of the people of Israel enslaved in the land of Egypt. Subsequently that people found God in the midst of the agonizing process of their national struggle for independence. The God who hears is the God who intervenes in history. It is this recurrent theme of a God who intervenes that makes the Bible stories so exciting to read. To give another example: In the story of the flood, when Noah offered offerings on the altar after the great ordeal was over, "the Lord smelt the soothing odour." Whereupon God said, "Never again will I curse the ground because of man . . ." (Gen. 8:20–21). God smells our sorrow, anxiety, fear, and sin! The God who can smell human odor is the God who can save. He must be very near us to be able to smell us. Indeed, he is near us in that he has become one of us. Jesus Christ is God close to us. He is God with us. Our prayers make sense because God is near. To him we can unburden ourselves in real earnest like the Psalmist who prayed to him out of great distress:

> Lord, hear my prayer
> and let my cry for help reach thee.

Hide not thy face from me
when I am in distress.
Listen to my prayer
and, when I call, answer me soon;
for my days vanish like smoke,
my body is burnt up as in an oven (Ps. 102:1-3).

A genuine prayer is a prayer offered to the God who hears, sees, feels, and smells us. He is the authentic and relevant God. He is the power of love that relates all things to himself.

This historical God, who is both authentic and relevant, is at the same time a faithful God. A faithful God is not an unchanging God. In fact, he changes. An unchanging God is a metaphysical God who has removed himself from history. A metaphysical God who maintains always a stoic composure is not a historical God. For history changes. Today is of necessity different from yesterday, and tomorrow will be different from today. This simply means that history is conditioned by its inner dynamics to move toward the future. History is a creation of the power that brings the past into the present and the present into the future. This power of history is God. It constantly makes openings in a history that is apt to become enclosed, past, and dead. God is faithful to his creation precisely because he is this power. In forgiving us sinners, he creates a new possibility for us who are trapped in self-reproach and self-contradiction. In reconciling himself to us, he gives hope to us who are consumed by hate and despair. In dying with us, he bestows life to us who are consigned to the past and to death. Jesus Christ is this faithful God's forgiveness for our sins; he is God's hope and future for humanity; and he is God's reconciliation for the world. This God who became flesh in Jesus Christ is the God who was, is now, and ever shall be, world without end. But he is everlasting because he has become temporal. This God who changes is a faithful God. Only the God who changes can save.

We must direct our thoughts once again to the Christians of Korea as they continue to fight for freedom and human rights, giving witness to the authentic, relevant, and faithful God. They could have chosen to remain on the mountain of the transfiguration and forget about the suspension of democracy in their nation. But they had to come down from the mountain, realizing that there was no tent to pitch there. They opened the door of their church and joined the battle of conscience with their fellow citizens. They had to translate the experience of the transfiguration into efforts to bring about justice and freedom in their own society. They had to bear the cross of the risen Christ into the struggle of their nation.

The Christians of Korea might have opted for the joy of the resurrection and put behind them the pain of the cross. The cross might have been to them an awkward reminder of the past they wanted to forget as quickly as possible. That Easter morning service on Namsan mountain in Seoul might have been a joyful celebration, filled with angelic voices of a huge choir. The Easter sermon might have been an eloquent exhortation that lifted the hearts of the worshipers up to the high heavens. "Rabbi, how good it is that we are here!" (Mark 9:5) But the distribution of pamphlets appealing for the restoration of democracy shattered their tranquility. It reminded them that the true ministry of the cross carried out by the disciples began only after Jesus' resurrection. With the resurrection the mission of the disciples in the world began. Namsan mountain was to be a Galilee and a Sea of Tiberias for the Christians of Korea. There they heard the command of the risen Christ to feed the lambs and tend the sheep, not on a peaceful mountain but in the busy streets of Seoul, in prisons, and among the poor and the oppressed. They might have remained in the safety of their sanctuary to attend to their "spiritual" needs. But the silent cry of the people was too loud not to hear, too tragic not to heed, too urgent not to pay attention to. They had to transform their resurrection experience into a call for repentance directed to those in power. In so doing, they are also gripped by the power of the resurrection, the power that can change life and history. This is evident in the concluding words of the "Theological Declaration by Christian Ministers in the Republic of Korea, 1973":

Jesus, the Messiah, our Lord, lived and dwelt among the oppressed, poverty-stricken, and sick in Judea. He boldly stood in confrontation with Pontius Pilate, a representative of the Roman Empire, and he was crucified in the course of his witness to the truth. He was risen from the dead to release the power of transformation which sets the people free.[24]

Through Christians committed to give witness to the cross of the risen Christ, the Christian faith has become an authentic and relevant faith in Korea. The history of Korea can no longer disown the Christian faith as an alien faith. The people of Korea have no reason to regard Christians as strangers in their land. Korea has ceased to be a mission field of churches from outside. Instead, it is the mission field of God, and these confessing and witnessing Korean Christians are God's workers in God's vineyard.

In this way the cross of the risen Christ has proved to be a powerful language addressed to the historical realities of the peoples and nations in the Third World today. It is powerful not because it is armed with external power, be it political or economic, but because it is equipped with a compelling force that calls people to chart the "highway of freedom from Alexandria to the Cape of Good Hope,"[25] from the Caribbean Sea to Argentina's Cape Horn, or from Hokkaido, the northernmost island of Japan, to Bandung in Indonesia. As the cross of the risen Christ summons people to the way, the truth, and the life, it ceases to be the spiritual symbol of the Christian church alone. It becomes a sign and a symbol, expressing the hope as well as the suffering of people who long for liberation from the bondage of the body and the spirit. What is important here is not the physical shape of the cross with which a Christian community is identified. It stands for hope for a people in despair, for the future for those who see no way out of the present, and for life for those who are threatened by death. The cross of the risen Christ is a declaration that God is at work with men and women who struggle to bring about justice and freedom. It is, above all, the power of a God who is actively engaged with the world to realize the fulfillment of the purpose for which all things are created.

This cross of the risen Christ is therefore the full exposition of the mystery of the incarnation. It affirms that God has never lost touch and will never lose touch with human history. It declares that the face of his son Jesus is his face, Jesus' suffering is his suffering, Jesus' death is his death, and Jesus' resurrection is his resurrection. Furthermore, it testifies that just as Jesus is God, who has become one with humanity, so in the face of suffering, death, and the longing for eternal life on the part of men and women in their daily struggle, we are confronted with the face, suffering, death, and assurance of eternal life of God. The incarnation means therefore above all things that nothing—literally nothing—that happens in human life and in the world here and now can be regarded as having no relationship with God. The world is God's and God is in the world. All men and women are God's people and God is in us all—God near us, God with us, God in us, IMMANUEL.

An important conclusion can be drawn from the reflection we have just made: this historical God is a political God; this historical faith is a political faith; this historical Christian community is a political community and a historical Christian is a political Christian. To become historical is therefore to become political. How can we avoid this fundamental thesis of faith once the cross of the risen Christ is accepted as the center of Christian witness? The conclusion we have drawn from our discussion of the cross of the resurrection in this chapter will be a premise we shall want to explore further under the theme "A Political God" in the following chapter.

# CHAPTER 10

# A POLITICAL GOD

What is historical is political. This basic understanding of the relationship between history and politics is essential for the Christian churches in Asia today as they try to wrestle with the political implications of the Christian faith. Our discussion in the preceding chapter made it clear that the Christian faith is a historical event. For the center of this faith is the incarnation, the Word become flesh. Flesh is, of course, the stuff of history—the substance of life that is expressed in historical realities. And Jesus Christ is the flesh and stuff of history. By the same token, the transfiguration of Jesus Christ is the transfiguration of humanity's historical existence. The transfigured Christ must thus become flesh. He must become a power working within history to transform it. The resurrection is no exception. The resurrected Christ must become flesh, he must eat again with his disciples by the Sea of Tiberias, and must give them a new vision of his messianic mission. He must impart the power of the resurrection to all peoples and to all history. With the resurrection of Jesus Christ from the dead, a new life becomes not only a possibility but a reality, and a new history ceases to be just a future projection. History can now become part of a new creation in the present time. From the beginning to the end, history is the arena of God's creating-redeeming activities. It follows that the faith that refuses history also refuses God, and that the faith that rejects the world also rejects the Word become flesh in Jesus Christ.

But insofar as Christian faith is a historical event, it is also a political event. History has to do with human affairs. It deals with the rise and fall of empires and dynasties. It tells about endless efforts on the part of human beings to build their *polis*—the Greek word for "city" from which the term *politics* is derived—and to make a revolution within this *polis,* pulling down an old *polis* and putting up a new one. Thus history is a cycle of making and unmaking one *polis* after another. In poetic language Lao-tzu, whom we quoted in Chapter 1, expresses the cycles of power at work in human society in the following way:

> He who is to be made to dwindle (in power)
> Must first be caused to expand.
> He who is to be weakened

Must first be made strong.
He who is to be laid low
Must first be exalted to power.
He who is to be taken away from
Must first be given.
—This is the Subtle Light.[1]

Lao-tzu saw history as cycles of power. The cycles move forward, leaving destruction and decay behind and making room for a new future and new days yet to be born. Thus:

Man models himself after the Earth;
The Earth models itself after Heaven;
The Heaven models itself after Tao;
Tao models itself after Nature.[2]

History is the work of one grand cycle after another in which humanity seeks to discern the law of nature. And the fulfillment of history in conformity to nature is the supreme art of politics.

## Israel's God and the Politics of Liberation

As far as the Christian faith is concerned, God is experienced as a historical God confronting the world as a political God. God takes seriously political actions in the life of a people and in the history of nations. It is from such a historicopolitical dimension that the people of Israel came to know Yahweh their God. The history of the Old Testament is therefore not just a history. It is in fact a *political* history of Israel, which began with the Exodus—a historical event that became the chief political paradigm that played a decisive role in the formation of Israel's spirituality. As Gutiérrez puts it:

The liberation of Israel is a political action. It is the breaking away from a situation of despoliation and misery and the beginning of the construction of a just and fraternal society. It is the suppression of disorder and the creation of a new order.[3]

Salvation experienced as a liberation from the land of enslavement is first and foremost a political salvation. It is thus true to say that Moses' mission in Egypt had all the characteristics of a political expedition. What happened between Moses and the pharaoh was a political tug of war. It was a contest of political will and political power. Behind Moses were the people of Israel condemned to inhuman conditions of slavery and hard labor. Deprived of freedom, they nevertheless constituted a volatile political strength which could change into a revolutionary power. The massiveness of their will and power could be seen in their groans under extreme conditions of oppression. Their cries and groans were so massive, power-ful, and loud that even God heard them. "I have indeed seen the misery of my people in Egypt," God said to Moses. "I have heard their outcry against their slave-masters. I have taken heed of their sufferings, and have come down to rescue them from the power of Egypt . . . " (Exod. 3:7–8).

What makes human history tragic is the fact that slave masters and oppressors are determined not to hear what God has heard, are resolved not to see what God has seen, and condition themselves not to feel what God has felt. They thus put themselves in an impossible position of rivalry with God. In this story of the Exodus, which is the core of biblical political history, we read that if the cries and groans of the oppressed people of Israel failed to move the pharaoh, they moved God. They made heaven and earth shake and tremble. Armed with the powerful cries and groans of his people, Moses confronted the pharaoh with a tough political de-mand: "Let my people go!" But of course the pharaoh was not impressed. As master of the imperial court and inheritor of the divine power to rule the vast land of Egypt, he was full of disdain for Moses and his fellow slaves. His response to Moses' impudent demand was an even harsher command designed to break the will of the people to rebel and to crush their power to revolt. Here was the pharaoh's new order to his task-masters:

Let them go and collect their own straw, but see that they produce the same tally of bricks as before. On no account reduce it. They are a lazy people, and that is why they are clamoring to go and offer sacrifice to their god. Keep the men hard at work; let them attend to that and take no notice of a pack of lies (Exod. 5:8–9).

This is the classical language of an oppressor who scorns the oppressed. And as long as the oppressor reinforces oppression with this kind of language, the struggle of the oppressed against the oppressor is bound to reach a point not negotiable through peaceful means. When the people of Israel under Moses finally made their way out of the land of bondage, they left the place strewn with the corpses of their former oppressors. Before the terrible night of the bloody coup was over, "Pharaoh rose, he and all his courtiers and all the Egyptians, and a great cry of anguish went up, because not a house in Egypt was without its dead" (Exod. 12:30).

In this way the people of Israel stepped onto the historical stage of the ancient Near East through a political act of liberation. The political system of the pharaoh was synonymous with violence. If such a systematic vio-lence was to be broken, it must be through the organized resistance of the oppressed people. This is how the political history of the world is written. The organized violence on the part of an oppressed people after all peaceful means have been exhausted to bring the oppressor down from the seat of destructive authority is revolution. Political history, including the history of Israel, is in actual fact a record of revolutions. The people of Israel understood their revolution as a liberation, and their liberation as divine salvation. Rubem Alves's observation on the relation between violence and revolution can be aptly applied to our discussion here. According to Alves:

God's politics . . . is subversive of the stability created by the violence of the old. The false peace of unfreedom is out of balance and its walls of defense are made to crumble.

There is violence involved in the process. God does not wait for the dragon to become a lamb. He knows that the dragon will rather devour the lamb. It must be opposed and defeated by the power of the lamb. . . . [God] does not wait for the master to decide freely to liberate the slave. He knows that the master will never do that. So, he breaks the yoke and the erstwhile master can no longer dominate. The power of God destroys what makes the world unfree. This use of power looks like violence because it destroys the equilibrium and peace of the system of domination. But . . . what looks like the violence of the lion is really the power of counter-violence, that is, power used against those who generate, support, and defend the violence of a world of masters and slaves. Violence is power that oppresses and makes man unfree. Counter-violence is power that breaks the old which enslaves, in order to make man free. Violence is power aimed at paralysis. Counter-violence is power aimed at making man free for experimentation.[4]

Commenting on this passage with approval, Paul Lehmann speaks of violence as:

that apocalyptic possibility that thrusts all who are caught up in the correspondence between the biblical and the human meaning of politics . . . into the agony and abandon of "a life of absolute insecurity . . . and safety" (Bonhoeffer) in which all idolatry and self-justification crumble and the freedom of the divine ordination shapes once again the involvement in a world that God is making over and making new.[5]

Revolution, understood in Christian terms, is this apocalyptic possibility of violence at work in the present situation of oppression and unfreedom.

The political God who leaps out at us from the pages of the Book of Exodus is not a casual God. He is a God who takes the historico-political affairs of our world with the utmost seriousness. His political engagement with the world is always of an ultimate kind. For after all, only when men and women are liberated from the power that enslaves and dehumanizes them can they be free for God and for their neighbors. That is why the enslaved Israelites wanted to leave Egypt. They had to become free so that they could worship Yahweh their God. They must come out of their bondage in order to enter a new history with other nations. All this makes it evident that political involvement is not something alien to the nature of God or unessential to the life of the community of faith. The Exodus shows us the God engaged in political action with his people. The God who commissioned Moses to lead his people out of Egypt is a political God.

Throughout the history of ancient Israel, Yahweh never ceased to be a political God. The liberation movements against alien lords such as the pharaoh later became internalized and took the form of struggles against the dehumanizing power of the kings of Israel and Judah. Prophets now confronted the kings as Moses had confronted the pharaoh long before with the demand to set the people free form exploitation and oppression. Therefore, the mission of the prophets was a political mission aimed at the ruling elites of their times. In the northern kingdom a farmer-prophet, Amos, declared dramatically in the hearing of high officials:

> Assemble on the hills of Samaria,
> look at the tumult seething among the people
> and at the oppression in her midst;
> what do they care for honesty
> who hoard in their palaces
> the gains of crime and violence? (Amos 3:9–10).

In the south there was Micah, a contemporary of Isaiah's, who exposed the crimes in high circles of Samaria and Jerusalem and denounced the cruelty and injustice committed against a defenseless people. It must have been an excruciating anguish that prompted him to say:

> Listen, you leaders of Jacob, rulers of Israel,
> should you not know what is right?
> You hate good and love evil,
> you flay men alive
> and tear the very flesh from their bones;
> you devour the flesh of my people,
> strip off their skin,
> splinter their bones;
> you shred them like flesh into a pot,
> like meat into a cauldron (Mic. 3:1–3).

God's politics is politics against the barbarism of power. Oppressing the powerless and the defenseless is political barbarism. Exploiting the poor is economic barbarism. Intimidating the dissenters into silence is spiritual barbarism. The rulers of Israel and Judah, as the prophets proclaimed, committed such barbarism of power against their own people. They became a terror instead of a blessing to their subjects.

### The Barbarism of Power

This barbarism of power has continued down through the centuries. It has not ceased to bedevil the lives of peoples and to disturb the peace of the world. It is like a primordial monster lurking in the depths of the sea and seeking to throw human life into a bitter and painful confusion. Facts and statistics show that more and more people in the world today have to bear the brunt of political, economic, and spiritual barbarism. It is said, for instance, of the situation in Latin America:

Factors many times mentioned keep their actuality: a growing rate of unemployment, a constant increase of the cost of living, inadequate health provision, the desperate situation of rural families, never fulfilled official promises, the boom of corruption and gambling, the lack of freedom of expression, varied forms of violence, repressive legislation calculated to intimidate the people, the lack of participation of the people in decisions, etc. . . . . If anything, all these problems are escalating at a frightening speed.[6]

This is hardly what we would expect after all the hue and cry about the "development" that promises to turn Latin America into a modernized democratic region. In many instances, "development" has in fact become a political ideology in the hands of the rulers to expand and consolidate their political and economic power at the cost of the freedom and welfare of the people. "Consequently," writes Míguez Bonino:

social unrest is rampant on the continent, and populist regimes have been replaced, with the aid and support of the U.S.A., by military, repressive governments which can guarantee the stable conditions required by foreign investment.[7]

Here is an international conspiracy to fight God's politics of freedom and justice, to combat the Gospel for the poor and the oppressed!

The situation in Asia is not more encouraging. Traditionally, Asia has been a seething cauldron of feudalism, dictatorship, and colonialism. But a number of nations in Asia claim that they have taken a big step toward modernization and democratization. Have they indeed? Here facts are more eloquent than rhetoric. On September 21, 1972, martial law was declared in the Philippines, ending efforts toward the construction of a democratic society. On October 16, 1976, a referendum took place under the vigilant eyes of the armed forces to make the citizens demand the continuation of martial law. Despite all this, God's politics has not been entirely frustrated. Voices of protest have come from concerned citizens, bishops, and other Christians despite the threat of arrest and imprisonment. A manifesto was signed on September 21, 1976, by members of the Christian community who met in the Cosmopolitan Church of downtown Manila to protest the unconstitutionality of the October 16 referendum. The manifesto also presented some hard figures and statistics showing that an era of economic prosperity has yet to dawn for the masses of the people. The economic miracle claimed by the government has not taken place. What martial law accomplished instead was a growing gap between

the rich and the poor and a consolidation of power around the ruling
elite. The manifesto points out:

Today, the Philippines had the highest per capita external debt in all Asia.
. . . After four years of one man rule under martial law, the Philippine foreign
debt soared, according to Central Bank statistics, to $4.5 million as of June 30,
1976. While our technocrats go abroad shopping for more loans and begging for
roll-overs and extensions, the martial law administrators are busy emptying the
public treasury at home.

Two examples are cited to show how the people in real need have not
benefited from the declared intentions of martial law:

—US$440 million [were used] for the International Convention Center and a
dozen new private hotels financed at public expense, but less than US$1 million
for the National Housing Authority.
—US$60 million [were used] to finance and stage the Miss Universe contest in
1974, but only 1.15% of the 1976 budget for agrarian reform.

Such a show of extravagance is surely not conducive to the welfare of the
people in the streets. "So debt-ridden to international banking and financ-
ing institutions," says the manifesto, "is the regime that it cannot implement economic and social policies that will truly benefit the more than
80% of our people who are poor and deprived."[8]

This manifesto and other expressions of Christian conscience are God's
politics against the pretensions of martial law. Martial law carried out in
the Philippines and in other countries in Asia today is subversive to God's
politics of justice and freedom. The consolidation of political power
against the people—this is political barbarism that has become a threat to
human integrity and a challenge to the God from whom, according to St.
Paul, all authorities come (Romans 13). Under such circumstances, more
and more Christians will find themselves having to work with various
forces in their society to throw off the barbarism of power. Increasingly
they will be made to appreciate and practice evangelism as the proclamation of the good news of liberation from oppression, inhumanity, and
poverty.

In this matter Christians do not seem to have a choice. Both justice and
freedom—two of the key concepts of the biblical message—are political as
well as spiritual in nature. Because God is the God of justice, he cannot
allow the poor and the powerless to be oppressed. Justice is therefore a
sociopolitical concept that has immediate sociopolitical consequences. It
cannot be confined to a spiritual realm divorced from what is going on in
the world. Justice that does not extend beyond the sanctuary of Christian
fellowship in a church has little to do with the justice of God in the Old and
the New Testaments. The biblical meaning of justice or righteousness
(tsedaqah) makes this clear:

Righteousness is in the OT the fulfillment of the demands of a relationship, whether that relationship be with men or with God. Each man is set within a multitude of relationships: king with people, judge with complainants, priests with worshipers, common man with family, tribesmen with community, community with resident alien and poor, all with God. And each of these relationships brings with it specific demands, the fulfilment of which constitutes righteousness.[9]

It is thus clear that in the Old Testament understanding and practice of justice, the spiritual dimension of life intersects with its sociopolitical dimension. Justice is a sociopolitical demand as well as a spiritual quality. We cannot speak of being right with God without at the same time being right with our fellow human beings socially and politically. Injustice in society is a spiritual or religious offense as well as a sociopolitical offense. At the same time religious practices that condone and justify injustice in society are doubly offensive to a sensitive mind attuned to God's justice. That is why Isaiah relentlessly attacked the pseudoreligiosity of his day and exposed its banality. God is fed up and "sated with whole-offerings of rams and the fat of buffalos," declared Isaiah. God has "no desire for the blood of bulls, of sheep and of he goats" (Isa. 1:11). This is what those in positions of power should do:

> Cease to do evil and learn to do right,
> pursue justice and champion the oppressed;
> give the orphan his rights,
> plead the widow's cause (Isa. 11:17).

What the prophets of the Old Testament have shown us is a God intensely concerned about humanity's social and political well-being. God is justice. The violation of justice is a sin against God. Since the ordering of society is based on justice, a distortion of justice is therefore a disturbance of the just ordering of the world created by God. Since God's justice and sociopolitical justice cannot be separated, the prophets are thrust into the struggle against kings and rulers who abuse their power to infringe upon God's justice and violate the people's rights.

At this point the parable of the lamb, which Nathan told to bring King David to his knees, comes at once to mind. David had used his kingly authority to commit a breach of trust and a violation of justice toward his loyal general, Uriah. David first usurped Bethsheba, Uriah's wife, and he then caused Uriah's death on the battlefield (2 Sam. 11). Unaware that Nathan's parable of the lamb that the rich man took by force from his poor neighbor to entertain his visitor was directed against himself, David exclaimed in indignation: "As the Lord lives, the man who did this deserves to die!" Then came the thunderous voice of judgment from Nathan to the king: "You are the man!" This encounter between King David and the prophet Nathan is a dramatic illustration of how God's justice must be translated into sociopolitical justice. God's justice weighs heavily on the social and political conscience of those who profess to embrace the biblical faith.

Another example is Jeremiah's condemnation of Jehoiakim, the despotic king of Judah. Although Jeremiah knew the risk he was taking, his language was sharp, bitter, and indignant. Here was a defenseless man who dared to stand against a powerful tyrant and point out the ruler's sin against God's justice and his crime against the people's rights:

> Shame on the man who builds his house by unjust means
> and completes its roof-chambers by fraud,
> making his countrymen work without payment,
> giving them no wage for their labour!
> Shame on the man who says, "I will build a spacious house
> with airy roof-chambers,
> set windows in it, panel it with cedar
> and paint it with vermillion!"
> If your cedar is more splendid,
> does that prove you a king?
> Think of your father: he ate and drank,
> dealt justly and fairly; all went well with him.
> He dispensed justice to the lowly and poor;
> did not this show he knew me? says the Lord.
> But you have no eyes, no thought for anything but gain,
> set only on the innocent blood you can shed,
> on cruel acts of tyranny (Jer. 22:13–17).

"Here is the strongest condemnation," says one commentator, "the prophet uttered against any of the Judean kings."[10] At a time when the nation of Judah was in imminent danger of invasion by the Babylonians, Jehoiakim was using his kingly power to exploit the people to satisfy his own greed and whims. No wonder the prophet Jeremiah, who was commissioned to speak for the God of justice, came to a showdown with him. Here Jeremiah clearly stood on the side of a people victimized by their brutal ruler. He was thus the hope of God for a beleaguered nation.

### Obedience or Submissive Acquiescence?

What does this political history of Israel teach us? What are some practical implications we can draw from it? What are some of the main convictions underlying the involvement of prophets in political affairs? How does this picture of a political God with his stern judgments tally with the image of God as all-loving and all-forgiving? To these questions we will now turn.

First of all, I must emphasize that political disobedience can be an essential form of service that a Christian community can render to its nation, particularly at a critical time. This insight gained from the involvement of the prophets in Israel's political history is of the utmost importance, especially to the Christians of Asia. For the Christians of Asia are under a twofold pressure to regard obedience as the supreme virtue. On the one hand, they are part of a society that traditionally upholds obedience as the basis of social relations and the political order. We may even go so far as to say that obedience is the basis on which feudalism is constructed and by which the loyalty of individuals to their society and nation is judged. This is the case, for instance, with the traditional sociopolitical order of China and Japan that has been profoundly influenced by Confucianism. In Confucius' *Analects* we find Confucius' exhortation to a son:

As you serve your parents you should remonstrate with them only slightly. If on doing so you find that they are set in having their own way, be even more respectful and do not thwart them. Even though this overwhelm you with toil, do not become angry with them.[11]

And further: "If for the three years [of mourning] one does not change from the ways of the father, one may be called filial."[12] Here a rigid observance of the father-son relationship on the one hand and the preservation of the status quo on the other are considered essential to filial piety. The relationship between ruler and ruled is the extension of this order of the family relationship. Thus, when Duke Ching of the state of Ch'i asked Confucius about the nature of good government, the reply was: "Let the prince be as a prince. Let the minister be as a minister. Let the father be as a father. Let the son be as a son."[13] It has to be admitted that Confucius and particularly his greatest follower Mencius (371–289 B.C.) speak of the love and compassion of the ruler for the ruled.[14] But the underlying principle that governs these sociopolitical relationships is obedience of the inferior to the superior. Obedience, almost absolute obedience, is the foundation stone of the hierarchical society in traditional China and Japan. Protest against the ruler or the superior is not only an expression of disrespect but also a disturbance of the predetermined order of society and human relationships. Therefore the authority of the ruler cannot be infringed upon with impunity.

Nurtured in such a social ethos and political tradition, Asian Christians quickly came to identify obedience to God with obedience to the political authorities. If obedience is considered essential to the relationship with God, it is also regarded as uncontestable in the relationship with the rulers. And when salvation is understood almost totally in terms of the spirit rather than of the whole person, that is, body as well as spirit, Christians in Asia, particularly Christians belonging to Chinese-speaking churches, disavow the involvement in social and political affairs as unspiritual—even worse, they think of it as harmful to salvation. A concern for social injustice and political anomalies is dubbed "interference in politics" and banned by the church. It seldom occurs to them that their unquestioning obedience to the ruling authorities is also a form of involvement in politics—and a lamentable form of political involvement at that. By being obedient to the political authorities—even when the latter commit injustice, exploit the people, and deprive them of their freedom—Christians become accomplices of political evil and social malaise. They have lost the freedom of the Old Testament prophets to speak to the rulers in the name of God their Lord. No wonder that personal salvation has become the single important subject matter of the Christian faith for many Christians under an authoritarian government.

This shows that mere obedience is not enough, for it often turns into submissive acquiescence. The Christian who advocates submissive acquiescence as part of what he understands by Christian obedience fails the God who has been politically involved not only in the history of Israel but in the history of all nations. Dorothee Sölle is therefore right when she says:

. . . man is not unconditionally placed under the demands of a sovereign ruler, whose lordship is analogous to that of an oriental despot. In the Old Testament obedience is always related to justice. Under no circumstances is it related to the ruler in a completely authoritarian manner.[15]

### St. Paul on Civil Obedience

In this connection, how are we to understand the thirteenth chapter of Paul's letter to the Romans? "Every person must submit to the supreme authorities," St. Paul counseled the Christians living in the heart of the Roman Empire. Why does one have to obey the state authority? To this political question St. Paul gives a theological answer. "There is no authority but by the act of God," he theologizes, "and the existing authorities are instituted by him" (Romans 13:1). The argument appears to be conclusive. God is the source of all authority, and the state authority is part and parcel of divine authority. Hence, just as we obey God's authority, so we must submit to the state authority. It is therefore not surprising that Romans 13 has become the text used as a proof by Christians who regard political involvement as not the business of the church. Submission to the state authority seems to have a solid biblical basis.[16]

But the conclusion drawn by "nonpolitical" Christians from Romans 13 is an oversimplification of the Pauline theology of authority. It takes for granted that, since the state authority is derived from God, it must be obeyed without further question. It does not take into consideration the fact that the state authority, though instituted by God, can and does go astray, can and does become reactionary, and can and does pose a challenge to God's authority. Moreover, the conclusion drawn by nonpolitical Christians does not raise the following question: if and when the state authority goes astray and practices oppression and injustice, what should Christians do? It is agreed that they are to submit themselves to God's authority, which is good, loving, and redemptive. But does submission to such an authority of God require at the same time Christians to submit themselves to a state authority that has become evil, unloving, and destructive?

This brings us back to the problem of how to interpret Romans 13. Here Karl Barth can help us gain a better insight into this controversial passage. In his famous *Epistle to the Romans* he treats the passage in question, namely, vv. 1–7, by attaching Romans 12:21 to it. It reads as follows:

Do not let evil conquer you, but use good to defeat evil. Every person must submit to the supreme authorities. There is no authority but by the act of God, and the existing authorities are instituted by him. . . .

To understand Romans 13:1–7 in the light of Romans 12:21, or the whole passage of Romans 12:17–21, is very important. In this latter passage Paul deals with the problem of evil and discusses ways to combat it. He advocates a positive attitude when he says: "Use good to defeat evil." In the true spirit of Christ, Paul is here saying that evil is not to be condoned but to be defeated with good. The negative that is evil must be overcome with the positive that is good. Thus Christians are not to be complacent about evil or withdraw from it.

By evil Paul does not only mean something that has to do with the morality of private individuals. Evil is not just a vice affecting the moral integrity of individuals. It can also be social and political. It affects social and community life; corrupts political systems; involves the misuse of political authority; and disturbs the sociopolitical order conducive to the well-being of the people. Evil therefore must be defeated. And as far as Christians are concerned, they are to overcome evil with good—good in the sense of justice, truth, and love. Evil cannot be defeated with evil, for this will only lead to a greater evil. One evil cannot be exposed by another evil. It is truth that discloses the falseness of evil. It is justice that exposes the injustice inherent in evil. And it is love that can effectively confront the destructive power of evil. Ultimately, the good with which Christians are to defeat evil resides in and comes from God. He is the criterion of what it means to be good. It is from God as goodness itself that the state derives its authority. And insofar as the state authority reflects the goodness of God, it is to be respected and obeyed. For this reason Paul stresses that the existing authorities are instituted by God. But if the state authority turns evil, the implication from Romans 12:21 is that evil must be defeated with good, that is, with truth, justice, and love that comes from God. Existing authorities instituted by God cannot thus escape the judgment of God when they become evil. Submission to such evil authorities is not only absurd but unethical and unholy. This means that criticism of existing authorities is a religious obligation as well as a political duty of Christians as children of God and citizens of this world.

The interpretation of Romans 13:1–7 in the light of Romans 12:21 yields the insight that Christian submission to the existing authorities should by no means lead to a slavish obedience. It involves active efforts by Christians to insure that the existing authorities do conform to the goodness of God. In Barth's words:

> He of whom the *power* is and by whom every existing authority is ordained is God the Lord, the Unknown, Hidden God, Creator and Redeemer, the God who elects and rejects. This means that the mighty *powers that be* are measured by reference to God, as are all human, temporal, concrete things. God is their beginning and their end, their justification and their condemnation, their "Yes" and their "No". If we adopt an attitude of revolution towards them—and this is the attitude adopted in the Epistle to the Romans, as is shown by the unmistakable fact that the passage dealing with human *rulers* follows immediately after the passage dealing with the *enemy* and is prefaced by the quite clear statement that men are to overcome *evil*, the attitude of revolution is, nevertheless, crossed by the reflection that it is only in relation to God that the evil of the existing order is really evil.[17]

Fundamentally speaking, evil is to be judged as evil not because it offends our personal taste, is at odds with our moral codes, does not respect our sense of decency, and infringes upon our precious private conscience. Evil is evil primarily and ultimately because it seeks to abolish God and turn his creation into chaos. Evil is a public challenge to God before it becomes a private attack upon all of us.

Commenting further on the concept of "defeating evil with good" in Romans 12:21, Barth leaves us without a shadow of doubt as to what Christian obedience to the state authorities means in the context of Romans 13:

> There is here no word of approval of the existing order; but there is endless disapproval of every enemy of it. It is God who wishes to be recognized as He that *overcometh* the unrighteousness of the existing order. This is the meaning of the commandment; and it is also the meaning of the Thirteenth Chapter of the Epistle to the Romans.[18]

If Barth's exegesis is correct, we must accept the following implications Disobedience to the existing authorities can sometimes be judged as an act that seeks to defeat evil with good. This is no doubt a political action, and we must acknowledge it as such. But insofar as an act of disobedience to an existing authority that has turned evil is an act of obedience to God, it ceases to be a purely political action. It becomes a confession of faith. One thing becomes therefore very clear: Christian political action rooted in faith in God is not motivated by ambition for political power but by obedience to God who wants to defeat evil with good. It is, in the final analysis, a work of love—the love that seeks to bring good even to those involved in evil as well as to those victimized by evil. It is thus no accident that St. Paul links our political duties with love. In his words, "Love cannot wrong a neighbor; therefore the whole law is summed up in love" (Romans 12:10). Love that becomes disobedient to a political authority that has become oppressive and evil is a love that heals, restores, and redeems. The political involvement of Christians ought to be a politics of love.

So much for submission to the existing authorities. We must now consider a second point in relation to the prophets' attitude toward kings and rulers. It can be summarized as follows: the political God of the Old Testament prophets is the God who takes sides. In a sense it is true to say that politics is essentially a matter of taking sides in accordance with your views and convictions. This is most obvious in a nation that practices a democratic system of government. In a democratic society people exercise the freedom of taking sides through elections. Elections are a political process that enables us to say either yes or no, to vote for this candidate and not for another candidate, to express our approval for this particular issue and our disapproval for other issues. It is the constitutional responsibility of a truly democratic government to protect the people's right to take sides politically without being harrassed or threatened. A totalitarian nation, in contrast, is marked by the suppression of this basic political right of the people. Under a totalitarian system of government, the right to take political sides especially in opposition to the official position is nonexistent or severely curtailed. Political dissidents, namely, those people who openly take sides in opposition to the government, must therefore pay the price of imprisonment, expulsion, or even death.

But the God of the prophets, and for that matter the God of Jesus Christ, is a God who takes sides. Under a totalitarian regime, God will be branded as a dissident God. He takes the side of the poor against the rich. In the words of Isaiah, God "has been a refuge to the poor and a refuge to the needy in his trouble" (Isaiah 25:4). Jesus is even more unequivocal about God's taking the side of the poor. After the rich young man had left him in sadness when asked to sell his wealth and give it to the poor, Jesus said to his disciples:

I tell you this: a rich man will find it hard to enter the kingdom of Heaven. I repeat, it is easier for a camel to pass through the eye of a needle than for a rich man to enter the kingdom of God (Matt. 19:23–24).

And as pointed out earlier, Jesus considers his mission as that of "announcing good news to the poor, proclaiming release for prisoners, letting the broken victims go free." In essence, these constitute for Jesus the mission "to proclaim the year of the Lord's favour" (Luke 4:18–19).

### The Crisis of Conscience

How then is it possible for the church to be the church of God if it refuses to take sides when a social and political situation demands it? In fact, not to take sides often amounts to taking the side of the rich and the powerful, which from the standpoint of biblical faith is the wrong side. We do not lack examples of the church taking the wrong side. In a letter to Pope Paul VI, for example, the Bureau of the Latin American Committee of Christian Trade Unions, which has some 5 million Catholic members, said during the Eucharistic Congress of 1968:

> Beware, brother Paul. Religion and the church have constantly been used in Latin America to justify and buttress injustice, oppression, repression, exploitation, persecution, the murder of the poor.[19]

Míguez Bonino, the Argentine theologian, calls this "a crisis of conscience." "It is a crisis of conscience," he writes, "when Christians discover that their churches have become the ideological allies of foreign and national forces that keep the countries in dependence and the people in slavery and need."[20] This crisis of conscience has been very much a force motivating many Christians in Latin America to become actively involved in efforts for a sociopolitical transformation. They participate in sociopolitical movements to bring about a new day that will be marked by justice, freedom, equality, and love—qualities foreshadowing the coming kingdom of God. In the words of Míguez Bonino again:

> When Latin American Christians tentatively speak of "a theology of liberation," "a Church of the poor," "the Church of the people," "revolutionary Christianity," and many other expressions which are always quite inadequate and sometimes even misleading, what really is at stake is the urgency to understand what it means to be the people of God in the new Latin America which is painfully emerging.[21]

A crisis of conscience has thus led many Christians to be on the side of those who suffer economically and politically. The Latin American theology of liberation is a theology that attempts to give articulation to the power of a political God at work among the suffering people. It is a theology that takes sides.

Another example of a church taking the wrong side comes from the experience of the United Church of Christ in Japan (Kyodan) during World War II. Under the pressure of a militaristic government, the Kyodan found itself giving a tacit, though unwilling, support to the war of aggression against China and the countries of Southeast Asia. Apart from a few exceptions, notably some leaders in the so-called non-church movement,[22] there was no resistance or open protest against what can be termed "the crime of the century" that Japanese imperialists committed against their fellow Asians. The following statement by Daikichi Tagawa is an explanation for the silence of the church and Japanese Christians at this critical time in the history of Japan and of Asia:

We Japanese Christians have been very severely criticised, especially by American and Chinese Christians, on account of our attitude toward the so-called Manchurian problem. The main point of such criticism seems to be that we did nothing at the time of the outbreak of the trouble there. Why were we silent? Were we in favour of our government's policy or against it? Were we living or dead with respect to the issues involved? These are questions which our fellow Christians in other lands could not understand at all.

I do not say that these criticisms are entirely wrong, but in reply to them I would say that at the time we Christians did not understand what to say or how to act. There was nothing for us to do except to keep silent. In Japan there is not a single Christian daily newspaper or a single Christian magazine devoted to the discussion of political, economic, or financial problems. Therefore Japanese Christians, as a whole, stand outside the sphere of political, economic, and financial interests, and are unfitted to judge the right and wrong and the merits and demerits with respect to such problems. This is the situation at present, and has been the situation for many years, being in fact the traditional Christian attitude toward these subjects.[23]

This is not so much an explanation as a "cop-out," so to speak. It may be true, as Junichi Asano, a Japanese theologian, states:

that the historic foundations within the tradition of the church in Europe out of which critical decisions in relation to issues of state and society could emerge were lacking for the Christians in Japan.[24]

But at the same time one has to bear in mind that obedience to the state authority, as has been discussed above, tended to be accepted by Christians in Asia in general not only as a civil virtue but as a religious virtue also. It is this virtue that produces blind obedience to the state authority and results in an uncritical alliance with it. When a religion is dominated by this kind of blind obedience, it can easily become an instrument of the state authority in pursuit of its destructive ambition. By keeping silent when tens of millions of people in Asia were suffering from the insane pursuit of power by the Japanese military leaders, Japanese Christians became willy-nilly the latters' accomplices in a war of destruction.

The conduct of the Kyodan during the war must have been a heavy burden to the conscience of Japanese Christians in the postwar period. We may surmise that there was a lot of repentance among them after the terrible nightmare was over. On Easter Sunday, March 26, 1967, the

Kyodan made public its "Confession on the Responsibility of the United Church of Christ in Japan during World War II."[25] While we may wonder why it took twenty-one years to express their repentance, nonetheless their decision to confess their sin was an important step in asking God's forgiveness for the past and his guidance for the future. The Confession is therefore an act of catharsis, or purification. It says:

The Church, as "the light of the world" and as "the salt of the earth," should not have aligned itself with the militaristic purposes of the government. Rather, on the basis of our love for her and by the standard of our Christian conscience, we should have more correctly criticized the policies of our motherland. However, we made a statement at home and abroad in the name of the Kyodan that we approved of and supported the war, and we prayed for victory.

This is an acknowledgement in humility and repentance of the fact that the Kyodan had taken the wrong side. By aligning itself with the wrong party and praying for its victory, the church involuntarily turned itself against the God who was on the side of Asia's people who suffered under the relentless cruelty of Japanese militarism. The Confession thus continues:

Indeed, as our nation committed errors we, as a church, sinned with her. We neglected to perform our mission as a "watchman." Now, with deep pain in our heart, we confess this sin, seeking the forgiveness of our Lord, and from the churches and our brothers and sisters of the world, and in particular of Asian countries, and from the people of our own country.

Toward the end of the Confession, a vision of the Kyodan is directed to the future. Forgiveness must bear fruits. "At this moment," concludes the Confession, "so that the Kyodan can correctly accomplish its mission in Japan and the world, we seek God's help and guidance. In this way we look forward to tomorrow with humble determination."

The Confession makes it clear that taking sides politically is an extremely risky business. When the church and Christians take the wrong side, they set themselves in opposition to God. We are thus reminded of the bold pronouncement of Peter when he was brought to trial before the High Priest. "We must obey God rather than men," he declared (Acts 5:29). This is not a question of divided loyalty. As far as Christians are concerned, there is only one loyalty—loyalty to God. This is the loyalty that can bring justice, freedom, and love to those to whom these basic qualities are denied. At the same time, this kind of loyalty may enable the state authority to use its power in fulfillment of the purposes for which it was instituted.

The political God to whom Christians owe their ultimate loyalty is a constructive God. This is a third point that engages us in our discussion here. God is the God of construction and not of destruction. He creates and recreates. He redeems and reredeems. He constructs and reconstructs. The political activity of God is therefore always positive because it is directed to the creation of new human relationships, the redemption of the cosmic order, and the construction of new creatures. One of the most dramatic examples of this is found in the Second Isaiah. The message of comfort delivered to those in exile is a message of reconstruction from a constructive God.

> Comfort, comfort my people;
> —it is the voice of your God;
> speak tenderly to Jerusalem
> and tell her this,
> that she has fulfilled her term of bondage,
> that her penalty is paid;
> she has received at the Lord's hand
> double measure for all her sins (Isa. 40:1-2).

Here is the essence of the political theology of the Old Testament. The politics of God working in the history of Israel is the politics of his redemptive love in construction and reconstruction. The Exile—a national calamity that brought shame, destruction, and despair to the people of Israel—was after all a part of God's constructive work with them.

This leads us to re-examine whether Christian involvement in sociopolitical change can be termed insurrectional or subversive. It is insurrectional in relation to the powers that be that refuse to replace oppression with freedom. It is subversive only insofar as the state authority turns a deaf ear to the cry of justice. It becomes rebellious when the rulers become incapable of love and compassion. In other words, Christian political action is in itself *not* insurrectional, subversive, or rebellious. On the contrary, it is redemptive, constructive, and creative. But for the powers that be that regard it as a challenge and threat to its authority, it does become insurrectional, rebellious, and subversive. What happens in Christian political action is the confrontation of the politics of the existing authority and the politics of God. The history of Israel in the Old Testament is the history of this confrontation. In many dictatorial and semidictatorial nations today, we see re-enactments of such confrontations with varied degrees of intensity. And there is no question about the fact that it is the existing authority that proves to be insurrectional, rebellious, and subversive vis-à-vis the politics of God.

Can we not draw from this a rather dangerous conclusion? The more Christian political concern takes on an insurrectional, rebellious, and subversive character under a repressive state authority, the more it resembles the politics of God. To state it more clearly, if the church has no message of justice to proclaim to a ruling authority that practices injustice toward its people, the church has opted out of the politics of God. If a Christian community speaks of peace and prosperity in a nation facing an imminent danger of traumatic sociopolitical change, that community of Christians is less true to the political God who exposes a false peace and a deceptive prosperity. The politics of God in such a situation must be a politics of repentance. It is a call to the rulers to repent of their sins of oppression and injustice. It is also a call to the people as a whole not to accept false security at the cost of freedom. The politics of repentance must then become a politics of change. It is a demand for a radical change in the structure of the governing power and its political behavior. It is a change dictated by what is good and true for the people as a whole and not just for a handful of powerholders. It is a change that brings about a democratization of power. It is the politics of repentance and change that is at the same time a politics of comfort. For within the framework of this politics of repentance and change, the restoration of humanity in accordance with the image of God becomes possible. Humanity becomes free again. Justice becomes a reality, and love becomes the way of sociopolitical life.

The politics of God is therefore not only a politics that liberates an oppressed people from oppression and injustice but also liberates the oppressors from the false pretenses and acts of violence with which they strengthen their rule. In fact, an oppressive state authority is a bundle of contradictions and a chain of vicious circles. Their power is built on lies and the illegitimate use of the power entrusted to them. In that power are combined ideological lies and military power. They enforce their lies with the points of bayonets. It is a violation of the truth. Dictatorship is thus a nightmare of whatever is true, good, and decent in humanity. The violence it practices leads to the dehumanization of what it means to be created in the image of God. The politics of God aims to do away with such a bundle of contradictions created by dictatorial rule. It attempts to break the chain of vicious circles that bind people to injustice, oppression, and a lack of freedom. When this vicious circle of contradictions is broken, liberation not only comes to the oppressed but also to the oppressors. The oppressors no longer have to pretend to be what they are not. They can stop their lies. They can be liberated from the illusions of power with which they justify their rule. They will, in a word, be set free from a politics of make-believe. After all, the politics of God is incompatible with the politics of make-believe, for it confronts injustice with justice, deception with truth, bondage with freedom, and terror with love. God's politics of construction begins by exposing the politics of make-believe under the light of truth, justice, and love. The participation of Christians in this politics of God is thus a part of God's redemptive work.

*Statements of the Presbyterian Church in Taiwan*

We have already made mention of the Christians of South Korea and the Philippines and their struggle for justice and freedom. Another example can be cited to illustrate how God's politics of construction is at work in the midst of the politics of make-believe. This is the case of the Christians of Taiwan. I am here referring to the "Public Statement on Our National Fate" issued by the Presbyterian Church in Taiwan on December 30, 1971. For a quarter of a century the Nationalist government on Taiwan had been practicing the politics of illusion. In 1945 it had emerged from the tragic war of resistance against Japan as a victor, having sustained cruel devastations and an enormous loss of life. But the civil war with the Communists flared up again quickly, giving the Nationalist party no time to recover from the war of resistance against Japan. This time the Communists were victorious. In confusion and chagrin the defeated Nationalists fled to the safety of Taiwan, an island separated from mainland China by the hundred miles of the Taiwan Strait. The tide of history had definitely turned against the Nationalists, but they refused to face the historical reality of their situation. As a result, the international and domestic policies of the Nationalist government were based on two claims: (1) that it was the sole legitimate government of China, and (2) that its sacred duty was to liberate the mainland from the Communists. In the early days of its exile in Taiwan, these two claims were real and urgent enough to constitute rallying points for the people. But as time went on and nothing came of them, the claims began to lose their impact. They became mere words that had no relationship to reality. And in proportion to the loss of real meaning in these claims, their ideological rigidity was intensified. They became dogmas defying any challenge to their validity or authority. They were elevated to the status of sacred cows that devour anyone who dares to interfere with them. Open allegiance to these dogmas became the test of correct thinking and loyalty to the ruling authorities.

Then came the expulsion of the Republic of China—the official name for the Nationalist government—from the United Nations in the winter of 1971. This blow shook the whole island like a hurricane buffeting a small ship at sea. After almost thirty years the people awakened from a bad dream to realize the vulnerability of Taiwan's international situation. There was a great deal of heart searching, especially among university students and teachers. They understood quickly that their national destiny was at stake and that they could no longer entrust their future to a one-party government without a murmur of complaint. But as a Chinese saying goes, misfortune is seldom unrepetitive. Even as a fierce battle was being fought at the United Nations in New York City, United States

Secretary of State Henry Kissinger was negotiating in Peking with the rulers of Communist China. An early result of these negotiations was President Richard M. Nixon's visit to China, which the Japanese called the *Nixon shokku.* This put an end to Communist China's isolation from the rest of the world. President Nixon himself later called his visit to China "a week which changed the world." The confusion and panic on Taiwan could hardly be suppressed. And in this critical situation the Presbyterian Church in Taiwan, as mentioned, broke its long silence and took the unprecedented action of issuing the "Public Statement on Our National Fate." It spoke aloud what the people of Taiwan were thinking, and perhaps even what many enlightened Nationalist Chinese officials were thinking too.

The church's statement was, in the first place, an appeal for the unity of all the people on Taiwan regardless of their origin. It affirms the desire of the people of Taiwan to live in peace, freedom, and justice. It rejected an attempt on the part of foreign powers to take over Taiwan. And it claimed in no uncertain terms the right of self-determination for Taiwan. In the words of the statement:

We oppose any powerful nation disregarding the rights and wishes of fifteen million people and making unilateral decisions to their own advantage, because God has ordained and the United Nations Charter has affirmed that every people has the right to determine its own destiny.

In this assertion of faith in a specific political situation, God's politics and human politics were joined in the politics of self-determination. The "self" that here claimed the right to be directly involved in the settlement of Taiwan's political future was not a wilful self seeking to gratify its own private interests. It was rather the self created in the image of God, and thus it shared the anguish and glory of all humanity. This self was thus inviolable, just as the image of God is inviolable.

The last part of the statement was pointedly directed to "the leaders of the Republic of China," that is, the heads of the Nationalist Party. It reminded them that this critical moment had to be grasped as an opportunity to commit themselves to justice and freedom and to a "thorough internal renewal." It boldly called for a general election through which a new government might come into existence to charter the future course of Taiwan. It voiced its conviction that the democratization of political power was a true, sure way to a secure, hopeful future for Taiwan.

Once the Presbyterian Church in Taiwan had set out on the course that caused its members' involvement in God's politics, the church became aware of its growing ability to say what had to be said about a political situation that continues to be critical and vulnerable. The immediate question facing the people of Taiwan had to do with the fear that they might be abandoned by the United States, which was beginning to pursue both openly and covertly, the goal of normalizing its relations with Communist China. And yet there was no sign that the ruling party of Taiwan would take effective steps to ensure the independence and freedom of Taiwan. The only thing the people could hear was the government's hollow claim to be the sole legitimate ruler of mainland China.

On August 16, 1977, the Presbyterian Church in Taiwan published another public statement, "A Declaration on Human Rights." Its occasion was the political uncertainty caused by the Nationalist government's stubborn refusal to change its policies in spite of the United States government's new attitude toward Peking. The Declaration, published when Mr. Vance, Secretary of State of the Carter government, was about to make his Peking visit, made it clear that self-determination was a right of the 17 million people of Taiwan which could neither be ignored nor taken away without serious consequences. It expressed the determination to oppose any use of force on Taiwan by Communist China. The Declaration then concluded with words that came right from the heart of the people, even though they could not have been spoken previously without a serious threat to those who proclaimed them.

In order to achieve our goal of independence and freedom for the people of Taiwan in this critical international situation, we urge our government to face reality and to take effective measures whereby Taiwan may become a new and independent country.[26]

The die was cast. It was now up to the government either to take "effective measures" by which the independence and freedom of Taiwan could be secured, or to resort to its usual "repressive measures" once again in order to silence the voice of the great majority of the people on the island state of Taiwan. No wonder the Declaration was drafted and made public only after much prayer.

What we have seen here is God's politics of construction at work through the Presbyterian Church in Taiwan. We must reject as a fallacy the concept that politics must be left in the hands of professional politicians and the ruling authorities. Since policies and the political behavior of those in power directly affect the well-being of a people and their destiny, each person in a nation should be both the subject and the object of political decisions and actions. There is no question that an involvement in politics is both a right and a duty of responsible citizens. Christians, who are citizens of this world and partners in God's politics of making all things new, have no reason to give up their political rights or to avoid their political duties. For our God is a political God. And above all ours is a God who judges repressive powers, condemns tyranny, and puts down the authorities that have become an instrument of evil rather than of good.

# CHAPTER 11

# THE TRANSPOSITION OF POWER

In politics "the analytical element most stressed is power. A political act is one performed in power perspectives."[1] Power is the root of all things political. Politics is basically a power struggle among contending parties and the possession of power is therefore the chief concern of all human political activities. By way of contrast, God's politics does not consist of attempts to seize power. What it aims at is the transformation of power. God's politics is therefore a transformation of human politics. It does not seek to rule and dominate but rather to effect a repentance of power. And in this transformation, or *metanoia* of power, is found the essence of God's politics.

The appearance of John the Baptist in the Jordan Valley is an example of God's politics in the New Testament. That stern preacher of repentance attracted all kinds of people who listened anxiously to his message of God's judgment and forgiveness. Among his listeners were some who had direct power over the people. "Master, what are we to do?" they asked John. He replied to the tax collectors: "Exact no more than the assessment." In other words, they must replace dishonesty and injustice by honesty and justice in the exercise of their power to tax the people. To soldiers he said: "No bullying; no blackmail; make do with your pay" (Luke 3:12–14). The power of the soldiers should be for the protection of the people. The power of the sword must not be used to terrify but to maintain order and justice. The Gospel for those who have power is therefore a Gospel of repentance aimed at a transformation of social, military, or political power.

The *metanoia* of power occupied a central place in everything Jesus said and did. From the beginning to the end he was confronted by the naked power of the religious and state authorities of his day. Soon after his birth, he had to be taken to Egypt to escape the ruthless power of King Herod, who rightly sensed in Jesus a potentially formidable threat to his throne. Throughout Jesus' ministry his enemies sought to undermine him with the combined strength of their religious and political power. In one sense the cross marked the success of the religious and political plot to do away

222

with him. Power was a reality that determined the fate of the people, even the fate of a Messiah. No wonder Jesus dedicated his entire life to the *metanoia* of power, trying to bring about a transformation of power through the power of the kingdom of God. This is the kernel of his political action. Through the transformation of power he sought to translate God's politics into messianic politics. In Jesus Christ we encounter the political God as the messianic politician.

From this perspective of power we must now look at the parable of the three servants in Luke 19:11–27. If we compare it with the parallel version in Matthew 25:14–30, Luke's parable appears very different in setting, plot, and intention. The parable in Matthew is preceded by the parable of the faithful and unfaithful servants (Matt. 24:45–51) and the parable of the five foolish and five prudent girls (Matt. 25:1–13). Both stories stress the unpredictability of the arrival of the kingdom of God. Hence the warning: "Be vigilant always!" Jesus uses these parables to bring home to people what he had already told them: "But about that day and hour no one knows, not even the angels in heaven, not even the Son; only the Father" (Matt. 24:36). Thus the faithful servant is found loyally carrying out his duties on the master's sudden return, whereas the unfaithful servant has spent his time mistreating the other servants and indulging himself in eating and drinking. What distinguishes the five prudent girls from the five foolish ones is essentially the same—the unpredictability of the bridegroom's arrival, the preparedness of the five wise girls, and the lack of preparedness of the five foolish girls. The lesson is: "Keep awake then; for you never know the day or the hour" (Matt. 25:13).

### The Parable of the Three Servants: Versions of Matthew and Luke

The parable of the three servants in Matthew carried the theme of the kingdom of God a little further. On the one hand there was approval of the first two servants who had worked hard to double the capital received from their master. The third servant, on the other, was severely reprimanded and punished for his miscalculation of the master's intention by hiding the money in the ground and then producing it intact on his master's return. "You lazy rascal!" thundered his profit-oriented business master: "You knew that I reap where I have not sown, and gather where I have not scattered. Then you ought to have put my money on deposit, and on my return I should have got it back with interest" (Matt. 25:26–27). In the first two parables the servants and the girls miscalculated the time of the master's arrival. In this parable the third servant miscalculated his master's thought. On account of their miscalculation, all of them have brought down the master's judgment on themselves.

In Luke's version of the parable of the three servants, we encounter a strikingly different situation. For we immediately realize that it is no longer a business transaction but a highly explosive political situation that provides the parable with its context. It is prefaced by an account of the setting in which Jesus told the parable. "While they [the people] were listening to this," so begins the text, "he [Jesus] went on to tell them a parable, because he was now close to Jerusalem and they thought the reign of God might dawn at any moment" (Luke 19:11). The atmosphere must have been full of tension and expectation. Jesus and his followers who hoped for liberation from their foreign rulers were now pressing toward Jerusalem, the religious and political center of the nation. Consistent with the social and political concern visible throughout his Gospel, Luke begins the parable about a nobleman who went on a journey to seek a kingdom and returned one day as a king. Needless to say, we are not dealing with a business transaction, as was the case in the parable in Matthew's Gospel. Instead, this is a political event with political consequences. According to Joachim Jeremias:

In these features we may possibly have a second, originally independent, parable about a claimant for the throne, reflecting the historical situation of 4 B.C. At that time Archelaus journeyed to Rome to get his kingship over Judaea confirmed; at the same time a Jewish embassy of fifty persons also went to Rome in order to resist his appointment.[2]

If this is true, then the political nature of Luke's parable is confirmed. As a result, the profits the servants made or did not make on the ten pounds left with them during the nobleman's absence become quite pointless. In other words, this was not Jesus' main concern when he told the parable. What then was Jesus trying to communicate through Luke's parable? Let us look at the parable more closely for an answer.

In the first place, our attention is drawn to Luke 19:14, which says that after the nobleman's departure, "his citizens hated him and sent an embassy after him, saying, 'we do not want this man to reign over us.' " It is conceivable that the nobleman in question was a powerful man who kept his little domain under tight control. In all probability he was a tyrant or dictator who had seized power at the expense of his subjects. Now he had gone to another country to request the rank of king, and he intended to return with greater power than ever. His subjects feared that life under such a despot would become even more intolerable. They thus decided to take their fate into their own hands and sent word after him declaring: "We do not want this man to reign over us" (v. 14). Fear for their ruler had turned into hatred, and then into disdain. "This man," they said, showing contempt by calling him in this way. When the nobleman heard of his subject's move, he must have exploded in anger. He saw their action as treason, mutiny, or rebellion. But insofar as the people were concerned, this was a revolution on behalf of social and political change.

The stage was thus set for a conflict between the ruler and his people. The nobleman, who had been crowned as king, now probably returned in great haste in order to bring the situation under control again. Upon his return the second stage of the conflict unfolded. The confrontation between the king and the third servant became the focus of this political drama. Previously the first and the second servants had been called upon to give an account of the money entrusted to them. They seem to have been shrewd people, and perhaps they had vested interests of their own. In any case they had worked hard during the nobleman's absence, surmising that it would be more prudent to cast their lot in with the nobleman who would probably return with kingly power than to throw their lot in with their fellow citizens who were trying to depose him as their ruler. As expected, they were amply rewarded for their labor: the first servant was given ten cities, and the second servant five cities by the king. They would henceforth share power with the hated ruler.

The third servant, however, was different. He seems to have shared the hatred of the masses for the ruler and to have decided to stand on their side. How else can we interpret the way he casually treated the pound entrusted to him by the nobleman? Instead of burying it in the ground like the third servant in Matthew's parable to ensure its safety, he just wrapped it in a handkerchief and put it away, thus "neglecting the most elementary safety measure."[3] This action on his part was self-explanatory and he was prepared to maintain his calm before the enraged King. But now that the first two servants had spoken, he could no longer remain silent. He was forced to explain himself in front of the ruler and his fellow citizens. He had lost his defense and knew it. His reply to the king was bitter. "Lord," he said, "here is your pound, which I kept laid away in a napkin; for I was afraid of you, because you are a severe man; you take up what you did not lay down, and reap what you did not sow" (Luke 19:21,RSV).

Read in the context of the social and political background to the parable, these words were highly poignant. They were no longer the servant's defense of why he did not do as the others had done. As a matter of fact, with these words he turned his defense into an accusation against the ruler. In saying these words, he involuntarily became the spokesman for his people. The people, including the third servant, had suffered under the severe ruler. They were expected to produce results for him despite harsh conditions. The ruler insisted on taking up what he had not laid down and on reaping what he had not sown. This must have reminded the people of the plight of the captive people of Israel in Egypt under a cruel pharaoh. They had to make bricks without straw! This touched off the Exodus from Egypt, changing the course of their history. The nobleman in the parable was a severe man and the third servant dared to say this to his face. He said what the people had long wanted to say but did not have the courage to. Now the chips were down, and the third servant and the people had to bear the consequences.

The parable ends with a gruesome picture of the outcome of the confrontation. A cruel suppression of the revolt took place. In great anger the king commanded that all the culprits be brought forward to be slaughtered: ". . . as for those enemies of mine, who did not want me to reign over them, bring them here and slay them" (Luke 19:27,RSV). The dissident elements were thus wiped out and the revolt put down. A bloodbath put an end to the abortive coup.

### Jesus as a Revolutionary

If this political interpretation of the parable is not entirely misleading, we may ask why Jesus told it. Was it because he was sympathetic to revolution as a possible means of changing the sociopolitical status quo? Or did he tell the parable to discourage people from becoming involved in revolutionary action because of possible fearful consequences? The revolt in the parable was suppressed with extreme cruelty. Was this meant to be a warning against involvement in opposition to the powers that be? Furthermore, was Jesus himself a revolutionary? If so, what kind of a revolutionary was he? A Zealot? Or a more peaceful revolutionary who refrained from violent means?

These are not easy questions to answer. To do so affirmatively or negatively would certainly amount to an oversimplification of the fairly complex situation in which Jesus was involved. In his conversation with his disciples, for instance, Jesus more than once referred to the sword. According to Matthew's Gospel, Jesus, in sending out his disciples on a preaching mission, included the following instruction: "You must not think that I have come to bring peace to the earth; I have not come to bring peace, but a sword" (Matt. 10:34). We may agree that the reference to sword here should not be taken literally. As Cullmann observes:

Jesus by no means *recommends* a holy war, but rather confirms that the decision to which his sermon calls men will cause dissension, and at the same time prepares his disciples for the persecution.[4]

At any rate, here is an allusion to situations that might involve his followers in a violent confrontation with the opponents of his mission.

A more striking mention of the sword was made by Jesus during the final hours he spent with his disciples after the Last Supper. The room where they had the last meal together must have been filled with an air of foreboding and expectation. The decisive hour was about to strike, and the disciples must have sensed it. They were probably gripped with anxious excitement—though they carefully suppressed it and refrained from verbalizing it—as if they were going out of that solemn meal to plunge into an uprising against the Roman authorities. Luke captured this scene with unusual sensitivity in recording the final conversation between Jesus and his disciples. He stressed the importance of preparedness in the face of an imminent ordeal. According to Luke:

He [Jesus] said to them, "When I sent you out barefoot without purse or pack, were you ever short of anything?" "No," they answered. "It is different now," he said; "whoever has a purse had better take it with him, and his pack too; and if he has no sword, let him sell his cloak to buy one. For Scripture says, 'And he was counted among the outlaws,' and these words, I tell you, must find fulfillment in me; indeed, all that is written of me is being fulfilled." "Look, Lord," they said, "we have two swords here." "Enough, enough!" he replied (Luke 22:35–38).

This is a curious saying indeed. Jesus seems, at this critical hour, to be reversing his earlier attitude. Earlier he had sent out seventy-two disciples in pairs with this instruction: "Carry no purse or pack, and travel barefoot" (Lk. 10:4). But here Jesus was urging preparedness and even the purchase of a sword at any cost, that is, by selling one's cloak. Jesus must have known for certain that such an instruction would be received as the signal of a revolutionary action, especially by the Zealotist elements among his disciples. Cullmann, for example, asserts that "one of the Twelve—Simon the Zealot—*certainly* belonged to the Zealots; others *probably* did, like Judas Iscariot, Peter, and *possibly* the sons of Zebedee."[5]

Then why did Jesus say these words attributed to him in Luke's Gospel? An easy way out of the difficulty of answering this question is to deny the authenticity of these words as coming from Jesus himself. They might have been attributed to him later by members of the early Christian community. But Cullmann regards the saying as authentic, and his explanation is consistent with the one he made in connection with Luke 10:34. In his words, the saying:

warns the disciples against believing that they will have the gospel to preach in a peaceful atmosphere. On the contrary, they will be exposed to attacks (even armed) when they preach the good news. This is no summons to a holy war. There may be times when the disciple individually is to defend himself if he is attacked while carrying out his mission, but he is not to take part in military ventures.

As to Jesus' response when the disciples produced two swords, Cullmann suggests that:

this was Jesus' way of breaking off the dialogue. As soon as he realized that the disciples, by their immediate display of two swords, understood his recommendation to buy a sword in the sense of Zealotism, he restrains them: It is enough![6]

This explanation is at least plausible and we may want to give it the benefit of the doubt. But the difficulty is that in the context in which the saying occurred, or at least as Luke recorded it, we do not see at all that Jesus was talking about the mission of preaching the good news. The cross was imminent, but Jesus' wrestling with the religiopolitical implications of his mission was not yet over. He was yet to pray in the Garden of Gethsemane: "Father, if it be thy will, take this cup away from me. Yet not my will but thine be done" (Luke 22:42; also Matt. 26:39). Perhaps the option of leading his followers in an act of challenge against the Roman authorities remained open for him until the last moment.[7]

On the other hand, there are clear evidences in the Gospels that Jesus did not identify the cause of the kingdom of God with the establishment of a new social and political order. From time to time he struggled with great effort against the temptation of exercising political and military options. But the no with which he fought back this temptation every time seemed categorical. A short while ago we discussed the rather baffling discourse between Jesus and his disciples about the purchase of a sword. How seriously and literally the disciples took his instruction concerning the sword can be seen in what happened during the excitement and confusion surrounding his arrest. On seeing what was coming, the disciples asked him: "Lord, shall we use our swords?" (Luke 22:49) Without waiting for an answer, one of them acted quickly, drew a sword, and attacked the High Priest's servant. It was then that Jesus' opposition to the use of sword became absolutely clear. According to Matthew's account, Jesus said firmly: "Put up your sword. All who take the sword die by the sword" (Matt. 26:52). This put an end to the issue about the sword that had been raised during the discourse after the Last Supper. A sword was no option for the kingdom of God. The politics of God was not a politics of the sword but the politics of the cross and suffering. This must be one of the thoughts that took hold of Jesus during the agonizing hours he had spent in the Garden of Gethsemane praying to God.

### Jesus Before Pilate

We must now consider the confrontation between Jesus and Pontius Pilate described in John 18:33–38a. In this confrontation two authorities and powers come into sharp conflict—one representing the formidable Roman Empire, and the other standing for a potential threat and challenge to it. This must have been the first face-to-face encounter between the two men. For Pilate, Jesus was a man to reckon with. He had the audacity to call King Herod a fox. Once he had said to those who warned him about Herod's attempt on his life: "Go and tell that fox, 'Listen: today and tomorrow I shall be casting out devils and working cures; on the third day I reach my goal' " (Luke 13:32). Apparently, this was not the only incident that had brought Jesus into the limelight of political conflicts with the ruling authorities. Herod's people were out to get him by various means. Once they sought to entrap him on the issue of loyalty by asking him about paying taxes to the Roman emperor. Jesus was undaunted and replied with unusual candor and authority: "Pay Caesar what is due to Caesar, and pay God what is due to God" (Mark 12:17). The way he said it and the tone with which he said it must have made its implication clear: loyalty to God must come before loyalty to Caesar. Therefore we must decide.

Pilate must have been aware that he was not confronted with an ordinary man. The ways in which Jesus had taken the religious and political leaders to task and had attracted enthusiastic crowds wherever he went must have impressed and at the same time worried Pilate greatly. He probably realized that standing in front of him was a formidable political figure endowed with immense spiritual power and authority. As we read the interlocution between Jesus and Pilate in this light, we cannot but conclude that Pilate was on the defensive. The questioner became the one who was questioned, and the judge became the one who was judged. "Are you the king of Jews?" asked Pilate. Instead of answering his question, Jesus countered with his own question: "Is that your own idea, or have others suggested it to you?" (John 18:34). This is hardly what a ruler would expect from his prisoner.

What actually happened in this intense hour of trial is what we have described as a transposition of power. The power to question and to judge was dramatically transposed from Pilate the judge to Jesus the prisoner. Pilate was taken aback. "What! Am I a Jew?" he shouted in disbelief. Still he must have an answer to his question about the man standing before him. "What have you done?" This he must know. What came back to him from Jesus was, however, not so much a reply as a declaration. "My kingdom," said Jesus, "does not belong to this world. . . . My kingly authority comes from elsewhere" (John 18:36). Pilate in his shrewdness did not fail to catch a political overtone in this declaration. And so he asked again: "You are a king, then?" (John 18:37). The whole proceeding must have been unsettling for him. He probably felt a threat to his power to rule and judge. He was unable to realize that the kingly power that transposed and changed the power relationship between himself and Jesus came from God. The tragedy was that, Pilate being used to the power struggles of this world, could see in Jesus' assertion of power and authority only a claim to political autonomy for a colonized people. This blindness to the significance of the transposition of power between himself and Jesus must have caused Pilate's secret decision to comply with the Jewish demand for the execution of Jesus as a political offender against the Roman authority. According to Cullmann:

The actual trial [of Jesus] was the trial before Pilate, and hence a political trial. . . . Thus Jesus suffered the Roman death penalty, crucifixion, and the inscription, the "titulus," above the cross named as his crime the Zealotist attempt of having strived for kingly rule in Israel, a country still administered by the Romans.[8]

But by the time of the confrontation with Pilate, Jesus was already beyond the Roman power represented by Pilate. He was on his way to complete the transformation of power under the authority of the reign of God. But this is to anticipate our discussion in the second part of this chapter.

### The Third Temptation

From the transposition of power that Jesus accomplished in his confrontation with Pilate, we must now return to Jesus' confrontation with Satan at the beginning of his ministry (Matt. 4:1–11; Luke 4:1–13). We focus our attention on the third temptation in Matthew's account (in Luke it is the second temptation).[9] After failing to induce Jesus to demonstrate his miracle-working power by turning stones into bread or by jumping down from the pinnacle of the temple, Satan now decided to come straight to the heart of the issue, that is, the power to rule "all the kingdoms of the world in their glory" (Matt. 4:8). What a temptation! And who could resist it? Is this not why you, Jesus, have come into the world? Think of David and the kingdom he established! Think of the long and tortuous history of that kingdom in the succeeding generations! It has been a history of captivity—one captivity after another. The northern kingdom collapsed under the attack of the Assyrians. The people of the southern kingdom were taken as captives to Babylonia. And now the Romans ruled the whole land. Think of those courageous fighters like the Zealots who are struggling against the Roman domination. The time is now ripe, and at one stroke all these kingdoms will be yours! The dream of restoring the Davidic kingdom to the promised land will be realized. Now is the time for you to act as the political messiah the people have been waiting for. The kingdom of God you represent must become a concrete reality. It must be translated into the system and structure of a kingdom on earth. It must not remain hidden. What is there to hold you back? It is entirely up to you. If you are ready, all these kingdoms of the world in their glory will be yours! Now is the hour of decision!

Jesus may have had to confront this same intense inner struggle many times throughout the course of his ministry. The attempt to take over political power from the Romans must have been offered to him more than once as a genuine political option. The Jewish people tended to read a literal meaning into any appeal to political messianism. At times Jesus must have felt a tremendous pressure to respond to their political summons. Political messianism seems therefore to be the central issue in the temptation story. As Cullmann puts it:

One is tempted only by those things which are close to him. In light of the burning expectation of the Zealots, which was shared by several disciples of Jesus, and in light of his great success with the crowd which offered him kingly rule, the idea must have come to his mind that perhaps he was to realize already on earth the kingdom of God.

But Cullmann goes on to say:

Whatever the historical core of the temptation narrative may be, certainly behind it stands the fact which can be followed throughout the Gospels, namely, that Jesus viewed the Zealotist political concept of Messiah as a satanic temptation.[10]

This seems to be the implication of Jesus' no to the political call of his people when he exclaimed: "Begone, Satan!"

The evidence that Jesus repudiated the cause of the kingdom on earth thus seems conclusive. But some questions still remain. Why, for example, did Jesus identify the cause of the earthly kingdom with a satanic temptation? Why did he not hesitate to use a strong word like "Satan" about the Zealotist political movement to which he was not entirely unsympathetic? He used the word again, this time about Peter, on the way to Caesarea Philippi. When Peter tried to disuade him from the role of a suffering Messiah, Jesus severely rebuked him saying: "Away with you, Satan, you think as men think, not as God thinks" (Mark 8:33). If the conjecture that Peter was also a Zealot is correct, then by repudiating him as Satan, Jesus repudiated at the same time the ways in which the Zealots tried to achieve their political goal. Theirs was definitely not the way of suffering but the use of force in violent revolts. Did Jesus see in this use of violence a satanic element he could not share? For Cullmann this repudiation of the use of violence is rooted in a much deeper theological reason. In his view, "It is certain that . . . Jesus did not reckon with the continuation of the world."[11] In other words, Jesus was counting on the imminent arrival of the kingdom of God with its new order. "The violent use of force in such a context," writes Lehmann in interpreting Cullmann's view, "would have signaled a loss of confidence in God's action and a disobedient repudiation of Moses and the prophets."[12]

However plausible Cullmann's argument may be theologically, it does not seem to carry with it a valid proof in human history. For as Lehmann goes on to ask: "Since the world obviously has continued for centuries, where does that leave us? With the conversion of heart? And with the ultimately stultifying or frustrating distinction between goals and methods?"[13] How is the dilemma here to be accounted for? Is Jesus' vision of the new order essentially incompatible with the transitoriness of the existing order? Does this mean that Jesus made a clear distinction between the kingdom of the new order, which was imminent, and the kingdom of the existing order, which was going to end in any case? Does this not leave us Christians wondering what to do with the kingdom of this world, which is still very much with us after two thousand years? Would all this lead us to think that we are here facing problems which Jesus did not have to face on account of his belief in the arrival of the new order possibly during his own lifetime? If the answer is yes, it is then perhaps futile for us to seek guidance from Jesus for the issues and questions that arise out of our political involvements, for he simply would have no answer for us. Clearly this cannot be the case. We are therefore compelled to examine more deeply how this apparent dilemma between the politics of the sword and the politics of love posed to us in the Gospels may be resolved.

There are sufficient indications in the Gospels to show that Jesus did not take lightly the social, political, and religious demands on the people in their daily contacts. He exhorted them to be peacemakers (Matt. 5:9), to be the salt to the world (Matt. 5:13), and to be light for the world (Matt. 5:14). Teachings such as these would have certainly sounded strange if Jesus had been indifferent to the present world. Not only this, he even had some emphatic things to say about the religious traditions of his own nation. He stressed:

Do not suppose that I have come to abolish the Law and the prophets; I did not come to abolish, but to complete. I tell you this: so long as heaven and earth endure, not a letter, not a stroke, will disappear from the Law until all that must happen has happened (Matt. 5:17–18).

Coming from the one who treated the world as something already *passé*, this would have made little sense. The kingdom of God might be imminent, but it is apparent that Jesus did not write off life in the kingdom of this world. In fact, he himself is the kingdom of God. In him and with him the reign of God is already present. The call to accept new values and practice new ethical codes becomes therefore urgent not because of the kingdom of God, which is still to come in the future, but because of its presence in Jesus Christ in the world here and now. The present world is not to be abolished simply; it has to be transformed.

It must be for this reason that Jesus felt a passionate concern for the poor and the oppressed. He did not commit the religious crime of painting a pie in the sky. His deliberate choice of Isaiah 61:1–2 as the opening manifesto of his mission was significant. He set out "to proclaim liberty to the captives, to set free the oppressed, and to bring the good news to the poor" (Luke 4:18–19). If the fulfillment of his message regarding the kingdom of God was to be achieved outside the historical realm, he would have displayed little passion for injustices committed by the religious and political leaders of his day.

Another incident (Matt. 17:24–27) can be cited to show how Jesus did not make light of the social and political demands imposed on the Jews by the Roman authorities. On one occasion the collectors of the temple tax asked Peter whether Jesus had paid his temple tax. Peter answered yes. After the temple-tax collectors had gone, Jesus used the occasion to discuss with his disciples the government tax. "What do you think about this, Simon?" he asked. "From whom do earthly monarchs collect tax or toll? From their own people, or from aliens?" The question was no longer related to the temple tax but to the tax levied by the Roman rulers. Peter replied that it was the foreigners who were taxed. "Why then," said Jesus, perhaps with suppressed indignation, "their own people are exempt!" This must have been a protest against the injustice of Roman colonialism. The Romans lived and thrived on the sweat and blood of their colonial subjects, and their tax system was the very embodiment of injustice and oppression. But Jesus' indignation against this unjust political system did not cause him to refuse to pay the tax. Rather he instructed Peter to find a silver coin to pay it for them both, because, to use his own words, "We do not want to cause offense."[14]

This incident must be understood in the same way as Jesus' aphorism about rendering to Caesar what is his due and rendering to God what belongs to God. On the one hand, the expectation of the kingdom of God does not divest us of our duty to pay our taxes. On the other hand, the political reality of the Roman rule dictated that both discretion and loyalty were needed to bring about a change in the status quo. Loyalty to God as the only Lord required that we should not give to Caesar more than he deserved. In other words, there was a limit to what Caesar could exact from his colonial subjects. At the same time, discretion was needed because an armed conflict was not the only way to achieve freedom and independence. Perhaps Jesus could already foresee the results of the armed confrontation advocated and practiced by the Zealots. In 70 A.D. the Jewish rebellion came to a catastrophic end when Jerusalem was sacked by Titus. As far as Jesus was concerned, he must have regarded it as necessary to let practical political considerations inform our confrontation with the powers that be. At the same time, a fine distinction had to be drawn between paying taxes to the earthly authority and rendering honor to the kingdom of God.

In this confrontation of the politics of kings and rulers and the politics of God, it is important to realize that the transposition of power has been achieved. Power has shifted its base. The power of this world intent on judging the power of God in Jesus Christ comes under divine judgment. By effecting this shift and transposition of power, Jesus sought to bring about the transformation of the power that works against God and against the people. Of course, there is no systematic description in the Gospels of how this transformation of power might take place. But from the parables given by Jesus and the incidents in which he was involved, we gain some insights into the shape and nature of the reign of God characterized by the transforming power of the redemption.

### The Parable of the Workers in the Vineyard

Let us first of all take a look at the parable of the workers in the vineyard (Matt. 20:1-15). As analyzed by Joachim Jeremias, the parable "describes two episodes: 1. the hiring of the labourers and the liberal instructions about their payment (vv. 1-8), 2. the indignation of the injured recipients (vv. 9-15)."[15] Jeremias calls this one of "the double-edged parables" whose emphasis lies on the second part, namely, the anger expressed by the early comers who had received the same wages as the late comers. Thus the purpose of Jesus in telling this parable is to show his critics, the Pharisees for example, "how unjustified, hateful, loveless and unmerciful was their criticism. Such, said he, is God's goodness, and since God is so good, so too am I. He vindicates the gospel against its critics."[16] What does this lead to? Here we come to the heart of the parable. As Jeremias explains:

We are suddenly transported into a concrete situation in the life of Jesus such as the Gospels frequently depict. Over and over again we hear the charge brought against Jesus that he is a companion of the despised and outcast. . . . Repeatedly is Jesus compelled to justify his conduct and to vindicate the good news. So too here he is saying, This is what God is like, so good, so full of compassion for the poor, how dare you revile him?[17]

If this interpretation is accepted, the parable can be seen as paradigmatic of the reign of God that has already begun in Jesus Christ.

We have said that politics has to do essentially with power. How power is used and how it is shared are therefore most crucial in determining the nature of politics practiced in a certain situation. In this parable Jesus makes it clear that that power is the goodness of God. It is the power of mercy, goodness, and love that becomes evident in the demonstration of God's reign. His kingdom is to be characterized as the power that does good, manifests mercy, and embodies love. Furthermore, since the poor and the oppressed are deprived of the protection of the power possessed by the rich and the powerful, God's power of mercy and love will be at work in them to support and strengthen them. By this Jesus seems to be stressing that the poor and the oppressed occupy a special place in the reign of God. That is why he stands on their side, identifies with them, and defends their rights. In word and in deed he shows that the transformation of the power that oppresses and exploits the poor and the powerless into the power that protects and cares for them is central to his ministry. It is at this point that Jesus inevitably comes into conflict with the institutions and structures of political power in the world.

The parable of the wicked tenants in the vineyard, which will be considered next, brings out again the radical nature of the politics Jesus inherited from the Old Testament prophets (Mark 12:1–11; parallels in Matt. 21:33–44; Luke 20:9–18).[18] There are variations of details in the three versions of the parable, but they do not need to concern us here. What is important is the judgment to be meted out on the wicked tenants who not only dealt with the messengers sent by the landlord brutally and shamelessly, but also killed his son so that they could usurp his property. But who are these wicked tenants? This is the central question in this parable, and not only those in the audience of Jesus but we too would like to know the answer. The clue to the question should be found in the obvious similarity between this parable and the Song of the Vineyard in Isaiah 5:1–7. That the parable derives its setting and framework from the Song of the Vineyard seems unmistakable if we compare the beginning and the ending of the two episodes.

|                      *Isaiah 5*                      |                      *Mark 12*                      |
| --- | --- |
| *vv. 1b–2a:* | *v.1:* |
| My beloved had a vineyard<br>high up on a fertile hill-side.<br>He trenched it and cleared it of stones<br>and planted it with red vines;<br>he built a watch-tower in the middle<br>and then hewed out a winepress in it. | A man planted a vineyard and put<br>a wall round it, hewed out a wine-<br>press, and built a watch-tower . . . |
| *v. 5:* | *v. 9:* |
| Now listen while I tell you<br>what I will do to my vineyard:<br>I will take away its fences<br>and let it be burnt,<br>I will break down its walls<br>and let it be trampled underfoot. . . . | What will the owner of the vineyard<br>do? He will come and put the ten-<br>ants to death and give the vine-<br>yard to others. |

The comparison indicates that Jesus' allusion to the Song of the Vineyard must have effectively driven home to his listeners the central point he was trying to make in his parable of the wicked tenants.

The question as to who these wicked tenants might be is now answered. The clue is Isaiah 5:7, which concludes the Song of the Vineyard with these words of judgment:

> The vineyard of the Lord of Hosts is Israel,
> and the men of Judah are the plant he cherished.
> He looked for justice and found it denied,
> for righteousness but heard cries of distress.

Who are the people chiefly responsible for the denial of justice and cries of distress in Israel and Judah, the vineyards of the Lord? Of course, it is the rulers and leaders of the people. They practice injustice, exploit the powerless, and violate the laws of God. They have betrayed the trust of God and destroyed the confidence of the people in their rule. This is precisely what the wicked tenants in Jesus' parable have done also. They proved to be unjust, wicked, and brutal. And worst of all, they completely betrayed the landlord by killing his son. At this point the people listening to Jesus must have realized who these wicked tenants might be. Just as the Song of the Vineyard directed its judgment to the leaders of Israel in Isaiah's time, so the parable of the wicked tenants in the vineyard points to the religious and political leaders of Jesus' day. Those who wield power over the powerless and defenseless people are the wicked tenants who are now plotting to do away with the Son who has come in the name of God.

By exposing the wickedness of the religious and political leaders, Jesus was not instigating a coup or preparing the people for a revolution. He was waging a moral war against the misuse of power and the abuse of privilege on their part. In fact Jesus was urging openly and boldly what Amos, the rustic prophet from Tekoa, had declared centuries earlier in the immediate hearing of the king:

> Let justice roll on like a river
> and righteousness like an ever-flowing stream (Amos 5:24).

Justice is one of the most fundamental principles of God's politics. It implies order in society and human relationships informed by love, freedom, and integrity. Justice should prevail in the courts of kings, the palaces of monarchs, and the executive offices of presidents and prime ministers. It is the responsibility of those who believe in the justice of God to be vigilant observers of the right use of power. This was the mission of the prophets in the Old Testament. It was the mission of Jesus. And it must be also the mission of the church and of all Christians. In this mission the position of power relations is transposed. Christians as such do not hold political power. Neither do they have the physical power to overcome the violent use of political power. But the power of God's love given to them through Jesus Christ becomes their power to judge abuses of power by those in positions of political authority. Herein is the essence of the political mission of the church, namely, the transposition of power.

It must be pointed out that power exercised in the sociopolitical realm does not exist as a neutral element since power does not exist in the abstract. It acts and works on people and events, and it thus produces results. It is in the service of both good masters and bad masters. Poverty, oppression, exploitation, and similar forms of injustice are all results of power in the service of wicked and ruthless masters. Freedom, peace, love, justice, and similar positive developments are some of the visible signs of power in the service of good masters. And since the concentration of power takes place in the state, the state becomes of necessity the most obvious target of the concern of the church and Christians. In the hands of state officials, power can be used to save or to destroy, to achieve well-being or to bring about chaos, to create blessings or to provoke curses. Power lodged in the state authority is therefore a crisis both for those with direct access to it and for those who are remote from it. In power we all face a crisis at the personal, social, and national levels. As Jacques Ellul observed:

When the state has all power, no boundary remains between what is just and unjust, true and false, good and bad. The effective boundary then is between what can and what cannot be done. What the state can do, the state will do, and what it does will *a priori* become just and true.[19]

This precisely points up the crisis of power.

It follows that the more concentrated power becomes, the greater is its crisis. This is most evident in a totalitarian or a semitotalitarian system of government. Of course, we do not mean that what the state does will "*a priori* become just and true." As a matter of fact the situation is often just the opposite. For this reason the politics of God comes dangerously close to the center of the state authority. Then the inevitable happens. The politics of God becomes closely involved in a contest for the transposition of power with the politics of the state. The Old Testament prophets appeared in the courts of kings and approached the seats of authority to pronounce judgment on the rulers and judges of the people. Jesus singlehandedly took to task the religious and political leaders, urging them to practice mercy and justice. This biblical prototype of political engagement has been repeated over again and again in the history of the Christian church. And as we have seen in the previous chapters, Christian communities in Asia today are increasingly finding themselves drawn into a struggle for the transposition of power. All this happens principally because what the state does is not *a priori* just and true. The state often errs terribly and thus brings misery to millions of people. The crisis of power at the state level is the root of the crisis in the sociopolitical life of the people. The transposition of power has to take place at that level in order to bring about repentance and the transformation of power.

But let us stop and ask whether we are not oversimplifying the very complicated reality of our political world. Have we not fallen into a political naiveté when we believe in the possibility of change in the nature of the political power exercised by high officials? As Jacques Ellul warned:

An all-powerful state, whatever its nature or doctrine, has never thus far accepted external values and the limits they impose. This is a historical fact, and I do not see how the situation could change; to claim that tomorrow things will be different is a jump into the absurd to which we are in no way entitled.[20]

We must concede that in a way this is very true. In considering the political conduct of those who hold power, especially of those who employ their enormous power to oppress and suppress people, we have to admit ruefully that those holding political power will not give it up unless they are forced to do so by a greater power. This means revolt and revolution. But this sad fact of life should not lead us to conclude that truth, justice, and love are religious virtues that are irrelevant in the world of politics. The repentance of those in power can and often does result in a more humane use of power.

In commenting on the civil war in Biafra, Nigeria, Dorothee Sölle points out in her book *Political Theology* the complexity of our political world on the one hand and stresses on the other hand the importance of Christian involvement in it on the basis of an informed judgment of actual situations. She writes:

> The war broke out when the oil companies, which had prospected in the Nigerian delta, switched their payment of royalties from Gowon to Ojukwu. They hastened the secession, because it was easier to gain access to the incredibly cheap oil . . . in tiny Biafra than in huge Nigeria. Half a nation starved for the sake of their business interests—and this is political information that must be taken into account. It seems to be the case that an economic system based on competition between private firms has a definite proclivity toward war. We can hardly reproach the oil companies, or even the expendable generals, for looking after their own interests, because it is contradictory for the spirit of instrumental reason simply to abandon the cheapest oil to the competition. Political theology takes this network of information into consideration; it is not the naive moralism of a country preacher berating the evil world, which in other respects is left in the care of instrumental reason.[21]

By *instrumental reason* Sölle means "reason that is no longer concerned with goals and final objectives, but only with the best rational methods."[22] It is a reason detached from concern for the whole person, the whole society, and the future of the whole nation. It pursues its objectives regardless of moral considerations. A political struggle is often the struggle of such an instrumental reason. Immediate political and economic gains become the chief focus of contention. The tragedy of the war in Biafra, according to Sölle, was the tragedy of the instrumental reason that subjected the lives of people to the tyranny of political and economic competition. It was therefore a *theological* problem as well as a political and economic problem. The call to repentance and the transformation of power dictated by instrumental reason is thus not illusory. It is imperative.

There can therefore be no doubt that faith cannot help being political, and that theology, which is a reflection on faith, is of a necessity also political. For this reason we speak of political theology, which does not deal with political systems, economic structures, and social institutions as such. Rather it has to deal first and foremost with the power on which these systems, structures, and institutions are constructed. It seeks to confront this power with the message of the Gospel that the power in the hands of human beings comes ultimately from God and that it must be exercised with due respect for truth, justice, and love. As Johannes Metz puts it:

Today more than ever, when the Church is faced with the modern political systems, she must emphasize her critical, liberating function again and again, to make it clear that man's history as a whole stands under God's eschatological proviso. . . . There is no subject of universal history one can point to in this world, and whenever a party, a group, a nation, or a class sought to see itself as such a subject, thereby making the whole of history to be the scope of its political action, it inevitably grew into a totalitarian ideology.[23]

The word *eschatological* used here clearly does not refer to the end of time in some distant future. What it refers to is here and now—the here and now of a political system, of an economic structure, in short, of the human institutions of power, criticized and evaluated in the light of the truth of the Gospel. This "eschatological stand" must be the basic political stand of Christians in the world, especially in a country where political power has been turned into a totalitarian power. This is the "eschatological" confrontation of the truth of the Gospel with the powers that be, motivated solely by instrumental reason.

### The Kingship of Jesus

Let us now resume our discussion of the encounter of God's politics with human politics, as seen in Jesus' encounter with Pontius Pilate. That encounter was the culmination of the power conflicts Jesus had had with the religious and political authorities during his ministry. And as we have seen, this confrontation between Jesus and Pilate demonstrated the nature of God's politics with the politicians of this world as essentially the transposition of power. As John, the author of the fourth Gospel, tells us, the question about the kingship of Jesus was now turned into a question about the truth Jesus represented. Kingship for Jesus had to be established on the truth of God's creating and saving love, whereas kingship for Pilate was simply a matter of the relentless pursuit of power inspired by instrumental reason. This is precisely the crux of the matter in the final interlocution between Jesus the prisoner and Pilate the judge. To Pilate who had asked him whether he was a king

Jesus answered, "'King' is your own word. My task is to bear witness to the truth. For this I was born; for this I came into the world, and all who are not deaf to truth listen to my voice." Pilate said, "What is truth?" (John 18:37–38)

The two men who confronted each other in that bizarre religious and political complexity stood on entirely different terrain. For Pilate Jesus was a potentially dangerous political rival to himself and to the Roman Empire. He was therefore obsessed with the alleged claim of Jesus to kingship. This seems clear from the fact that he directed the question about kingship to Jesus more than once. But Jesus turned Pilate's question around and reminded him: "It is you, Pilate, who used the word 'king,' not I." For Jesus the matter of kingship was secondary, especially when it came to the kingship of this world. He finally rejected it categorically, and in his last hour he was completely free from its temptation. His primary concern now was the truth to which he had come to bear witness. It was the truth that God is love, justice, and freedom. It was the truth that liberates the world from the bondage of sin and sets men and women free for God and for one another. It was the truth of salvation. This is the truth that should become the central concern of any power that rules over the people, even the power of the Roman Empire. This is the truth a political power must serve in the fear of God and in the service of the people. Standing before Pilate was this truth in all its power. Pilate, who represented the power of the kingdom of this world, must have been staggered when Jesus declared himself to be God's truth. In bewilderment and perhaps also in dismay Pilate asked: "What is truth?" This question must have come out of his mouth in a weak and confused manner.

The truth—namely, the truth of God—must be the battleground on which God's politics and the politics of humanity cross swords with one another. In the final analysis, this is how Christians should try to see and understand their social and political responsibilities. Their primary interest as Christians bearing witness to the truth of God's love, justice, and freedom does not lie in overthrowing one state authority and constructing a new one. History has taught us that a Christian state can be as bad and corrupt as a secular state; in some cases a Christian state has been worse and more corrupt. It is therefore not possible to identify God's truth with a particular state, even a state that calls itself Christian. This does not mean that any sociopolitical revolution must be excluded from the purview of the Christian faith. As Metz pointed out:

If love is actualized as the unconditional determination to freedom and justice for the others, there might be circumstances where love itself could demand actions of a *revolutionary character*. If the status quo of a society contains as much injustice as would probably be caused by a revolutionary upheaval, a revolution in favour of freedom and justice for the sake of "the least of our brothers [and sisters]" would be permissible even in the name of love.[24]

Revolution is certainly a political option even for Christians. However, what I want to stress is as follows: the politics of God's truth is not dictated by a revolution through which a change in a state authority with its power systems and structures might be realized in a systematic and forceful way. A sociopolitical revolution may become a part of Christian witness to God's truth, but it certainly cannot subsume this truth under it. God's truth continues to seek the transposition of power, even within a revolution initiated in the name of justice and freedom. Maybe this is the reason that Jesus, though sympathetic to the Zealotist cause, finally did not take it up as his own cause. Instead he took up the cross and carried the politics of God to Golgotha. His is therefore the revolution of the cross. It is this revolution of the cross that has succeeded in revolutionizing the world for the past two thousand years, and we do not see how it will be any different in the future. The revolution of the cross will surely continue its revolutionary work in the days to come and until the end of time. It will not cease to confront the powers of this world with its eschatological power of the truth of God to bring about a *metanoia* of power that may bear fruit through the transformation of the nature and quality of political power.

The transposition of power with its basis in God's truth is therefore a most revolutionary kind of politics. It is a *radical* politics—radical in its original sense of being fundamental, of going to the root of things. It is the invasion of God's politics into humanity's politics. It is the confrontation of God's truth with the sham truths held by the rulers, leaders, and politicians of the nations. Here *the* truth becomes the final and supreme issue—the truth that judges and saves with the justice and love of God. In this truth God's political realism and humanity's *realpolitik*, to use Paul Lehmann's expressions, come into collision with each other. This is the moment of truth for the powers of this world. It is a decisive and eschatological moment. Lehmann's excellent formulation of the difference between political realism and *realpolitik* is very helpful to our discussion. He writes:

The confrontation between Jesus and Pilate underscores the great gulf between *political realism* and *Realpolitik*. *Realpolitik* is politics with the accent upon the primacy of power over truth. *Political realism* is politics with the accent upon the primacy of truth over power. *Realpolitik* increasingly succumbs to the temptation of confusing immediate goals and gains with ultimate outcomes and options and seeks validation by increasingly dubious authority. *Political realism,* on the other hand, involves an increasing struggle against the temptation to overcome irrelevance through premature ventures to close the gap between the ultimate and the immediate, thus overdrawing on the truth in its power. Ever and again the successors of Jesus have sought to convert the moment of truth exposed by his presence into a blend of political realism and power politics (Caesaro-papism, theocracy, sectarian withdrawal) that seeks to effect the triumph of Jesus over the "prince of this world" in this world. Meanwhile, the successors of Pilate follow him in opting for the view that the state can have no interest in truth, i.e., in radical reality. In so doing, they convert the moment of truth exposed by the presence of Jesus into a politics of power that disregards the real and exalts the possible as necessary.[25]

This is an important theological analysis of the nature of politics. When humanity's politics is confronted by God's politics, it is compelled to ask itself whether, in the exercise of its power, it leaves room for the ultimate truth in fulfillment of the ultimate goal of human life.

In this confrontation is the hope for a redemption of human politics. Redemption takes place in the life of a people when the politics of power begins to respect the politics of God's truth. Humanity's politics will not be considered merely as an exercise of naked power in self-fulfillment. It comes to partake of the power of the truth in the service of God's love, justice, and freedom. This is the transformation of *realpolitik* into political realism. This is the goal of Jesus' messianic politics. Jesus has shown us that this transformation is a possibility because of the cross. He has also shown that this transformation can be a reality on account of the reality of the resurrection. The messianic politics of Jesus is thus built on the cross and the resurrection. In Chapter 9 we discussed the cross of the resurrection. In the next and final chapter we must concern ourselves with the politics of the resurrection.

# CHAPTER 12

# THE POLITICS
# OF THE RESURRECTION

Messianic politics is the politics of the resurrection. This is the thesis to which I wish to address myself in the concluding chapter. As a point of departure, let me quote a poem entitled "I Believe" that was composed by a seventeen-year-old girl from Singapore, Lai Leng Woon:

I believe that there's
Still hope to live,
—not merely to exist,
Somewhere in this
Hopeless whirlpool of life,
—a hand extends to help.
In these battered days,
You will find, if you search,
—one who has offered to mend.
I know that somewhere,
In this canyon of despair,
—there's a place of relief.
Somewhere, in this
Turmoil of confusion,
—a right path to follow
Within this world
Of make-believe,
—a faithful friend awaits you.
In this polluted time,
We lead,
—a hope to be made clean.[1]

In the poem we find no idealization of the world as a projection of our unfulfilled dreams. Nor is there an attempt of the soul to escape from this world as an illusion. The harsh realities of life grip us so tightly that we cannot take flight into a land of fantasy and illusion. What we must do is to look for signs of hope, however small and insignificant they may be, in order to continue life's journey. We must seek strength in our today to live tomorrow. "The soul," writes Simone Weil, "has to go on loving in the emptiness, or at least to go on wanting to love, though it may only be with an infinitesimal part of itself. Then, one day, God will come to show himself to this soul. . . . "[2] Christian hope begins with an "infinitesimal" sign of love in this whirlpool of life, in this canyon of despair, and in this world of make-believe, to use Lai Leng Woon's phrases. This is how both Lai Leng Woon and Simone Weil perceive the hand of God working in the world. For them God is not a sensational giver of hope. Their God is not a headline-making God. For them he is the God who begins with infinitesimal signs of love. And this is God's politics of the resurrection.

In comparison with the great commotion and excitement about the crucifixion, the resurrection of Jesus could have come and gone without attracting much public notice. There seemed to be little expectation that Jesus might rise from the dead. In order to put an end to rumors about this possibility, the Pharisees even persuaded Pilate to post soldiers at the tomb to prevent Jesus' body from being stolen (Matt. 27:62–66). It is therefore no wonder that Mary of Magdala, who visited the tomb early on Sunday morning, was at first not able to recognize the risen Christ when he accosted her (John 20:10–15). The two disciples on their way to Emmaus were not even aware of the presence of the risen Christ until they reached the destination of their journey (Luke 24:13–32). Some years later when St. Paul stood before the court of Areopagus in Athens and spoke about Jesus and his resurrection, the Athenians were either skeptical or derisive (Acts 17:16–34). Undaunted, Paul continued to preach the gospel of the resurrection, staking his faith on Jesus Christ who had risen from the dead. He wrote to the Christians in Corinth with a tone of finality: " . . . if Christ was not raised, then our gospel is null and void, and so is your faith; and we turn out to be lying witnesses for God . . . " (1 Cor. 15:14–15).

## The Eschatological Meaning of History

The resurrection is not only decisive for Christian faith but also vital to our understanding of world history. For the resurrection is the very source of the infinitesimal signs of hope that enable us to affirm life despite our failures and despair, and to see a positive meaning in history despite acts of atrocity and insanity. The resurrection is therefore an essential part of God's politics of the cross in the world. For this reason we must now speak of the resurrection in the cross as we spoke of the cross in the resurrection in Chapter 9. To put it another way, the resurrection did not take place as an afterthought on the part of God. It did not take place as if God felt compelled to repair the damage done through the crucifixion. The resurrection of Jesus was not an accident, not even a *divine* accident. Jesus did not stumble, as it were, into the resurrection. The resurrection was the affirmation of the cross. As such it was already present in the crucifixion. According to John's Gospel, Jesus' last word on the cross was: "It is accomplished" (John 19:30). The Greek word *tetelestai* literally means "completed." It "announces the victory of the victim. The Christ has accomplished his mission, and the salvation of the world is attained," says Edwyn Hoskyns. He goes on to add:

The word sums up the messianic interpretation of Psalm 22 applied to Jesus. The Psalm begins with My God, my God, why hast thou forsaken me? and after describing the sufferings of the man of God, breaks out into an almost eschatological cry of victory.[3]

The resurrection enables us to hear the echo of victory in the pain and suffering of the cross.

Furthermore, Jesus' cry of victory on the cross anticipates the advent of God's ultimate victory in the ultimate future. As Raymond Brown puts it in commenting on the last word of Jesus:

If "It is finished" is a victory cry, the victory it heralds is that of obediently fulfilling the Father's will. It is similar to the "It is done" of Rev. 16:17, uttered from the throne of God and the Lamb when the seventh angel pours out the final bowl of God's wrath. What God has decreed has been accomplished.[4]

The victory of Jesus on the cross connects the work of creation done through the Word and the redemption of all creation through the Lamb. Resurrection as the victory of life over death is the eschatological meaning of the cross on Golgotha. The resurrection therefore vindicates all the pain and agony of history.

From the Old Testament to the New Testament, from the past to the future, from the beginning of time to the end of time, and from the old creation to the new creation, God's politics of the resurrection constitutes the meaning of history. The resurrection then means that God relates himself to history and is active in it creatively and redemptively. Jesus Christ is the concentration of God's politics of the resurrection in the movements of history. In him the meaning of the cross comes to a full disclosure in the resurrection. To see history, be it the history of individuals, nations, or the world, in the light of Jesus Christ is to see it eschatologically—if we take eschatological in the sense that something decisive has taken place, no matter how infinitesimal that something might be. This is in essence the decisive—and thus the eschatological —meaning of history: each tear shed, every sacrifice made, each and every effort toward transformation of the power that enslaves and de-humanizes people—all these moments, whether small or great, become decisive events in our lives and in the history of humanity's progression toward its fulfillment in God. History is not autonomous. It is not left to its own devices. It is the arena in which God engages all men and women in a struggle for love, truth, and justice. And the resurrection is the affirma-tion that the final victory is on God's side. The cry of victory on the cross is a declaration that even as the battle is being fought, we can count on God as the victor. The resurrection is therefore the proclamation of the triumph of life over death even as death seems to be wrecking God's work of redemption on the cross. It is a new beginning right in the midst of the old ruins. It is a promise of life even as an attack from the power of destruction is under way. And it points to a future of hope within our present of despair.

### Religion in Communist China

There must be a great number of silent witnesses to this eschatological meaning of the resurrection in situations where a profession of faith is considered by the state to be a sign of reactionary behavior. Let me cite a story about a "reform-through-labor" (forced labor) camp in Communist China in the early 1960s as an illustration of this point. Bao Ruo-Wang (Jean Pasqualini), who was born to a French father and a Chinese mother, had lived all his life in China until 1962 when he was released from a reform-through-labor camp and permitted to leave the country. He had spent the last part of his imprisonment in the *Ching Ho* camp from which no prisoner was expected to come out alive. His recollection is at once moving and depressing:

The last extraordinary experience I had at *Ching Ho* was the Christmas mass of Father Hsia. Our teams had spent most of the month of December 1961 in miscellaneous agricultural housekeeping, such as making boundaries for rice paddies, cleaning out irrigation ditches and cutting brush. The morning was bright and clear that Christmas Day, but the temperature was close to zero, and a force five wind was roaring down from the northwest. . . . It was around 9:30 when I noticed a solitary figure approaching me across the strip. Even quite far away, I could tell from his gait that it was Hsia. The earflaps of his ragged old cotton hat danced in the wind as he hurried over to me, and his faded khaki army overcoat and black padded pants were splattered with mud. With the exaggerated politeness characteristic of him, Hsia asked me if he could have a break for a few minutes. I had nothing against that, but he knew we had a deadline for the paddy job—couldn't he wait until lunch time? Embarrassed and pained, he looked down at his boots, toying absently with the red-and-white markers he still held in his mittens. "Don't you remember what day it is today, John?" he asked me in English. "Of course." I had been thickheaded. "Good old man," I said, "but be careful." He smiled gratefully and scurried away across the road and down the embankment to a dry gully where a bonfire was burning, and where he was shielded from the wind and the view of the warders. A quarter of an hour later, I saw a bicycle against the sky in the distance—a warder was on his way. I hustled over to the gully and warned Hsia. As I looked down the embankment, I saw that he was just finishing up the mass in front of a mound of frozen earth which he had chosen as an altar. He was making the traditional gestures of priests all over the world. But his vestments here were ragged work clothes; the chalice, a chipped enamel mug; the wine, some improvised grapejuice; and the host, a bit of *wo'tou* he had saved from breakfast. I watched him for a moment and knew quite well it was the truest mass I would ever see. I loped down the embankment, and when the warder passed on his bike, he saw only two prisoners warming hands.[5]

Without any exaggeration this was a truly extraordinary experience. The author called the primitive celebration on that Christmas Day "the truest mass" he would ever see. Why? Perhaps at that moment the ultimate meaning of life based on the death and rising of Jesus Christ dawned on him for the first time. In this mass of Father Hsia, there was no pretension, no glory, and certainly no sermonizing. And yet how eloquent, compelling, and convincing it was! This was a personal experience of a particular individual and should not be taken as typical of what Christians are doing in China today. Still the story gives us much to think about.

China has been in the extremely tight grip of Communist ideology for nearly three decades. By persuasion, coercive measures, appeals to patriotism, and the formidable machinery of the Communist party, China seems to have succeeded in demonstrating how the Communist ideology can shape not only the external life of the people but also their minds and hearts. What we may encounter in China today, on the surface at least, is "an ideological human being in an ideological society." From top to bottom China is unashamedly ideological. The ideology of Marxism-Leninism, as adapted and transformed by the thought of Mao Tse-tung, has been translated into the practical language of China's 900 million people of whom 80 percent are peasants. Today China is on the move, and its leaders are determined to make Marxism-Leninism and the thought of Mao Tse-tung the political daily food of the people. The Chinese people are taught that dialectical materialism is an absolute law governing not only the course of nature but also the life and history of humanity. They are told that the dictatorship of the proletariat will ultimately bring into existence a classless society; that religion is a superstition and an illusion; and that religion has no role to play in the class struggle and the construction of a socialist nation. By now such official claims and teachings have flooded the minds and thoughts of the Chinese people. These doctrines were preached with redoubled emphasis and vigor during the Great Proletarian Cultural Revolution in 1966–1969. All religions, including Christianity, have now lost their status in the nation. Christian believers such as the Father Hsia mentioned in the story above have had to go underground and practice their faith in private.

Christians outside China who are looking for some faint signs of Christian faith in that country should find the example of Father Hsia informative. Here is evidence of faith and hope in Christ demonstrated by Christians in the teeth of hardship and ostracism. Surrounded by the vigilant eyes of party cadres and prison guards, some Christians still cling to the hope actualized in the event of Christmas. By celebrating mass on Christmas morning behind the backs of the forced-labor camp officials, Father Hsia undoubtedly served as a symbol of Christian hope. So long as there are Christians in China who keep faith in Christ in their hearts and celebrate Christmas or Easter in a clandestine way, are they not witnesses to God's presence? Is not the very existence of these Christians an assurance that God continues his work there? Are they not sacramental in the sense that because of them God's purpose of redemption has not departed from that vast country?

This may be so. But recent developments in China should warn us against false feelings of optimism about Christianity's ability to survive as an organized religion. True, freedom of religion in China is constitutionally provided. In the Constitution approved by the First Session of the Fourth National People's Congress on January 17, 1975, the citizens of the People's Republic of China are said to be entitled to various freedoms such as freedom of speech, correspondence, publication, gathering, association, demonstration, and even the freedom to strike. Of course, it would be misleading to interpret these freedoms in the sense in which they are understood in the West. They must be interpreted in accordance with a special semantics developed in strict conformity to the national ideology of communism. It is interesting to note that the Constitution also mentions religious belief, and one of its clauses states: "Citizens . . . enjoy freedom of religious belief." But this provision for religious belief is immediately followed by the "freedom of nonbelief and the freedom to propagate atheism."[6] If we read this in the light of Article 2 of the Constitution, which states that "Marxism, Leninism and the thought of Mao Tse-tung are the theoretical foundations that guide the thinking of our nation,"[7] then we understand that freedom of religious belief has little practical meaning in the life of the people and the policy of the Communist party. What this really means is that the atheistic propaganda is sanctioned constitutionally at the expense of the freedom of religious belief.

Furthermore, if religion is equated with superstition, Christianity with western imperialism, and belief in the gods with "the fantastic reflection in men's minds of those external forces which control their daily life,"[8] religion has really no chance to coexist with Communist ideology. In the long run religion must be eliminated from China. An article entitled "The Correct Recognition and Handling of the Problem of Religion," states:

The active leadership of the masses in the class struggle and the production struggle is of decisive significance for the elimination of religion. This is because in order to promote the death of religion, we must first eliminate the roots by which religion is given birth and exists—the pressure from natural forces and social forces. Only with the abolition of class warfare and exploitation and the extensive development of the capacity to control nature, and on this foundation raising the people's degree of consciousness and level of knowledge, may the death of religion be brought about. Comrade Mao Tse-tung pointed out that the removal of the religious superstitions of the masses is "the natural result after victory in the political struggle and the economic struggle." For this reason, the Party should first lead the masses in carrying out the political struggle and the economic struggle.[9]

This is a shrewd observation, to say the least. The policy adopted by the Chinese Communist party toward religious beliefs is at least logical and is proving to be effective. Under tight Communist control and a fantastic drive for political unification, socialist reconstruction, and economic development, the Chinese Communist leaders apparently have been able to change a fatalistic dependence of the masses on the whims of heaven into an active reliance of the people on themselves and the Communist party to overcome natural disasters and social evils. But some fundamental questions must be raised: Is religion to be identified simply as a superstition? Can the longing of the human spirit for the eternal be obliterated by the powerful wand of the Communist party? Is there not a possibility that religion might play a constructive role in a socialist-communist state without posing a threat to the party's political power? In some eastern European countries like Rumania and Czechoslovakia coexistence between church and state has proved to be a possibility. Of course, the church needs to be prepared for opposition if the church finds it necessary to take a firm social and political stance on the basis of the Christian faith. Will the political and ideological situation in China evolve in such a way that this kind of coexistence between church and state might become possible in the future? Should such a time arrive, we might surmise that the form of Christian faith that would develop in Communist China would differ radically from the past model. The new form of faith would probably show all of us outside China how quietly, forcefully, and unobtrusively God has been at work inside the country. It would definitely show us that God is not only the God of the people in the so-called free world but also the God of the people in a socialist-communist nation. But most important of all, this new form of faith would probably teach Christians in the affluent West what it means to follow Christ, what it means to lose a false way of life in order to gain the true life.

But for the time being, at least, religion is officially considered a phenomenon of the past in China. China has, so to speak, grown out of religion and needs no support from religion in its national reconstruction.

The Communist ideology practiced in China is tough in the sense that it needs no sanction apart from its own practicability and apart from the truth believed to be inherent within it. In the 1950s when the Chinese Communist party was struggling to bring order out of chaos, to achieve recovery from the vast devastation caused by years of war, and to feed hundreds of millions of people, the church was led to believe that it would have a role to play in the national effort of reconstruction. This was clear from the United Declaration of the Delegates of the Chinese Christian Churches issued in April 1951 at a conference of 151 Protestant church leaders. The conference had been convened by Chou En-lai at Peking. Among other things the Declaration called upon the Christians in China

to support the Common Programme, support the Government land reform policy and support the Government in the repression of anti-revolutionaries, obey all Government laws, positively respond to the Government commands, and exert every effort in the reconstruction of the nation. We want to be more alert, to resolutely reject the blandishments of imperialism, to assist the Government to discover and punish anti-revolutionary and corrupt elements within the Protestant church, . . . and with the highest enthusiasm [we] welcome the unlimited, glorious future of the People's Republic of China.[10]

This effort on the part of the churches to survive under a totalitarian state has failed, however. The voice of the church is now muted. The church was totally submerged in the fanatical class struggle and incessant battle over ideological power. The institutional church seems to have had its day in China, and to have been lost in the movements of history that shook and convulsed the country.

The end of the institutional church is, however, not the end of faith in God the creator and redeemer. In certain situations, especially in a situation of adversity under an authoritarian government, faith in God really begins. Although the church has been destroyed and the Christian community dispersed, faith has taken on a deep dimension for believers. Examples of this are too numerous to cite. But the case of Christians in the Soviet Union, for instance, in the 1920s and 1930s when they came under severe persecution, is a sober and revealing lesson to us all. It was reported that "when the last church building has been closed in a town," the priests and monks

take their staff and go from place to place. They teach everywhere, in the villages, in the houses and in the stables, in the forests and under the open sky in the field. They look pale and miserable, and often their clothing is torn. A few crumbs of bread are their only nourishment. In their little sack they carry a Bible, their most precious belonging. They are warmly received by the people, but woe to them if they fall into the hands of the stool-pigeons of the police.[11]

God has not ceased to work. He lives in the hearts of the people, who know that God is the God of the cross *and* the resurrection. He quietly and firmly continues his creating and redeeming work to transform humanity and history.

We must remember that Jesus himself died outside the institutional church. He was crucified outside the holy city, thus fulfilling the prophecy of the Servant Songs in the time of the exile:

> He was afflicted, he submitted to be struck down
> and did not open his mouth;
> he was led like a sheep to the slaughter,
> like a ewe that is dumb before the shearers.
> Without protection, without justice, he was taken away;
> and who gave a thought to his fate,
> how he was cut off from the world of living men,
> stricken to the death for my people's transgression?
> He was assigned a grave with the wicked,
> a burial-place among the refuse of mankind,
> though he had done no violence
> and spoken no word of treachery (Isa. 53:7–9).

The servant was not designated as God's servant because he had served the church with distinction, nor because he was held with respect and honor in society. He became God's servant because he shared a common fate with the wicked and with "the refuse of humankind." The end of the institutional church can therefore be the beginning of the mission of God in ways quite incomprehensible to Christians. This is at least true in a totalitarian country in which the propagation of the Christian faith is considered by the state to be reactionary. When the institutional church is closed down, God enables the church to go to the people, to "the wicked" and to "the refuse of mankind."

"In the climate of our Marxist society," says the Czech theologian Jan Milic Lochman:

> this presence of the Christians in the unexpected places was difficult to achieve or maintain for an organized church. Christian possibilities of entering the secular realm were limited. The collapse of the Constantinian era narrowed the chances in this respect.[12]

In Communist China the Constantinian era came to an absolute end in 1949 when the People's Republic proclaimed its existence. But the end of the Constantinian era must have been the beginning of Christ's mission of the cross and the resurrection in China. For Lochman goes on to tell us out of his experience in his own country:

And yet the decisive Christian witness often occurred in individual acts of obedience and love, in secular places, outside any immediate contact with a congregation. It occurred in the personal risk of word or act which in a given secular environment was easily misunderstood, opposed, even ridiculed, but which sometimes and with some people evoked a genuine curiosity, sympathy, and trust.[13]

Who can say this is not what may be happening in China today? God in the Bible is the God of surprises. He always has a surprise in store for those who believe. A God who has ceased to surprise us does not interest us. Such a God is too predictable to forgive and forgive again, to redeem and re-redeem, to create and re-create. A predictable God cannot raise Christ from the dead. He cannot surprise and thrill the world with the resurrection after the crucifixion. Perhaps in China God may have a very big surprise for us all, for it is there that he may be engaged in the birthpangs of new men and women who have come to encounter a new Christ risen from the dead.

### The Politics of Freedom

Thus in the resurrection God's politics in the world has taken a drastic turn. It has become a "secular" politics, that is, a politics conducted not primarily in the holy of holies or in the company of like-minded religionists. It takes into account the world of human suffering and the world of political power. It is the politics that enables "the refuse of humankind" to rise from the death of self-consciousness and empowers the weak and the powerless to strive for freedom and justice. Resurrection is therefore the birth of a new human being. It is the emergence of a new life not only for the world to come but for the world here and now. Resurrection is essentially the power that forms and reforms, sustains and resustains, empowers and re-empowers those who are regarded as refuse, nonentities, or good-for-nothings. It is the power that enables slaves to become their own masters, and that fills empty hearts with hope in the future. Resurrection is the foretaste of a new world in which each and every human being will be free for God and for all creation. It is the realization that, to use Rubem Alves's words:

Man ceases to be a one-dimensional being, whose consciousness is submerged into the facts exterior to it. It gains distance. It looks at the facts as something against which it is opposed. Man no longer is a reflexive repetition of his contacts with the world. He is born to freedom as he becomes critical.[14]

The experience of the resurrection is thus the experience of becoming truly free and truly human. Resurrection life is a life in which our human potentiality comes to its full expression. And a fully human life is the life that reflects the glory and pride of the image of God.

It follows that God's politics of the resurrection is a politics without fear, for the resurrection overcomes fear. It conquers the fear of the cross and overpowers the fear of darkness and death. Fear makes us morbid and inactive. It immobilizes us, drains something vital from us, and makes us less human. When we become captives of fear, we are likely to act and react solely on the basis of the instinct for survival and self-protection. Fear turns us into animals of instinct, corrupts human relationships, and destroys human integrity. It silences our conscience, makes us betray our friends, and may even compel us to be unfaithful to God. Resurrection sets us free from such fear and makes us free for what is truly human. That is why the angel at Jesus' tomb told the women on that resurrection morning: "You have nothing to fear!" (Matt. 28:5).

Resurrection is the power that casts out fear. It enables us to face the world with equanimity and conviction. The fearless Jesus in front of Pilate is therefore already the resurrected Christ. The power of the resurrection is already at work in him. Pilate is confronted with the power of a new life radiating from Jesus. Pilate, who has no real reason to be afraid because of his position of power, is now afraid. He is reduced to being a petty ruler trying to please all power groups except the power of God. The ominous silence of Jesus makes him all the more afraid. In desperation he asks: "Do you refuse to speak to me? Surely you know that I have authority to release you, and I have authority to crucify you?" (John 19:10). These words must have sounded hollow, and Pilate knew it. He knew well that he might have had the authority to crucify Jesus but no authority to release him. Jesus' reply must have put an end to Pilate's illusion of authority. "You would have no authority at all over me," says Jesus, "if it had not been granted you from above" (John 19:11). The power of resurrection is the power of divine authority over all earthly authorities. It exposes an authority like Pilate's as a sham authority.

St. Paul has put this politics without fear supported by the power of the resurrection into a most passionate and moving language. To the Christians in Rome who live under the immediate authority of the powerful Roman Empire, St. Paul confesses his fearlessness on account of Jesus' resurrection. He writes:

It is Christ—Christ who died, and, *more than that, was raised from the dead*—who is at God's right hand, and indeed pleads our cause. Then what can separate us from the love of Christ? Can affliction or hardship? Can persecution, hunger, nakedness, peril, or the sword? "We are being treated like sheep for slaughter"—and yet, in spite of all, overwhelming victory is ours through him who loved us. For I am convinced that there is nothing in death or life, in the realm of spirits or superhuman powers, in the world as it is or the world as it shall be, in the forces of the universe, in heights or depths—nothing in all creation that can separate us from the love of God in Christ Jesus our Lord (Rom. 8:34–39).[15]

The politics of the resurrection which has done away with fear has come to a full expression in St. Paul. This Paul, reputedly a man of small stature, must have stood before King Agrippa like a towering spiritual giant when he proclaimed to the king the message about the resurrection of Christ (Acts 26). And in a scene reminiscent of Jesus' trial before Pilate, Paul the prisoner was on the offensive and King Agrippa found himself on the defensive. Hence the following dialogue between Paul and Agrippa:

> *Paul:* What I am saying is sober truth. . . . King Agrippa, do you believe the prophets? I know you do.
> *Agrippa:* You think it will not take much to win me over and make a Christian of me.
> *Paul:* Much or little, I wish to God that not only you, but all those also who are listening to me today, might become what I am, apart from these chains.

The reversal of positions here is as dramatic as it was at Jesus' trial. The transposition of power has taken place. It is not Paul who wears the chains but those who are to judge him that wear the chains. The chains of earthly power that they wear are like the ones Pilate wore. Just as Pilate, who did not have the power to release Jesus even though he had found Jesus innocent of the accusation brought against him, so Agrippa who found no grounds to the criminal charge brought against Paul was not free to let him go. Chained, Paul was free. Though free, Agrippa and his entourage were chained to the so-called power of a sham authority.

Thus St. Paul shows us how the powers of this world come under the politics of the resurrection. In fact, this has been the case ever since the Gospel was carried from Jerusalem to other parts of the world. Christian witnesses in adverse political situations in Asia today are repetitions of this politics of the resurrection. Catholic Bishop Daniel Chi of Korea, the director of the Young Christian Workers, denounced the regime of President Park "for violence, intimidation and fraud."[16] At his trial by the military court, he said defiantly:

> I have done nothing wrong. I in no way support violent revolution. I did give money to the students for a peaceful demonstration . . . [because] I wanted to make the government realize that there is such a thing as a loyal opposition.[17]

Here again the positions of the judge and the judged, of the prosecutor and the prosecuted, of the interrogator and the interrogated are reversed. It is not Bishop Chi who had denounced the government for "violence, intimidation and fraud" who was on trial. It was the government that had committed the crimes of violence, intimidation, and fraud against its people that was on trial before the bishop and the whole people of Korea. In Bishop Chi, God's redemptive power for the nation was at work. Blessings to the rulers who are able to heed and accept such "loyal" opposition— the opposition loyal to God's love and justice, and loyal to the cause of freedom and democracy! But woe to the persons in power who suppress loyal opposition, stifle the voice of conscience, and set their sham authority over the authority of God!

The power of the resurrection makes it possible to reverse and transpose the relationships of power. The state authority may still have the power to imprison, silence, and even liquidate those opposed to it. But the power of such a state authority is a mere physical power that may kill the body but cannot kill the soul. Jesus tells us not to fear such power (Matt. 10:28). Such power is powerless in front of the moral force that defends truth, freedom, and justice. To fight against such a moral force is to fight against the divine power of creation and redemption. It is an audacious but self-defeating challenge to the authority of divine power. In the case of Bishop Chi and similar witnesses, the whole of creation rallies around to support them and anxiously anticipates the victory that will be theirs ultimately. This is nothing new. It has been demonstrated by the presence of the power of the resurrection in the cross of Jesus. That is why the last word of Jesus on the cross, as mentioned earlier, was the word of accomplishment, the word that sealed the victory, the word that announced the completion of God's redemptive work.

This enables us to say that the politics of the resurrection, since it is free from fear, is also the politics of freedom. The resurrection liberates us from the captivity of fear and leads us into the freedom of life. We are no longer subject to the animal instincts of survival and self-protection. We learn to transcend our personal interests and even our national interests conceived in a narrow and destructive patriotism. The radical transformation that took place in Peter and his fellow disciples is in this sense absolutely remarkable. The risen Christ freed them from the fear of the Roman authorities and their own religious leaders. And what is most important, the risen Christ liberated them from their narrow political messianism. Summoned to the Sanhedrin by the high priest to give an explanation, Peter declared: "We must obey God rather than men!" (Acts 5:29). What made it possible for Peter and his companions to distinguish between obedience to God and obedience to human authorities? What was the criterion that enabled them to decide what belonged to God and what to Caesar? And what was the basis on which they were now able to put messianic politics before political messianism? Peter himself has told us what this power, criterion, and basis were immediately after his forceful declaration. He said:

The God of our fathers raised up Jesus whom you had done to death by hanging him on a gibbet. He it is whom God has exalted with his own right hand as leader and saviour, to grant Israel repentance and forgiveness of sins. And we are witnesses to all this, and so is the Holy Spirit given by God to those who are obedient to him (Acts 5:30–32).

Here Peter spoke under the powerful impact of the resurrection of Jesus Christ. He could now look back on the ministry and teachings of Jesus and, above all, on the cross under that impact. He has now grasped the true meaning of all this and was prepared to act in this new light. He had been under the captivity of political messianism and perhaps also of fear, but now he has come under the captivity of the risen Christ. He had been in bondage to the political power of this world, but now has submitted himself to the bondage of the power of the resurrection. At the foot of the cross he had denied Jesus and left him to the fate of death, but now he pledged his allegiance to the resurrected Christ. He had not been free before, but now he was entirely free. He had become so free that he could declare in humility and exaltation: "We must obey God rather than men!" The power of resurrection has brought about the transposition of power between Peter and the religious authorities—a transposition that also took place between Jesus and Pilate, between Paul and Agrippa. The powerful people sitting in judgment of Peter and his fellow apostles must have felt a peculiar sense of powerlessness when they heard Peter's declaration. In contrast, from the powerless Peter and the other apostles flowed the power of truth and life which no power on earth could suppress or overcome.

The risen Christ sets us free. In his letter to the Galatians, Paul says: "Christ set us free, to be free men. Stand firm, then, and refuse to be tied to the yoke of slavery again" (Gal. 5:1). Many Christians in Asia today are learning to be free from the powers and authorities that try to enslave the human spirit and imprison the human conscience. By taking up this politics of freedom, they have become part of God's politics of the resurrection. What St. Paul said to the Corinthian Christians is therefore also true in their case:

. . . Where the Spirit of the Lord is, there is liberty. And because for us there is no veil over the face, we all reflect as in a mirror the splendour of the Lord; thus we are transfigured into his likeness, from splendour to splendour; such is the influence of the Lord who is Spirit (2 Cor. 3:17–18).

Our transfiguration takes place when we exercise our freedom under the influence of the risen Christ. The life of freedom under the power of the resurrection is thus the life that moves from splendor to splendor, as Paul says. This is the splendor of our being seen as "Christ's likeness." This likeness to Christ does not automatically happen. It does not appear in us at the waving of a magic wand. It does not come to us when we indulge in plenty of food or plenty of leisure when millions of people are starving or working themselves to death. Christ's likeness does not just pop out of us the way a Jack-in-the-box pops out of a box. We are transfigured into Christ's likeness only when we overcome the powers and principalities of this world by the power of the risen Christ. Transfiguration takes place in us only when we become engaged in the politics of freedom under the impact of the resurrection. Then, and only then, what the powers of this world have to reckon with in us is not pitiful criminals but a powerful Christ, not helpless rebels but a revolutionary Lord, not mere human beings but a transfigured Christ, not men and women condemned to death but the risen Christ.

## The Politics of Openness

This brings us to the final words of this chapter. The politics of the resurrection, like the politics manifesting itself in the freedom of Christ, is the politics of openness to the future. Openness is the key word here. What it means essentially is as follows: the politics of God that moves from darkness to light, from despair to hope, from death to life, and from the cross to the resurrection is a politics that creates the future in the present, that makes an opening at a dead end. History is now an open book. The resurrection has forced open the closed doors of history. History has been gripped by the power of the resurrection and has now to do with the future in the present and also in the past. All that happens in history, whether in the past or in the present, is not dead. It will be brought before the tribunal of the resurrection to be judged, redeemed, and re-created and to become a part of the future of God. God is the God of alpha and omega. He is the God who brings the beginning into the end and the end into the beginning. He is the God of *the beginning* and of the end. He is also the God of *the end* and of the beginning. History consists of interactions between the beginning and the end. And when the beginning and the end collide in the present, the future appears on the horizon. Resurrection therefore beckons us not from some distant future. It resides in the present to usher us into the future.

History, as understood under the profound impact of the resurrection, can best be described as an apocalyptic vision. The Book of Revelation is therefore a history—a history perceived as a vision in which the past and the future converge in the present. The extraordinary vision of the sealed book seems to give us a glimpse into history not just as a record of the human past but as a drama of divine and human actions encompassing the whole span of time. "Then I saw in the right hand of the One who sat on the throne a scroll, with writing inside and out," so begins the vision of the sealed book,

and it was sealed with seven seals. And I saw a mighty angel proclaiming in a loud voice, "Who is worthy to open the scroll and to break its seals?" There was no one in heaven or on earth or under the earth able to open the scroll or to look inside it. I was in tears because no one was found who was worthy to open the scroll or to look inside it. But one of the elders said to me: "Do not weep; for the Lion from the tribe of Judah, the scion of David, has won the right to open the scroll and break its seven seals" (Rev. 5:1–5).

The sealed book is the sealed history—history that has been rendered past and dead, history that defies the power of resurrection. As long as it remains sealed, our fate is sealed too. We become things of the past and remain forever things of the past. Our destiny in the beginning becomes at the same time our destiny at the end. Our final destination is a sealed tomb guarded by the power of death. There would be no empty tombs; even the tomb of Jesus would not become empty. No wonder the seer who found no one capable of opening the sealed book wept. Confronted with the sealed history and sealed past, we could only sing a dirge, for eternal darkness returned and everlasting death devoured every vestige of life. But to his great relief and unspeakable joy, the seer was told that the risen Christ was the one to open the sealed book. Then at once he heard a heavenly chorus singing in praise to the Lord of the resurrection:

Thou art worthy to take the scroll and to break its seals, for thou wast slain and by thy blood didst purchase for God and men of every tribe and language, people and nation; thou hast made of them a royal house, to serve God as priests; and they shall reign upon earth (Rev. 5:9–10).

Now all the inhabitants of heaven joined in the chorus. It must have sounded like the sound of a mighty stream and lofty mountains touched by the divine hand of creation. The whole cosmos was now in jubilation as "countless angels, all living creatures, myriads upon myriads, thousands upon thousands" cried aloud:

Worthy is the Lamb, the Lamb that was slain, to receive all power and wealth, wisdom and might, honour and glory and praise! (Rev. 5:12)

What a magnificent opening of history to a new future! As one seal after another was opened, history was summoned to give an account of itself before the Lamb who was slain and rose again. The whole of creation was thrown into a great convulsion. It was going through a tremendous birthpang. And when the seventh seal was broken, "there was silence in heaven" (Rev. 8:1). The chorus stopped; the jubilation came to a halt; the entire cosmos was enveloped in a deep silence just as in the beginning when God's Spirit moved over the deep and dark abyss in preparation for his work of creation (Gen. 1:1).

It must have been a terrifying silence. The power of primordial dark-ness seemed to have returned to thwart God's work of re-creation. But this silence did not last for long. The first angel broke the silence by blowing a trumpet. Then the whole universe was thrown into a terrible agony and chaos. An absolute end seemed to have descended upon the earth. All the powers in heaven and on earth were let loose to make a holocaust of all creation. But this absolute end proved to be the start of an absolute beginning. Through that horrible convulsion history was set free from its dead past and was given the power to break out to a living future. As the seer tells it:

Then I saw a new heaven and a new earth, for the first heaven and the first earth had vanished, and there was no longer sea. I saw the holy city, new Jerusalem, coming down out of heaven from God, made ready like a bride adorned for her husband. I heard a loud voice proclaiming from the throne: Now at last God has his dwelling among men! He will dwell among them and they shall be his people, and God himself will be with them. He will wipe every tear from their eyes; there shall be an end to death, and to mourning and crying and pain; for the old order has passed away (Rev. 21:1–4).

God's history begins when humanity's history comes to an end. And it is this history of God that is our history now.

A new history is born each time the politics of the resurrection breaks into the life of people and into the history of nations. This history is new because it is open to the future. It is a history created and sustained by the truth, freedom, and love given to all humanity through the resurrection of Jesus Christ. It is the history of hope because it has been molded by the power of God's creating and redeeming love. As Teilhard de Chardin, who lived so close to God and to this earth, puts it:

We may imagine perhaps that creation was finished long ago. This is not true. It continues more graciously than ever. . . and we serve to complete it, even with the humblest work of our hands. . . . In each of our works we labor, in a very minute but real way, to build the Pleroma. . . . In action I adhere to the creative power of God; I coincide with it; I become not only its instrument but its living extension.[18]

The power of the resurrection makes us into "the living extension" of God's creating power. Together with the risen Christ we become makers of a new history. As we take part in this divine politics of the resurrection, we experience the glory of the transfiguration in the transposition of all meanings, values, and powers. And under the irresistible grace of God we become witnesses to the risen Christ as the way, the truth, and the life (cf. John 14:6).

# NOTES

## Introduction

1. *The New English Bible.* All biblical quotations in this book are from *The New English Bible* unless otherwise indicated.

2. Paul Tillich, *Christianity and the Encounter of the World Religions* (New York: Columbia University Press, 1965), p. 75.

3. Hajime Nakamura, *Ways of Thinking of Eastern Peoples: India, China, Tibet, Japan* (Honolulu: East-West Center Press, 1964), p. 3.

4. R. H. S. Boyd, *India and the Latin Captivity of the Church* (London: Cambridge University Press, 1974), p. xiii.

5. Shusaku Endo, *Silence,* trans. William Johnston (Rutland, Vt., and Tokyo: Sophia University in cooperation with the Charles E. Tuttle Co., 1969), pp. 266–67.

6. William Johnston, Preface to Shusaku Endo's *Silence,* p. 11.

7. Endo, *Silence,* p. 272.

8. Lin Yutang, ed., *The Wisdom of China and India* (New York: Random House, 1942), pp. 831–32.

9. Boyd, *India and the Latin Captivity of the Church,* p. xiii.

10. Daisetz Suzuki, *Essays in Zen Buddhism,* First Series (London: Luzac & Company, 1927), p.1.

11. Quoted by Kazo Kitamori in his *Theology of the Pain of God* (Richmond, Va.: John Knox Press, 1965), p. 130.

12. James Burns, *The Christ Face in Art* (New York: E. P. Dutton & Co., 1907), p. 3.

13. In *The Christ Face in Art,* James Burns distinguishes more than a dozen types of artistic works on the Christ face, such as the Tuscan, North Italian, Venetian, Flemish, Spanish, etc.

14. Ibid., p. 16.

15. Ibid., p. 30.

16. Ibid., p. 110.

17. See Masao Takenaka, *Creation and Redemption through Japanese Art* (Osaka, Japan: Segensha, 1966), plate 71. Cf. also his more recent work, *Christian Art in Asia* (Tokyo: Kyo Bun Kwan in association with Christian Conference of Asia, 1975).

## Chapter 1    The Double Darkness

1. Cf. Wade Baskin, ed., *Classics in Chinese Philosophy* (New York: Philosophical Library, 1972), p. 62.

2. John S. Mbiti, *African Religions and Philosophy* (New York: Praeger Publishers, 1969), p. 15.

3. Rudolf Otto, *The Idea of the Holy,* trans. John W. Harvey (London: Oxford University Press, 1950), p. 39.

4. Karl Barth, *The Epistle to the Romans,* trans. Edwyn C. Hoskyns (London: Oxford University Press, 1933), p. 250.

5. *The Wisdom of Laotse,* ed. and trans., Lin Yutang (New York: Random House, The Modern Library, 1945), p. 41.

6. Lin Yutang, *The Wisdom of China and India,* p. 819.

7. Ibid., p. 829.

8. Ibid., p. 819.

9. Ibid., p. 826.

10. Paul Tillich, *Systematic Theology* (Chicago: University of Chicago Press, 1951), 1:212.

11. Kosuke Koyama, *Waterbuffalo Theology* (Maryknoll, N.Y.: Orbis Books, 1976), p. 85.

12. According to Ronald L. Johnstone, "There are more people attracted to religious cults in the United States today than were in the past. . . . There are over a million and a half Americans in the cult movement today." Among these religious cults are Transcendental Meditation, Nichiren Shoshu, Hari Krishna. See Ronald L. Johnstone, *Religion and Society in Interaction* (Englewood Cliffs, N.J.: Prentice-Hall, 1975), p. 317.

13. Hu Shih, *Wen–ts'un,* collection 3, pp. 1–11, in William Theodore de Bary, Wing–tsit Chan, and Burton Watson, comps., *Sources of Chinese Tradition* (New York: Columbia University Press, 1960), p. 854.

14. Mao Tse-tung, *Selected Works* (Peking: Foreign Language Press, 1961), 4:411.

15. Stuart Schram, *Mao Tse-tung* (New York: Penguin Books, 1967), p. 270.

16. C. K. Kurien, *Poverty and Development* (Madras: The Christian Literature Society, 1974), pp. 51–52.

17. Ibid., p. 53.

18. Ibid., p. 54.

19. *Newsweek,* November 11, 1974, p. 17.

20. Gunnar Mydal, *Asian Drama: An Inquiry into the Poverty of the Nations* (New York: The Twentieth Century Fund, 1968), 1:112.

21. H. A. Jack, ed., *The Gandhi Reader* (Bloomington, Ind.: Indiana University Press, 1956), p. 23.

22. Quoted in Lerone Bennet, Jr., *What Manner of Man: Martin Luther King, Jr.* (Chicago: Johnson Publishing Company, 1968), p. 38.

23. Martin Luther King, *Strength to Love* (New York: Harper & Row, Publishers, 1963), p. 138.

24. Eberhard Bethge, *Dietrich Bonhoeffer: Man of Vision, Man of Courage* (New York: Harper & Row, Publishers, 1970), pp. 329–30.

25. Ibid., p. 332.

26. *The Cost of Discipleship,* rev. ed. (New York: Macmillan, 1963).

27. Karl Barth obviously was not amused by Bonhoeffer's plan to visit India. In writing to Bonhoeffer in October 1936, he says: "Do you remember that business of 'the next ship but one'? And yet the only thing I have heard about you in ages is the strange news that you intend to go to India so as to learn some kind of spiritual technique from Gandhi or some other holy man and that you expect great things of its application in the West" (quoted in Bethge, *Dietrich Bonhoeffer,* p. 330).

28. Harvey Cox, *The Seduction of the Spirit* (New York: Simon and Schuster, 1973), p. 304.

29. No. 14; see *The Gospel of Peace and Justice,* Joseph Gremillion, ed. (Maryknoll, N.Y.: Orbis Books, 1976), p. 391.

## Chapter 2        God's Heartache: The Beginning of Theology

1. John Skinner, *Genesis,* 2nd ed. (Edinburgh: T. & T. Clark, 1930), p. 171.

2. James B. Pritchard, ed., *The Ancient Near East: An Anthology of Texts and Pictures* (Princeton, N.J.: Princeton University Press, 1958), p. 34.

3. Ibid., p. 35.

4. E. H. Speiser, *Genesis,* The Anchor Bible 1 (New York: Doubleday & Company, 1964), p. 10.

5. Hermann Gunkel, for example, made the following observation: "Die Lehre, dass die Welt aus Finsternis geworden sei, finden wir auch bei Babylonien, Agyptern, Indern, Phönizien, Griechen, Chinesen. . . und sonst: die Nacht ist das Erste, Ursprüngliche, das Licht der Anfang der gegenwärtigen Welt" (Gunkel, *Genesis,* Göttingen: Vandenhoeck & Ruprecht, 1919), p. 103.

6. Lin Yutang, ed., *The Wisdom of China and India,* p. 15. The *Rigveda,* songs of spiritual knowledge, says Lin Yutang, embodies Hindu "preoccupation with God and the mystic conception of the universe" (ibid., p. 11).

7. This is a lamentation psalm that combines individual laments and the lament of the

nation. According to Artur Weiser, "The subject of the lament is not personal suffering, such as illness or personal persecution of the worshipper, but the affliction of the people that became the occasion for that crisis in the worshipper's own faith" (see *The Psalms*, trans. Herbert Hartwell, Philadelphia: The Westminster Press, 1962, p. 530). In any case the meaning of life is at stake here.

8. *Tehom*, the cosmic abyss, "is unquestionably connected with the Babylonian Tiamat, that primeval dragon of chaos" (Gerhard von Rad, *Genesis*, trans. John H. Marks, Philadelphia: The Westminster Press, 1961, p. 48).

9. Hajime Nakamura, *Ways of Thinking of Eastern Peoples*, p. 163.

10. See Choan-Seng Song, *Christian Mission in Reconstruction: An Asian Attempt* (Madras: The Christian Literature Society, 1975, and Maryknoll, N.Y.: Orbis Books, 1977). Chapters 2 and 3 are especially relevant to our discussion here.

11. Dwight Goddard, ed., *A Buddhist Bible* (Boston: Beacon Press, 1966), p. 9.

12. C. K. Barrett, *The Fourth Gospel* (London: Faber and Faber, 1947), p. 127.

13. Ibid.

14. Justo L. Gonzalez, *A History of Christian Thought* (Nashville and New York: Abingdon Press, 1971), 2:76.

15. The statement is found in the General Introduction to *Christology of Later Fathers*, Library of Christian Classics, vol. 3 (London: SCM Press, 1954), p. 17.

16. T. F. Torrance, "Theses on Truth," *The Irish Theological Quarterly* 39, no. 3 (1972):217, quoted in R. H. S. Boyd, *India and the Latin Captivity of the Church*, pp. 88–89.

17. T. F. Torrance, *Theological Science* (London: Oxford University Press, 1969), p. 11.

18. T. F. Torrance, *God and Rationality* (London: Oxford University Press, 1971), p. 196.

19. Ibid., p. 200.

20. Ibid., p. 201.

21. Ibid.

22. We must be careful not to overgeneralize modes of thinking characterized as eastern and western. Even within Asia a wide difference exists between different peoples, as Hajime Nakamura repeatedly reminds us in his *Ways of Thinking of Eastern Peoples*. He says, for example, "It is often said that the peoples of the East are intuitive, and accordingly not systematic or orderly in grasping things; by contrast the Westerners are said to be 'postulational' or logical, and that they try to grasp things systematically and by orderly planning. Indeed, the ways of thinking of the Chinese or Japanese may be characterized as 'intuitive'. But in the case of the Indians this label is hard to apply. For example, the intricate arguments of the Abhidharma literature are logical and can never be called intuitive" (Hajime Nakamura, *Ways of Thinking*, p. 13).

23. Ibid., p. 575.

24. Daisetz Suzuki, *Essays in Zen Buddhism*, First Series, p. 216.

25. Ibid., p. 221.

26. To quote Calvin: "If we desire to provide in the best way for our consciences—that they may not be perpetually beset by the instability of doubt or vacillation, and that they may not also boggle at the smallest quibbles—we ought to seek our conviction in a higher place than human reasons, judgments, or conjectures, that is, in the secret testimony of the Spirit" (Ford Lewis Battles, trans., and John T. McNeill, ed., *Institutes of the Christian Religion* [Philadelphia: The Westminster Press, 1960], Book I. 7.4, p. 78).

27. Dwight Goddard, ed., *A Buddhist Bible*, p. 27.

28. Ibid., p. 22.

29. Ibid., p. 33. The Noble Eightfold Path which leads to the extinction of suffering is (1) Right Understanding, (2) Right Mindedness, (3) Right Speech, (4) Right Action, (5) Right Living, (6) Right Effort, (7) Right Attentiveness, (8) Right Concentration.

30. John Bunyan, *The Pilgrim's Progress* (New York: Macmillan Company, 1948), p. 27.

31. Dwight Goddard, ed., *A Buddhist Bible*, p. 59.

32. See George Elton Ladd, *A Theology of the New Testament* (Grand Rapids, Mich.: William B. Eerdmanns Publishing Company, 1974), pp. 481–83, for a short historical survey on theological discussions relative to the mysticism of St. Paul. It was Deismann who interpreted the Pauline expression "in Christ" in terms of mystical fellowship. Bultmann and Conzelmann, for example, now reject such a view.

33. Paul Tillich, *Christianity and the Encounter of the World Religions* (New York: Columbia University Press, 1963), pp. 65–66.

34. See Nakamura, *Ways of Thinking*, p. 412. This is a poem which Ryonin (1072–1132), the founder of the Yuzu Nembutsu sect, is supposed to have received from Amida Buddha in his meditation.

35. Dwight Goddard, ed., *A Buddhist Bible*, pp. 31–32.

36. See Gustaf Aulen, *Christus Victor*, trans. G. Hebert (New York: Macmillan, 1951), p. 81.

37. Ibid.

38. Ibid., p. 82.

## Chapter 3    Love as the Possibility of Theology

1. Paul S. Minear, "Theology: Vocation or Profession?" in Choan-Seng Song, ed., *Doing Theology Today* (Madras: The Christian Literature Society, 1976), p. 14.

2. Psalm 139:23, RSV. The New English Bible renders the verse as follows: "Examine me, O God, and know my thoughts; test me, and understand my misgivings." RSV's rendering of the Hebrew word *lēbāb* as "heart" is more literal and forceful than the NEB's "thoughts."

3. Gerhard Kittel, ed., and G. W. Bromiley, trans. *Theological Dictionary of the New Testament* (Grand Rapids, Mich.: Wm. B. Eerdmans Publishing Company, 1975), 1: 606–7.

4. Ibid., p. 610.

5. Ibid., p. 616.

6. Daisetz Suzuki, *Outlines of Mahayana Buddhism* (New York: Schocken, 1963), p. 25.

7. Kazo Kitamori, *The Theology of the Pain of God* (Richmond, Va.: John Knox Press, 1965), p. 19.

8. Ibid., p. 27.

9. Ibid.

10. Carl Michalson, *Japanese Contribution to Christian Theology* (Philadelphia: The Westminster Press, 1960), p. 79.

11. Jürgen Moltmann, *The Crucified God*, trans. R. A. Wilson and John Bowden (New York: Harper & Row, Publishers, 1974), p. 152.

12. "Theological Trial between God and God" in the German original is "Der theologische Prozess zwischen Gott und Gott." See *Der gekreuzigte Gott* (Munich: Chr. Kaiser Verlag, 1972), p. 145.

13. Kitamori, *Theology of the Pain of God*, p. 47.

14. Ibid., p. 140.

15. Ibid., p. 148.

16. Ibid., p. 135 and p. 177, n. 9.

17. This parable is commonly known as the parable of the prodigal son, but it would be more accurate to call it the parable of the father's love. Joachim Jeremias states: "But we have not yet spoken of the third line of attack, by far the most decisive, with which Jesus vindicates the proclamation of the Good News to the despised and outcast. It appears most clearly in the Parable of the Prodigal Son, which might more correctly be called the Parable of the Father's Love" (Jeremias, *The Parables of Jesus*, S. H. Hooke, trans., New York: Charles Scribner's Sons, 1963, p. 128).

18. Shusaku Endo, *Sikai no Hotori* (By the Side of the Dead Sea) (Tokyo: Shin-cho Shia, 1973), pp. 37–38. My translation.

19. There are several conjectures as to the historical background of this oracle. Perhaps it is correct to say that "the basic substance of the text relates to the . . . situation that existed after the siege of Jerusalem by the Assyrian King Sennacherib in the year 701." See Otto Kaiser, *Isaiah 13–39* (Philadelphia: The Westminster Press, 1974), p. 139.

20. Admah and Zeboyim are the cities of the plain that perished along with Sodom and Gomorrah.

21. Kitamori, *Theology of the Pain of God*, p. 150.

22. The verb used in John 3:16 is *egapesen*, the noun form of which is *agape*. This is of course the unconditional love that God has shown to the world in Jesus Christ. It is the love that suffers.

23. Daniel D. Williams, *The Spirit and the Forms of Love* (New York: Harper & Row, Publishers, 1968), p. 117.

24. Gerhard Kittel, ed., *Theological Dictionary of the New Testament*, 4:627.

25. "In form, as in substance, the passage has all the characteristics of a hymn or a poem, and must have been composed deliberately with this end in view. It has been argued . . . that Paul has here inserted a Christian song with which his readers would be familiar, and which expressed his own ideas more forcefully and beautifully than he could do himself." (See *The Interpreter's Bible* [New York: Abingdon Press, 1955], 11:46–47.)

26. The following is a succinct description of *The Bhagavad-Gita:* "The Bhagavadgita is a religious classic rather than a philosophical treatise. It is set forth not as a metaphysical system thought out by an individual thinker or school of thinkers but as a tradition which has emerged from the religious life of mankind. . . . The Gita derives its main inspiration from the Upanishads and integrates into a comprehensive synthesis the different elements of the Vedic cult of sacrifice, the Upanishadic teaching of the Absolute Brahman, the Bhagavata theism, the Samkhya dualism, and the Yoga meditation. It is a part of the Mahabharata, and its authorship is attributed to Vyasa." See S. Radhakrishnan and Charles A. Moore, eds., *A Source Book in Indian Philosophy* (Princeton, N.J.: Princeton University Press, 1957), p. 101.

27. Ibid., p. 162.

28. Rudolf Otto, *India's Religion of Grace* (London: SCM Press, 1930), p. 55.

29. Ibid., pp. 54–55.

30. See Kenneth K. S. Ch'en, *Buddhism, The Light of Asia* (New York: Barron's Educational Series, 1968), p. 181.

31. Ibid., pp. 180–81.

32. See Otto, *India's Religion of Grace*, p. 18.

33. Karl Barth, *Church Dogmatics* I/2, trans. G. T. Thomson and Harold Knight (Edinburgh: T. & T. Clark, 1963), p. 340.

34. Ibid., p. 343. Yodoism or Jodoism, the Pure Land Sect, was founded by Honen (1133–1211). His disciple Shinran developed it into Jodo Shinshu, the Pure Land New Sect.

35. Radhakrishnan and Moore, eds., *A Source Book in Indian Philosophy*, p. 8. Most of the hymns in the Rigveda go as far back as the fifteenth century B.C.

36. Williams, *Spirit and the Forms of Love*, p. 4.

37. Vine Deloria, Jr., *God is Red* (New York: Grosset & Dunlap, 1973), p. 123.

## Chapter 4        Theology as the Love of the God-Man in Action

1. T. F. Torrance, *Theological Science*, p. 9.

2. Ibid., p. 26.

3. Ibid., pp. 26–27.

4. Juan Luis Segundo, S.J., *The Liberation of Theology*, trans. John Drury (Maryknoll, N.Y.: Orbis Books, 1976), p. 8.

5. James Cone, *The God of the Oppressed* (New York: The Seabury Press, 1975), p. 15.

6. James Cone, *Black Theology and Black Power* (New York: The Seabury Press, 1969).

7. Cone, *God of the Oppressed*, p. 136.

8. Ibid., p. 238. See also Deotis Roberts, *Liberation and Reconciliation: A Black Theology* (Philadelphia: The Westminster Press, 1971).

9. Oh Jae Shik and John England, eds., *Theology in Action, A Workshop Report*, September 1–12, 1972, Manila, the Philippines (Singapore: Asian Christian Conference), p. 10. The second workshop on Theology in Action was held in Kuala Lumpur, W. Malaysia, March 1–6, 1973.

10. Ayako Miura, *Hyo-ten* (The Freezing Point) (Tokyo: Asahi Shin-bun-sha, 1965). The quotations from *Hyo–ten* are my translation from the Japanese original. In the order they occur in the text, readers are referred to pp. 69, 281, and 403.

11. Martin Buber's *I and Thou* was first published in Germany in 1923 under the title *Ich und du.*

12. Martin Buber, *I and Thou*, Walter Kaufmann, trans. (New York: Charles Scribner's & Sons, 1970), p. 57.

13. Ibid., p. 62.

14. Unfortunately the source of this poem is lost to me. I first heard it from my philosophy teacher Professor Fang Tung-mei of National Taiwan University in his course on the Chinese philosophy of life. I therefore quote the poem from memory.

15. The Song of Songs has been interpreted in many ways—allegorically, as a collection of Jewish wedding songs, and as a secular love song. It owes its canonical status to its stress on human love as an analogy of divine love. Theophile J. Meek observes: "The phrase 'the Song of Songs' would seem to be a superlative, 'the best of songs' like 'the Lord of lords' and kindred expressions. Hence Rabbi Akiba (early second century), according to the Mishnah (yedaim 3:5), called it 'the holy of holies' and said that 'no day outweighed in glory the one on which Israel received the Song of Songs.' " See Meek, *The Interpreter's Bible*, vol. V (New York: Abingdon Press, 1956), pp. 91–96.

16. Wing-Tsit Chan, for example, compares Mo Ti and Confucius as follows: "The motive of benefits is behind all Maoist doctrines. Confucianists throughout history have condemned benefits as motivation instead of righteousness. For Confucius, a main difference between a superior man and an inferior man is that the former is after righteousness and the latter after benefits. Not that Confucianism renounces benefits. On the contrary, it promotes them. But they should be the *results* of good deeds, not the *motivation* for them. Mo Tzu does emphasize righteousness, but to him righteousness is to be understood in terms of beneficial results." See Wing-Tsit Chan, *A Source Book in Chinese Philosophy* (Princeton, N.J.: Princeton University Press, 1963), p. 215.

17. Family-ism is the ideology that constitutes the basis of Confucianist China. According to Joseph M. Kitagawa, "Traditional Chinese society rested upon the principle of 'Family-ism,' which, in turn, was based on the Confucian concept of filial piety. The nation-state in the modern sense never existed in China until recently. Instead, the state was regarded as a super family . . . in which the relationship among members of different social strata were governed by Confucian moral principles. In short, the family in China has been a 'metaphysical' focus as well as a 'sociological' unit" (*Religions of the East*, Philadelphia: The Westminster Press, 1968, p. 43).

18. See Wing-Tsit Chan, *A Source Book in Chinese Philosophy*, p. 213.

19. Ibid., p. 214.

20. See C. P. Fitzgerald, *China: A Short Cultural History*, C. G. Seligman, ed. (London: The Cresset Press, 1935), p. 98.

21. See Ninian Smart, ed., *Historical Selections in the Philosophy of Religion* (London: SCM Press, 1962).

22. Swami Mikhilanada, ed., *The Upanishads* (New York: Harper & Row, Publishers, Harper Torchbooks, 1964), p. 189.

23. Kierkegaard deals with the thesis that truth is subjectivity in Chapter 2 of his *Concluding Unscientific Postscripts*, David Swenson and Walter Lowrie, trans. (Princeton, N.J.: Princeton University Press, 1941), pp. 169–224.

## Chapter 5   The Cross and the Lotus

1. "The symbolism of the lotus-flower was borrowed by the Buddhists directly from the parent religion Brahmanism. Primarily, the lotus-flower appears to have symbolized for the Aryans from remote times the idea of superhuman or divine birth, and secondarily, the creative force and instrumentality. The traditional Indian and Buddhist explanation of it is that the glorious lotus-flower appears to spring not from the solid earth but from the surface of the water, and is always pure and unsullied, no matter how impure may be the water of the lake" (*Encyclopedia of Religion and Ethics*, James Hastings, ed., Edinburgh: T. & T. Clark, 1975, vol. 8, p. 144).

2. Arthur Schopenhauer, *The World as Will and Representation* (The Falem's Wing Press, 1945), 2:443–44. Quoted by O Hyun Park in *Oriental Ideas in Recent Religious Thought* (Lakemont, Ga.: CSA Press, 1974), p. 116.

3. See Piero Gheddo, *The Cross and the Bo-tree: Catholics and Buddhists in Vietnam* (New York: Sheed & Ward, 1970), pp. 242–43.

4. Paul Tillich, *Dynamics of Faith* (New York: Harper and Brothers, Publishers, 1957), p. 45.

5. Mircea Eliade, *Images and Symbols: Studies in Religious Symbolism*, trans. Philip Mairet (New York: Sheed & Ward, 1952), p. 12.

6. Charles Allen Clarke, *First Fruits in Korea* (New York: Fleming H. Revell Company, 1921), p. 101.

7. Tillich's following remark concerning sexual rites and symbols is very much to the point: "In judging the sexual rites and symbols of many religions, one should remember that it is not the sexual in itself which is revealing but the mystery of being which through the medium of the sexual manifests its relation to us in a special way. This explains and justifies the rich use of sexual symbols in classical Christianity. Protestantism, rightly aware of the danger of a demonization of these symbols, has developed an extreme distrust of them, often forgetting the mediating character of sex in revelatory experiences. But the goddesses of love are in the first place goddesses, displaying divine power and dignity, and only in the second place do they represent the sexual realm in its ultimate meaning. Protestantism, in rejecting sexual symbolism, is in danger of losing much symbolic wealth but also of cutting off the sexual realm from the ground of being and meaning in which it is rooted and from which it gets its consecration." See Tillich, *Systematic Theology* (Chicago: University of Chicago Press, 1951), 1:119, note 4.

8. Eliade, *Images and Symbols*, p. 174.

9. See also Isaiah 40:18–20.

10. See *The Interpreter's Dictionary of the Bible*, 2:676.

11. Ibid., p. 673.

12. Ibid., p. 676.

13. Protestant Christianity has not been able to make a fine distinction here and tended to play down the visual aspect of religious devotion in favor of the aural aspect. It has always appealed to the ear to the exclusion of the eye. Tillich's historical observation on this point is very important. He writes: "If we look at the history of Protestantism, we find that it has continued and often surpassed the achievement of the early and medieval churches with respect to religious music and hymnical poetry but that it has fallen very short of their creative power in all the visual arts. . . . This is related to the turn in the late Middle Ages from the emphasis on the eye to the emphasis on the ear. . . . The background of this rejection of arts of the eye is the fear—and even horror—of a relapse into idolatry. From early biblical times up to the present day, a stream of iconoclastic fear and passion runs through the Western and Islamic world, and there can be no doubt that the arts of the eye are more open to idolatrous demonization than the arts of the ear. But the difference is relative, and the very nature of the Spirit stands against the exclusion of the eye from the experience of its presence" (*Systematic Theology*, Chicago: University of Chicago Press, 1963, 3:200).

14. Eliade, *Images and Symbols*, pp. 174–75.

15. Joseph M. Kitagawa, *Religions of the East*, p. 210.

16. Arend T. van Leeuwen, *Christianity in World History* (London: Edinburgh House Press, 1965), p. 146.

17. For the origin and meaning of the symbolism of the lotus, see note 1 above.

18. It is certain that Jesus did not use parables to hide the truth about the kingdom of God from the people. As is pointed out, "for those who came to Jesus expecting or demanding either a revolutionary or a wonder-worker a different approach was necessary." Thus the parables provided an alternate approach. See W. F. Albright and C. S. Mann, eds., *Matthew: The Anchor Bible* (New York: Doubleday and Company, 1971), p. cxlii.

19. Kenneth Ch'en, *Buddhism*, p. 11.

20. Ibid., pp. 11–12.

21. See *The Gospel of Buddha*, Paul Carus (Chicago: The Open Court Publishing Company, 1894), p. 159.

22. See William Theodore de Bary, ed., *The Buddhist Traditions in India, China, and Japan* (New York: Vintage Books, 1972), pp. 89–90.

23. John Knox, for example, says in his exegesis on Romans 1:19–23: "It now becomes apparent that Paul is to speak first to the Gentiles; and that the first and most important item in his indictment of the Gentile world is its idolatry." See *The Interpreter's Bible*, 9:398.

24. Paul Tillich, *Systematic Theology*, 3:102.

25. Edward Conze, comp. and trans., *Buddhist Scriptures* (Baltimore: Penguin Books, 1959), p. 54.

26. Christmas Humphreys, *Exploring Buddhism* (London: George Allen and Unwin, 1974), p. 89.

27. The population of Indonesia is made up of the following elements: Muslims 85

percent; Christians 6.3 percent; Hindu-Bali 2 percent; Buddhists 0.9 percent; and others 5.9 percent. See Frank L. Cooley, *Indonesia: Church and Society* (New York: Friendship Press, 1968), p. 125.

28. Thich Nhat Hanh, *The Lotus in the Sea of Fire* (London: SCM, 1967), p. 9.

29. Ibid.

30. Frances FitzGerald, *Fire in the Lake: The Vietnamese and Americans in Vietnam* (Boston: Little, Brown and Company, 1972), p. 81.

31. Thich Nhat Hanh, *Lotus,* p. 118.

32. Ibid.

33. "Afterward" by Alfred Hassler in Thich Nhat Hanh, *Lotus,* pp. 109–110.

## Chapter 6    The Seed of Hope in the Womb

1. Nguyen Ngoc Bich, ed., *A Thousand Years of Vietnamese Poetry* (New York: Alfred A. Knopf, 1975), pp. 204–5.

2. Frances FitzGerald, *Fire in the Lake,* pp. 428–29.

3. Nasatosh Doi, "Dialogue Between Living Faiths in Japan," in *Dialogue Between Men of Living Faiths,* papers presented at a consultation held at Ajaltoun, Lebanon, March 1970, S. J. Samartha, ed. (Lucknow: Lucknow Publishing House, 1972), p. 42.

4. Gerhard von Rad, *Genesis: A Commentary,* trans. John H. Marks (Philadelphia: The Westminster Press, 1972), p. 207.

5. This is a controversial text in the history of Old Testament interpretation. Otto Kaiser has summarized the situation as follows: "The interpretation of the sentences that follow is among the most disputed in all scripture. Exegetes are not agreed either as to whether they form a promise or a warning, or who is meant by the child Immanuel. Since Matt. 1:22f, and to some extent even up to the present day, a hidden prophecy of the marvelous birth of Jesus Christ has been seen in the passage" (Otto Kaiser, *Isaiah 1–12: A Commentary,* Philadelphia: The Westminster Press, 1972, p. 88).

6. "John's mission is like that of Elijah, according to the proof-text of Mal. 3:22–3 and the account of Elijah in Sir. 48. He is to prepare a penitent and faithful Israel as God's people" (Matthew Black and H. H. Rowley, eds., *Peake's Commentary on the Bible,* London: Thomas Nelson and Sons, 1962, p. 828).

7. "The Lord is with you." This greeting of the angel gives Mary the assurance that she is in God's care and that God is favorably disposed toward her.

8. According to Cassuto, the name is usually explained to mean "smith" on the basis of the Arabic *qaynum,* and the Aramaic *qenaya* or *qena'a.* . . . The primary significance of the stem *qyn* in Arabic, too, is "to fashion," "to shape," "to give form to. . . . " In regard to the verb *qanithi,* it appears, especially in view of what we have learned in recent years about the usage of the root in the ancient Canaanite tongue, that its connotation here is: "I have formed (created), gave birth to. . . ." See U. Cassuto, *A Commentary on the Book of Genesis* (Jerusalem: The Magnes Press, Hebrew edition, 1944, English edition, 1961), pp. 197–99.

9. Ibid., p. 201.

10. Speaking of pain in childbearing, Genesis 3:16 presents a problem, for the pain of childbearing is associated with the punishment inflicted on woman on account of the part she played in the fall. Many Old Testament scholars and exegetes have tried to explain the passage without adding an undue moral burden to the mother who undergoes the pain of childbearing while everybody else waits for the birth with expectation and joy. Von Rad, for example, says: "The woman and the man are not cursed (it is unthinking to speak of their malediction!), but severe afflictions and terrible contradictions now break upon the woman's life. 'In the bondage of compulsive drive and yet most immediately involved in the work of creation, groaning in pain, cramped in travail, humiliated, overburdened, care-worn, and tear-stained. . . .' (see W. Vischer, *Christus-Zeugnis,* p. 80.) Whence these sorrows, contradictions and degradation in a woman's life? It is not a small matter that our narrative absolves God's creation for a part in all this. Here a primeval offence receives its consequence, which faith recognizes as a punishment" (Gerhard von Rad, *Genesis: A Commentary,* p. 93). Perhaps more deserving of our attention is Claus Westermann's explanation of this passage. On the one hand he stresses the fact that "no eternally valid norm is pronounced; it is a question of the lot of woman's life as it was understood at that time. . . . On the other hand, it must be

said just as clearly that there is something here belonging to the very being of women. . . . The whole process of conception, pregnancy, and birth, from the moment the child begins to be right up to its definitive separation from the mother, belongs to the life of woman" (Claus Westermann, *Creation,* John J. Saillim, S.J., trans., Philadelphia: Fortress Press, 1974, p. 101).

At any rate, a passage such as the one we are discussing presents hermeneutical difficulty for the church today. It is therefore all the more important for us to take seriously what Phyllis Trible calls "depatriarchalization." This is a beginning of a new hermeneutics, as she points out: "I know that Hebrew literature comes from a male dominated society. I know that biblical religion is patriarchal, and I understand the adverse effects of that religion for women. . . . Nevertheless, I affirm that the intentionality of biblical faith . . . is neither to create nor to perpetuate patriarchy but rather to function as salvation for both women and men. . . . The hermeneutical challenge is to translate biblical faith without sexism" (Phyllis Trible, "Depatriarchalizing in Biblical Interrelation," *Journal of the American Academy of Religion* 41, no. 1 (March 1973):317.

11. Thanks to the Women's Liberation Movement, women theologians are beginning to make their contributions to Christian theology from their unique point of vantage. Their theology, like the Third World theologies, will disclose important dimensions of Christian perception of the mystery of God's creation and redemption.

12. It has been argued that Elizabeth should be the one who utters the Magnificat. But as has been pointed out, "The dispute is academic, for neither Mary nor Elizabeth can seriously be considered as the author of the psalm. Almost every phrase in the Magnificat has its parallel in 1 Sam. 1:11, 1 Sam. 2:1–10, or elsewhere in the Old Testament. Luke or his source took a Jewish (or Jewish-Christian) hymn of praise and fitted it to the situation" (*The Interpreter's Bible,* 8:42).

13. I again refer to Phyllis Trible's effort to depatriarchalize the interpretation of the Old Testament. See note 10 above.

14. We have already touched upon this point in Chapter 3 when we discussed Kazo Kitamori's theology of the pain of God.

15. The Hebrew word *toledoth* means "family tree," "genealogy" (literally "generations").

16. Walter Eichrodt, *Theology of the Old Testament,* trans. J. A. Baker (Philadelphia: The Westminster Press, 1967), 2:244.

17. David M. Paton, ed., *Breaking Barriers, Nairobi 1975,* Official Report of the Fifth Assembly of the World Council of Churches, Nairobi, November 23–December 13, 1975 (London: SPCK, 1976), p. 74. Nothing conclusive is said in this section of the report, which can be regarded only as an exploratory attempt. One wishes that a bolder step had been taken with the faith in Jesus Christ who frees and unites.

## Chapter 7      The Rice of Hope

1. From Nguyen Ngoc Bich, ed., *A Thousand Years of Vietnamese Poetry,* pp. 200–201.

2. The wording is from the RSV. "Psalm 6 is regarded as the first of the seven penitential psalms of the ancient Church. The others are: Psalms 32, 38, 51, 102, 130 and 143. However, the theme of penitence is not particularly prominent in the present Psalm . . . " (Artur Weiser, *The Psalms: A Commentary,* The Old Testament Library, Philadelphia: The Westminster Press, 1962, p. 132). Lamentations and petitions, according to Weiser, constitute the main part of this psalm.

3. See Augustine, *Confessions and Enchiridion,* The Library of Christian Classics, vol. 7, trans. and ed. Albert C. Outler (Philadelphia: The Westminster Press, 1955), pp. 216–17.

4. Ibid., p. 217.

5. Ibid., p. 223.

6. "A Messiah who suffers and dies as a substitute for all men in the New Testament sense was unknown in Judaism. To be sure, there is evidence for suffering *or* for death of the Messiah, but not for a Messiah who suffers *and* dies" (*Interpreter's Dictionary of the Bible,* vol. K–Q, p. 365). Therefore there is a basis for the relation of Peter's denial to his disillusionment in Jesus.

7. There have been attempts to absolve Peter of his denial of Jesus. For example,

"Guguel, the distinguished French Protestant scholar, has recently concluded that the story of Peter's denial has no historical value. His chief arguments are that Peter's place of leadership in the earliest days of the Church would have been impossible, had he been guilty of such a serious defection as the one described" (B. Harvie Branscomb, *The Gospel of Mark,* The Moffat New Testament Commentary, New York and London: Harper and Brothers Publishers, 1941), p. 281.

8. "Christians are to enact the whole actions of the Lord's Supper . . . in recollection of Jesus, and this not merely in such sort that they simply remember, but rather, in accordance with the active sense of anamnesis. . . . The making present by the later community of the Lord who instituted the Supper, and who put the new into effect by His death, is the goal and content of their action." See Gerhard Kittel, ed., Geoffrey W. Bromley trans., *Theological Dictionary of the Bible,* 5:349.

9. C. H. Dodd is quoted in Donald Baillie and John Marsh, eds., *Intercommunion.* See Donald Baillie, *The Theology of the Sacraments* (New York: Charles Scribner's Sons, 1957), p. 105.

10. Ibid., p. 106.

11. Kenneth Scott Latourette, *A History of Christian Missions in China* (New York: Macmillan Company, 1929), p. 154.

12. Ibid., p. 152.

13. Ibid., p. 154. Matteo Ricci, the greatest of the Jesuit pioneers, who was assigned to China in 1582, took a rather liberal view of ancestor worship. According to Latourette, "Ricci, after prolonged study, took the moderate position, deciding that the rites in honor of Confucius and ancestors had only a civil significance and that Christians could engage in them insofar as the laws of the Empire required . . . and he hoped that the Catholic practices concerning burial and honoring the dead would gradually supplant those of the older China" (ibid., p. 134).

14. *Breaking Barriers, Nairobi, 1975,* Official Report of the Fifth Assembly of the World Council of Churches, p. 70. In the course of the debate following the presentation of the draft report, Dr. Lynn A. de Silva from Sri Lanka made a number of observations that deserve our attention. He said among other things: "Dialogue is urgent and essential for us in Asia in order to repudiate the arrogance, aggression, and negativism of our evangelistic crusades which have obscured the gospel and caricatured Christianity as an aggressive and militant religion. As a result of this Jesus Christ appears in the eyes of people of other faiths as a religious Julius Caesar, as one of our honored guests from another faith present in this Assembly put it in one of our Section's meetings. Let us remind ourselves that Jesus Christ was not a Christian—he belongs to all—but we have made him appear as a Western Christian of an affluent society, somewhat like a Julius Caesar" (*Breaking the Barriers,* p. 72).

15. Baillie, *Theology of the Sacraments,* p. 70.

16. I think the point that ancestor worship has to do more with life than with death needs to be borne in mind. This is in a sense a belief in the continuation of life through the continuation of the family. We may recall Confucius' saying that he who fails to raise a male heir commits the greatest unfilial act. This Confucian teaching has been misused in China in a practice such as concubinage. But it can be also seen as the Chinese way of believing that our life is continued in the lives of our posterity.

17. Walter Eichrodt, *Theology of the Old Testament,* trans. J. A. Baker (Philadelphia: The Westminster Press, 1967), 2:221.

18. *Encyclopedia of Religion and Ethics,* 1:427.

19. Emily M. Ahern, *The Cult of the Dead in a Chinese Village* (Stanford, Cal.: Stanford University Press, 1973), p. 91.

20. That the deceased persons are not regarded as gods can be seen in the kinds of food offered to them in comparison with the food offered to the deities. Emily M. Ahern makes an interesting observation: "Supernatural beings are offered food that is less transformed, and therefore less like human food, according to their difference from the humans making the offerings. For example, of all the supernaturals, the ancestors are probably the most like those who offer them food. As ancestors in halls or domestic shrines they are well-known kinsmen with distinctive, individual identities; they can be spoken to, apologized to, thanked, and so on. They are generally accessible and familiar beings. Consequently, they

are offered food that is precisely like the food consumed by those who offer it. The gods, on a more distant level, receive different offerings according to their ranks . . . " (ibid., p. 167).

21. In Eichrodt's words: "If any circumstance at all can be pressed into service to provide some sort of effective proof of the existence of ancestor worship, then the only one worthy of real consideration is the strikingly high regard in which the ancestral graves were held. Genesis in particular is absolutely full of traditions about the graves of the patriarchs and their families. . . . " Then he cites examples such as Abraham's purchase of the cave of Machpelah (Gen. 23), the grave of Rachel (Gen. 35:19), and so on. See *Theology of the Old Testament,* 2:217.

22. Baillie, *Theology of the Sacraments,* p. 71.

## Chapter 8    Suffering unto Hope

1. Richard D. N. Dickinson, *To Set at Liberty the Oppressed* (Geneva: World Council of Churches, 1975), p. 34.

2. Ibid., pp. 20–21.

3. Rubem Alves, a Latin American theologian, speaks, for example, of the theology of captivity.

4. The poem is by Denis Murphy. It is quoted in *CCA News* (Christian Conference of Asia) 2, no. 10 (October 15, 1976):5.

5. Williston Walker, *A History of the Christian Church* (New York: Charles Scribner's Sons, 1959), p. 209. Henry IV obtained absolution on January 28, 1077, but was excommunicated again in March 1080.

6. John K. Fairbank, ed., in *The Missionary Enterprise in China and America* (Cambridge, Mass.: Harvard University Press, 1974), p. 271.

7. Gerhard von Rad, *Old Testament Theology,* trans. D.M.G. Stalker (New York: Harper and Brothers, 1962), 1:17.

8. The Suffering Servant, in a sense, can be seen as a redemptive element in the history of Israel, which, as has been pointed out, was much involved in the use of its military power against other nations.

9. See the temptation story in Matt. 4:8–10 and Luke 4:5–8.

10. Stuart Miller, in *The Missionary Enterprise in China and America,* ed. John K. Fairbank, p. 273.

11. D. Bonhoeffer, *Letters and Papers from Prison,* enlarged ed. (London: SCM Press, 1971), p. 360f.

12. In Jürgen Moltmann's words: "Jesus' death cannot be understood as 'the death of God,' but as death in God. The 'death' of God cannot be designated the origin of Christian theology, even if the phrase has an element of truth in it; the origin of Christian theology is only the death on the cross in God and God in Jesus' death" (*The Crucified God,* p. 207).

13. Ibid., p. 205.

14. Elie Wiesel, *Night,* 1969, p. 75f. Quoted by Moltmann in *The Crucified God,* pp. 273–74. The story also appears in Dorothee Sölle, *Leiden* (Stuttgart-Berlin: Kreuz-Verlag, 1973), p. 178.

15. See Corretta King, *My Life with Martin Luther King, Jr.* (New York: Holt, Rinehart and Winston, 1969), pp. 239–40.

16. Paul Tillich, *Courage to Be* (New Haven: Yale University Press, 1952), p. 181.

17. From unpublished paper "Hunger Priority of the Christian Conference of Asia," prepared by Carmencita Karagdag, Harry Daniel, and Harvey Perkins, staff of the Christian Conference of Asia, Singapore, April 1976.

18. Ibid.

19. Ibid.

20. See Gerhard von Rad, *Old Testament Theology,* 1:129–35, for the meaning of convenant in the Old Testament.

21. *Study Examiner, Catholic News of the Week,* May 10, 1974. Quoted in an unpublished paper "The Theology of Liberation," prepared by the Institute of Labor and Manpower Studies in the Philippines.

22. Quoted by Moltmann in *The Crucified God,* p. 124.

23. Bonhoeffer, *Letters and Papers from Prison,* p. 125.

## Chapter 9      The Cross in the Resurrection

1. Karl Barth says, for example: "Christian faith naturally says Yes to the created world—a secure, definitive and absolute Yes. What is it essentially but an echoing and mirroring of the divine Yes which God Himself spoke in this matter when He raised Jesus Christ from the dead? And if it conforms to this archetype, how can it say even a partial or provisional No when God has spoken His unqualified and everlasting Yes?" (Karl Barth, *Church Dogmatics* III/1, *Doctrine of Creation*, Edinburgh: T. & T. Clark, 1958, p. 385).

2. Guenter Rutenborn, *The Sign of Jonah*, trans. Bernhard Ohse and Gerhard Elston (Chicago: Lutheran Student Association of America, 1954), p. 75.

3. Nicholai Berdyaev, *The Fate of Man in the Modern World*, trans. Donald A. Lowrie (London: SCM Press, 1935), p. 29.

4. See *Documents on the Struggle for Democracy in Korea*, edited by the Emergency Christian Conference on Korean Problems (Tokyo: Shinkyo Shuppansha, 1975), pp. 37–43.

5. Ibid., p. 35. See also *Kan-koku ka-ra no tsu-sin* ("Correspondence from Korea") (Tokyo: Iwanami Shoten, Publishers, 1974), pp. 5–8; in English see T. K., *Letters from South Korea* (Tokyo: Iwanami Shoten Publishers, 1976).

6. *Documents on the Struggle for Democracy in Korea*, p. 36.

7. Ibid., p. 14.

8. Ibid., p. 36.

9. Dorothy Pickles, *Democracy* (Baltimore: Penguin Books, 1970), p. 13.

10. *Documents on the Struggle for Democracy in Korea*, p. 47.

11. Ibid.

12. Kim Chi Ha, *Cry of the People and Other Poems* (Kagawa ken, Japan: Autumn Press, 1974), pp. 90–107; see also Kim Chi Ha, *The Gold-Crowned Jesus and Other Works* (Maryknoll, New York: Orbis Books, 1978).

13. Jürgen Moltmann, *The Crucified God*, p. 185.

14. Joachim Jeremias describes Mark 16:1–8 as a secondary construction at a later stage of the Easter tradition and as an "apologetic legend." He says: "It has been extremely unfortunate that until recently in considering this prelude scholars have begun from Mark 16:1–8, regarding it as the earliest literary account" (*New Testament Theology*, trans. John Bowden, New York: Charles Scribner's Sons, 1971, p. 304).

15. Karl Barth regards the empty tomb as "not the same as the resurrection. It is not the appearance of the Living; it is only the presupposition. Hence it is only the sign, although an indispensable sign. Christians do not believe in the empty tomb, but in the living Christ" (*Church Dogmatics* III/1, *Doctrine of Creation*, Edinburgh: T. & T. Clark, 1960, p. 453).

16. It is perhaps not accidental that the empty tomb was not mentioned explicitly in important creeds and confessions such as the Nicene Creed or the Westminster Confession of Faith.

17. This is the title of the book dealing with case studies of the experiences of persons declared to be "clinically dead." See Raymond A. Moody, *Life After Death* (New York: Bantam Books, 1976).

18. Paul Lehmann, *The Transfiguration of Politics* (New York: Harper & Row, Publishers, 1975), p. 86. The last part of Lehmann's quotation—"the Transfiguration is the prefiguration of the Resurrection"—is taken from Margaret E. Thrall, "Elijah and Moses in Mark's Account of the Transfiguration," *New Testament Studies*, 16, no. 4 (July 1970): 305–17. In this article Thrall points out the parallelism as follows: "The time with which the narrative begins, i.e., 'six days later,' in Mark 9:2 and 16:1; Jesus' garments become shining white (9:3) and the messenger has a white robe (16:5); the prominence of Peter in both narratives. . . . " Cf. Lehmann, *Transfiguration of Politics*, p. 314, n. 31.

19. According to Vincent Taylor, "The message is a declaration of the Messianic Sonship of Jesus which points back to the Confession of Peter (8:29). What Peter confessed is now divinely affirmed" (*The Gospel according to St. Mark*, London: Macmillan, 1959, p. 392).

20. Today missiologists in both the liberal and the conservative camps speak about a global mission. Here is, for example, a statement from a conservative viewpoint: "Certainly the East is no longer understood only as a mission field but has itself become a mission center, whereas the West is now also a mission field. So long as Christ's Commission to the ends of

the earth applies, the mandate of missions from one end of the earth to any other will pertain. So long as there is Gospel for the whole world, there will be mission in the whole world. And so long as the *Missio Dei* applies, we shall have the *Missio Ecclesiae*" (F. Dale Brunner, "A New Strategy: Statesmanship in Christian Mission," *Christianity Today*, August 1, 1960, p. 891), quoted by Arthur F. Glasser in "Confession, Church Growth and Authentic Unity in Mission," *Protestant Crosscurrents in Mission*, p. 192. But the fact is that even today the Third World provides the context for western mission theology and strategy.

21. Emerito P. Nacpil, "A Gospel for the New Filippino," in Gerald H. Anderson, ed., *Asian Voices in Christian Theology* (Maryknoll, N.Y.: Orbis Books, 1976), pp. 118–19.

22. Gerald H. Anderson and Thomas F. Stransky, eds., *Mission Trends no. 3: Third World Theologies* (New York: Paulist Press and Grand Rapids, Mich.: Wm. B. Eerdmans Publishing Company, 1976), pp. 132–34.

23. Williston Walker, *A History of the Christian Church*, pp. 72ff., and pp. 160ff.

24. *Documents on the Struggle for Democracy in Korea*, p. 43.

25. "The Confession of Alexandria," in *Mission Trends no. 3*, pp. 132–34.

## Chapter 10    A Political God

1. *The Wisdom of Laotse*, trans. Lin Yutang (New York: Random House, The Modern Library, 1948), p. 191.

2. Ibid., pp. 145–46.

3. Gustavo Gutiérrez, *A Theology of Liberation* (Maryknoll, N.Y.: Orbis Books, 1973), p. 155.

4. Rubem Alves, *A Theology of Human Hope* (Cleveland: Corpus Books, 1969), p. 125, quoted by Paul Lehmann in *The Transfiguration of Politics*, pp. 267–68.

5. Lehmann, *Transfiguration of Politics*, p. 268.

6. Mons. Alberto Devoto, "Pautas para una reflexión de la Iglesia de Goya al comenzar el año 1973," in *La Opinión* (Buenos Aires, February 13, 1973, p. 8), quoted by José Míguez Bonino in *Doing Theology in a Revolutionary Situation* (Philadelphia: Fortress Press, 1975), p. 22. Míguez Bonino, in the same context, quotes a United Nations' report that cites hard statistics on the sad situation of Latin America. The report states: "Two-thirds, if not more, of the Latin American population are physically undernourished to the point of starvation in some regions. . . . Three-fourths of the population in several of the Latin American countries are illiterate; in the others, from 20 to 60 percent. . . . About one-third of the Latin American working population (particularly the great majority of the millions of Indian laborers) continue to remain outside the economic, social, and cultural pale of the Latin American community. The consuming power of the Latin American Indian is in many areas almost nil. . . . An overwhelming majority of the Latin American agricultural population is landless. Two-thirds, if not more, of the agricultural, forest, and livestock resources of Latin America are owned or controlled by a handful of native landlords and foreign corporations. (In the recently opened Amazonia, in Brazil, sixty million acres have been bought by U.S.A. investors in the last five years.)"

7. Ibid., p. 25.

8. See *CCA* (Christian Conference of Asia) *News* 11, no. 10 (October 15, 1976):10–12.

9. *The Interpreter's Dictionary of the Bible*, vol. R–Z, p. 80.

10. *The Interpreter's Bible*, vol. 5, p. 982. Jehoiakim sought an alliance with Egypt to fend off the Babylonians. People were taxed heavily to enable him to pay tribute to Egypt. In all probability he died a violent death. "In December, 598, the Babylonian army marched. In that very month Jehoiakim died; in all likelihood, since he was responsible for the nation's predicament and persona non grata with the Babylonians, he was assassinated (cf. Jer. 22:18f; 36:30) in the hope of gaining milder treatment thereby" (John Bright, *A History of Israel*, 2nd ed., Philadelphia: The Westminster Press, 1972, p. 326).

11. James R. Ware, *The Sayings of Confucius, A New Translation* (New York: New American Library, 1955), IV. 18, p. 36.

12. Ibid., IV. 20, p. 37.

13. Ibid., XII. 11, p. 79.

14. Mencius stresses humanity and righteousness as the basic guiding principles of the sociopolitical order. He says, for example, in reply to King Hui with regard to the art of governing: "Even with a territory of a hundred *li* [one-third of a mile is one *li*], it is possible to

become the true king of the empire. If Your Majesty can practice a humane government to the people, reduce punishments and fines, lower taxes and levies, make it possible for the fields to be plowed deep and the weeding well done, men of strong body in their days of leisure may cultivate their filial piety, brotherly respect, loyalty, and faithfulness, thereby serving their fathers and elder brothers at home and their elders and superiors abroad. Then you can have them prepare sticks to oppose the strong armor and sharp weapons of the states of Ch'in and Ch'u" (Wing-tsit Chan, comp. and trans., *A Source Book in Chinese Philosophy*, Princeton, N.J.: Princeton University Press, 1963, p. 61).

15. Dorothee Sölle, *Beyond Mere Obedience*, trans. Lawrence W. Denef (Minneapolis: Augsburg Publishing House, 1970), p. 31.

16. Here we are reminded of 1 Peter 2:13–17. "The Pauline theme of obedient and respectful submission by Christians to governmental authorities," observes the editorial of *Journal of Church and State* 18, no. 3 (Autumn 1976):433–42, "was soon echoed in the admonition found in 1 Peter 2:13–17. In fact, Cullmann has described the Petrine passage as 'the first exegesis' of Romans 13:1–7."

17. Karl Barth, *The Epistle to the Romans*, trans. Edwin C. Hoskins (London: Oxford University Press, 1933), p. 484.

18. Ibid., p. 481.

19. Quoted by José Míguez Bonino, *Doing Theology in a Revolutionary Situation*, p. 17.

20. Ibid.

21. Ibid., p. 18.

22. This movement was also known as non-churchism. First advocated by Kanzo Uchimura, it has produced many fine Christian lay leaders. It stresses the study of the Bible and can be called "biblical orthodoxy."

23. D. Tagawa, "To an American Friend," *Japan Christian Quarterly* 10, no. 2 (April 1935):138, quoted in Charles H. Germany, *Protestant Theologies in Modern Japan* (Tokyo: The International Institute for the Study of Religions, 1965), pp. 173–74.

24. Recorded conference of the Fifth Section of the Research Institute on the Mission of the Church, May 5, 1958. See Germany, *Protestant Theologies*, p. 173.

25. This Confession is included in Appendix I: "Selected Creeds, Confessions, and Theological Statements of Churches in Asia," Gerald H. Anderson, ed., *Asian Voices in Christian Theology*, pp. 254–55.

26. Upon publication, the Declaration was immediately seized by the government. It became quickly known, however, both inside and outside Taiwan.

## Chapter 11    The Transposition of Power

1. Julius Gould and William L. Kalb, eds., *A Dictionary of Social Sciences* (New York: The Free Press, 1964), p. 316. Cf. also H. D. Lasswell and A. Kaplan, *Power and Society* (New Haven: Yale University Press, 1950), p. 240.

2. Joachim Jeremias, *The Parables of Jesus* (New York: Scribner's, 1963), p. 59.

3. Ibid., p. 61. Jeremias explains the difference between burying the money and wrapping it in a napkin as follows: "Burying (Matt. 25:18), according to rabbinical law, was regarded as the best security against theft. Anyone who buried a pledge or a deposit immediately upon receipt of it was free from liability. On the other hand, if anyone tied up entrusted money in a cloth, he was responsible to make good any loss incurred through inadequate care of the entrusted deposit."

4. Oscar Cullmann, *Jesus and the Revolutionaries*, trans. Gareth Putman (New York: Harper & Row, Publishers, 1970), p. 47.

5. Oscar Cullmann, *The State in the New Testament* (London: SCM Press, 1957), p. 83, quoted by Gutiérrez in *A Theology of Liberation*, p. 227.

6. Cullmann, *Jesus and the Revolutionaries*, pp. 48–49.

7. This is not to imply that Jesus might have joined the Zealotist movement. He was sympathetic to it, but he kept his distance because of the narrow nationalism of the movement. Thus the relation between Jesus and the Zealotist movement must have been a delicate one (cf. Gutiérrez, *A Theology of Liberation*, p. 227).

8. Cullmann, *Jesus and the Revolutionaries*, p. 34.

9. It is strange that the authors of the two most important treatises on political theology in recent years did not seem to find it important to discuss the temptation of Jesus. Gutiérrez's

*A Theology of Liberation* makes only a passing remark to it (p. 228 and p. 246, n. 88), while Paul Lehmann makes no mention of it at all in *The Transfiguration of Politics.*

10. Cullmann, *Jesus and the Revolutionaries,* p. 39.

11. Ibid., p. 55.

12. Lehmann, *Transfiguration of Politics,* pp. 92–93.

13. Ibid., p. 93.

14. Regarding the story in Matthew 17:24–27, we find the following explanation: "Since God is the true king of the earth, his children might easily think themselves free from any external authority, but it was necessary to remind them that they must give free and willing obedience to the state" (*The Interpreter's Bible,* 7:465).

15. Jeremias, *The Parables of Jesus,* p. 38.

16. Ibid.

17. Ibid.

18. Ibid., pp. 70–77, esp. p. 76.

19. Jacques Ellul, *The Political Illusion,* trans. Konrad Kellen (New York: Alfred A. Knopf, 1976), p. 81.

20. Ibid., p. 82.

21. Dorothee Sölle, *Political Theology,* John Shelley, trans. (Philadelphia: Fortress Press, 1974), p. 80.

22. Ibid., p. 78.

23. Johannes B. Metz, *Theology of the World,* trans. William Glen-Doepel (New York: Herder and Herder, 1969), p. 118.

24. Ibid., p. 120.

25. Lehmann, *Transfiguration of Politics,* pp. 56–57.

## Chapter 12     The Politics of the Resurrection

1. This poem by Lai Leng Woon appeared in *Suffering and Hope* (Singapore, 1976), p. 80, an anthology prepared by Ron O'Grady and Lee Soo Jin for the General Assembly of the Christian Conference of Asia held in Penang, Malaysia, in June 1977.

2. Simone Weil, "The Love of God and Affliction," in *Waiting for God,* trans. Emma Crauford with an introduction by Leslie A. Fielder (New York: G. P. Putnam's Sons, 1951), p.121, quoted by Dorothee Sölle in *Suffering,* p. 154.

3. Edwyn C. Hoskyns, *The Fourth Gospel,* ed. Francis Noel Davey (London: Faber and Faber, 1940), p. 531.

4. Raymond E. Brown, S.S., *The Gospel according to John (XIII–XXI),* The Anchor Bible (New York: Doubleday and Company, 1970), p. 930.

5. Bao Ruo-wong, *Prisoner of Mao* (New York: Coward, McCann and Geoghegan, 1973), pp. 257–58.

6. This is my translation from Chapter 3, Article 28, of the Chinese edition of *The Constitution of the People's Republic of China* (Peking: People's Press, 1975).

7. Ibid., Chapter 1, Article 2.

8. The phrase is from Engels. Cf. doc. 31 in Donald E. MacInnis, *Religious Policy and Practice in Communist China* (New York: Macmillan, 1972), p. 60.

9. The article is by Yu Hsiang and Liu Chun-wang. Cf. MacInnis, *Religious Policy and Practice,* pp. 67–68.

10. See Wallace C. Mewin and Francis P. Jones, eds., *Documents of the Three-Self Movement* (New York: National Council of the Churches of Christ in the U.S.A., 1963), pp. 41–43.

11. Trevor Beeson, *Discretion and Valour: Religious Conditions in Russia and Eastern Europe* (Glasgow: Collins, 1974), p. 61.

12. Jan M. Lochman, *Church in a Marxist Society* (London: SCM Press, 1970), p. 89.

13. Ibid.

14. Rubem Alves, *A Theology of Human Hope,* p. 11.

15. Italics mine.

16. *Newsweek,* August 12, 1974, p. 26.

17. *Newsweek,* August 12, 1974, p. 29.

18. Teilhard de Chardin, *The Divine Milieu* (New York: Harper & Row, Publishers, 1960), quoted by C. F. Mooney in *Teilhard de Chardin and the Mystery of Christ* (New York: Harper & Row, Publishers, 1966), pp. 151–52.

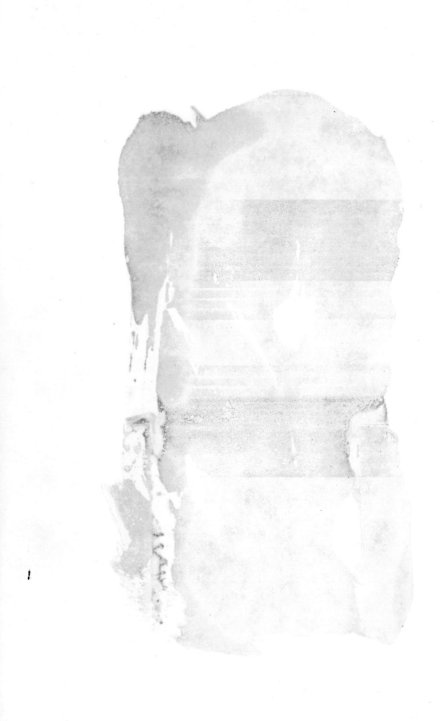